W0061629

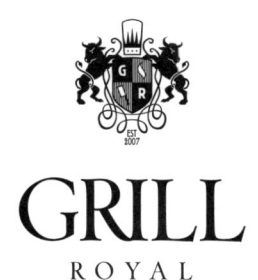

GRILL

ROYAL

DISTANZ

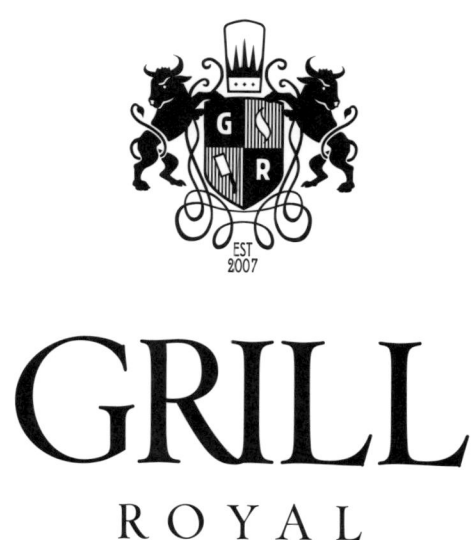

GRILL

ROYAL

Wir bedanken uns bei unseren Gästen und bei unserem Team.
We would like to thank our guests and our team.

Stephan Landwehr, Boris Radczun, Moritz Estermann

Inhalt/*Content*

INHALT/CONTENT

Der unverschämte Zauber des Grill Royal 9
The Outrageous Magic of Grill Royal 15
ADRIANO SACK

Grill Royal 21
STEFAN KORTE

Der Grill Royal oder die Gastlichkeit der Berliner Welt
seit dem neunzehnten Jahrhundert 61
Grill Royal—Berlin's Hospitality since the Nineteenth Century 81
ERWIN SEITZ

One Night 100
MAXIME BALLESTEROS

Der Dandy, der Fälscher und die Kurtisane 163
The Dandy, the Faker, and the Courtesan 169
RENÉ POLLESCH

A Day 174
PETER LANGER

Ein Gespräch über Wein 185
A Conversation About Wine 193
STUART PIGOTT

Fleisch – mehr als nur ein Stück Lebenskraft 201
Meat—More Than Just A Slice Of Vitality 223
THOMAS VILGIS

Autoren/*Authors* 245
Fotografen/*Photographers* 249
Impressum/*Imprint* 252

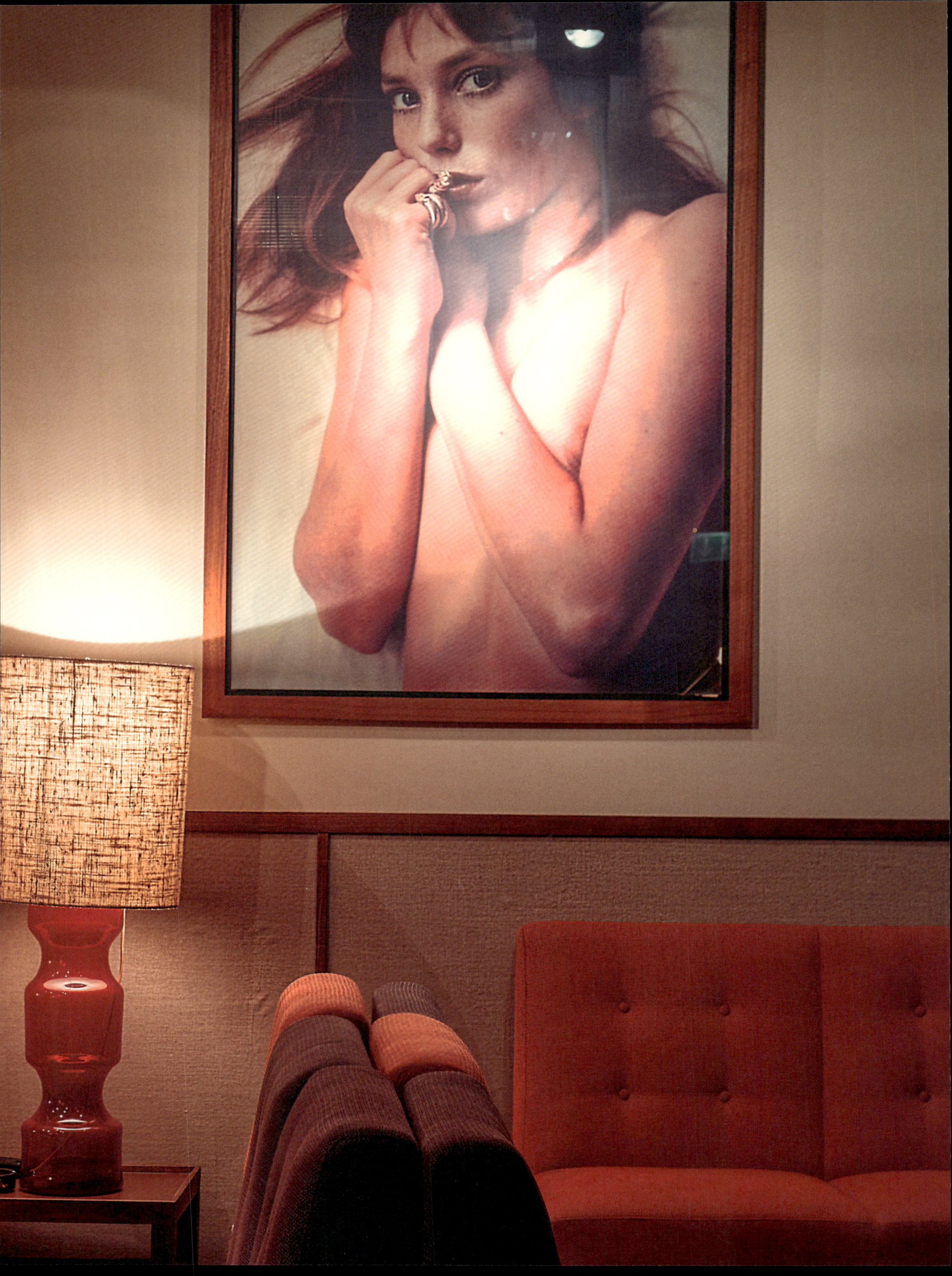

Der unverschämte Zauber des Grill Royal

Adriano Sack

Wir sprechen hier nicht von einem guten Restaurant. Wir sprechen hier nicht über die Qualität der Steaks. Wir sprechen auch nicht über die erlesene Weinkarte, die Kenner für sehr fair kalkuliert halten. Und schon gar nicht über die geschickte Beleuchtung. Oder die geschmackvollen Toiletten mit Verweilqualität.

Wir sprechen über die unverschämten Kunstwerke, den highly fuckable staff, die einzigartige Mischung aus Arroganz und Selbstironie der Besitzer. Wir sprechen also über den Grill Royal, der seltsamerweise von nicht wenigen Stammgästen „das Grill" genannt wird.

So oder so ist und bleibt der Name eine Frechheit. Ernst kann man ihn nicht nehmen. Oder aber als Zeichen verstehen, dass die Welt als solche, und alle auf ihr stattfindenden Äußerungen, nicht ernst zu nehmen sind. „Ja, wir sind (oder haben) die Größten. Und wissen, dass man das eigentlich nicht sagt. Tun wir aber trotzdem", verkündet einem der Name *Grill Royal* mit einem charmanten Grinsen. Es handelt sich also um durch Sichtbarmachung der eigenen Strategie erträglich gemachte Angeberei. Wie die meisten interessanten Dinge: total eins zu eins und gleichzeitig total meta.

Wenn man hier aber noch kurz hängen bleibt, by the way eine Tätigkeit, für die der Grill Royal wie geschaffen ist, verrät er noch ein bisschen mehr. Er beschwört Erinnerungen an „Gelée Royale" herauf, jenes Gemisch aus den Sekreten der Futtersaftdrüse und der Oberkieferdrüse der Arbeiterbienen, das vielleicht erste Superfood, das das Massenpublikum elektrisierte, auch wenn es bis heute den Beigeschmack von Halbseidenheit und Scharlatanerie nicht ganz loswerden konnte. Und natürlich verweist er auf die Serie *Kir Royal* von Helmut Dietl, in der Franz Xaver Kroetz einen Münchner Klatschreporter spielt und in dieser Funktion entscheidet, wer „drin ist" – also in seiner Klatschkolumne und damit Teil der sogenannten Schickeria. In der ersten Folge spielt Mario Adorf den erfolgreichen Mittelständler Heinrich Haffenloher, Herr über ein Klebstoffimperium. Dieser Mann kommt nach München und sehnt sich nach gesellschaftlicher Bestätigung. Als der Klatschreporter sich ihm trotz intensiven Werbens verweigert, setzt Haffenloher mit der Unbeirrbarkeit eines deutschen Panzers seine wirtschaftliche Potenz ein und lässt Baby Schimmerlos an den Pool des Hotels Bayerischer Hof bestellen. „Ich scheiß dich zu mit meinem Geld", droht der Industrielle im Bademantel dem Reporter. Und der knickt natürlich ein. Hier wird mit Brecht'scher Kälte – schließlich handelt es sich um Helmut Dietl auf der Höhe seines Schaffens – der Gesellschaftsreporter vom Zeremonienmeister zum Dienstleister degradiert. Und der Unternehmer als rücksichtsloses Tier gefeiert, mit kleinbürgerlichen Träumen und einer Faust aus Stahl.

Das Berlin des neuen Jahrtausends ist ein anderes Biotop als das München der achtziger Jahre. Statusdenken, Wohlstand und Hedonismus machen sich breit. Ein Tisch in einem Szenerestaurant ist nun Zeichen sozialen Erfolgs. Aber aufgrund der Sozial- und Geistesgeschichte von Berlin ist dessen Inszenierung nur in ironischer Halbaffirmation möglich. Deswegen das Zitat, das Distanz und Liebeserklärung zugleich ist, deswegen also „Grill Royal".

Das Gründertrio bestand aus dem Galeristen Thilo Wermke, einem spitzzüngigen Intellektuellen, der in Rafael Horzons Bestseller *Das weiße Buch* aus unerfindlichen Gründen als „Baron zu Wermke" auftritt, dem Rahmenbauer Stephan Landwehr, der seine ersten Schritte in der Berliner Gastronomie im legendären „Exil" von Oswald und Ingrid Wiener gemacht hatte, und dem DJ und Hobbykoch Boris Radczun, der höchst erfolgreich durch das Berliner Nachtleben irrlichterte. Der Nukleus für den Grill war ein kleines illegales Restaurant, das Boris ab 2002 in einem nicht genutzten Nebenraum des Clubs Cookies veranstaltete. Der völlig willkürlich erweiterte Freundeskreis erhielt im Laufe des Vormittags ein Codewort, mithilfe dessen man durch den am Frühabend noch leeren Club eine Treppe hochstieg und an einer Geheimtür eingelassen wurde. Die Speisekarte war überschaubar und schon für damalige Verhältnisse auf eine aus der Zeit gefallene Art fleischlastig. Und wer lang genug sitzen blieb, bekam von Boris noch ein Stück kurz gebratene Filetspitze auf den Teller geschnitten.

Die Location, die Landwehr, Radczun und Wermke sich für den Grill Royal aussuchten, zeugt von Vorstellungskraft und exzellentem Geschmack. Denn auf den ersten Blick scheint die Wahl abwegig. Das Souterrain von einem der scheußlichsten Hotels in Berlin-Mitte mit in Relation zur Größe des Hauptraums niedrigen Decken. Und dann auch noch der blöde Schiffbauerdamm mit seiner Eventgastronomie gleich gegenüber. Wer ausnahmsweise mal nicht mit dem Taxi oder der Limousine (oder dem Wassertaxi, wie die Sammlerin Julia Stoschek zu ihrer eigenen Geburtstagsfeier) zum Restaurant kommt, sondern sich zu Fuß über die Weidendammer Brücke nähert, sieht schon von Weitem die roten Markisen, die ein bisschen zu tiefen und gemütlichen Sessel mit den tweedartigen Bezügen, die keck auf der Mauer lungernden Raucher mit ihren Weißweingläsern, das einladende Leuchten aus der 24 Meter langen Fassade. Wer ein Herz für die Verführungen des großstädtischen Lebens hat, dem beschleunigt dieser Anblick den Puls. Und wer ein paar Mal hier war und die Herzlichkeit, Ruppigkeit und Energie dieses Ladens schätzt, der fühlt das Beste, was ein Restaurant wie dieses bieten kann: Heimatgefühle.

Der Abstieg die 31 Stufen runter auf das Restaurantlevel wird meist von zwei roten Samtkordeln so gebremst, dass man beim besten Willen nicht die Treppe runter und auf den ersten Terrassentisch stürzen kann. Sie erzwingen eine theatralisch langsame Annäherung. Der Abstieg, der ja in Wirklichkeit ein Aufstieg ist, vermittelt das Gefühl einer Showtreppe, die traditionell nur Stars hinunterschweben – insofern ist der Grill Royal überaschenderweise ein großer Demokratisierer und Gleichmacher. Hier aber schreitet man nicht frontal, sondern von der Seite herunter, schleicht sich also quasi an. „Capitalism Kills Love" verkündet die Lichtinstallation von Claire Fontaine über dem Eingang, und wem diese Geste an dieser Stelle keine gute Laune macht, der hat hier vermutlich nichts verloren.

Es gibt eine Form des guten Geschmacks, die erdrückt und erstickt. Der gute Geschmack der Richtigmacher. Und es gibt den anderen, der befreit und berauscht. Den Tyrannosaurus Rex aus Bronze auf dem Tresen. Der Vorhang aus obszön dickem Gummi am Eingang zum Raucherraum. Die nutzlose Riva-Yacht am Ende des Restaurants, wo normale Gastronomen eine VIP-Nische vorgesehen hätten. Die kleine Gestalt im Anorak, die wie ein obdachloses Kind auf dem Boden sitzt, eine Skulptur von Iris Kettner. Die vielen schicken Lampen. Das alles ist fantastisch ausgesucht und arrangiert. Ist aber auch geprägt von Maßlosigkeit und Humor.

In den Tresen sind Plaketten mit den Namen Stucki, Uslar und Fetisch eingelassen, eine Hommage von drei Kulturschaffenden an den Schauspieler Otto Sander, dessen Tresenplatz in der Paris Bar mit einer solchen Plakette markiert war. Eine Zeitlang stand auf der Karte des Grill Royal das „Hendl with care" – ein Brathähnchen, das man in Kombination mit *Das weiße Buch* erwerben konnte. Man kann sich an der latenten Ich-Sucht von solchen Witzen reiben. Oder sich freuen, dass man nicht selbst auf die Idee kommen musste.

Erfolgreiche Entertainer verstehen, dass sie ihrem Publikum eine Mischung aus Erneuerung und Überraschung bieten müssen. Aber auch ihre größten Hits. Im Grill sind das, je nach Veranlagung, die gebratenen Garnelen mit Knoblauch, die frittierten Süßkartoffelschnitze oder das Tomahawk-Steak für mindestens zwei Leute. Oder der ganze grüne Salatkopf, der mit einer Vinaigrette serviert wird. An einem Detail lässt sich manchmal die Welt erklären. Oder in diesem Fall, die Philosophie eines erfolgreichen Restaurants. Der grüne Salat ist ein aus der Mode gekommener Klassiker. Andere Sorten sind robuster, allen voran der schmerzfreie Eisbergsalat. Oder vermeintlich charaktervoller, wie der zum Allgemeinplatz verkommene Rucola. Der Kopfsalat dagegen wird schnell welk oder kriegt braune Stellen, schmeckt nach wenig außer vage nach grün.

So weit ich weiß, steht er seit Tag eins auf der Karte des Grill Royal. Er wird seitdem in einer verlässlichen Perfektion serviert. Er ist immer noch so schwer zu essen wie am ersten Tag, vor allem, wenn man der alten Schulweisheit anhängt, dass man die Blätter nicht schneiden, sondern nur mit dem Besteck falten darf. Der Kopfsalat im Grill Royal ist der Beweis, dass die zwei Herren vom Grill (der dritte hat sich bald in aller Freundschaft verabschiedet) zu Zärtlichkeit, Treue und Demut fähig sind.

Und darüber hinaus Meister darin sind, das Schwere leicht aussehen zu lassen. Gleich der erste Abend war programmatisch: viel zu viele Gäste, überforderte Gastgeber, die schließlich zur nahe gelegenen Currywurstbude vom Bahnhof Friedrichstraße rannten, um Kunstsammlern die Wartezeiten auf die Steaks zu verkürzen. Ich habe noch nie gehört, dass irgendjemand den ersten Abend bereut hätte.

Seitdem hat sich die riesige Vergnügungsmaschine, die der Grill Royal ist, eingespielt und läuft meist reibungslos wie ein Kreuzfahrtschiff. Selbst die Klofrau, vermutlich die bestverdienende der Stadt, wirkt inzwischen wie ein alter Hase. Was sich aber seit der ersten Nacht nicht geändert hat: Strudel und Kick, wie sie das Nachtleben bieten sollte. Man weiß nie genau, was oder wer einen erwartet. Oder in welchem Zustand, und mit wem man nach Hause geht.

George Clooney am Nebentisch. Leyla Piedayesh auf dem Tisch. Yung Hurn nackt am Tisch. Johann König mit grünem Slime im Haar. Gerhard Schröder im Gespräch mit einer teuren Flasche Rotwein. Rammstein beim Grölen am Tresen. Oder so.

Ein Großteil der anständigen Berliner würde keinen Fuß in diesen Laden setzen. Aber das kann man über das Berghain oder die Philharmonie auch sagen.

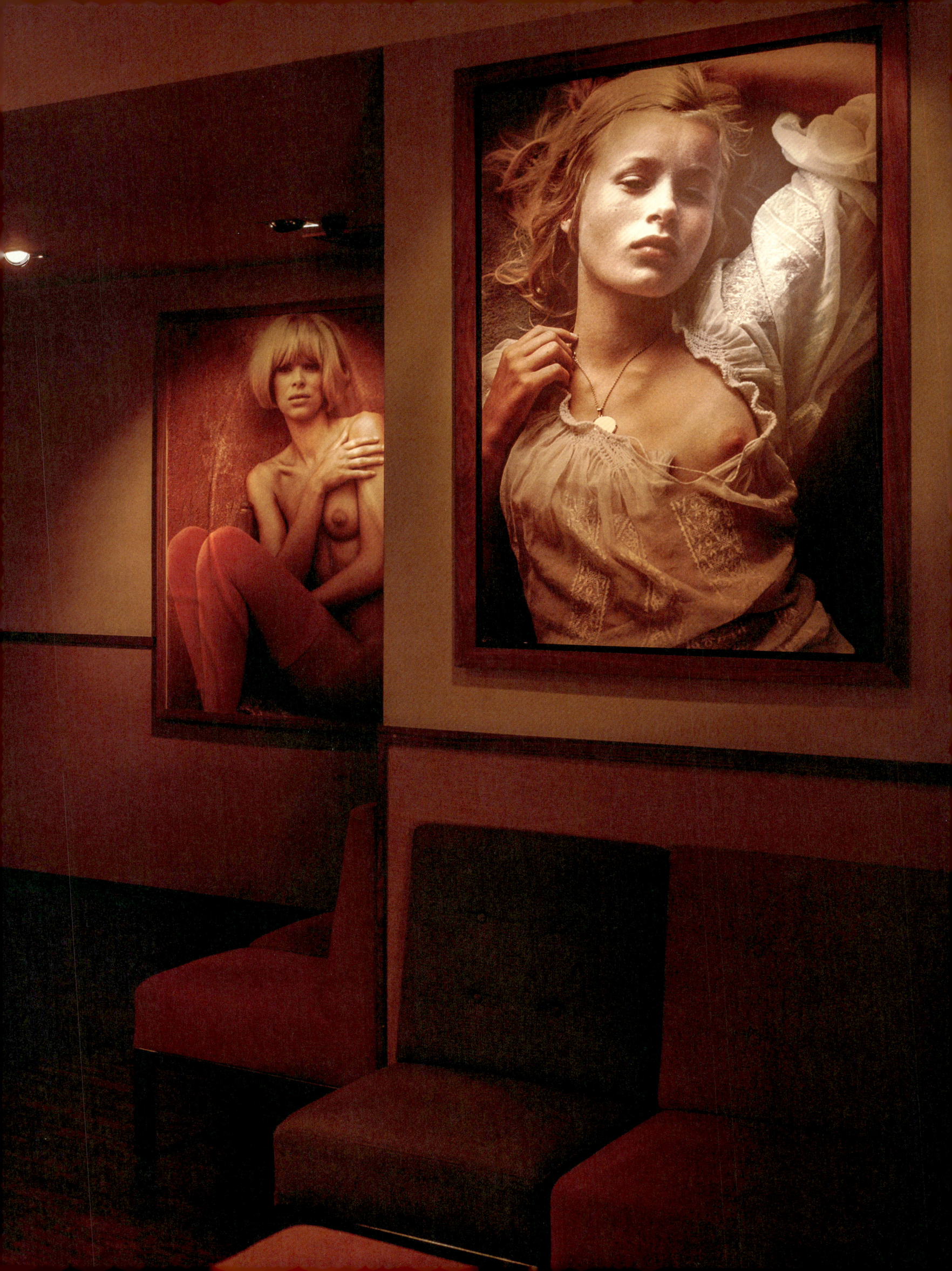

The Outrageous Magic of Grill Royal

Adriano Sack

We're not talking about a good restaurant here. We're not talking about the quality of the steaks. We're also not talking about the exclusive wine menu, which connoisseurs claim is more than fairly priced. And definitely not about the subdued lighting, or the tasteful bathrooms that invite us to linger in them.

We're talking about the audacious works of art, the highly fuckable staff, the owners' inimitable blend of arrogance and self-irony. We're speaking, of course, about Grill Royal, which many of its regulars strangely call "the Grill."

In any case, the name is an affront. It's impossible to take it seriously. Or you could interpret it as a sign that the world as such, together with every statement uttered in it, can't be taken seriously. "Yes, we're (or we have) the greatest. And we know that you don't really say that. But we do it anyway," is what the name *Grill Royal* proclaims with a charming grin. And so we're dealing with a form of bragging that becomes bearable because it exposes its own strategy. Like most interesting things: it's exactly what it is, and at the same time it's totally meta.

But if you hang out here for a little while, which, by the way, is exactly what the Grill Royal was made for, it reveals more as it conjures up memories of the royal jelly, that mixture of secretions given off by the hypopharyngeal glands of worker bees, probably the very first super food to electrify a mass public, even if it never could quite shake an aftertaste of dubiosity and charlatanism. And of course it refers to Helmut Dietl's series *Kir Royal*, in which Franz Xaver Kroetz plays a tabloid reporter in Munich who gets to decide "who's who"—in his gossip column and, by extension, in the so-called high society. In the first episode, Mario Adorf plays the successful Heinrich Haffenloher, who lords over a mid-sized glue empire. The man, newly arrived in Munich, longs to make it in society. When the gossip columnist turns him away in spite of his attempts to woo him, Haffenloher, with the relentlessness of a German tank, mobilizes his financial might and summons Baby Schimmerlos to the pool at the Bayerischer Hof Hotel. "I'll shit on you with my money," the magnate, wrapped in a bathrobe, threatens the reporter. Who gives in, of course. With Brechtian coldness—after all, we're talking about Helmut Dietl at the height of his craft: the society reporter is degraded from master of ceremony to service staff. And the businessman, a ruthless beast, is celebrated with his petit bourgeois dreams and his iron fist.

Berlin of the new millennium is a completely different ball of wax than Munich of the 1980s. Status worries, wealth, and hedonism are on the rise. A table at a very hip restaurant is a sign of social success. But because of Berlin's social and intellectual history, orchestrating this only works in the form of an ironic half-affirmation. That's where the quote comes in, which is both a declaration of distance and love; that's why it's called "Grill Royal."

The founding trio was comprised of the gallery dealer Thilo Wermke, a sharp-tongued intellectual who for unknown reasons made an appearance in Rafael Horzon's bestseller *Das weiße Buch* (The White Book) as "Baron zu Wermke"; the frame builder Stephan Landwehr, who took his first steps in Berlin gastronomy in Oswald and Ingrid Wiener's legendary Exil; and the DJ and hobby chef Boris Radczun, whose meanderings through Berlin nightlife were a great success. The Grill's nucleus was a small illegal restaurant that Boris began running in 2002 in an unused side room of the Cookies Club. Sometime in the morning, the randomly expanding circle of friends received a code word that they then used in the early evening to walk up a flight of steps leading to the still-empty club and be let in through a secret door. The menu was small, and for the time fairly heavy on meat, which in those days seemed from another era altogether. And anyone who stayed late enough got a piece of seared fillet tips carved onto the plate by Boris.

The location that Landwehr, Radczun, and Wermke picked out for Grill Royal attests to their powers of imagination and excellent taste. At first glance, though, the choice seems absurd: the basement of one of the ugliest hotels in Berlin-Mitte, with low ceilings in proportion to the size of the main room. And then there's the stupid Schiffbauerdamm, with its event gastronomy right across the way. Whoever makes an exception and doesn't arrive at the restaurant by taxi or limousine (or water taxi, as the collector Julia Stoschek did on her birthday), but comes on foot over the Weidendammer Bridge, already sees the red awnings from a distance, the armchairs with the tweed-like covers that are a bit too low and comfortable, the smokers loitering jauntily on the wall with their glasses of white wine, the lights beckoning from the 24-meter-long façade. Anyone with a heart for the seductions of big-city life feels their pulse quicken at the sight. And anyone who's been here a few times and values the warmth, surliness, and energy of the place feels the best of what a restaurant like this can offer: a sense of home.

Walking down the 31 steps to the restaurant level, you're usually held back by two red velvet cords that prevent you, hard as you might try, from falling down the stairs and landing right on the first terrace table. They impose a theatrically slow approach. The descent, which in reality is an ascent, speaks show business, a staircase that only stars would traditionally float serenely down. In this regard, surprisingly, Grill Royal is a great democratizer and equalizer. You don't stride in frontally here, but from the side, a kind of sidling up. Above the entrance, Claire Fontaine's light installation proclaims "Capitalism Kills Love," and whoever isn't instantly put in a better mood when they see this gesture probably doesn't belong here.

There's a form of good taste that oppresses and strangles: the good taste of those who do everything right. And then there's the other kind that liberates and intoxicates. The bronze Tyrannosaurus Rex on the counter. The curtain of obscenely thick rubber at the entrance to the smokers' room. The useless Riva yacht at the far end of the restaurant, where normal restaurateurs would have installed a VIP booth. The small figure in a parka, sitting like a homeless child on the floor—a sculpture by Iris Kettner. The many well-designed lamps. It's all been fantastically selected and arranged. But there's also a mark of extravagance and humor.

Badges with the names Stucki, Uslar, and Fetisch are imbedded in the bar, an homage by three cultural workers to the actor Otto Sander, whose place at the counter in the Paris Bar was marked with a badge of this kind. For a time, the "Hendl with care"—a roasted chicken that you could order together with *Das weiße Buch*—was on the menu of the Grill Royal. You could bristle at the latent selfishness of a joke like this—or be happy that you didn't have to come up with the idea yourself.

Successful entertainers know that they have to give their audience a mixture of renewal and surprise. But also their biggest hits. At the Grill, these are, depending on your taste, braised shrimp with garlic, fried slices of sweet potato, and the Tomahawk steak for a minimum of two. Or the very green garden lettuce, served with a vinaigrette dressing. Sometimes, a single detail helps explain the whole world. Or in this case, the philosophy of a successful restaurant. Green salad is a classic that's gone out of fashion. Other sorts are far more robust, above all the indestructible iceberg lettuce. Or they're perceived as having more character, like arugula, which has become a cliché. On the other hand, green lettuce wilts or gets brown spots very quickly, and it doesn't have a lot of taste, apart from being vaguely green.

As far as I know, it's been on the menu at Grill Royal from day one. And ever since, it's been served with reliable perfection. It's as difficult to eat as it was on the first day, especially if you subscribe to the old-school wisdom that you're not supposed to cut the leaves, but fold them over the fork. At Grill Royal, the green lettuce is proof that the two gentlemen managing the Grill (the third soon departed amicably) are capable of tenderness, loyalty, and humility. And that they're masters at making difficult things look easy. The very first evening was already a classic: way too many guests, overworked hosts who finally ran to the nearby fast-food joint in the Friedrichstrasse station to cut the time art collectors had to wait for their steaks. I've never yet heard that anyone's regretted this first evening.

Since then, the huge amusement machine that Grill Royal is runs as smoothly as a cruise ship, and almost always without a glitch. Even the toilet woman, presumably Berlin's best earner in her category, acts like a pro by now. But what hasn't changed since that first night is the whirl and kick the night-life has to offer. You never know who or what to expect, or in what state (and with whom) you'll go home.

George Clooney at the next table. Leyla Piedayesh on the table. Yung Hurn at the table, nude. Johann König with green slime in his hair. Gerhard Schröder in conversation with an expensive bottle of red wine. Rammstein bellowing at the bar. Or something like that.

A large number of respectable Berliners would never set foot in this place. But you can say the same thing about Berghain or the Philharmonie.

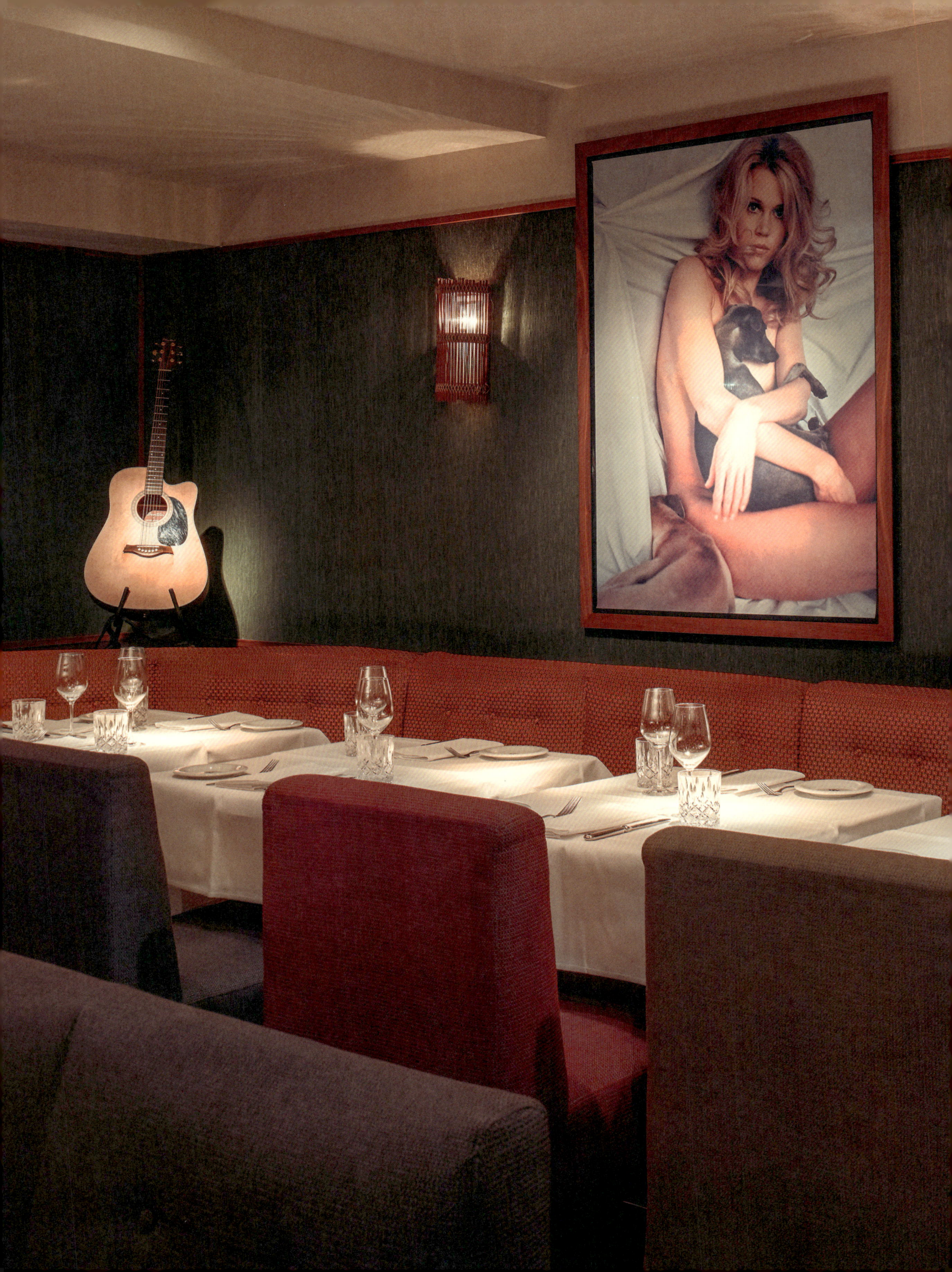

Grill Royal

Stefan Korte

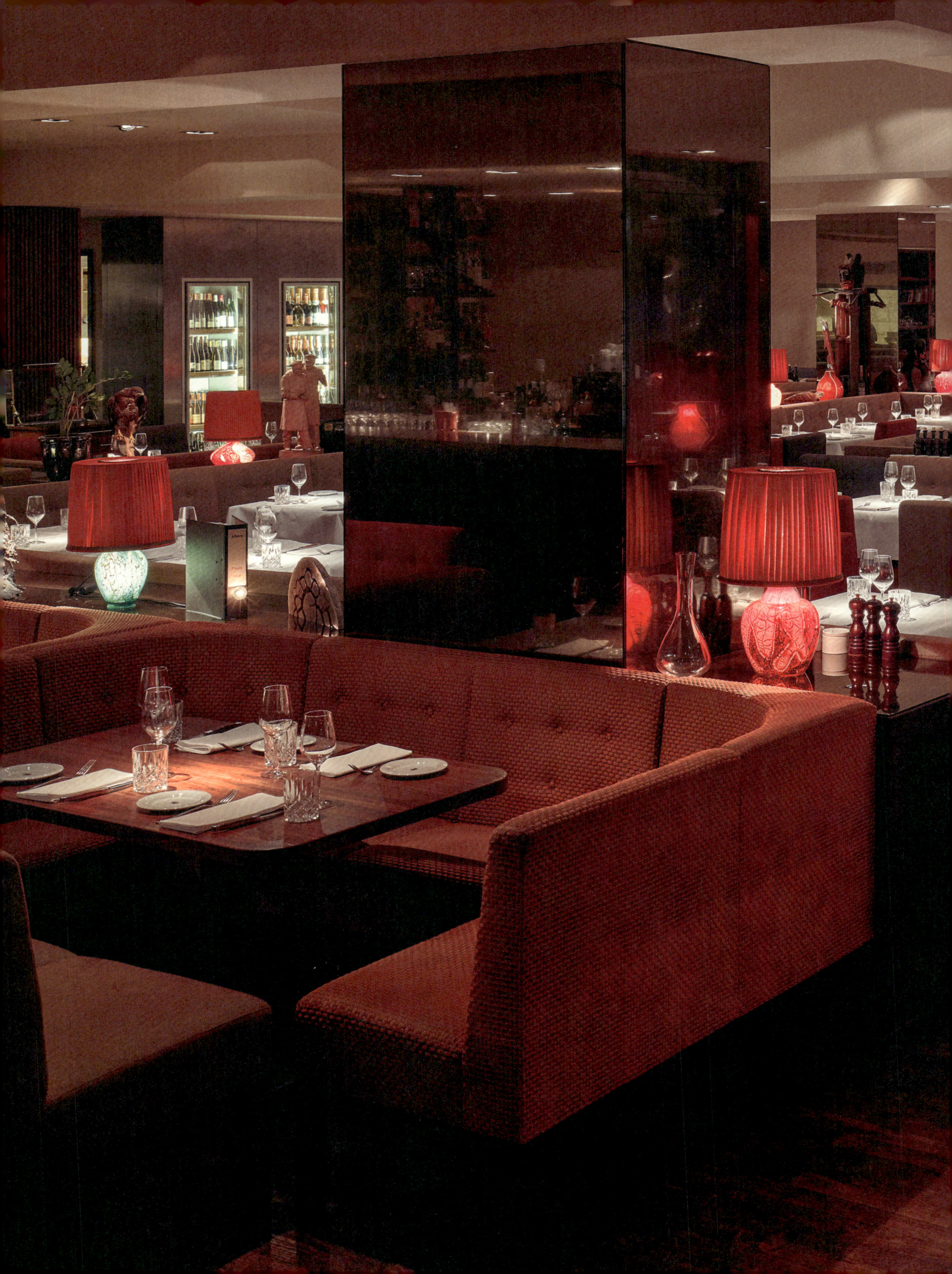

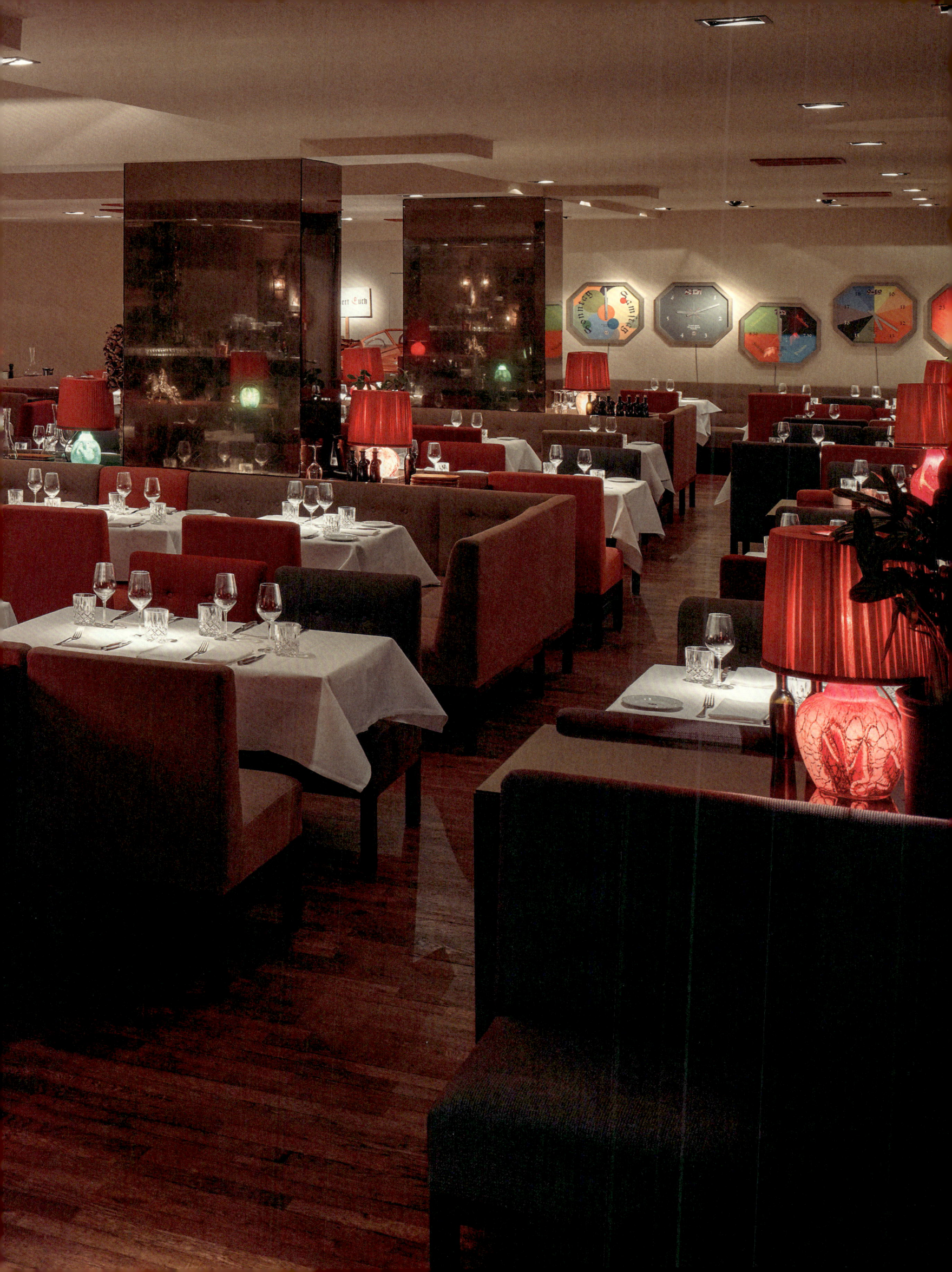

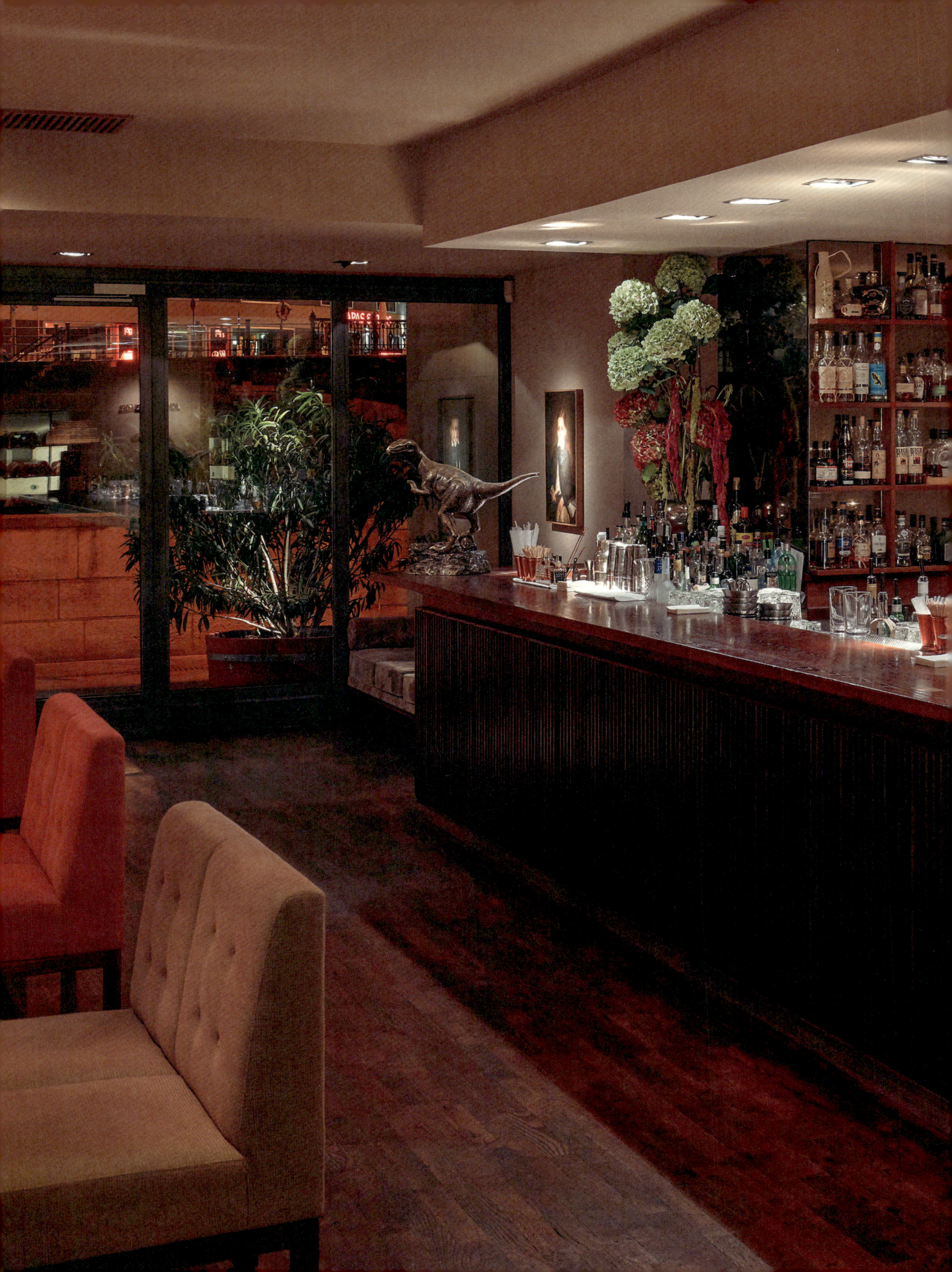

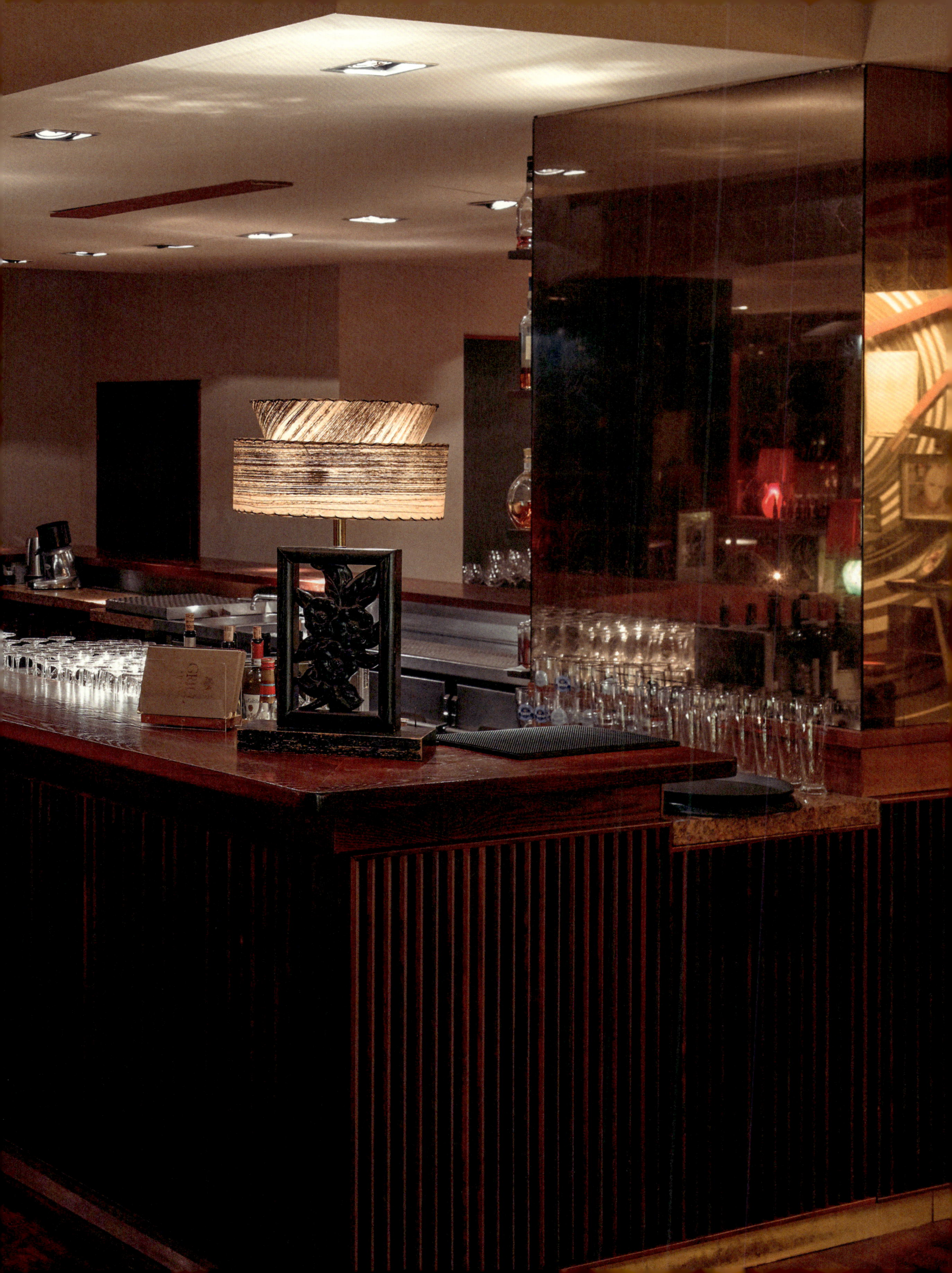

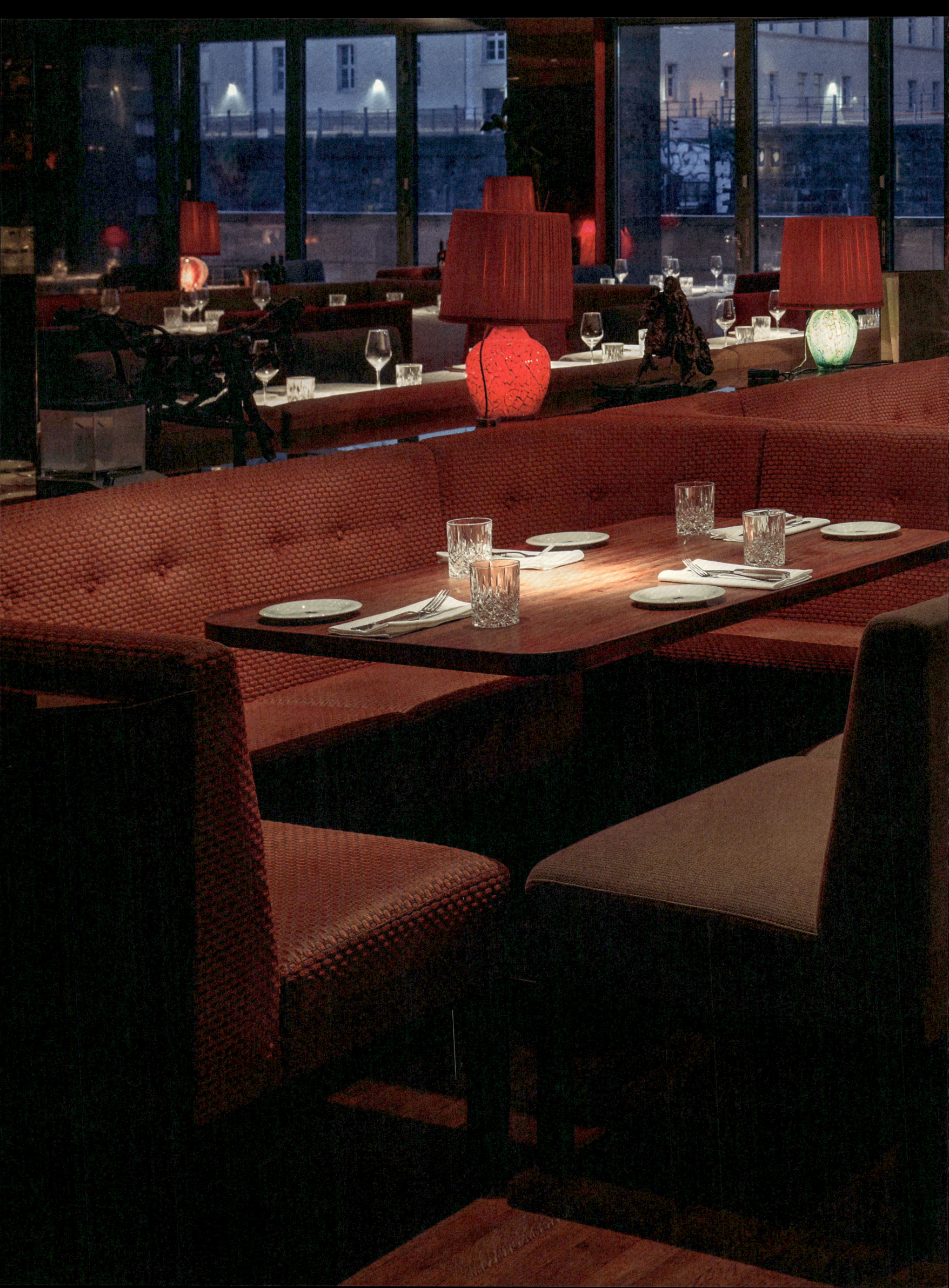

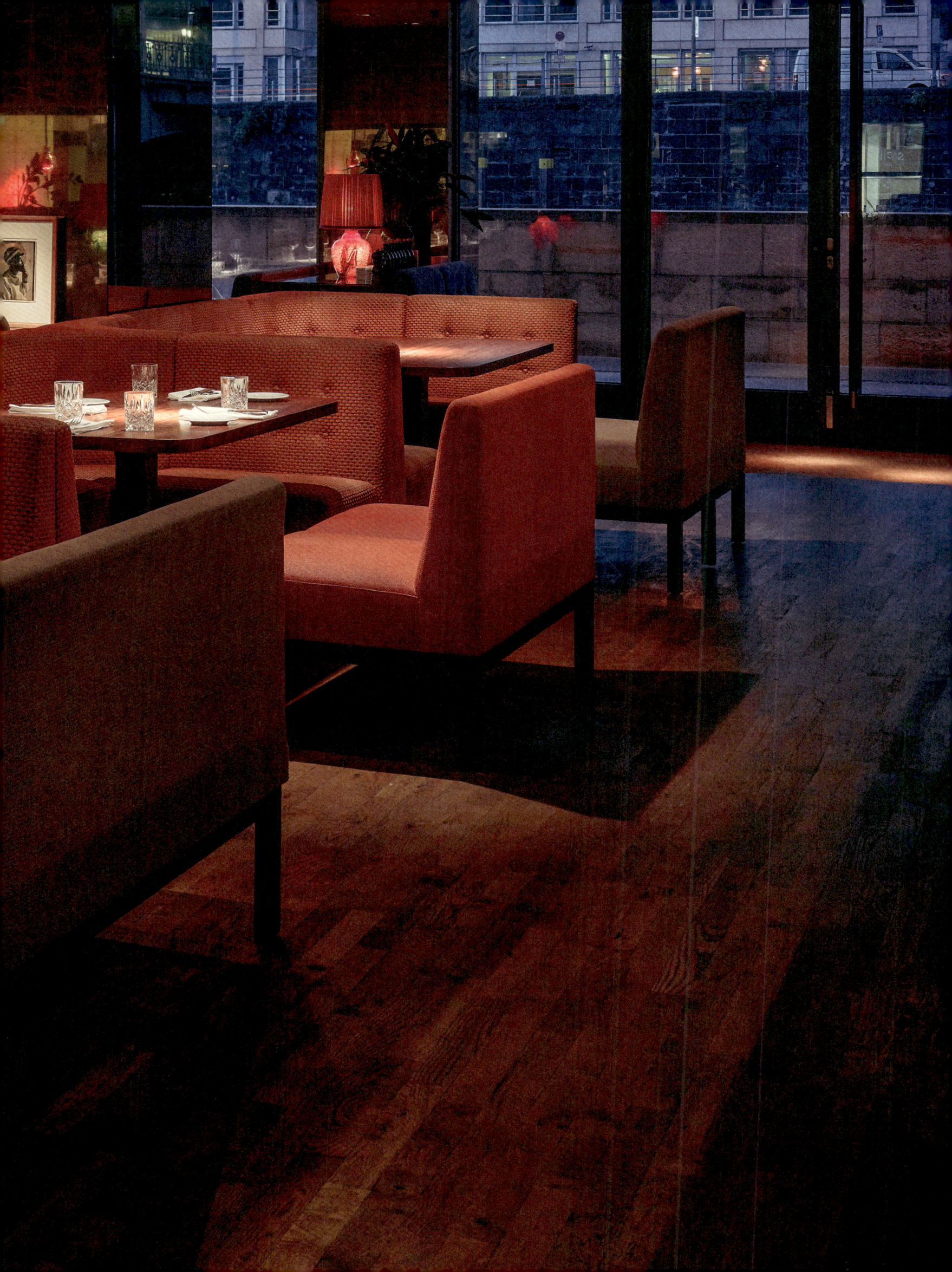

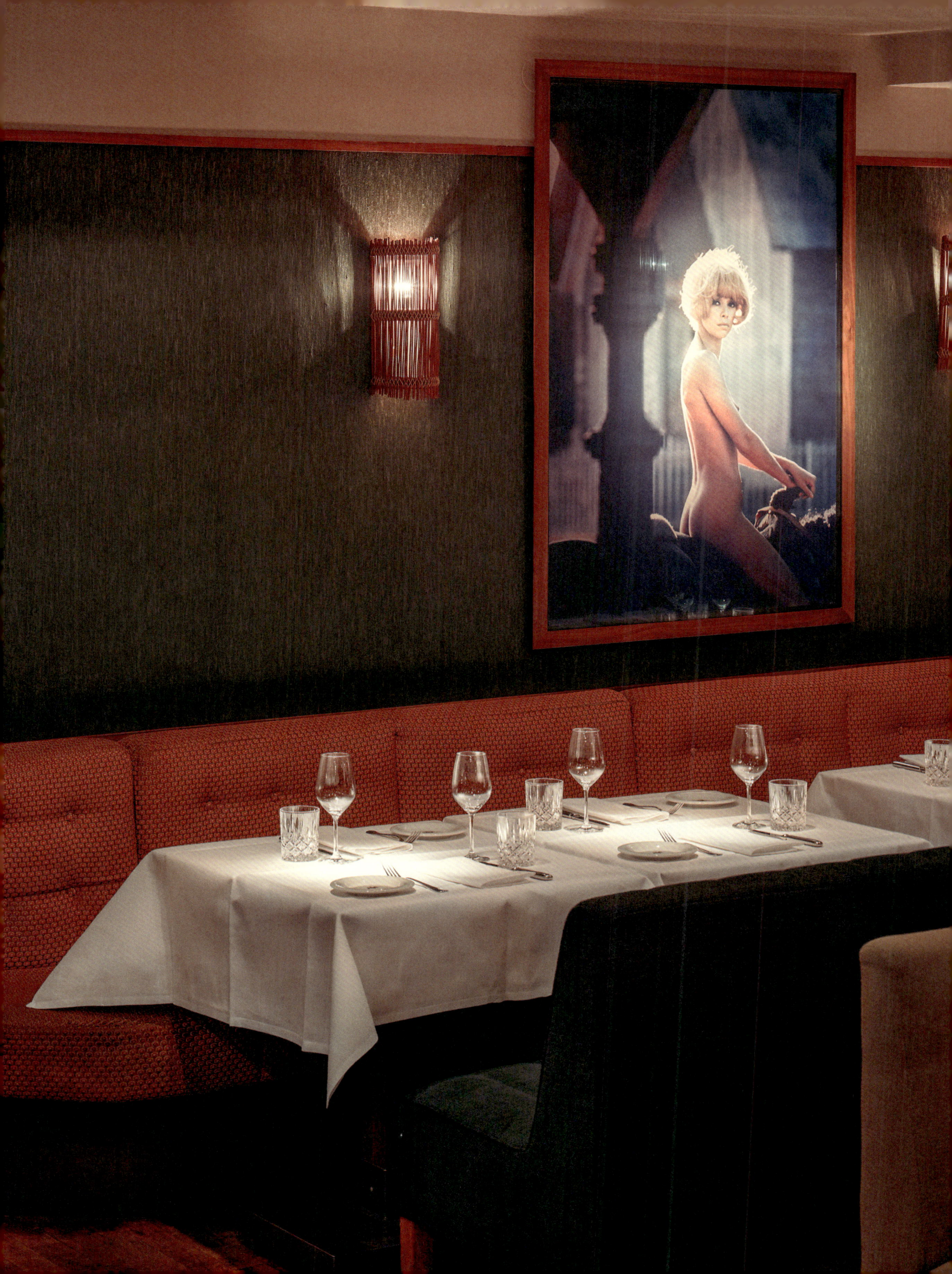

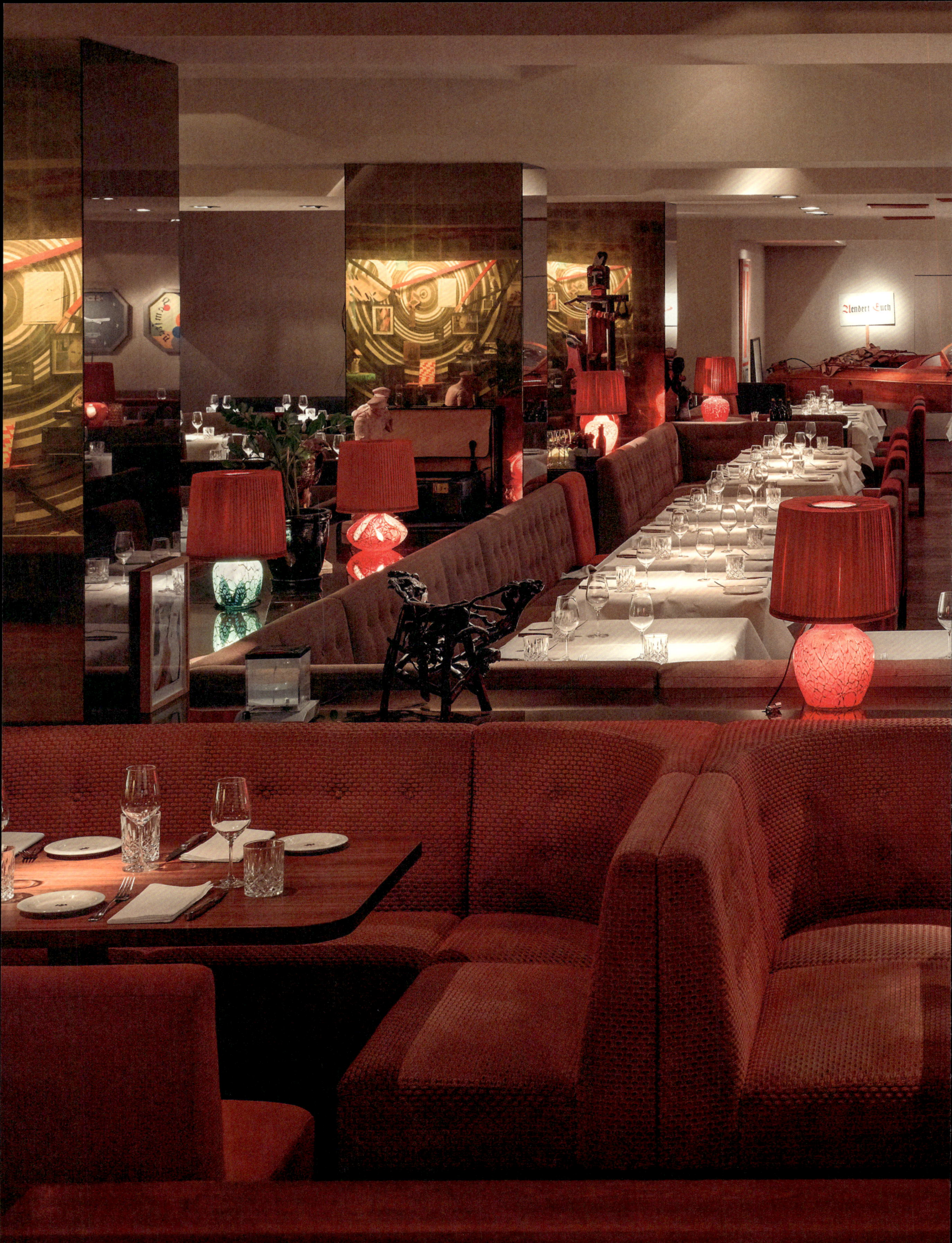

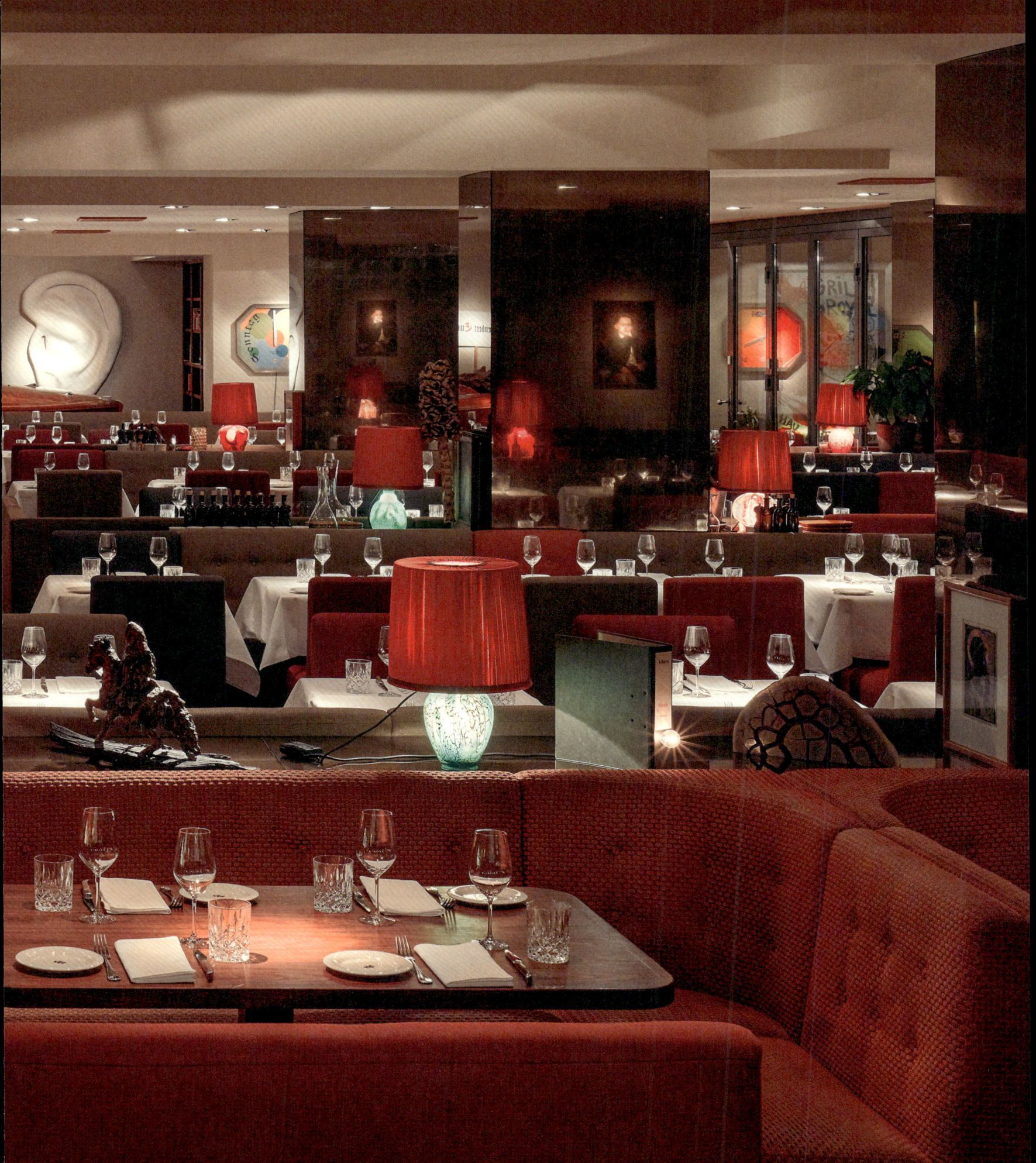

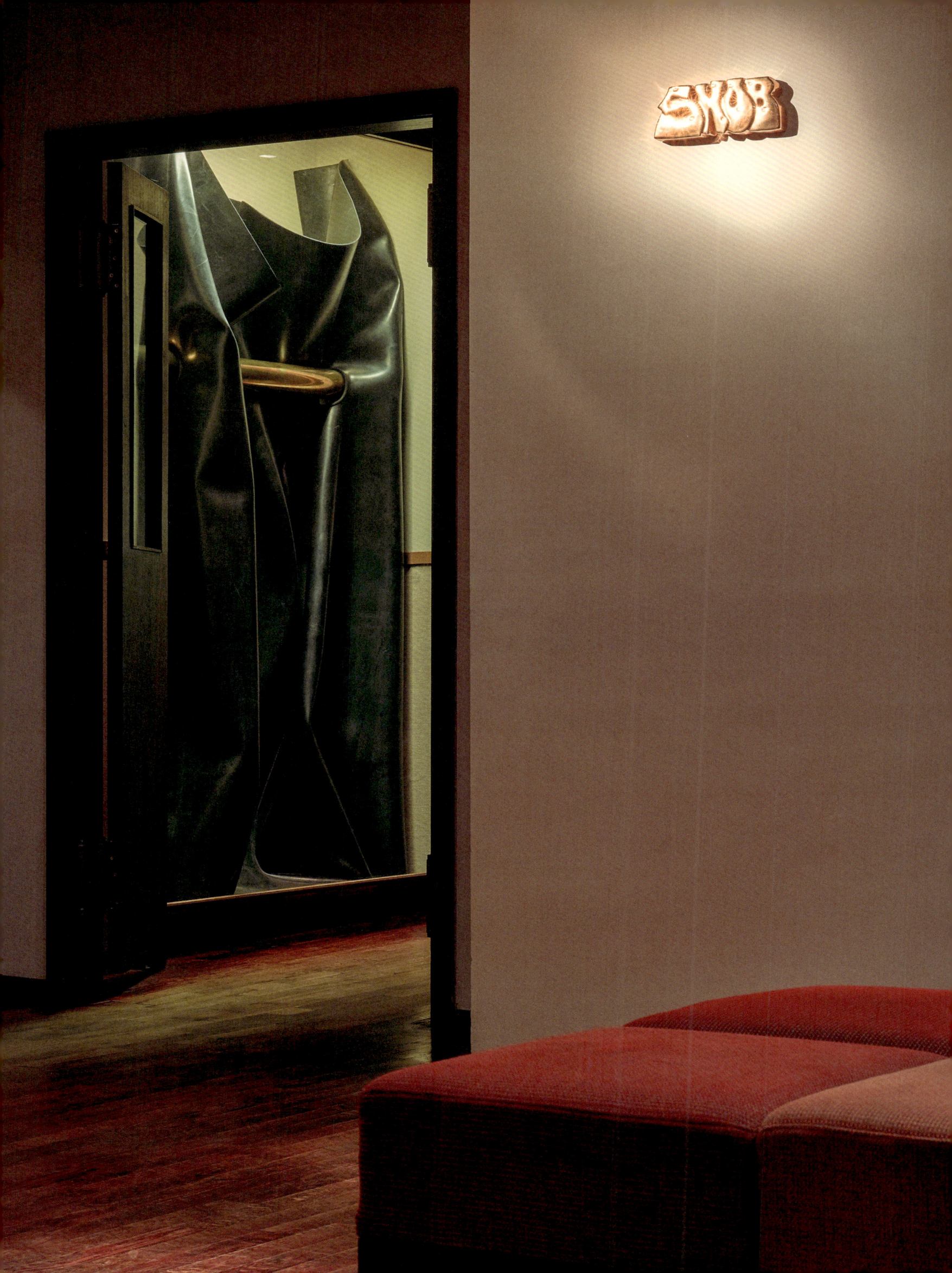

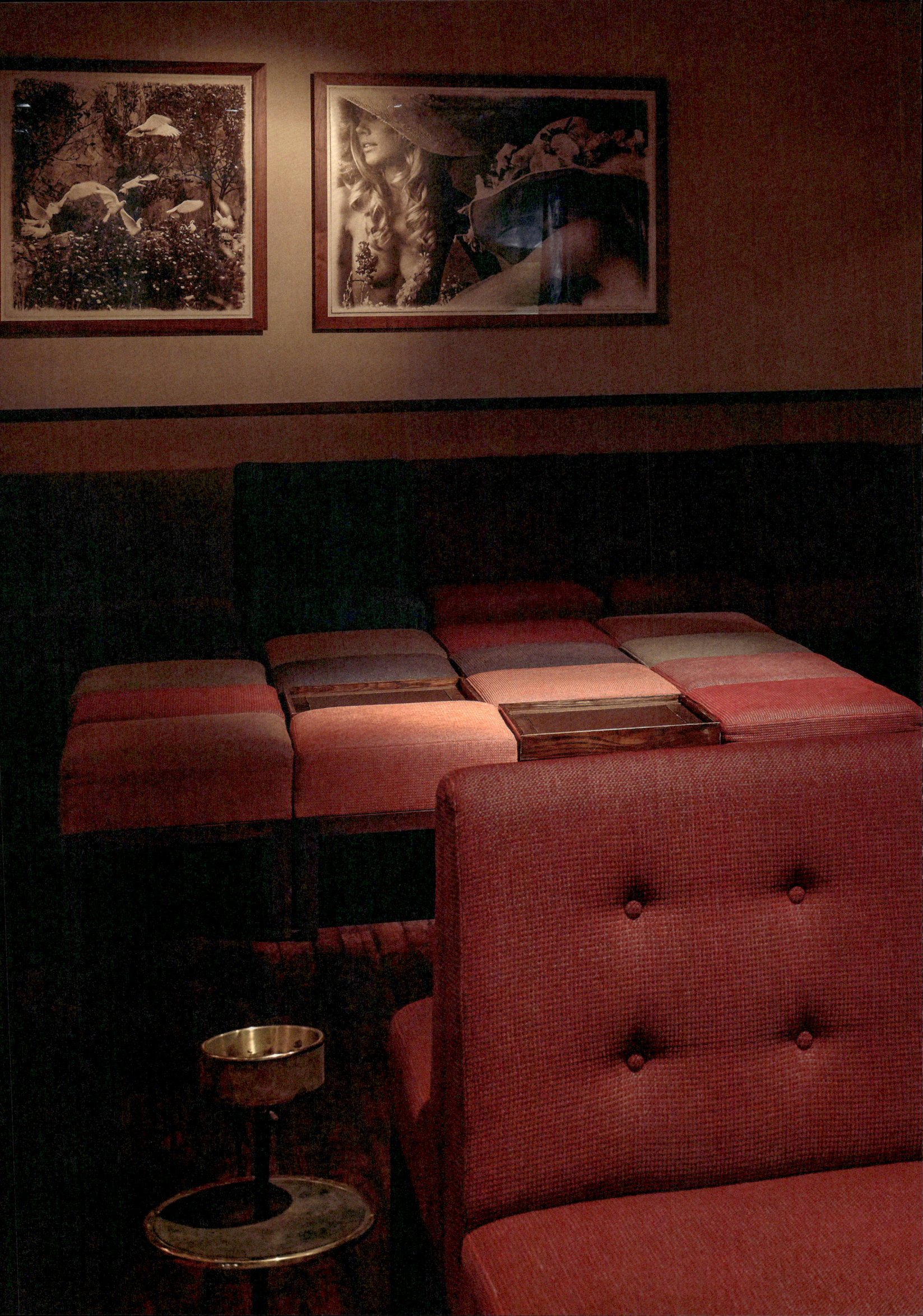

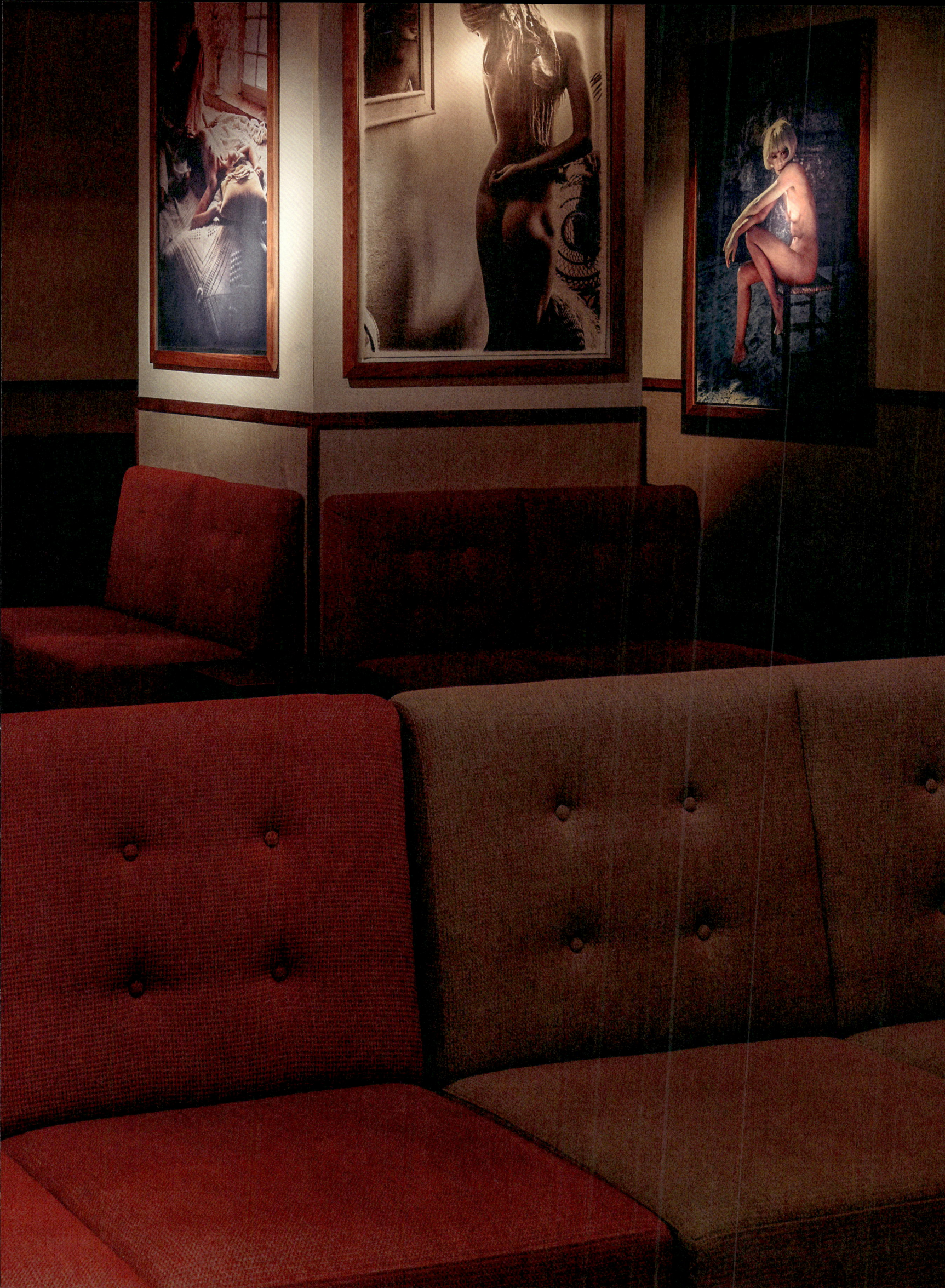

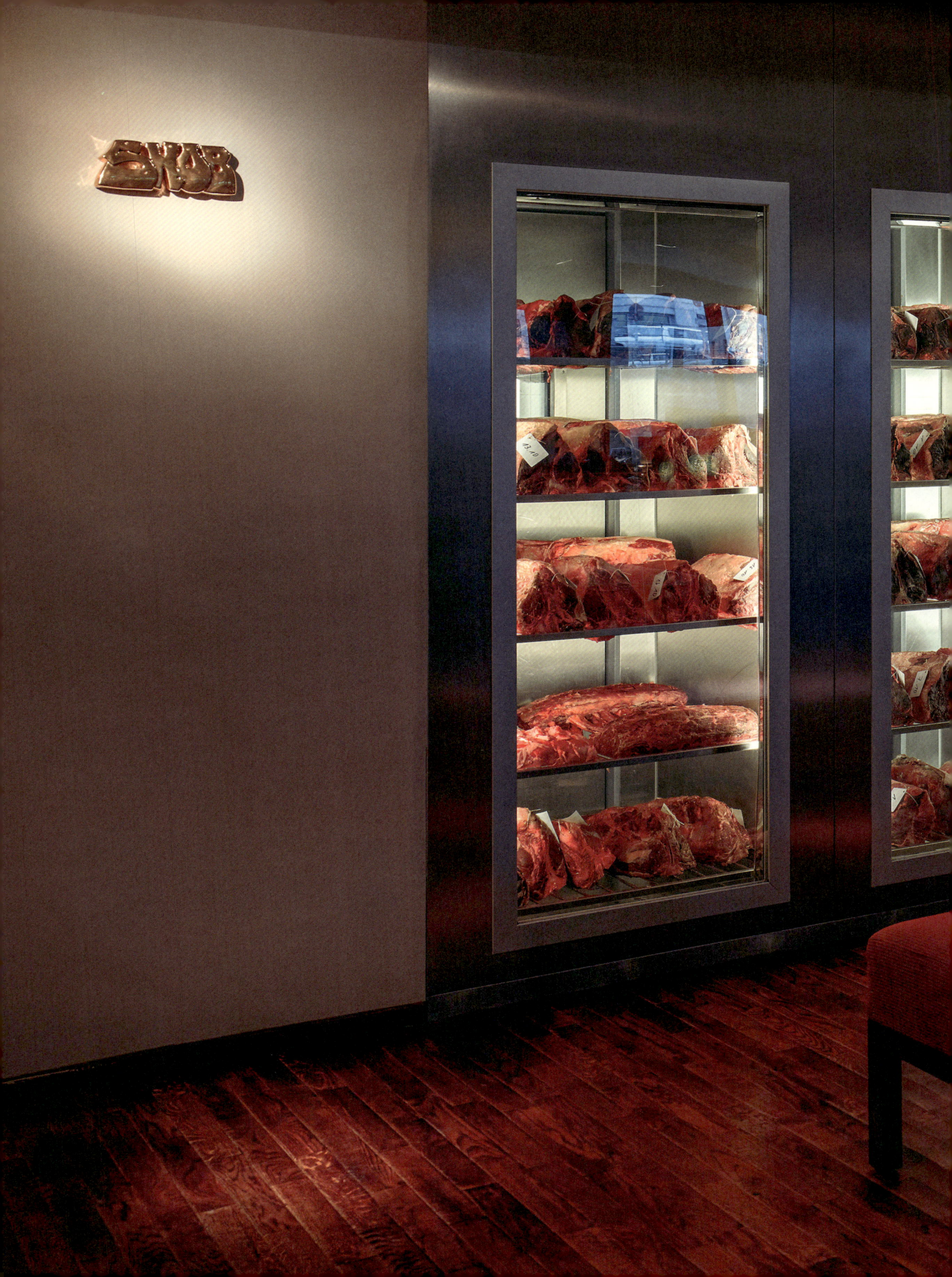

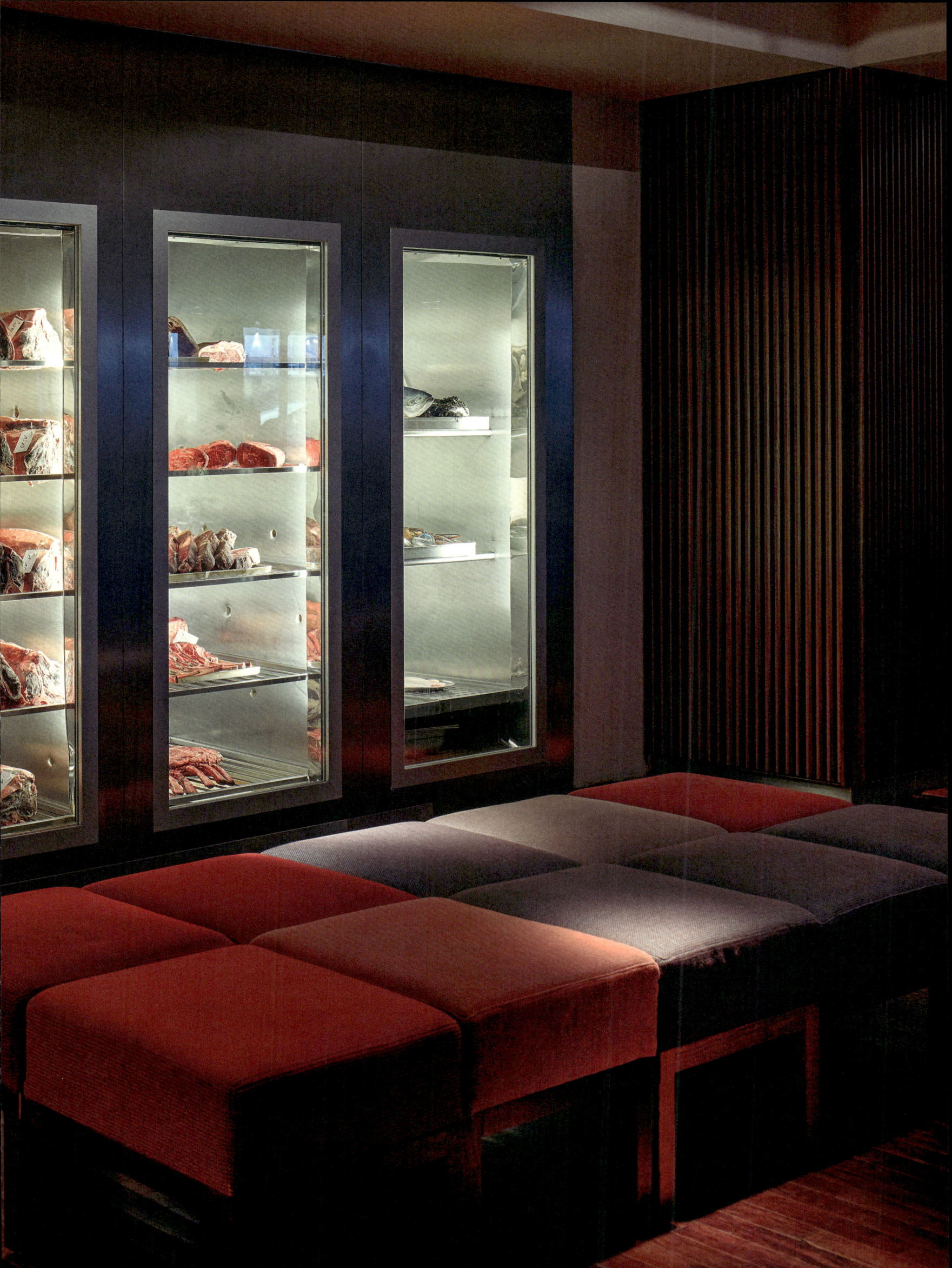

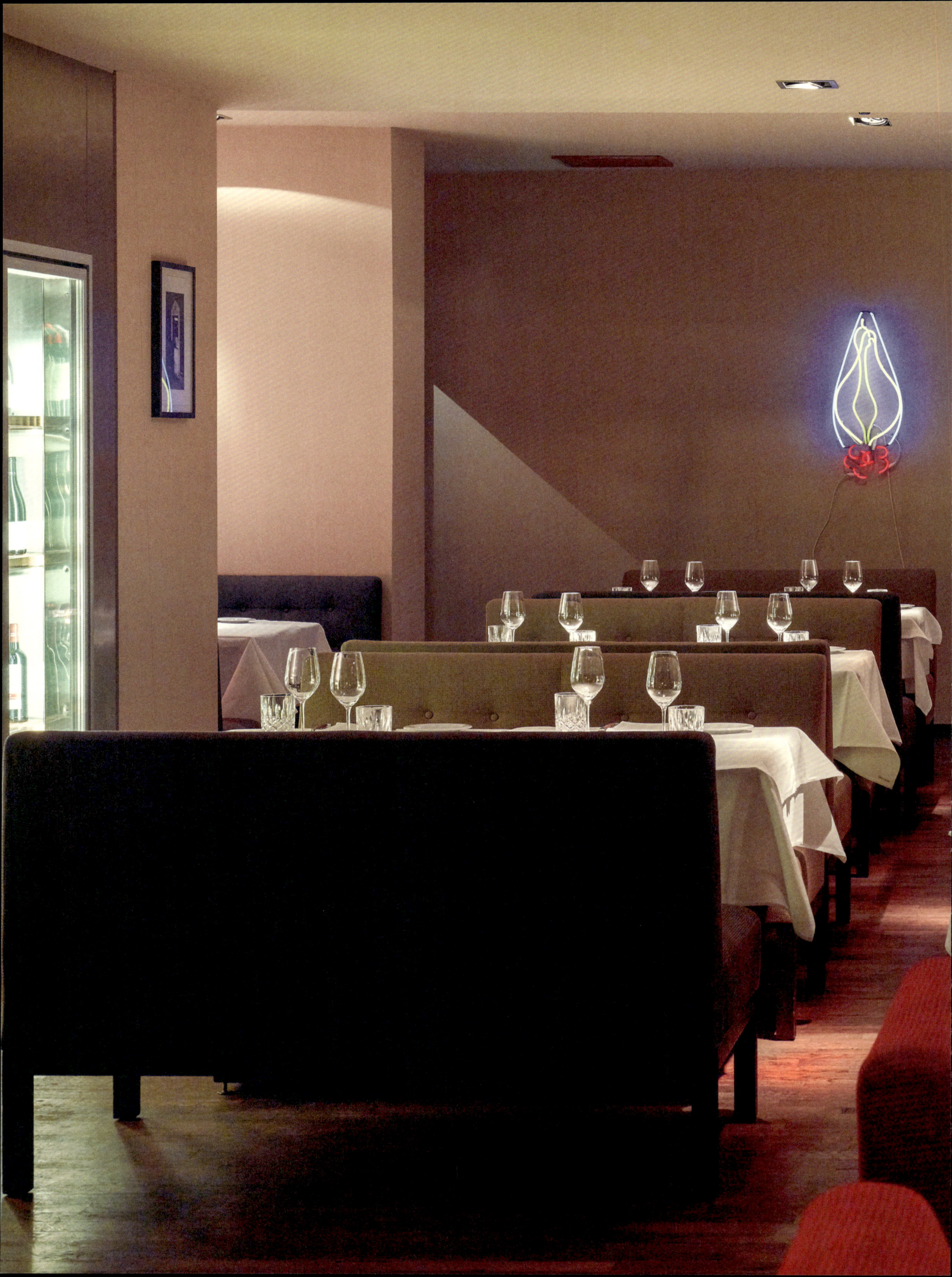

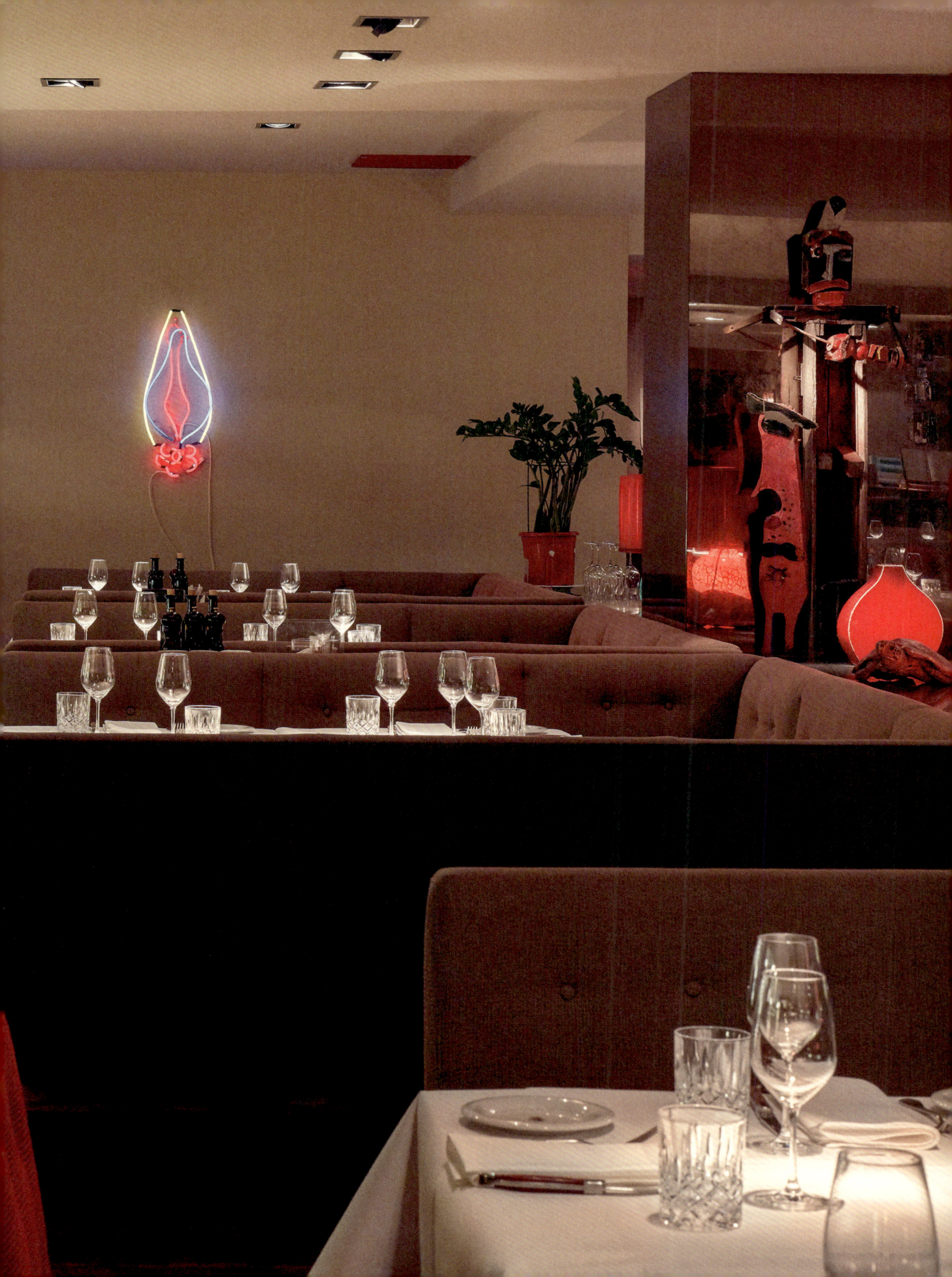

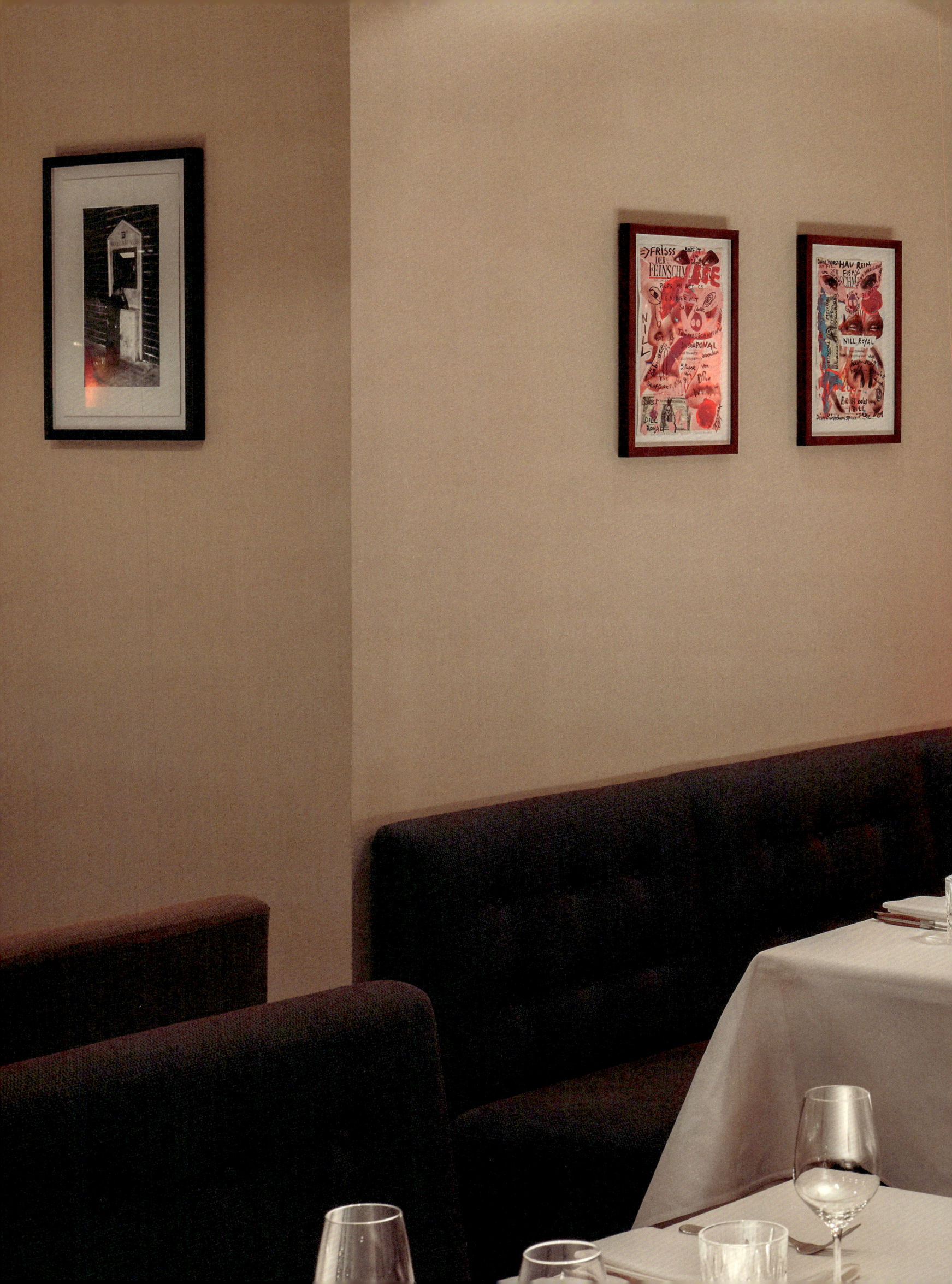

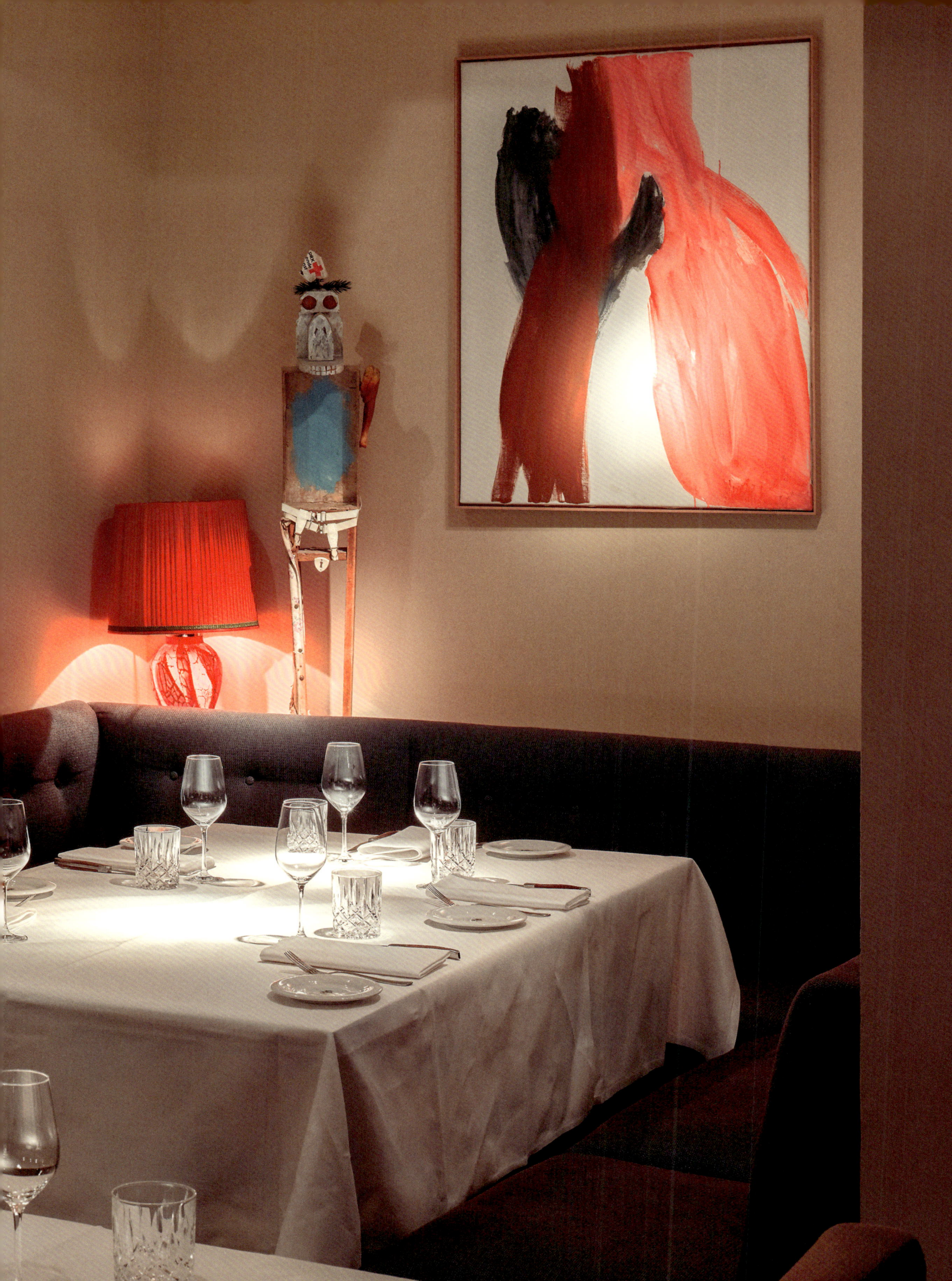

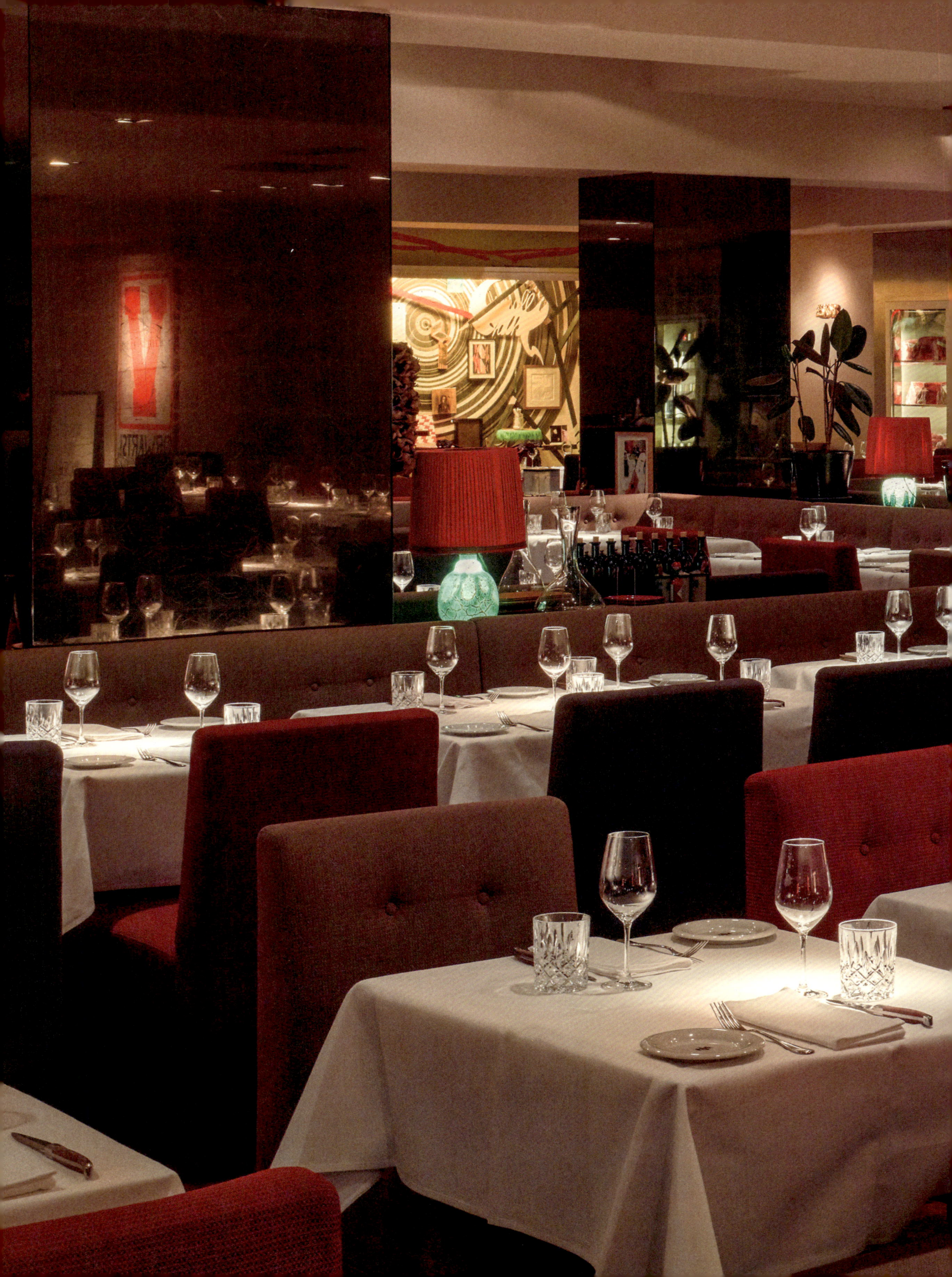

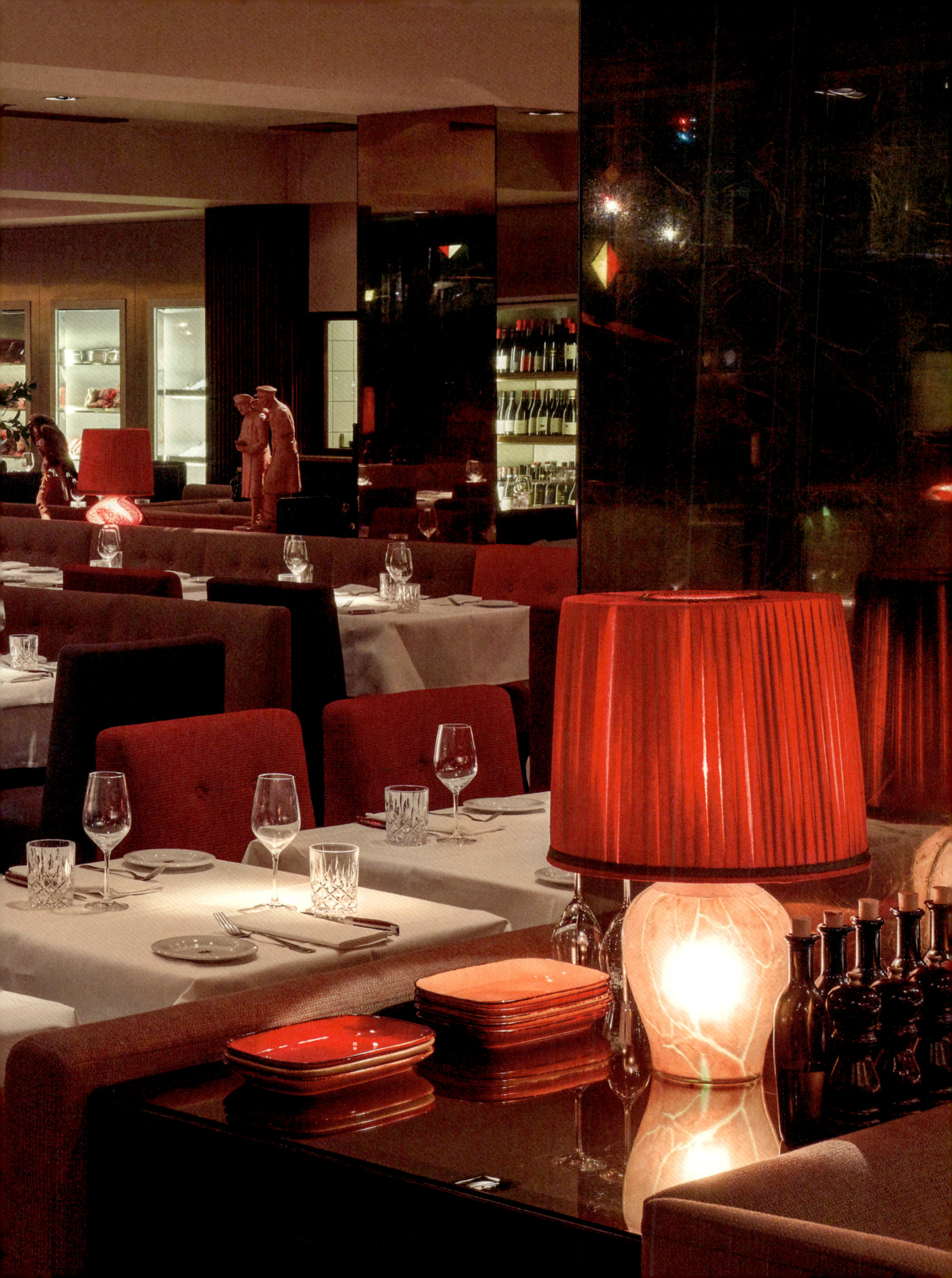

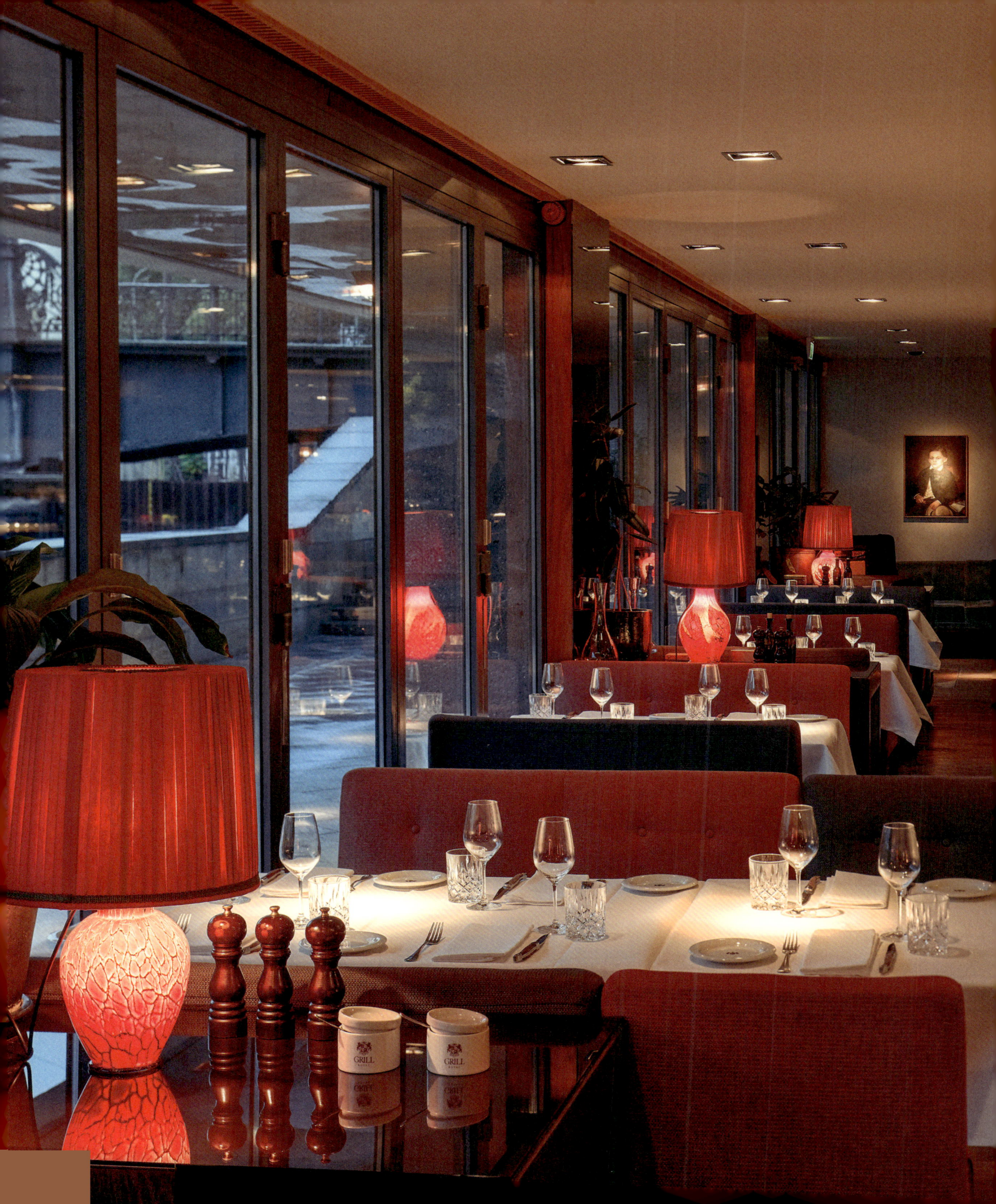

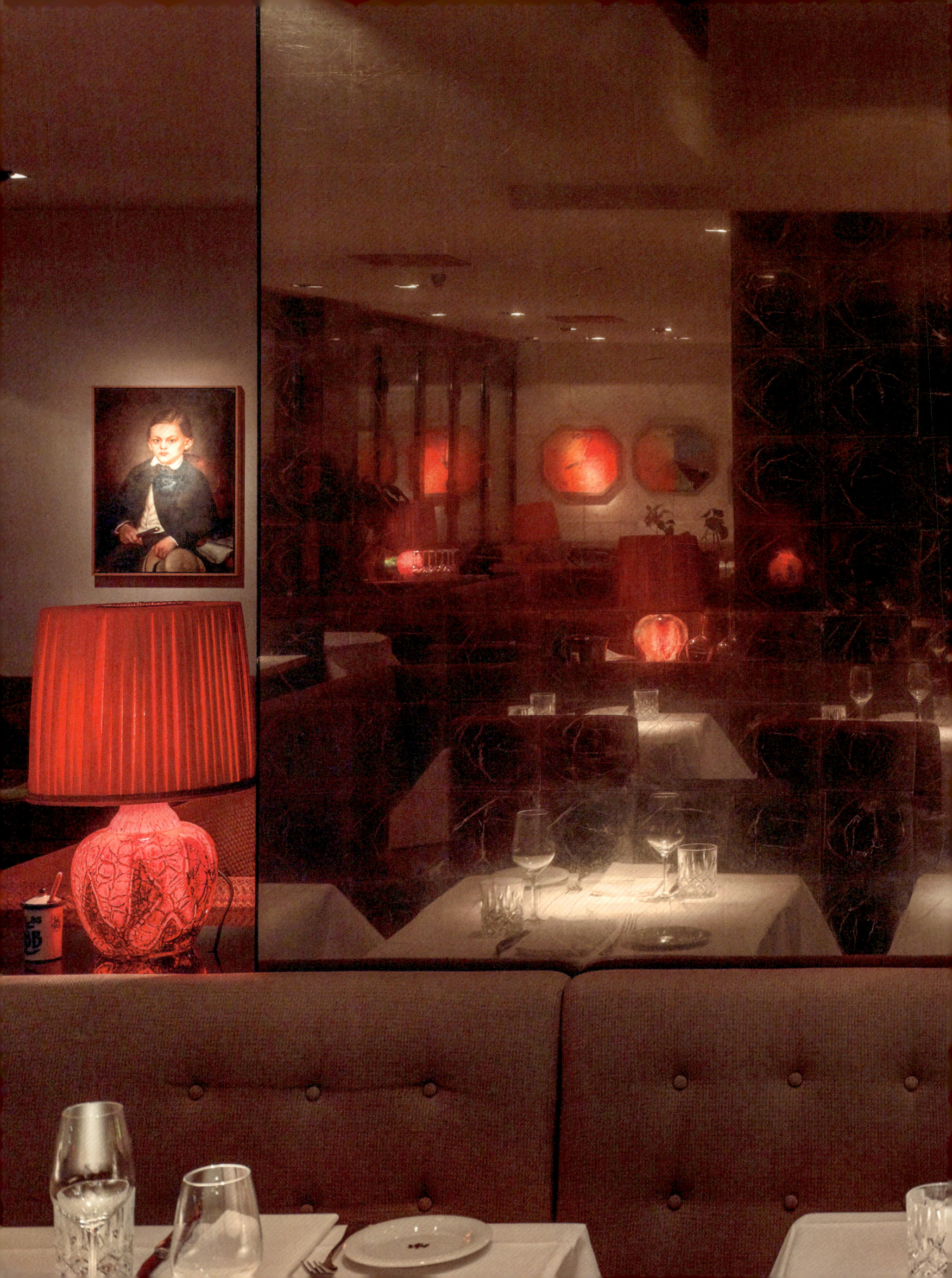

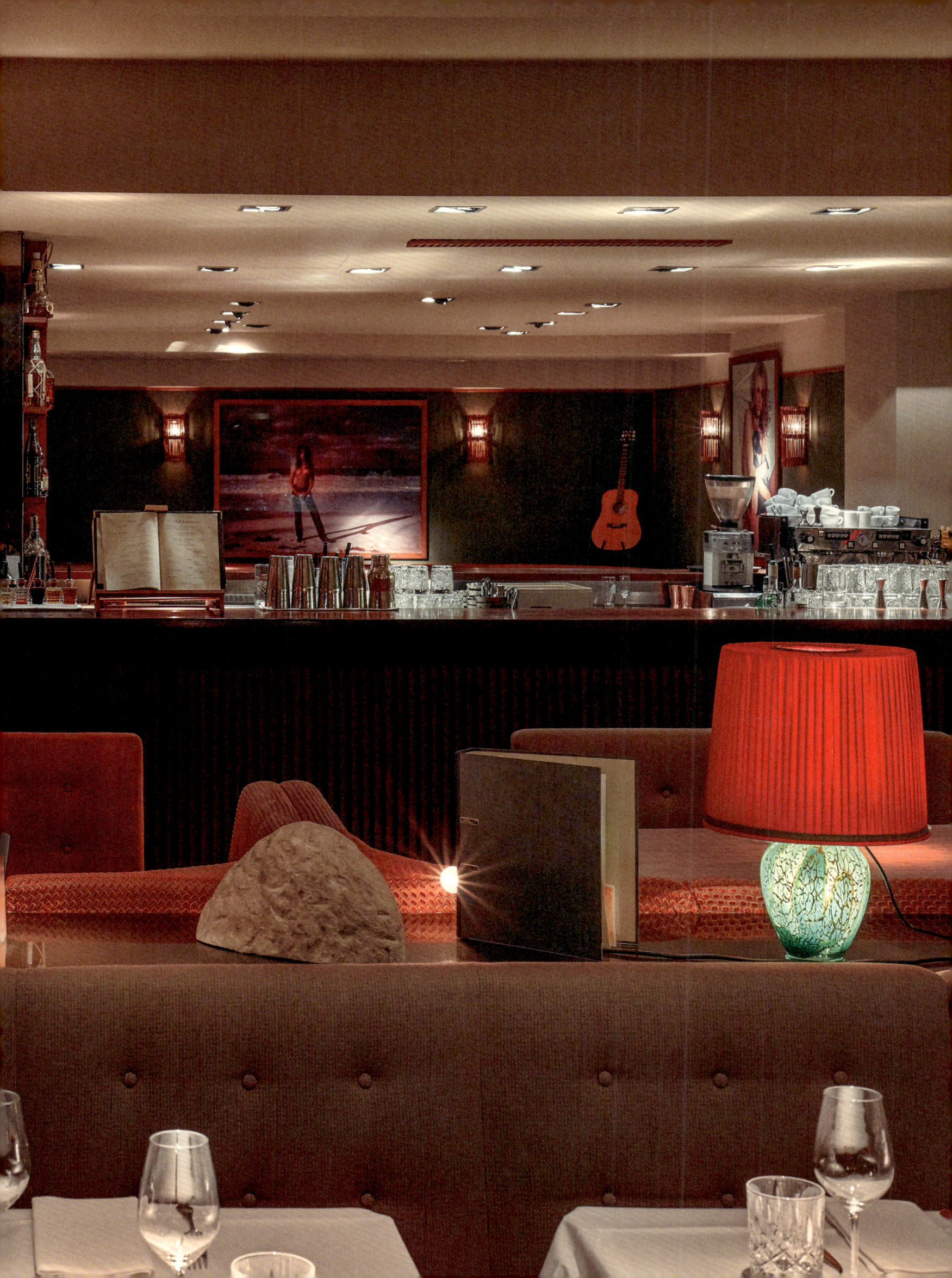

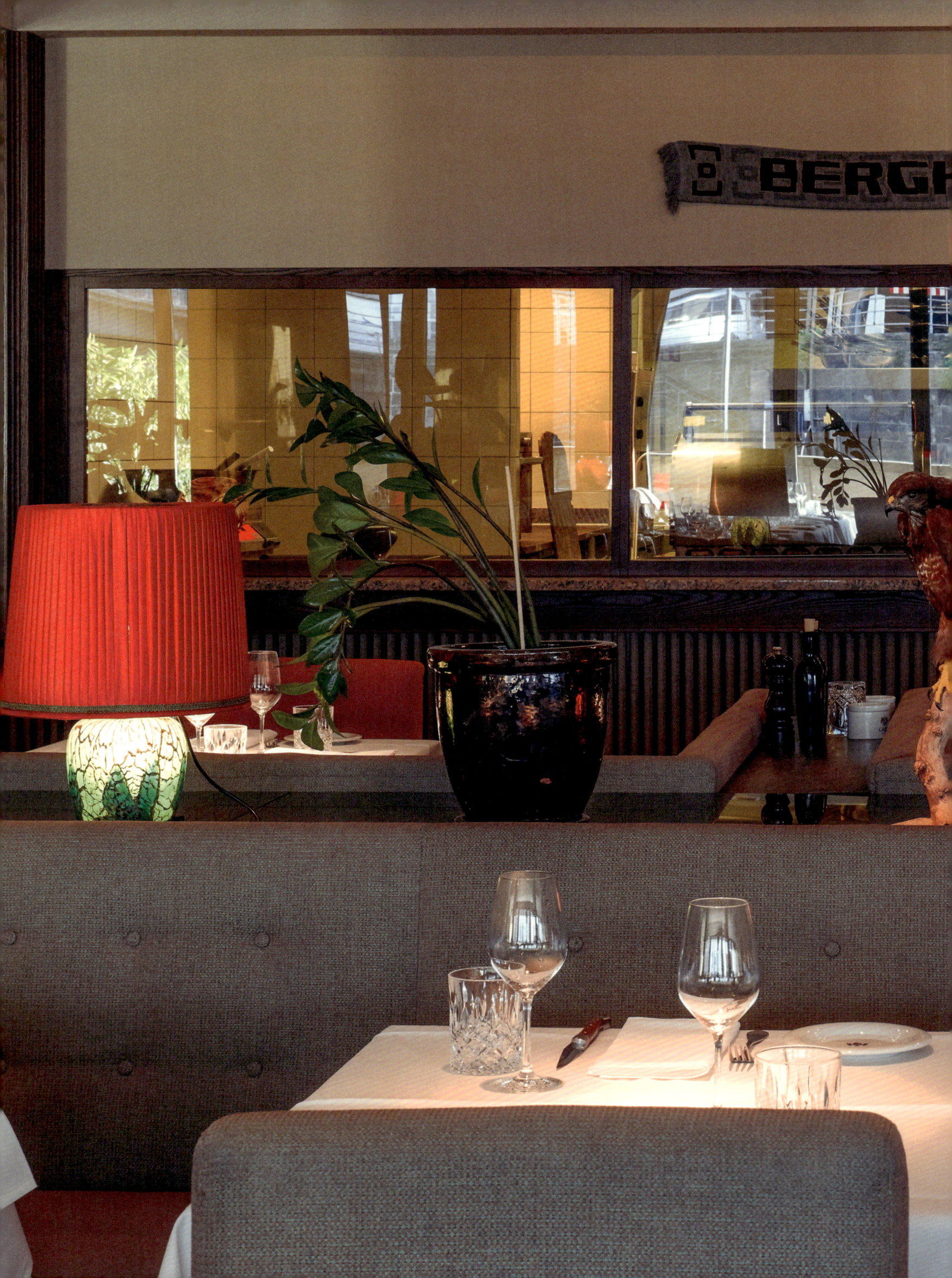

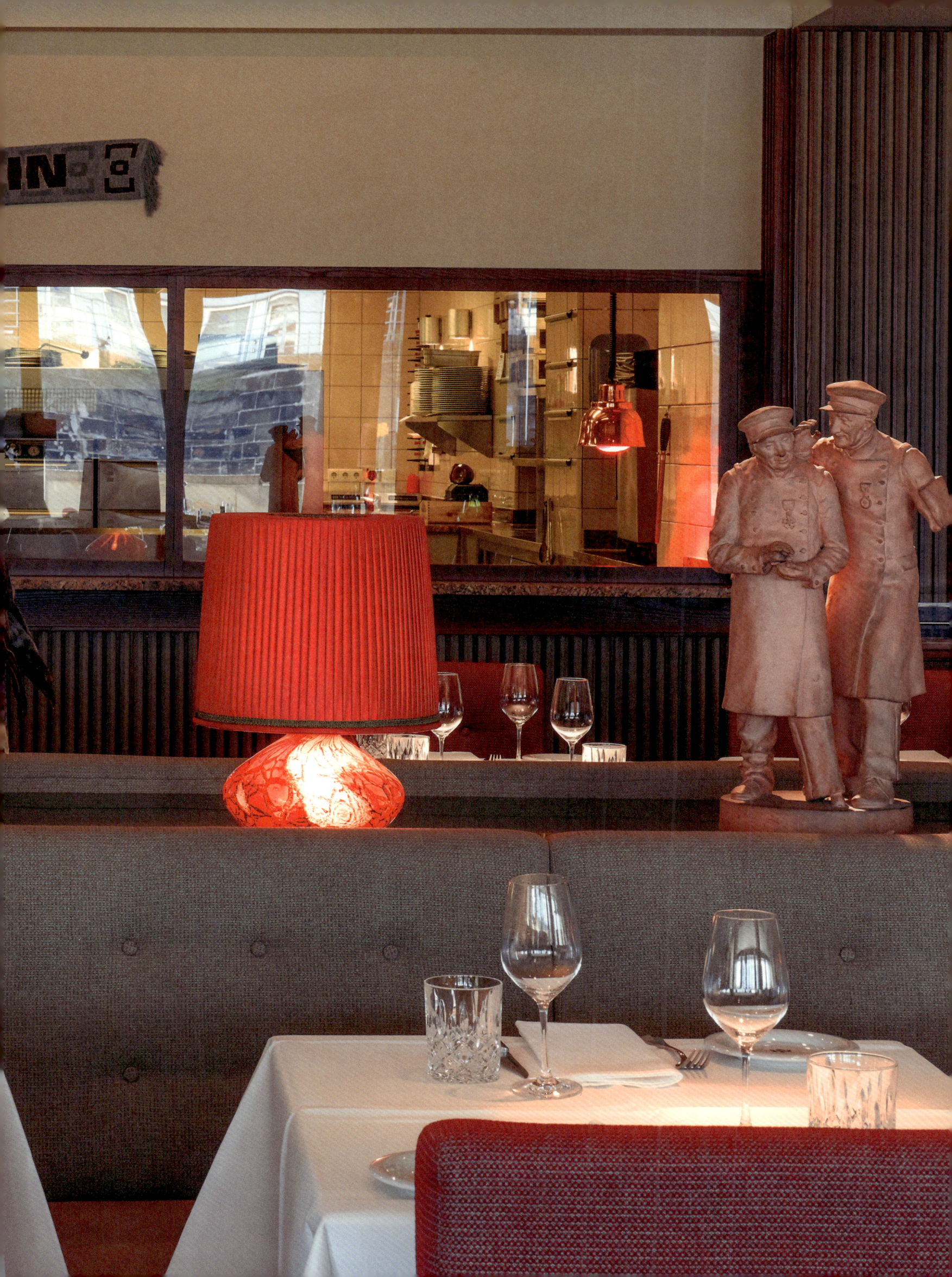

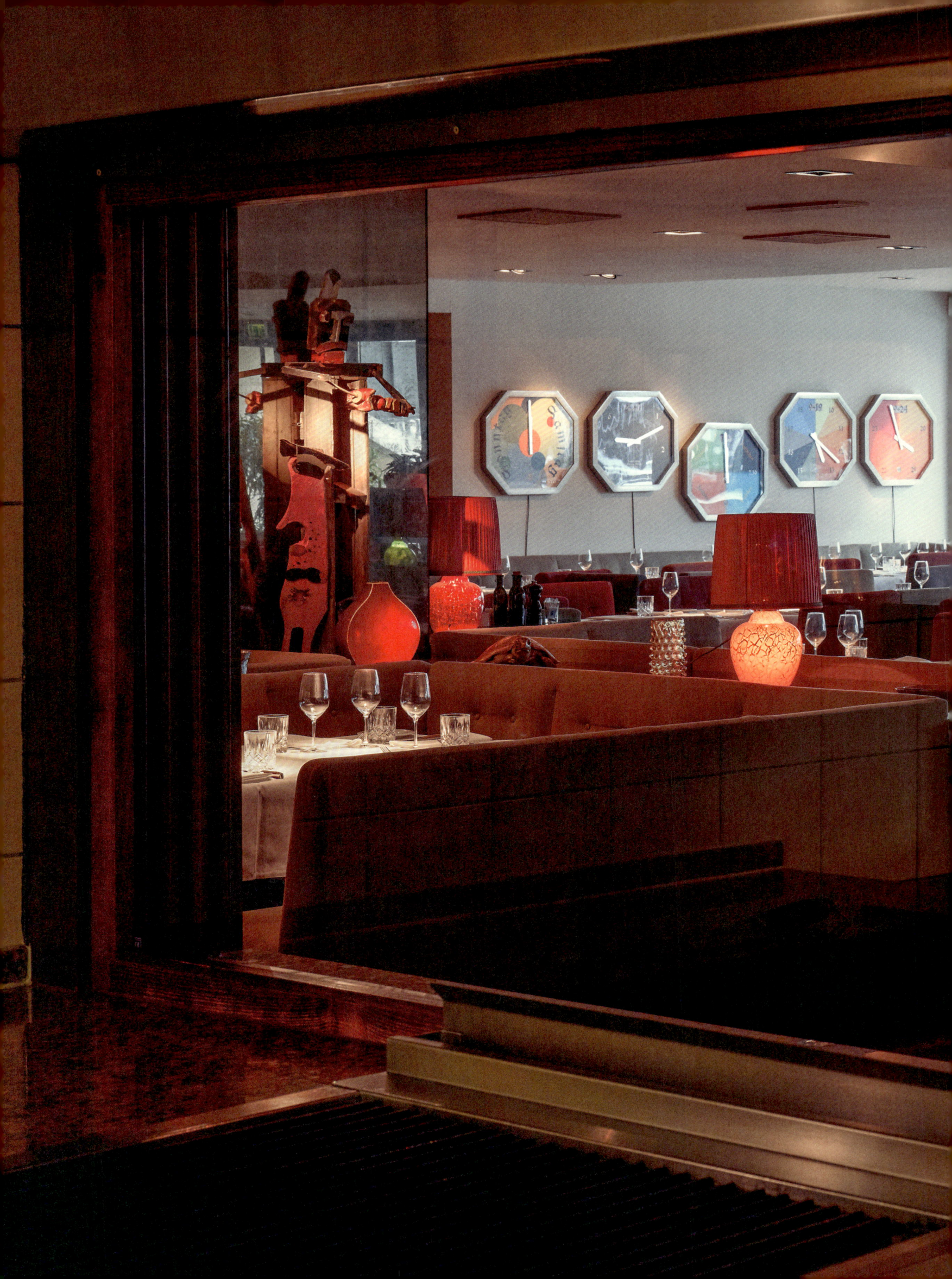

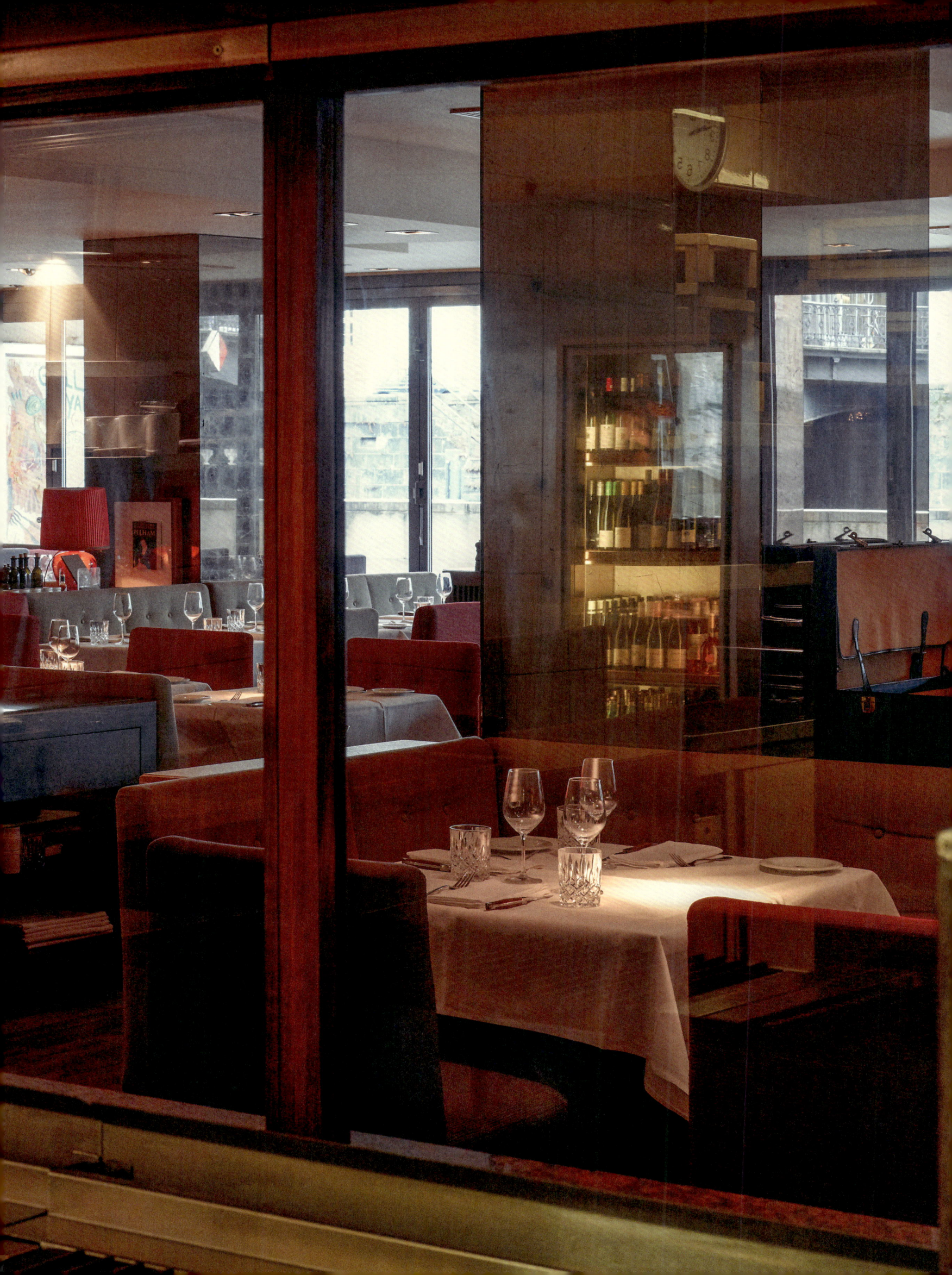

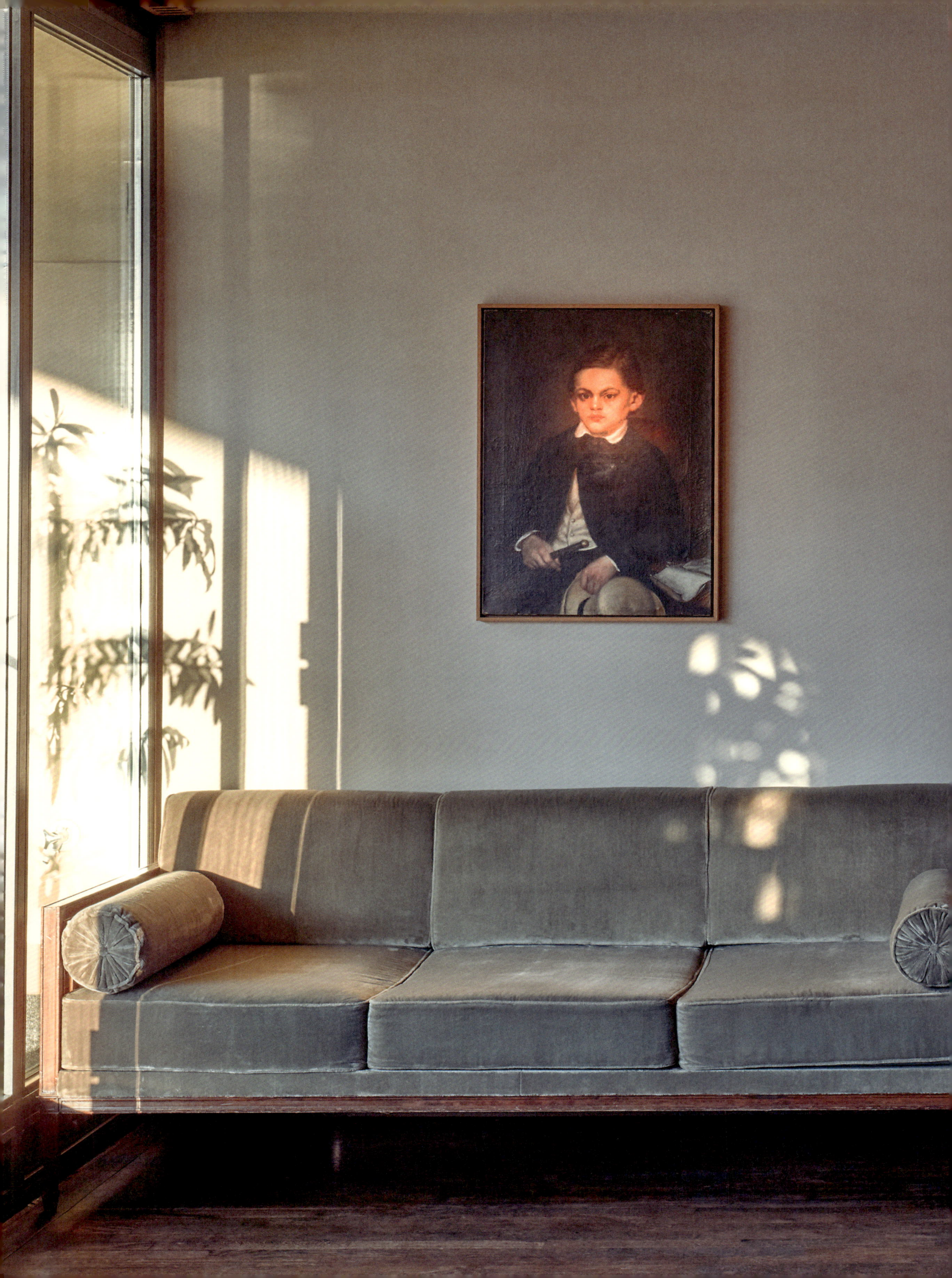

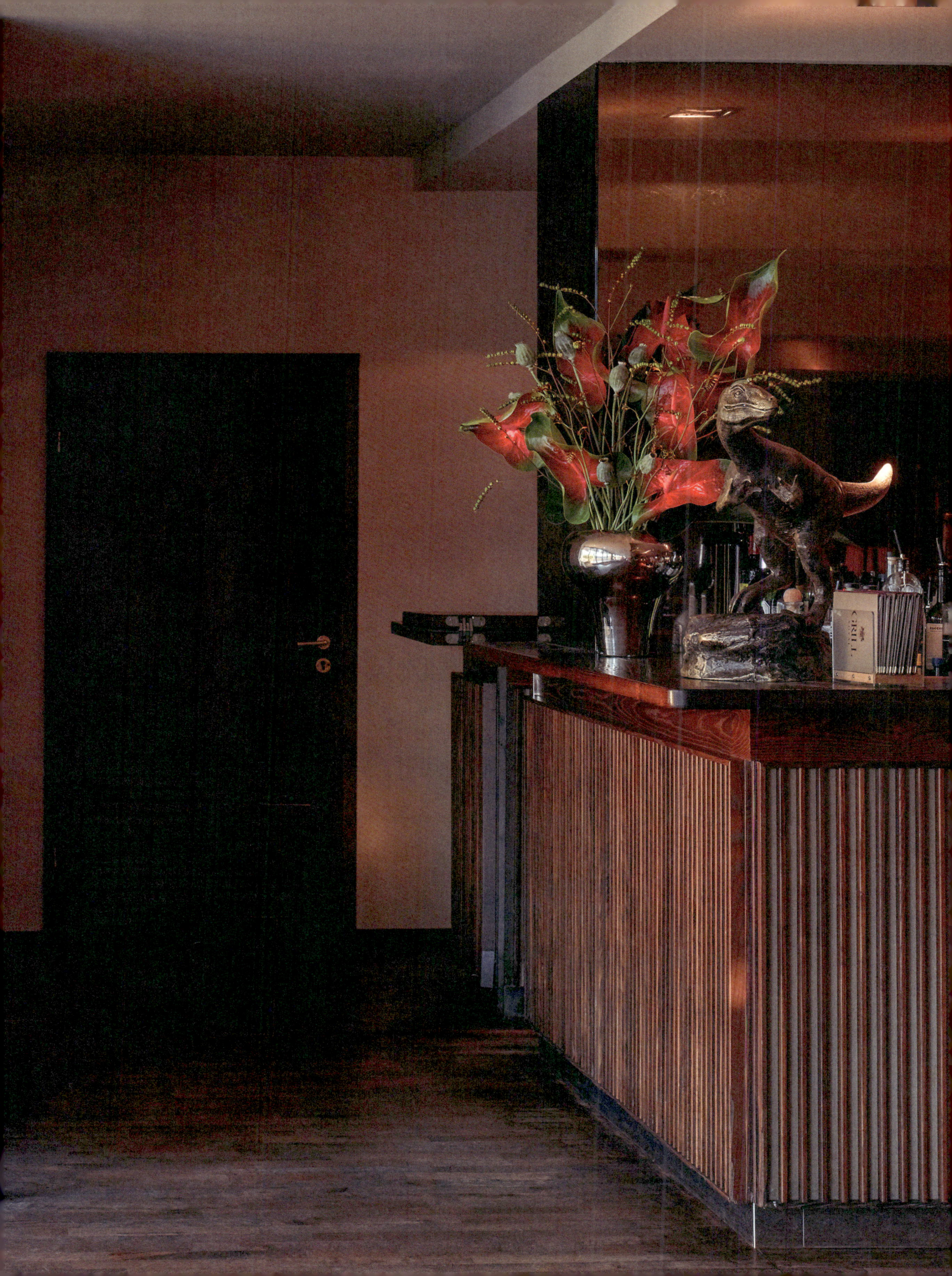

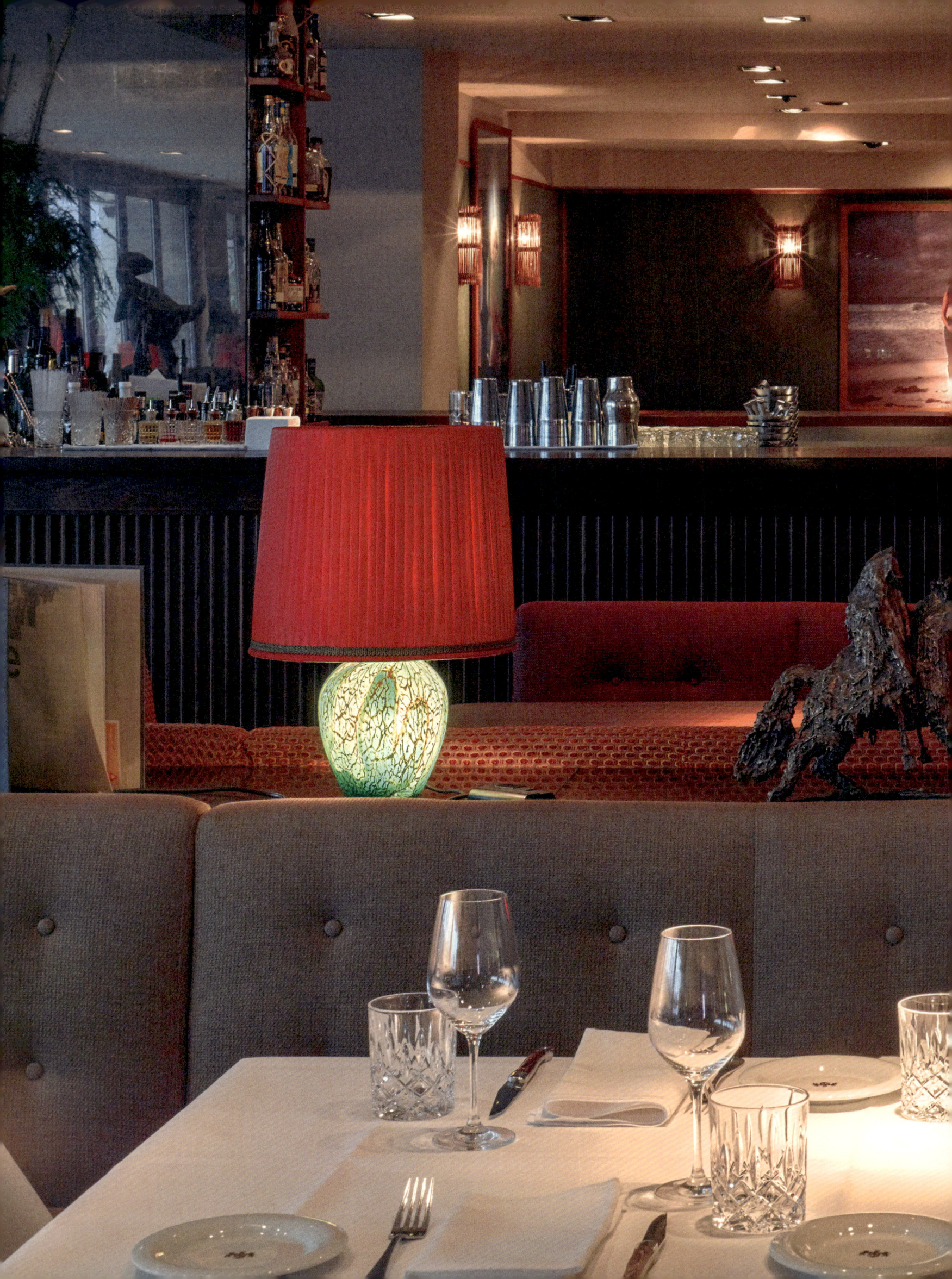

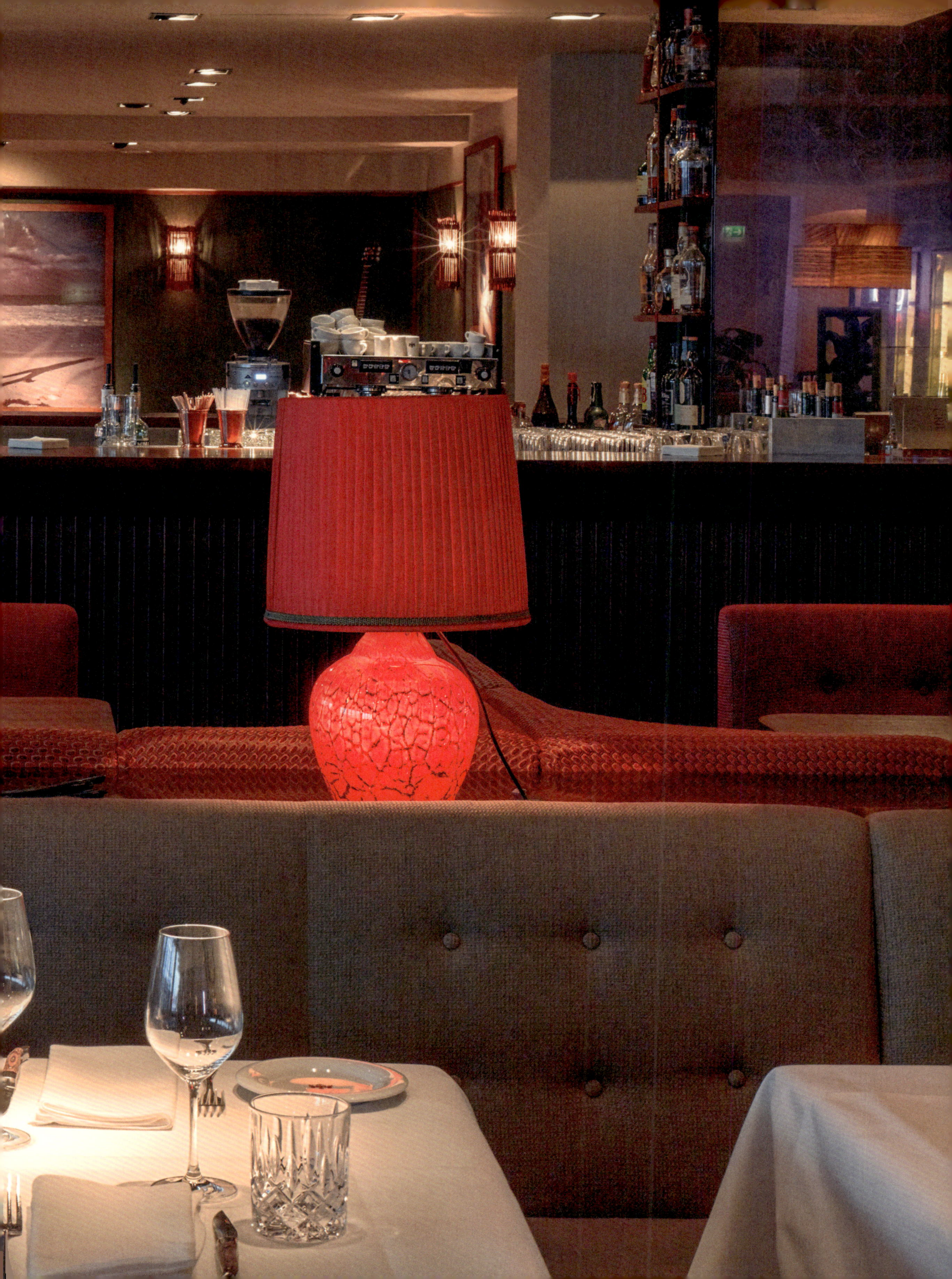

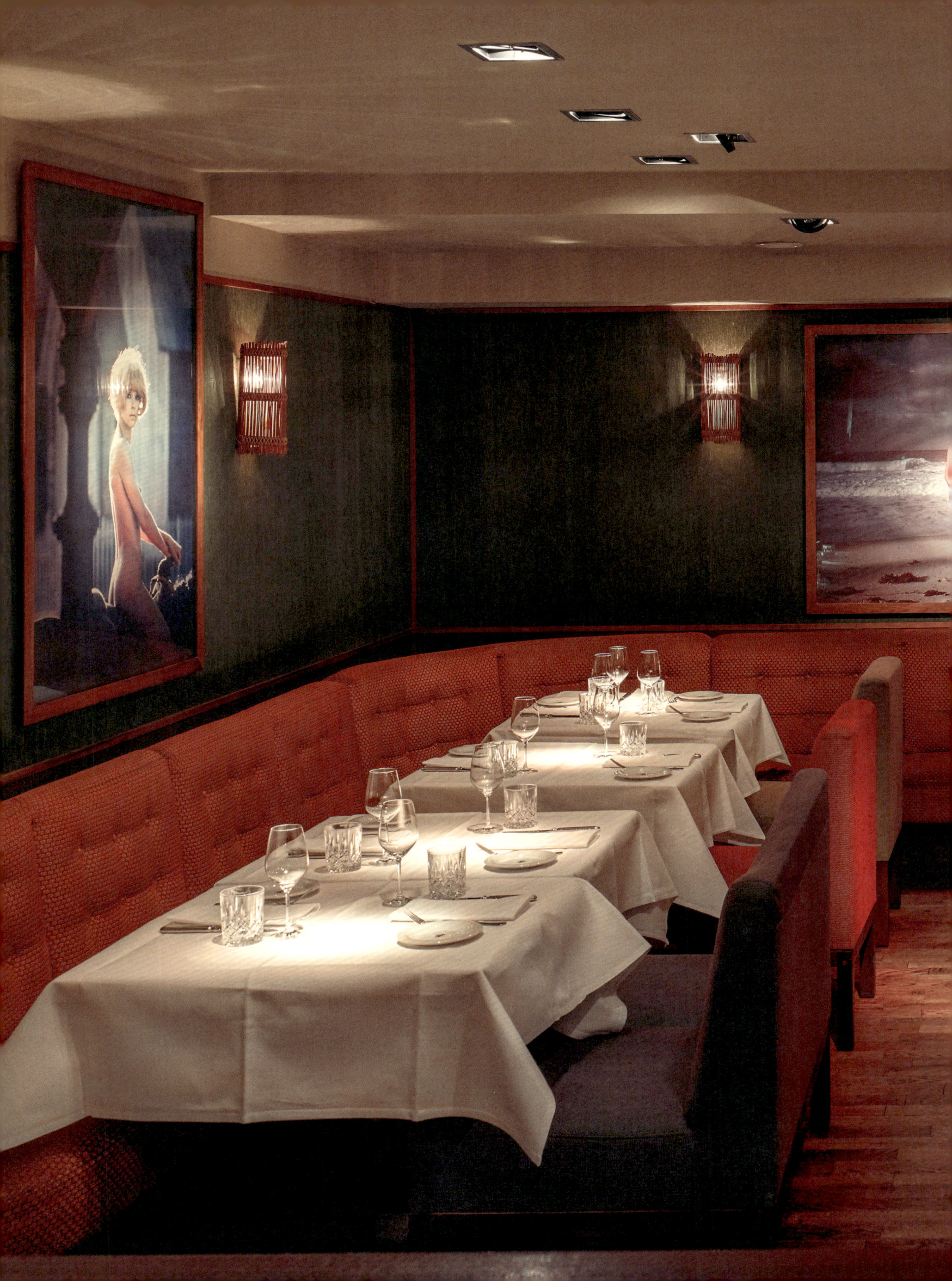

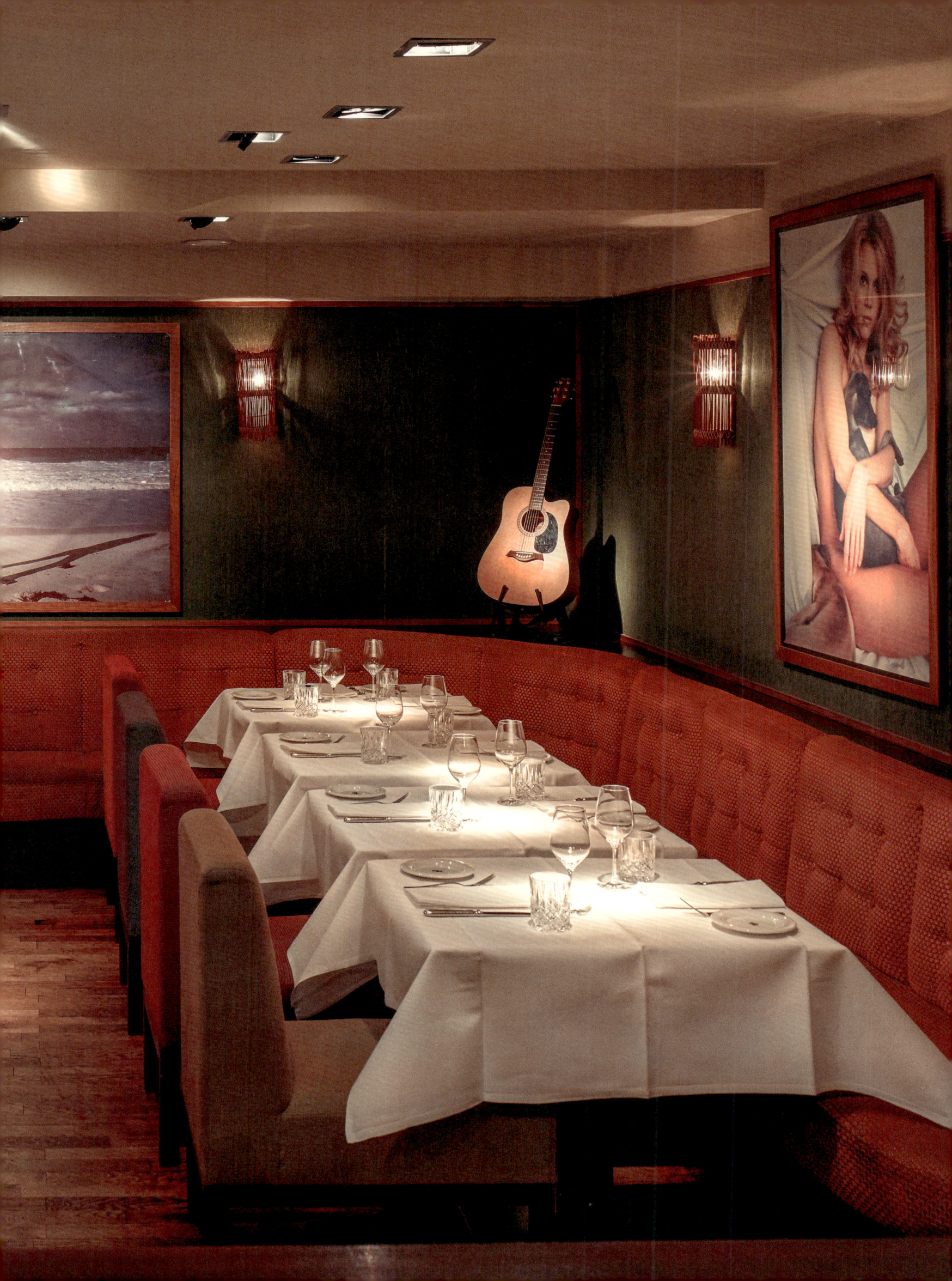

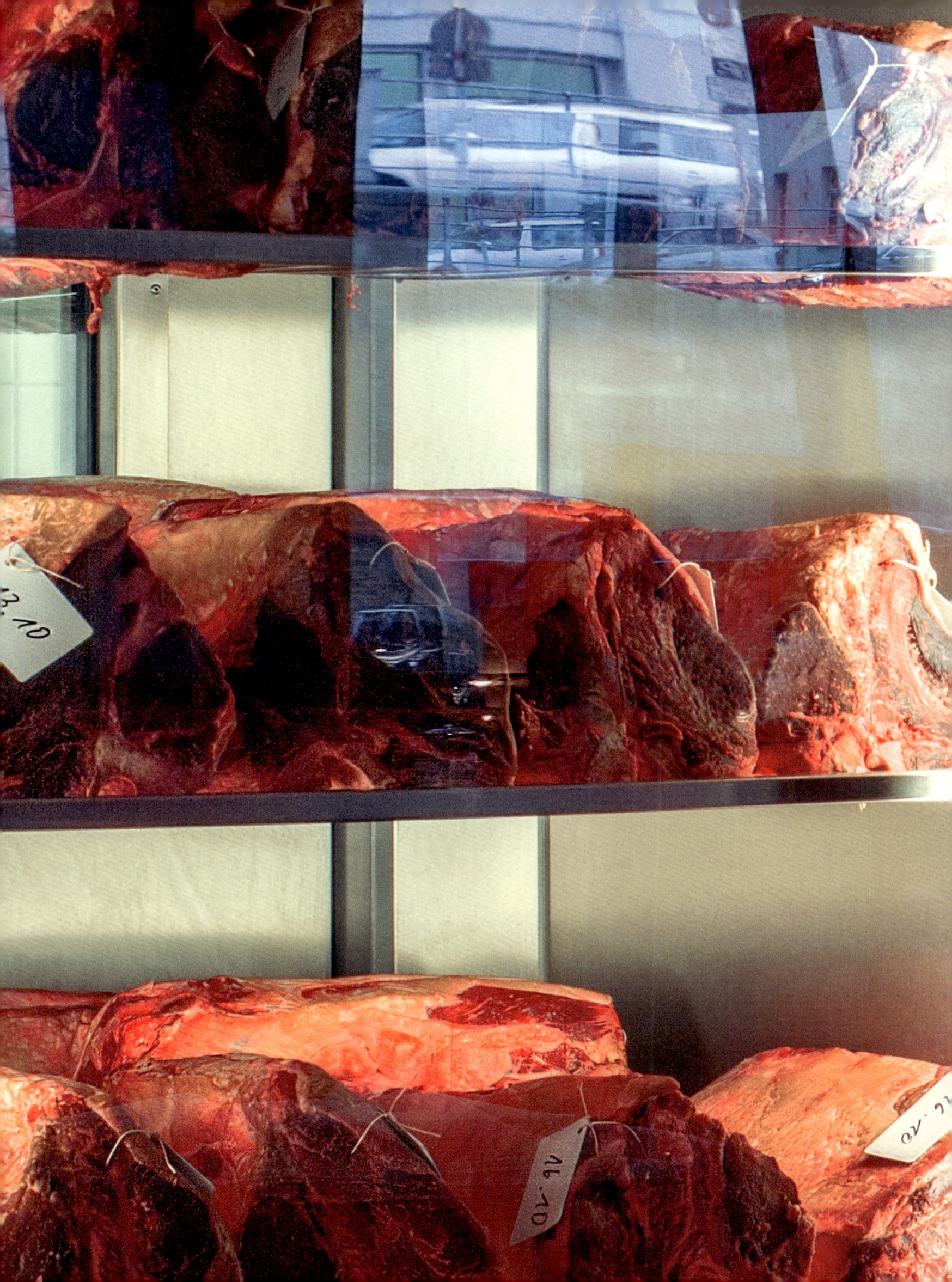

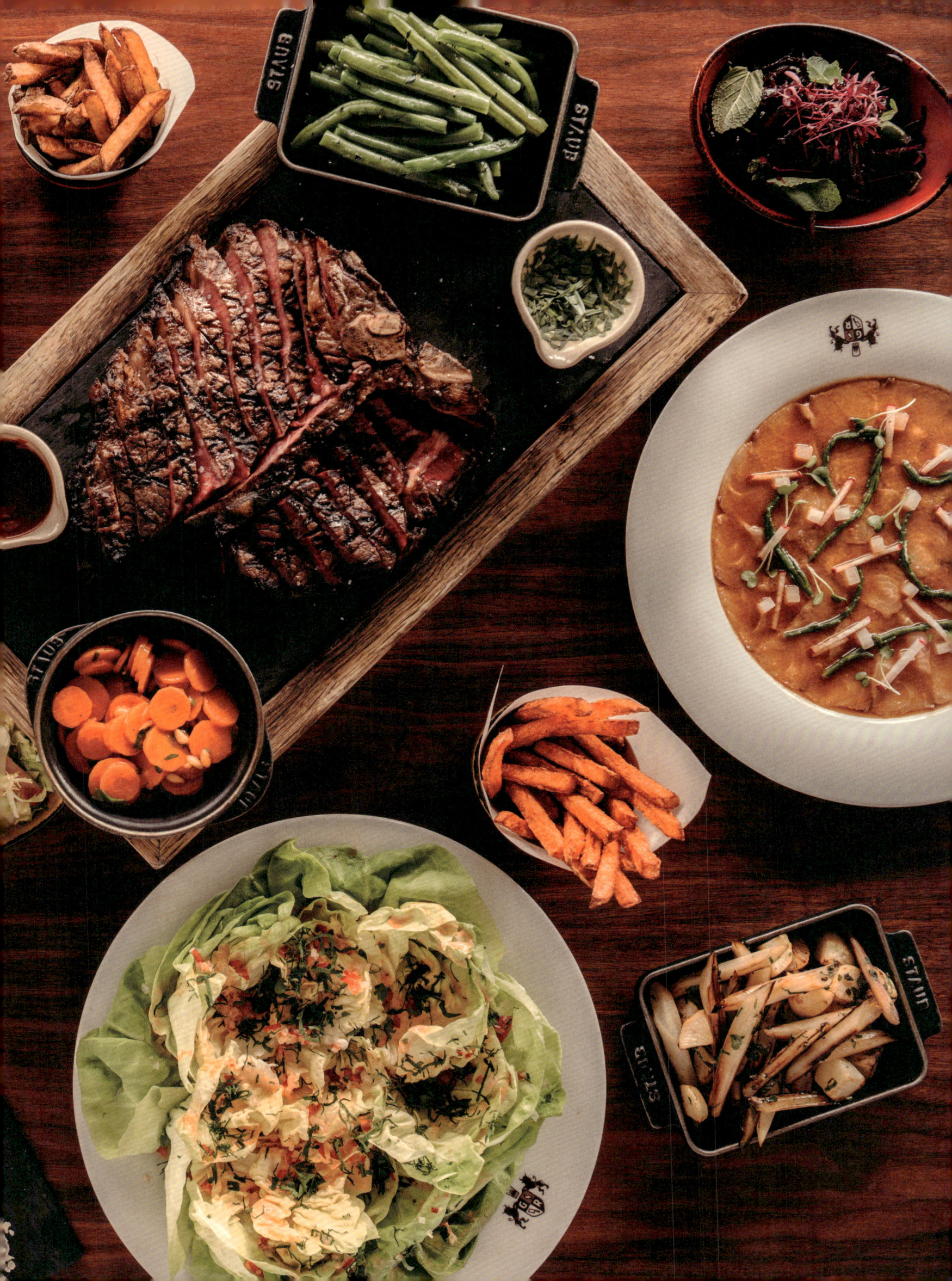

Der Grill Royal

oder die Gastlichkeit der Berliner Welt seit dem neunzehnten Jahrhundert

Erwin Seitz

Vorspiel auf der Bühne

Berlin, im Dezember 2016. Wir gehen ins Deutsche Theater in Berlin-Mitte, wo an diesem Abend Goethes *Iphigenie* gegeben wird. Wir wollen einfach vor Ende des Jahres noch einmal ausgehen und einen anregenden Abend erleben – und vertrauen darauf, dass in diesem Haus in der Regel gute Schauspielkunst zu sehen ist. Und Goethes Iphigenie? Nun, man wird sehen. Kein leichtes Stück für die Bühne. Es wird viel geredet, ohne dass äußerlich viel passiert.

Der kleine Bühnenraum erscheint ganz in Schwarz – und Iphigenie, die als erstes die Bühne betritt, trägt ein Kleid ganz in Weiß, aus leichtem Stoff, vielleicht auch nur ein Nachthemd, ohne sonstigen Schmuck, auf das Existenzielle reduziert: auf Vorgänge in der Seele. Die anderen Schauspieler treten hinzu; gemeinsam tünchen sie den Bühnenraum weiß. Doch es entsteht kein makelloses Weiß; es macht sich da und dort noch schwarzer Schimmer bemerkbar. So einfach geht das nicht, Lebensräume zu verwandeln: vom abgründigen Schwarz in unschuldiges Weiß.

Iphigenie fühlt sich von dunklen Schicksalsmächten getrieben. Sie scheint einer Familie anzugehören, die von den Göttern verflucht ist, verbannt auf eine Insel, wo König Thoas regiert. Dieser will sie heiraten; sie selbst aber will in die Heimat zurückkehren und ihren Bruder Orest wiederfinden. Sie hält Thoas hin, während Orest unversehens und heimlich auf der Insel eintrifft. Es wird der Plan ausgeheckt, Thoas zu hintergehen und zu fliehen. Aber das würde bloß bedeuten, dass sich Lug, Trug und blindes Schicksal fortsetzen. Iphigenie spürt das, geht in sich, ersinnt andere menschliche Spielräume, wird ruhiger, überlegter, setzt auf den vertrauensvollen Umgang mit Thoas und baut auf sein Entgegenkommen. Sie schlägt – alias Kathleen Morgeneyer – mehr und mehr einen gelassen-klassischen Ton an, ganz den Vorgaben des Dichters ergeben, ein bezauberndes Parlando, so, wie man es heutzutage im Theater selten erlebt. Im Saal ist es mucksmäuschenstill, alles lauscht.

Geht doch, denkt man sich. Es muss nicht immer Spektakel sein. Es kann auch feiner zugehen, selbst im Zeitalter der Hektik und Geschwindigkeit. Und vielleicht muss man, ob solcher Sprachkunst, gar nicht sagen: „Geht doch noch einmal", sondern: „Jetzt geht das wieder", nach all dem Turnen und Lärmen auf der Bühne in jüngerer Zeit. In sich gehen, sich selbst erkennen, ein Maß finden, sich verständigen, Lebensart erlernen – das sind doch die zeitlosen Elemente des Menschlichen.

Der Besucher schaut sich um im Saal, wo vormals, um 1900, die bürgerliche Spielkunst dem Königlichen Schauspielhaus am Gendarmenmarkt den Rang ablief, weil wirklichkeitsnaher, echter – und wo so viele berühmte Leute wirkten und zuschauten wie Max Reinhardt, Alfred Kerr und andere, wo Stücke der Klassiker ebenso aufgeführt wurden wie die der Zeitgenossen, Tradition und Moderne ineinander verwebend. Im Publikum sitzen heute auch junge muslimische Frauen, elegant gekleidet mit Kopftuch, in kleinen Gruppen, ohne männliche Begleitung, hören zu, was eine weibliche Figur der europäischen Hochaufklärung zu sagen hat; alle anderen im Saal spitzen ebenfalls die Ohren, ganz so, als sei Goethe immer noch einer von uns.

Auf der Suche nach der verlorenen Mitte in Berlin
Die Theorie des Preußentums sah einst nicht vor, dass man sich nach dem Theater abends noch anderweitig vergnügt. Der Bürger sollte sich als Untertan an hehren Gedanken delektieren und sich dann wieder einfacher Häuslichkeit widmen. Heinrich Heine, der in den 1820er Jahren in der preußischen Hauptstadt studierte, war empört über diese Knausrigkeit und entwich nach Paris. Selbst Bismarck, der zur selben Zeit als Gymnasiast und Student viele Jahre in Berlin verbracht hatte, dachte später als Reichskanzler und Fürst nicht gern an das frühere Berlin zurück. Julius von Eckardt notierte ein rückschauendes Gespräch mit ihm im Jahr 1884: „Das gab zu Erzählungen von dem alten Berlin, der Beschränktheit seines Zuschnittes, Veranlassung, an welchem gemessen es für verschwenderisch galt, wenn man (wie der Fürst bemerkt) ein Beefsteak für ‚acht Jute‘ im Café Royal zu verzehren und innerhalb der Altstadt mit der Droschke zu fahren den Mut hatte."

Natürlich war auch Goethe das spartanische Preußentum nicht geheuer. Sein Credo lautete: Gedenke zu leben! Strebe und genieße! Er selbst zelebrierte in seinem Haus am Frauenplan in Weimar die Kunst der Gastlichkeit, und so mancher preußische Asket, der ihn von Berlin aus mit hochfliegenden Gedanken besuchte, staunte, dass der Dichterfürst so nonchalant den sinnlichen Freuden zusprach.

So gut wie jeden Tag dinierte er zwei, drei Stunden mit Freunden und Bekannten. Die Palette der Speisen reichte von einfacher Hausmannskost bis zu luxuriösen Delikatessen wie Kaviar und Austern. Selbstverständlich wurde geredet, viel geredet bei Tisch, über leichte musische Themen, bildende Kunst, Lese- und Reiseerfahrungen, über das, was draußen in der Welt vor sich ging. Eine solche Lebensführung machte dann allmählich auch in Berlin Schule. Berühmte Tagebuch- und Memoirenschreiber des späten neunzehnten und frühen zwanzigsten Jahrhunderts wie Marie von Bunsen oder Harry Graf Kessler, welche für Neues aufgeschlossen waren, schätzten an Goethe und seinen Schriften genau das: die Kunst des Kommunizierens, die geistreiche Plauderei, den guten Umgang mit Menschen und Dingen, die gemütvolle wie gesellige Art, die Kennerschaft der Genüsse.

Wir, die wir an diesem Abend aus dem Goetheschen Schauspiel kommen, entscheiden uns, nicht gleich nach Hause zu gehen, sondern das Theatererlebnis anderswo noch fort- und ausklingen zu lassen und die Eindrücke zu vertiefen, an einem Ort mit ähnlich bühnenartiger Atmosphäre, nur um das Gastronomische bereichert. Wir laufen vom Theater aus zu Fuß, biegen in die Friedrichstraße ein und sehen, wie gerade aus dem Friedrichstadtpalast das Publikum herausströmt. Wir stehen bald, nur einen Katzensprung vom Bahnhof Friedrichstraße entfernt, auf der Weidendammer Brücke, wo ein altes schmiedeeisernes Geländer in der Mitte den preußischen Adler zur Schau stellt. Zu Zeiten der DDR posierte Wolf Biermann vor dem Adler, passend zu seiner Ballade vom preußischen Ikarus. Ein stolzer, doch flügellahmer Adler als Symbol des autoritären Staates, der nicht vom Fleck kommt und scheitert, ob Preußen, ob DDR. Wir lehnen uns über das Geländer, schauen hinunter auf die Spree und lesen über einem erleuchteten Kellerraum am Kai: „Capitalism Kills Love".

So ist das also: Vormals war es die dunkle Schicksalsergebenheit, die die Liebe zerstörte, dann der Sozialismus, nun ist es, wie es scheint, der Kapitalismus. Wir glauben nicht unbedingt an diesen Spruch, haben ein gewisses Zutrauen zu uns selbst und gehen auf breiten flachen Stufen zum Kai hinunter. An der Wand steht „Grill Royal", obwohl es – anders als noch in der Ära des Café Royal – gar keine preußischen Könige mehr gibt und die höfisch-aristokratische Gesellschaft längst perdu ist, überrollt zuerst von der bürgerlichen, dann nationalsozialistischen, später sozialistischen, schließlich kapitalistischen Gesellschaft. Lauter Widersprüche hier, Brüche, Mehrdeutigkeiten!

Wir, die wir die Treppe hinuntergehen, wissen allerdings so einigermaßen, was uns unten erwartet, und lassen uns locken. Wir kennen den Grill Royal, der 2007 im Kellergeschoss an der Kaimauer eröffnet wurde, in einem hohen Wohn- und Geschäftshaus in Edel-Plattenbauweise aus den letzten Tagen der DDR. Anziehend ist die Lage am Wasser allemal, die Situation des Untergeschosses, eine Art von Underground, hinzu kommt die Vieldeutigkeit der Baudenkmäler ringsum. Im Hintergrund lugt prachtvoll das neobarock gerundete Bode-Museum auf der Musemsinsel empor, ganz so, als habe es nie Brüche in der Geschichte Berlins oder der deutschen Vergangenheit gegeben.

Wie geht man damit um? Soll man das Büßerhemd anziehen? Oder soll man über den Kapitalismus jammern? Den Gründern des Grill Royal liegt so etwas fern. Sie wollen, wie der Begriff „Royal" sagt, einen Anklang der großen Welt nach Berlin-Mitte zurückbringen, und der Spruch „Capitalism Kills Love", ein Kunstwerk des Künstlerkollektivs Claire Fontaine, das über dem Eingang installiert ist, ist ein selbstironischer Wink. Unter den Gästen sind vornehmlich jene, die vom Kapitalismus profitieren.

Die Besitzer wagten es, den Ort zu verwandeln, Neues zu schaffen, Glamouröses, ohne das alte Grau ganz zu übertünchen. Berlin-Mitte nun als Ort der Bürger- und Zivilgesellschaft, die sich des Lebens freut, die strebt und genießt – quasi fürstlich mit bürgerlich-zeitgenössischem Zuschnitt. Ursprünglich waren es drei Initiatoren, Stephan Landwehr, Boris Radczun und Thilo Wermke, doch der Letztere scherte bald aus. Landwehr und Radczun sind die treibenden Kräfte des Grill Royal, beide gastronomische Quereinsteiger, mit frischem Blick auf das Metier. Zwischenzeitlich wurde das Duo wieder zum Trio. Moritz Estermann ist als Geschäftsführer hinzugekommen.

Landwehr studierte in den Achtzigern Gesellschafts- und Wirtschaftskommunikation an der Hochschule der Künste in Berlin, ohne das Studium abzuschließen. Früh fand er den Weg in die Berliner Kunstszene, arbeitete in Ateliers und eröffnete ein Bilderrahmengeschäft. Radczun studierte in den Neunzigern Architektur in Weimar und Berlin und schloss gleichfalls das Studium nicht ab. Es fehlte ihm, wie er sagt, in der Architekturlehre „das Werkstoffempfinden". Er jobbte in der Gastronomie, wurde Caterer und Clubmacher, bis er vorübergehend in Landwehrs Wohnung einzog, wo sie gemeinsam viele Freunde bewirteten. Es kam die Idee auf, doch gleich ein Lokal einzurichten, das einem Wohnzimmer nicht unähnlich sei. Gleichzeitig sollte ein weltläufiger Ort entstehen, groß und weiträumig. Nichts Nostalgisches, auch keine Coolness in Schwarz und Weiß, sondern komfortabel, mit warmer Atmosphäre und erstklassigem schnörkellosen Essen.

Wenn man es vorteilhaft deuten möchte, so steckte in den beiden Studienabbrechern vielleicht von je her eine gastronomische Mission, die sich früher oder später Bahn brechen musste. Vielleicht hängt nichts mehr mit Lebenskunst zusammen als Gastlichkeit. So oder so sollte ein neues Lebensgefühl für Berlin-Mitte gefunden werden. Landwehr spazierte eines Tages über die Weidendammer Brücke, entdeckte hinter einer breiten Glasfront den leeren Kellerraum am Kai und sagte sich: Das ist es (mit Gespür für den Genius Loci). Auch Radczun war gleich davon angetan. Der biografische Hintergrund der beiden, ihre Vernetzung mit dem Kunst- und Architekturmilieu sowie ihre Erfahrung in der Gastronomie: All das sollte hier zum Tragen kommen. Bloß keinen Trash mehr, auch kein überzogenes Design, keine hyperkreative Küche! Sondern eben eine neue Mitte: Sich elegant und gelassen geben, natürlich und unprätentiös, so gemütvoll deutsch wie kosmopolitisch.

Ethik des Mondänen

Das spartanische Preußentum war ja bereits seit der Reichsgründung von 1871 erodiert. Berlin wurde die Reichshauptstadt und wollte als solche eine „Weltstadt" werden, mondän, von internationaler Bedeutung. Die neue politische Stellung Deutschlands in der Mitte Europas sollte gerade auch in der Kapitale selbst eine kulturelle Entsprechung finden. Fixpunkt der großen Welt, der „monde", war vorläufig der königlich-kaiserliche Hof. Selbst modern ge-sinnte Chronisten wie Harry Graf Kessler in seinen Erinnerungen *Gesichter und Zeiten* schildern den ersten Kaiser des zweiten deutschen Kaiserreichs, Wilhelm I., als einen Grandseigneur, und auch die Kaiserin, Augusta, galt als eine Grande Dame, deren Salon im Alten Palais, an der Ecke Unter den Linden/Bebelplatz, nicht nur Adligen, sondern auch Bürgerlichen offenstand, zumal Wissenschaftlern. Ähnliches galt für das Kronprinzenpalais, Unter den Linden, nahe dem Schloss, wo Kronprinzessin Victoria, die Tochter der eng-lischen Königin Victoria, gleichfalls einen offenen, adlig-bürgerlichen Salon führte. Höhepunkte der Saison, die etwa von November bis April dauerte, waren die Empfänge und Hofbälle im Schloss, bei denen die Herren in Gala-uniform oder Frack und die Damen in großer Toilette erschienen.

Wenn man für Berlin kulturellen Rang beanspruchen wollte, dann musste man in der Lage sein, Schauplätze der Eleganz zu schaffen: Ballsäle im Schloss, Salons in den Palais, Opernhäuser, Konzertsäle, Theater oder Museen der bil-denden Künste. In Berlin stand der größte Teil dieser Institutionen um 1871 noch unter royalem, königlich-kaiserlichem Patronat.

Lediglich die Salons waren hauptsächlich adlig-bürgerliche Einrichtun-gen und vorläufig ein Ersatz für den Mangel an gehobener Gastronomie in der Stadt. Bereits im späten achtzehnten und frühen neunzehnten Jahrhundert hatten hier die Salons jüdischer Damen für Furore gesorgt, wie jener der be-zaubernden Henriette Herz. Im Zuge der Reichsgründung, bei der sich Ber-lin nach 1871 von der puritanisch-preußischen in die lebensfrohere deutsche Hauptstadt verwandelte, blühte die Salonkultur erneut auf, stets unter der Regie eleganter Frauen. So mancher Salon stand nur dem Adel offen, andere waren sozial durchmischt, adlig-bürgerlicher Art. Jene Damen, welche über das Ideal eines Salons nachdachten, hielten den sozial durchmischten Kreis für den wahren Salon, wo sich nicht nur die Aristokraten auf vornehme Wei-se langweilten, sondern wo neben den Leuten von Welt auch Personen aus der Wissenschaft, den Künsten, der Industrie und Hochfinanz vertreten waren, so wie im Salon der Marie von Schleinitz oder der Anna von Helmholtz.

In solchen Salons traf man sich nach dem Abendessen, zeigte sich in mo-discher Kleidung, bewies Anmut, Geschmack, übte taktvolles Benehmen, Gewandtheit, Haltung, gab sich aufgeschlossen gegenüber den Ideen der Zeit und war eher liberal gesinnt, plauderte, wechselte die Themen, zeichnete sich durch Esprit und Toleranz aus – quasi ein Labor der Moderne. Man sprach bei Gelegenheit über die Bilder und Stiche im Salon, musizierte, trank Tee und knabberte am Gebäck. Sabine Lepsius, selbst eine Berliner Salonière, berich-tete über die Soireen der Anna von Helmholtz: „Mit ihrem ausgesprochen äs-thetischen Sinn und der instinktiven Abneigung einer ‚Grande Dame' gegen alles Philistertum wusste Frau von Helmholtz ihrer Geselligkeit Schwung und Haltung zu geben und den widerspenstigsten Typen einen gewissen Stil aufzuzwingen."

Man erlernte die Kunst der Muße und des Müßiggangs und betrieb dafür einen gewissen Aufwand, eine Art Ethik des Mondänen: durch einen gewissen Komfort der Einrichtung, Kunstverständnis, Modebewusstsein, Lektüre, selbsterworbene Gedankenwelt, Weltkenntnis, Zuvorkommenheit, Großzügigkeit, Güte. Zwar ging es auch um Distinktion, Vernetzung, Vorwärtskommen, aber der wahre Salon strahlte zivilisierende Impulse aus, vermittelte ein paar angenehme Stunden, Vergnügen und Amüsement, Galanterie und Flirt. Viele Tagebücher, Briefe, Memoiren und Schriften der Berliner Salondamen bilden einen wahren Schatz feiner Lebensführung und privater Gastlichkeit – wenngleich diese Literatur heute oft nur noch antiquarisch erhältlich ist. Günter Erbe gibt aber in seinem Buch *Das vornehme Berlin* einen vorzüglichen Einblick. Und niemand falle mehr auf das Klischee herein, dass Berlin keine Tradition des eleganten Umgangs und der Freundlichkeit habe.

Restaurant-Society

Gehobene gewerbliche Gastronomie und Hotellerie konnte man in Berlin bis 1871 an einer Hand abzählen. Feineres Gastgewerbe hatte sich erst seit dem frühen neunzehnten Jahrhundert an der repräsentativen Achse in der Stadt, am Lindenkorso, zaghaft herausgebildet. 1819 wurde dort ein älteres Gasthaus, in dem einst Goethe 1778 übernachtet hatte, in ein Gourmet-Restaurant verwandelt, und zwar im neuartigen Pariser Stil: das Jagor, Unter den Linden, Nummer 23. Man speiste dort nicht länger, wie bis dahin in Herbergen üblich, an einer gemeinsamen Tafel, der Table d'Hôte, wo zu einer festgelegten Stunde unter dem Vorsitz des Wirts allen Gästen dasselbe Menü serviert wurde, sondern konnte an Einzeltischen Platz nehmen und à la carte bestellen.

Mit der Französischen Revolution kehrten nicht nur in der Politik, sondern auch in der Gastronomie neue Freiheiten ein. Für Paris hat diese Entwicklung der Gastrosoph Brillat-Savarin 1825 in seinem Werk *Physiologie des Geschmacks* dokumentiert. Für Berlin wurde der junge Heinrich Heine zum Kronzeugen solcher Veränderungen. Er jubelte in seinen *Briefen aus Berlin*: „Kniet nieder, ihr modernen Peruaner, hier wohnt – Jagor!" Mit den „modernen Peruanern" meinte er natürlich die arglosen preußischen Kartoffelesser. Dieses Lokal sei aber eine „Paradiesespforte", wo es geniale Erfindungen wie Trüffeleis gebe. Eine erhaltene Speisekarte des Jagor aus dem Jahr 1830 bietet exklusive Vorspeisen an, darunter: „Kleine Pasteten", „Geräucherter Rheinlachs", „Omelette au jus", „Frischer Caviar", „12 Austern", die am teuersten waren, weil sie vermutlich mit einer Expresskutsche frisch aus Hamburg geliefert wurden, hinzu kamen Kiebitz-Eier, Rinder-Mark, Kalbsbries-Kroketten, Kalbskotelett, schließlich Beefsteaks, wörtlich „Beef-stakes".

Noch lieber ging Heine ins Café Royal, Unter den Linden, Nummer 33, eröffnet 1820. „Ein Versammlungsort eleganter, gebildeter Welt", schrieb er wiederum in seinen *Briefen aus Berlin*. Ein netter Service empfange den Gast, aufmerksam, von feinem Betragen, ohne zu buckeln, zudem gäbe es Gutes zum Essen und zum Trinken. Man traf hier Talente und Koryphäen: Komponisten, Opernsänger, Theaterintendanten, Politiker, Journalisten. Auch der junge Otto von Bismarck bestellte ja hier, leicht verwegen, ein „Beefsteak für acht Jute".

Erst im Zuge der Reichsgründung von 1871, durch die Berlin von der preußischen zur deutschen Hauptstadt aufstieg, schossen an der Promenade Unter den Linden und an der Friedrichstraße beziehungsweise in der gesamten Dorotheen- und Friedrichstadt vornehme Cafés, Restaurants, Hotels und Grandhotels wie Pilze aus dem Boden, bürgerliche Gründungen mit salonähnlicher Geselligkeit. Neben der höfischen Gesellschaft bildete sich ein bürgerlich-großbürgerliches Smart Set heraus, das gewissermaßen auch die Restaurant-Society bildete. Die expandierende Industrie machte die Bourgeoise reich; die Eisenbahn veränderte das Tempo und den Lebensrhythmus, drang vor bis ins Zentrum der Stadt mit dem Bau des Bahnhofs Friedrichstraße, und mit den Zügen strömten mehr Touristen denn je in die Metropole. Nicht länger nur der Hochadel, auch Bürgerliche aus Industrie, Hochfinanz und Kunstmilieu waren jetzt europäisch vernetzt, kannten Paris und London, nicht selten auch New York, und beherrschten einen gewissen Weltton.

Am Wilhelmplatz, nahe dem damaligen Kanzleramt, wurde 1875 das Grandhotel Kaiserhof eröffnet, das nun als das erste Haus am Platz galt, schon nach außen hin in seiner Vierflügelanlage dem Berliner Schloss nicht unähnlich. Noch entscheidender war, dass auch das Raumprogramm einem Schloss gleichkam. Während sich der Gast vormals in einer Fürstenherberge nur an der Table d'Hôte vergnügen konnte, gab es hier jetzt eine Empfangshalle, Restaurants, Salons, Ballsäle.

Die königlich-kaiserliche Familie war sich nicht zu fein, dort zu logieren; wenngleich es auch Vertreter des Hochadels gab wie die Fürstin Marie Radziwiłł, die es als frivol empfanden, sich hier blicken zu lassen. Es hätte ja sein können, dass die Doyenne des eleganten Gesellschaftslebens in Berlin plötzlich neben bürgerlichen Parvenüs saß. Für Fürstin Marie, die am Pariser Platz einen exklusiven adligen Salon führte, war ein solches Luxushotel nichts anderes als ein „Wirtshaus".

Doch mit diesen Ansichten stand sie längst schon auf verlorenem Posten. In der Reichshauptstadt gewann neben dem Geburtsadel mehr und mehr der

Geld- und Geistesadel an Bedeutung, Industrielle, Bankiers, Wissenschaftler, Professoren, Schriftsteller, Verleger, Redakteure, dazu Vertreter der Bohème, der Halbwelt oder „demi-monde", wie man sagte, Maler, Musiker, Schauspieler, Schönheiten; über deren Rang entschied nicht mehr der Hof, sondern die Presse.

So versammelte sich im Kaiserhof ein sozial durchmischtes, illustres adlig-bürgerliches Publikum. Jules Huret beschrieb 1909 in seinem Berlin-Buch die Szenerie in diesem Grandhotel: „Ich bin diesmal im Kaiserhof abgestiegen, der mitten in der Stadt und in direkter Nähe der Gesandtschaften und Ministerien liegt und vortrefflich eingerichtet und geleitet ist. Man sieht viele reiche Fremde, und die fashionablen Berliner halten im Winter ihre Gastmähler und Bälle dort. / Narbenbedeckte Offiziere, jüdische Bankiers und ihre Gattinnen, durchreisende Gesandte, junge, nach reichen Erbinnen ausschauende Diplomaten treffen mit eben angelangten Yankees zusammen. Russische Damen, rieselnd von kostbarem Geschmeide, elegante Amerikanerinnen mit riesengroßen Federn, wallenden Schleiern auf dem Kopfe, die Handschuhe bis zum Ellbogen zurückgestreift, lachen und unterhalten sich laut an der Seite ihrer ernsten, glattrasierten, brillentragenden Männer."

Der Hof der Hohenzollern verlor langsam seine tonangebende Macht. Erst recht, seit Kaiser Wilhelm II. auf dem Thron saß. Er gab sich sprunghaft, bizarr, hielt skandalöse chauvinistische Reden, die auf Adlige wie Bürgerliche erschreckend wirkten und Deutschland in Europa politisch isolierten. Fürstin Daisy von Pless urteilte in den 1890er Jahren: „Der Kaiser und die Kaiserin haben keine Ahnung von Benehmen." Der Berliner Volksmund erfand den Spottnamen „Wilhelm der Plötzliche".

Immerhin förderte Wilhelm II. die Eröffnung des Grandhotels Adlon am Pariser Platz im Jahr 1907, so wie vorher sein Großvater, Wilhelm I., den Kaiserhof unterstützt hatte. Schon seit längerem bewirtschaftete der Hotelgründer Lorenz Adlon auch das Restaurant Hiller, Unter den Linden, Nummer 62/63. 1910 verkaufte er das Hiller an Alfred Walterspiel, der dort nun Patron und Küchenchef zugleich war. Beide Häuser, das Adlon wie das Hiller, erlangten gastronomischen Ruhm weit über die Grenzen der Stadt hinaus. Viel später, 1952, als Walterspiel längst schon in München war und das Hotel Vier Jahreszeiten leitete, verfasste er sein Buch *Meine Kunst in Küche und Restaurant* und erklärte: „Den größten Teil der in diesem Buche niedergelegten praktischen Erfahrungen sammelte ich während der Jahre als Inhaber des Restaurants Hiller in Berlin." Hier, am Lindenkorso, entwickelte er – in den Fußstapfen von Lorenz Adlon – seine gastronomischen und kulinarischen Maßstäbe; er konservierte sie in seinem Buch, das wiederum in den ersten Jahrzehnten nach dem Zweiten Weltkrieg zum einflussreichsten Werk für die gehobene Küche in Deutschland wurde, inspiriert von der Belle Époque in Berlin. Erst die Kochbücher von Eckart Witzigmann, die seit den 1970er Jahren erschienen, gingen darüber hinaus und stellten die Nouvelle Cuisine vor.

Walterspiel ließ so manche Eindrücke aus der Berliner Zeit in das Werk einfließen, und das stellte abermals Wilhelm II. in kein gutes Licht. So wie der Kaiser nicht in der Lage war, sich anhaltend mit etwas Ernstem zu beschäftigen, so war es ihm auch nicht gegeben, reizvolle Gastlichkeit zu entfalten: „Nach den Essen am Kaiserlichen Hof", fuhr Walterspiel fort, „durften wir uns immer eines regen Zuspruchs erfreuen, weil ein großer Teil der Geladenen infolge des dort gepflogenen schnellen Services nicht satt wurde. Ein Essen von manchmal sieben Gängen musste oft in einer Stunde herunterserviert werden. Und wenn gar Seine Majestät die Gnade hatte, einen der Geladenen ins Gespräch zu ziehen, bekam dieser meist überhaupt nichts, weil sich die Lakaien an ihre vorgeschriebene Zeit halten mussten und sogar unberührte Speisen einfach wegräumten."

Die Kunst der Gastlichkeit wurde nicht länger bei Hofe, sondern in bürgerlich-adligen Salons oder bürgerlich-großbürgerlichen Cafés, Restaurants und Grandhotels eingeübt. Im Hiller tummelten sich die Stars und Berühmtheiten – und der Patron achtete bravourös auf die Individualität und Wünsche seiner Gäste. „Gar viele von den großen Sängern", fuhr Walterspiel fort, „gingen bei mir ein und aus. (...) Ich lernte die Eigenheiten mancher weltbekannter Künstler kennen. Caruso zum Beispiel, stets begleitet von seinem Arzt, durfte nur Spiegeleier, auf beiden Seiten gebacken, Spinat, Makkaroni und einige andere italienische Nationalgerichte essen. Manchmal kam er auch allein, und dann durfte ich ihn verwöhnen. (...) Die große Sängerin Melba hatte einen besonders guten Geschmack. Für sie zu arbeiten war immer eine Freude, während Sarah Bernhardt als Sklavin ihrer Launen schwer zu befriedigen war. Viel Kummer bereitete uns auch die unvergessliche Eleonora Duse. Sie war im Leben wie auf der Bühne ein Nervenbündel; zwar von feinem Geschmack, nahm sie sich zum Essen zu wenig Zeit. Emmy Destinn, die gottbegnadete Prager Sängerin, hatte einen prächtigen Appetit und einen ausgezeichneten Humor." Quasi der ideale Gast!

An das Restaurant schlossen sich verschiedene kleine Salons an, in denen es zuweilen recht libidinös zuging. Es kam vor, dass der Salon-Oberkellner bei der Buchung übersah, dass in dem einen Salon der Geheimrat X mit Frau von Soundso speiste, während in dem anderen dessen Gattin mit dem jungen Schauspieler Y dinierte. Als „die Gnädige", so Walterspiel, im Nebenraum die Stimme ihres Mannes hörte, sei sie in fünf Minuten verschwunden gewesen.

Sittsamer waren die Verhältnisse im Restaurant Borchardt in der Französischen Straße, nahe dem Gendarmenmarkt (das heutige Borchardt befindet sich im ehemaligen Nebenhaus, wo sich damals die Feinkosthandlung des Restaurants befand). In diesem Lokal, gegründet 1855, blieb vorläufig etwas von der Geselligkeit aristokratischer Couleur erhalten, weniger kühn, weniger intensiv im Ausleben sinnlicher Freuden. So erzählt es jedenfalls Helene von Nostitz in ihrem Buch *Aus dem alten Europa*: „Die Gespräche, die sich in den Essenspausen entwickelten, waren auch meist ernster Natur. Ab und zu schwebte wohl ein Berliner Witz durch den Raum. Aber es lag kein Wagnis in der Luft. Nie würde sich eine internationale Kurtisane hierher verirren und den Raum lärmend erfüllen. Die Eltern schauten beruhigt auf ihre Töchter, die hier keiner Überraschung ausgesetzt waren."

Das Spektrum der Lebensführung wurde breiter; jeder konnte nach seiner Façon selig werden. Berlins Mitte verwandelte sich im Achsenkreuz der Promenade Unter den Linden und der Friedrichstraße sowie bald auch am Potsdamer Platz in ein Büro-, Einkaufs- und Vergnügungsviertel: mit Grandhotels, Restaurants, Cafés, Theatern, Varietés, Warenhäusern, Banken. Volker Wagner hat diese Citybildung in seiner Studie *Die Dorotheenstadt im 19. Jahrhundert* bestens dokumentiert. Etwas später vollzog sich dieselbe Entwicklung weiter westlich, südlich vom Bahnhof Zoo, an der Achse Tauentzien und Kurfürstendamm. Berlin nahm Maß an Paris, London, New York, Chicago. Tatsächlich kam es amerikanischen Beobachtern so vor, als sei Berlin das deutsche Chicago: mit rasantem Wachstum und industriellem Fortschritt, ein Ort unbegrenzter Möglichkeiten.

Die einen freuten sich darüber, die anderen schüttelten nur noch den Kopf. Fürstin Marie Radziwiłł war sowohl über die Dynamik bürgerlicher Industrialisierung und Großtuerei als auch über den Niedergang des königlich-kaiserlichen Hofes entsetzt; in einem Brief machte sie sich Luft: „Denn was ist Berlin jetzt? Eine riesige Stadt mit geschmacklosen Dekorationen und unglaublich hohen Häusern. Nur noch Banken und Hotels. Eine richtige amerikanische Stadt, ohne Hof, ohne eine Equipage der königlichen Familie, nur Automobile, die von Zeit zu Zeit durch sonderbarste Musik ein Signal geben, dass eine Fürstlichkeit die Straße durchfährt." Aber war dieses Urteil gerecht? War nicht sie selbst der beste Beweis, dass es in Berlin nach wie vor eine erkleckliche Zahl eleganter Salons europäischer Prägung gab? Übernahmen nicht große Hoteliers und Gastronomen wie Adlon und Walterspiel etwas von der spezifischen Art der Aufmerksamkeit und Freundlichkeit in den Salons?

Alfred Kerr begrüßte in seinen *Briefen aus der Reichshauptstadt 1895–1900* die bürgerlichen Neuankömmlinge, die Bildungsaufsteiger, Karrieremacher, Hochstapler, Abenteurer, ökonomischen Parvenüs, die gern mal auf die Pauke hauten. Diese Leute waren dem Journalisten lieber als die Hofschranzen oder Spießbürger. Er freute sich über das „Städtchen W", das neue westliche Berlin, entlang des Kurfürstendamms und darüber hinaus. Es war für ihn Sinnbild einer politisch-kulturellen Annäherung an den Westen. Über die Villenkolonie Grunewald schrieb er: „Hier nähert sich alles einem wohlhabenden deutschen Engländertum." Das hieß für ihn eine weniger chauvinistisch geprägte, sportlichere Lebensauffassung, die Sphäre des Liberalismus, ein taktvollerer Menschenschlag. Kerr zielte auf die Bürger- und Zivilgesellschaft, die im Hier und Jetzt lebt: „Wir neuen Menschen glauben ja, dass dieses Dasein auf der Erde die Hauptsache ist."

Grill Room

Neben dem gastronomischen Typus des Restaurants, der Ende des achtzehnten Jahrhunderts im Wesentlichen in Paris aus der Taufe gehoben worden war, entstand im Laufe des neunzehnten Jahrhunderts der sogenannte Grill Room. Während im feinen Restaurant die französische Grande Cuisine vorherrschte und hohen zeitlichen Aufwand in die Herstellung von Soßen und Schmorgerichten steckte, gehörte der Grill Room der angloamerikanischen Tradition an und stellte das Beefsteak vom heißen Eisenrost in den Mittelpunkt: Kurzgarstücke vom Rind, hauptsächlich Rumpsteak und Filet, aber auch Rib-Eye, französisch Entrecôte, deutsch Hohe Rippe genannt.

Genau genommen ging der Grill Room aus einem Ineinander von formellem Restaurant und unkompliziertem Steakhouse hervor, beziehungsweise aus der Mischung zwischen französischer und angloamerikanischer Kulinarik. Das Steakhouse konzentrierte sich ausschließlich auf das Beefsteak, während der Grill Room neben dem Beefsteak auch Gerichte der französischen Grande Cuisine ins Programm aufnahm. Umgekehrt schrieb das Restaurant neben den Speisen der Haute Cuisine gleichfalls das Beefsteak auf die Karte wie bereits das Berliner Jagor im Jahr 1830.

Das Beefsteak war ein edles Teil des Rindes, zugleich benötigte es nicht viel Zeit zum Garen und passte gut zu einer flotteren Epoche angesichts von Eisenbahn und Automobil. Auch der glühende Eisenrost fügte sich gut in die industrielle Revolution, die die Bourgeoisie reich machte. Das Steak ließ sich auf dem heißen Grill im Handumdrehen zubereiten, war in der Regel saftig und bot intensive Aromen mit Röst- und Rauchnoten. Der Gast konnte sich als wahrer Zeitgenosse fühlen, wenn er im Grandhotel nicht ins Restaurant, sondern in den Grill Room ging.

Habbo Knoch weist in seiner Studie über *Grandhotels* darauf hin, dass nach 1850 in New York und London Luxushotels damit begannen, neben dem klassischen Restaurant einen Grill Room einzurichten. Auch das berühmteste Grandhotel der Belle Époque, das Ritz in Paris, wo der große schweizerische Hotelier Cäsar Ritz und der französische Meisterkoch Auguste Escoffier seit

1898 zusammenarbeiteten, erhielt einen Grill Room. Und Hedda Adlon, die Schwiegertochter des Hotelgründers Lorenz Adlon, bezeugte in ihren Memoiren, dass im legendären Hotel am Brandenburger Tor nach 1907 ein „Grillraum" vorhanden war. Neben den Kurzgarstücken vom Rind servierte man in einem Grill Room normalerweise auch Austern, Kaviar, Hummer, Seezunge oder Gerichte mit Périgordtrüffeln, alles Speisen, die sich über einen jahrzehnte- oder jahrhundertelangen Selektionsprozess als Delikatessen bewährten. Der Grill Room bot die exklusivsten Dinge und nahm zuweilen im Grandhotel gegenüber dem Restaurant den höheren Rang ein.

Die Gründer des Grill Royal an der Weidendammer Brücke in Berlin mussten 2007 nicht bei null anfangen. Lokale mit königlichem Anspruch gab es an der Spree schon seit 1820 mit der Eröffnung des Café Royal – und ein nobler Grillraum existierte bereits seit 1907 im Adlon. Allerdings waren solche Kostbarkeiten der älteren Berliner Gastronomie zwischenzeitlich untergegangen, sei es im Zuge der Citybildung vor dem Ersten Weltkrieg, sei es durch den Bombenhagel im Zweiten Weltkrieg. Das Jagor, das Café Royal, der Kaiserhof, das Hiller, das alte Adlon: all das verschwand. Spätestens am Ende des Zweiten Weltkriegs lagen diese Schauplätze der Eleganz in Schutt und Asche.

Aber die Erinnerung daran lebte fort. Zwar hatte nach 1945 der Sozialismus im Ostteil der Stadt kein besonderes Interesse an bürgerlich-großbürgerlicher Vergnügungskultur und setzte eher wieder auf schlichte Häuslichkeit. Doch im Westteil der Stadt entstand schon kurz nach Kriegsende ein neues Kempinski Hotel am Kurfürstendamm, wo der Gast seit 1952 auch in einem „Grill" speisen konnte. Wenn Vertreter des internationalen Jetsets die Stadt besuchten, kehrten sie dort ein. Den Kempinski Grill gibt es noch heute, wenngleich die Kellner längst nicht mehr im Frack bedienen.

Es lässt sich nicht unbedingt behaupten, dass es zu Zeiten der Berliner Mauer eine Schickeria in der Stadt gegeben habe. Aber man entdeckte damals doch ein paar Lokale, wo sich die Kunstszene traf, wie im Exil am Paul-Lincke-Ufer (wo sich heute das Restaurant Horváth befindet); in der Paris Bar in der Kantstraße oder im Café Einstein in der Kurfürstenstraße. Nach dem Fall der Mauer entstanden ähnliche Lokale in Berlin-Mitte, wo sich auch ein paar Politiker mit Lebensart einfanden: das neue Borchardt in der Französischen Straße; das Café Einstein Unter den Linden; desgleichen konnte man seit 2000 die Empfangshalle des neuen Adlon zu den weltläufigen Bühnen der Berliner Gastlichkeit zählen. Aber man suchte vorläufig vergeblich nach einem royalen Grill.

Boris Radczun schwebte bei der Planung des eigenen Lokals bald ein Grill vor. Er kannte, wie er erzählt, das berühmte Steakhouse Gene & Georgetti in Chicago, beeindruckt vom Look, dem Touch von Kartell – komfortabel, aber nicht zu kompliziert. Überdies war er mit der Brasserie La Coupole in Paris vertraut, einem Großraumlokal aus der Epoche des Art déco, wo man so etwas wie Paris-Atmosphäre erlebt. Er wusste zudem, was im alten Adlon gastronomisch geboten worden war, und im Grill im Kempinski Hotel am Kurfürstendamm aß er gelegentlich selbst.

Hinzu kam, dass gerade auch altehrwürdige Grandhotels wie das Baur au Lac in Zürich, gegründet 1844, ihren ehemaligen Grill Room wiederentdeckten. Nach vorübergehenden Irrungen und Wirrungen mit euro-asiatischer Fusionsküche und Gartenmöbeln im Lokal wurde das Rive Gauche im Baur au Lac 2005 wieder in einen klassischen Grill verwandelt. Die dunkelbraune, clubmäßig-neogotische Vertäfelung aus der Zeit um 1890 verbindet sich seither wieder angenehm mit puristisch-komfortablen Möbeln: mit creme- und pistazienfarbenen Stühlen, Polsterbänken und Lampenschirmen. Innenarchitektonisch bewunderte Radczun auch die Räume in James-Bond-Filmen mit Motiven der Raumstation oder der luxuriösen Yacht, oft entworfen von Klaus Adam, der in Berlin geboren wurde und als Jude mit seinen Eltern vor den Nationalsozialisten flüchten musste.

Grill Royal
Berlin, im Dezember 2016, 22.30 Uhr. Wir betreten den Grill Royal, um hier das Theatererlebnis fort- und ausklingen zu lassen. Obwohl die Decke des Grill Royal nicht allzu hoch ist, öffnet sich ein großer und weiter Raum, der viel Platz bietet. Es sind um diese Zeit noch mehr als hundert Gäste anwesend, die essen, trinken, reden, lachen und Energie verströmen. Man fühlt sich gleich wie gefesselt davon. Die Beleuchtung ist gedämpft, aber nicht dunkel. Warme Farben leuchten; da und dort erkennt man das helle Braun oder das Graugrün grob gewebter Stoffe über gut gepolsterten Sitzbänken, dazwischen die weißen Tischdecken, weiße Teller, Speisen und gefüllte Gläser, kontrastiert vom Orangerot kleiner Lampenschirme auf den Ablagen zwischen den Polsterbänken, dazu das mattierte Glas der Stützpfeiler, die im Raum verteilt sind. Alles gleicht einer behaglichen Unterwasserstation, die gerade aus der Spree auftaucht.

Wir haben nicht reserviert und fragen im Eingangsbereich, ob es einen Tisch für zwei Personen gibt. Man bittet uns um einen Moment Geduld. Es wird nachgeschaut, ob irgendwo ein Platz freigeworden ist. „Ja, wir haben einen Tisch für Sie. Setzen Sie sich doch noch kurz an die Bar oder auf die Couch, bis der Tisch neu eingedeckt ist." Es verläuft alles unkompliziert und nett, ohne viel Getue von Seiten des Service. Ein paar Minuten später sitzen wir an einem angenehmen Tisch, nicht weit von der Fensterfront entfernt, die den Blick auf die Weidendammer Brücke sowie die dahinter aufsteigenden

Häuser freigibt, die ihrerseits beleuchtet sind und in der Nacht funkeln. Wir fühlen uns ein wenig wie in New York, doch in Wahrheit genießen wir Berlin-Midtown-Feeling.

Wir bestellen Austern, Sylter Royal, sechs Stück und fragen, ob wir zwei Teller dazu haben können, um die Portion miteinander zu teilen. „Selbstverständlich", sagt der freundliche Kellner. Unser Hunger ist um diese Zeit nicht mehr allzu groß, aber ein paar delikate Petitessen auf der Zunge dürfen es schon sein. Den Austern soll eine Hummer-Bisque folgen. Wir fragen den Kellner, was er uns dazu zum Trinken empfehlen könne, etwas im offenen Ausschank. „Ein Glas Champagner oder burgundischen Chardonnay". Wir entscheiden uns dieses Mal für den Chardonnay, weil er etwas mehr Würze hat, die im Winter der Seele guttut. Sommers wäre es Champagner gewesen.

Die sechs Austern werden auf gestoßenem Eis serviert. Obwohl das Licht im Raum insgesamt wohlig gedämpft ist, beleuchten doch kleine Spotlights die Mitte des Tisches und lassen das Perlmutt der geöffneten Muschelschalen glitzern, ganz so, als sei ihr Inhalt unendlich wertvoll. Die Sylter Royal ist eine eher kleine Auster, und man könnte sie leicht unterschätzen. Wir schlürfen sie in den Mund und drücken sie an den Gaumen. Sie schmeckt köstlich: cremig und mineralisch, mit einem Hauch von Meeresbrise und wunderbarer Frische. Für Momente sind wir still und genießen diese Caprice. Nicht minder frisch und leicht mundet dann die aufgeschäumte Hummerbrühe, mit fabelhafter feiner Würze, die von den gerösteten Hummerkarkassen und vom Cognac herrührt. Vermutlich ist so eine Bisque überhaupt das Beste vom Hummer. Wir reden wieder und schauen.

Man geht in den Grill Royal auch zum Leutegucken – sehen und gesehen werden. Der Gast ist Akteur und Zuschauer zugleich. Es bilden sich längere Wege zwischen den Nischen, gleich Laufstegen bei einer Modenschau. Der eine Weg führt zur Raucherlounge, quasi in einen kleinen Nebensalon, wo große Fotografien mit barbusigen Damen zu sehen sind. Ein Schelm, wer Schlechtes dabei denkt. Natürlich kommt es vor, dass sich dort Mann und Frau, ohne bislang miteinander bekannt zu sein, im Rauch der Zigaretten annähern. Wie schon einst in den Nebensalons im Hiller.

Im Restaurant erscheinen Stars und Berühmtheiten. Unversehens kann es sein, dass am Nebentisch ein Hollywoodstar Platz nimmt, wie die bezaubernde Scarlett Johansson oder der verdammt gutaussehende George Clooney. Berliner Galeristen und ihre Maler kommen herein, Modemacher, Schauspieler, Fußballstars, auch der ein oder andere Politiker mit Lebensart. Die Restaurantchefin Andrea Kauk passt unaufdringlich darauf auf, dass sich keine zu starken Grüppchen bilden, und sorgt für eine angenehme Durchmischung der Gäste aus unterschiedlichen sozialen Kreisen – eben gute Berliner Salonkultur, möchte man sagen. Für Radczun soll der Grill Royal ohnehin auch eine Art „Volksrestaurant" sein, in dem sich jeder wohlfühlt, der die Rechnung bezahlen kann.

So oder so hält sich der Kult um berühmte Gäste in Grenzen. Sie werden begrüßt von der Restaurantchefin oder den Patrons, wenn diese gerade da sind. Doch alles verläuft ohne viel Aufhebens. Lieber plaudern die Wirte etwas länger mit Stammgästen, die nicht selten persönliche Freunde oder gute Bekannte sind. Landwehr und Radczun haben auch immer ein gewitztes Wort für ihre Kellner und Köche übrig. Alle bilden eine große Familie: die Gäste, die Kellner, die Patrone.

Gelegentlich essen sie, die Patrone, mit ihren Familien oder mit Freunden am Wirtstisch, gleich am Eingang gegenüber der Bar. Entzückend, wie sie sich selbst über das Essen und Trinken sowie die Unterhaltung freuen. Irgendwie gewinnt man den Eindruck, als stecke ihre eigene gute Laune und ihre menschliche Art das Lokal an. Der Gast, der durch den Besuch des Restaurants lediglich auf Distinktion aus ist, ist nicht unbedingt am richtigen Ort. Natürlich kann man hier Networking betreiben, denn nicht wenige Gäste kennen sich und stellen anderen neue Freunde vor. Es findet sich hier so etwas wie die Berliner Restaurant-Society ein, vermischt mit Besuchern der Stadt. Aber viele sind einfach da, um sich zu vergnügen und angenehme Stunden zu erleben.

Beefkultur
Im Vordergrund steht das gastronomische Erlebnis selbst. Alles spielt zusammen: die Lage des Lokals, die Einrichtung, die Atmosphäre, die Gäste, der Service, die Küche. Selbstverständlich ist der hiesigen Küche durch den Begriff des „Grills" eine feste Struktur vorgegeben. An der Beefkultur führt kein Weg vorbei. Der Gast sieht in verglasten Kühlschränken das Fleisch am Knochen reifen, zumindest gilt das für das US-Beef. Es wird immer am Knochen geliefert, reifte in der Regel zuvor schon zwei, drei Wochen und bleibt dann die eine oder andere Woche zusätzlich noch hier im gläsernen Kühlschrank.

US-Beef ist in seiner Art wohl am zuverlässigsten für den Feinschmecker, weil es strengen staatlichen Regelungen unterliegt. In keinem anderen Land der Welt spielen Rinderzucht, Steakhouse, Diner, Burger eine so große Rolle wie in den Vereinigten Staaten von Amerika. Der Cowboy wurde dort zur nationalen Ikone, zu einer Figur, die das Selbstverständnis der Amerikaner stärkt: ein Bild von Freiheit und Abenteuer. Das Rind vermittelt Stärke und Kraft, ebenso dessen Fleisch, das Beef. Und auch die Gäste in einem Berliner Grill Room möchten sich davon ein wenig inspirieren lassen.

Diese amerikanische Tradition der Rinderzucht und Beefkultur entwickelte sich nicht von ungefähr. In den Weiten des nordamerikanischen Kontinents fanden sich die entsprechenden Areale dafür: die „Great Plains", die Ebenen der Prärie im Mittleren Westen. Kernregionen sind Nebraska oder South Dakota. In den westlichen Teilen dieser Gegenden, zu den Rocky Mountains hin, gibt es vor allem Grasland, das für den Ackerbau nicht geeignet ist und so der Viehzucht dient; in den östlichen Teilen, wo es mehr regnet, wird vorwiegend Weizen und Mais angebaut.

Die Tiere leben die meiste Zeit des Jahres nicht im Stall, sondern auf der Weide, fressen im Sommer Gras und Kräuter und im Winter Heu. Bevor sie geschlachtet werden, verbringen sie noch mindestens drei Monate in Gattern unter freiem Himmel und werden dort nicht nur mit Heu gefüttert, sondern auch mit Weizen und Mais gemästet, damit das Fleisch die begehrte Marmorierung erhält.

Das amerikanische Landwirtschaftsministerium führte bestimmte Qualitätsstufen ein, die den Grad der Marmorierung, der Fettsträhnen im mageren Fleisch, markieren. Die höchsten Stufen sind „Prime Grade", mit einem Anteil von über zehn Prozent, sowie „Choice Grade", mit einem Anteil von fünf bis zehn Prozent. Allerdings merkte man zwischenzeitlich auch, dass allein der Grad der Marmorierung noch nicht darüber entscheidet, ob ein Fleisch überdurchschnittlich gut ist.

Es kommen noch andere Dinge hinzu. Man braucht die richtige Rasse für die bestmögliche Entwicklung des Fleisches. Im Mittleren Westen stehen vorwiegend das Angus und das Hereford auf der Weide, reinrassige Rinder mit Tradition, ursprünglich in Schottland und England gezüchtet. Für die Fleischverarbeitung kommen nur die Färse, das ausgewachsene, weibliche Rind, das noch nicht gekalbt hat, und der Ochse, der kastrierte Stier, in Frage. Die ältere Milchkuh oder der Stier wären kaum in der Lage, eine reiche Marmorierung hervorzubringen. US-Beef ist sowohl kernig als auch zart, saftig und vollmundig, von intensivem Geschmack – pure Lust.

Man sollte ja meinen, dass zwei kulinarische Hauptbewegungen unserer Zeit – sowohl der Trend zur pflanzlichen Ernährung als auch die Beefkultur – nichts miteinander zu tun haben. Doch da wie dort wendet man sich von der industriellen Massentierhaltung ab, einmal mit, einmal ohne Fleisch. Beefkultur meint Fleisch aus artgerechter Tierhaltung für besondere Momente – die Steaks mittlerweile besser gereift und zarter als je zuvor, als es noch keine ausgetüftelten Kühlsysteme gab. Auch in der Art, wie man Tiere hegt und Fleisch verzehrt, gibt es eine Entwicklung.

Auf der Karte im Grill Royal stehen neben den Steaks vom US-Beef noch andere, die zu den besten zählen, die man finden kann: vom japanischen Wagyū-Rind aus Kobe, einfach auch Kobe-Rind genannt, über das australische Wagyū-Rind bis hin zur Temmener Queen, einem Bio-Weiderind aus der

Mark Brandenburg. Dieses frisst vornehmlich Gras und Heu, ohne besonders gemästet zu werden. Das Fleisch ist nicht ganz so stark marmoriert wie das US-Beef oder das Kobe-Beef und deshalb nicht ganz so zuverlässig zart. Doch dann und wann stellt das Steak von der Temmener Queen alles andere in den Schatten, durch eine ungemein mineralische Tiefe und Würze.

Auf der Tageskarte entdeckt man gelegentlich auch Steaks von älteren Kühen aus der Muttertierhaltung auf der Weide. Solche Kühe sind nicht so ausgemergelt wie jene aus der Milchwirtschaft und ihr Fleisch ist gut marmoriert. Ein Steak davon kann sagenhaft gut schmecken. Sowieso wünscht man sich, dass auch in Deutschland Landwirte, Ministerien, Händler und Köche besser zusammenarbeiten und eine ähnlich feine Beefkultur entwickeln wie in den USA.

Im Grill Royal wird jedes Steak in zwei Schritten gegart: Zuerst wird es auf dem heißen Grill, unter dem Gasflammen brennen, kräftig geröstet, dann zieht es schonend im Warmhaltefach noch die eine oder andere Minute nach und entspannt sich wieder. Urim Bytyci ist dort schon seit mehreren Jahren der erfahrene Grillmeister, ab und zu vertreten durch einen der beiden Sous-Chefs in der Küche, Christian Lorenz oder Enrico Melillo. Für den Gast wiederum wäre folgende Bestellung bestimmt keine schlechte Empfehlung: Austern, Hummer-Bisque, Entrecôte vom US-Beef, Sauce Bernaise.

Seit November 2016 ist Roel Lintermans der neue Küchenchef. Der geborene Belgier verbrachte seine Lehr- und Wanderjahre bei Köchen, die zu den berühmtesten unserer Zeit gehören, bei Alain Ducasse und Pierre Gagnaire, teils in Paris, teils in London, teils in Berlin. Er hat auch Erfahrungen in einem der legendären Grandhotels in der französischen Hauptstadt gesammelt, im Crillon. Natürlich kann er die Küche des Grill Royal jetzt nicht einfach auf den Kopf stellen; das wäre auch gar nicht seine Art. Er zeigt erst einmal Respekt vor dem, was bisher geleistet wurde. Ohnehin soll der Grill ein Grill bleiben. Grillmeister Bytyci bleibt eine der wichtigsten Stützen des Küchenchefs. Aber es lässt sich immer alles noch ein wenig besser machen. Die Austern werden jetzt etwas anders geöffnet und behandelt, die Hummer-Bisque wirkt um eine Spur leichter und frischer, der „Plateau de fruits de mer" bekommt allmählich einen stärkeren atlantischen Charakter, mit Strandschnecken, Schwertmuscheln und Krabbenfleisch. Salat und Gemüse erscheinen saisonaler. Bezaubernd reintönig und frisch munden die wechselnden Vorspeisen auf der Tageskarte.

Maître Andrea Kauk, die fast von der ersten Stunde an im Grill Royal dabei ist, ist auch die Sommelière, unterstützt vom stellvertretenden Restaurantleiter Stephan Schubert und den stellvertretenden Sommeliers Nikolaus Laurentius und Torben Gottwald. Wie im Grill Room zu Zeiten der Belle Époque gibt es auch im Grill Royal die klassischen Schwerpunkte beim Wein: Mosel, Rheingau, Champagne, Burgund, Bordeaux, Piemont. Man findet die großen Namen auf der Weinkarte, aber auch weniger bekannte Winzer, die feine Weine zu moderaten Preise anbieten.

Aufbruch

24 Uhr. Die Reihen im Grill Royal lichten sich langsam. Wir bitten um die Rechnung und geben ein anständiges Trinkgeld. Es ist mitten in der Woche, und wir wollen es mit der kleinen Eskapade nicht übertreiben. Erst jetzt, zum Schluss, da sich der Raum nach und nach leert, tritt so manches nachdenklich stimmende oder provozierende Kunstwerk stärker in Erscheinung. Man sieht ein Figurenpaar, zwei invalide Soldaten, offenbar in preußischer Uniform, an anderer Stelle prunken im Neonlicht weibliche Schamlippen, dann erscheint ein riesiges Ohr, als gäbe es hier viel zu lauschen. Überall Anspielungen, ohne dass irgendetwas aufdringlich erschiene. Eine Welt unterschiedlicher Entwürfe und Ideen – Anklänge des Postmodernen und Ironischen, aber allemal ein Ort mit echtem gastronomischen Kern, vielleicht insgesamt doch eher romantische Spätmoderne, ein Raum für Selbstentfaltung und gutes Leben. Wir verlassen das Lokal und freuen uns über diesen anregenden Abend: Iphigenie, Sylter Royal, wunderbare Gespräche.

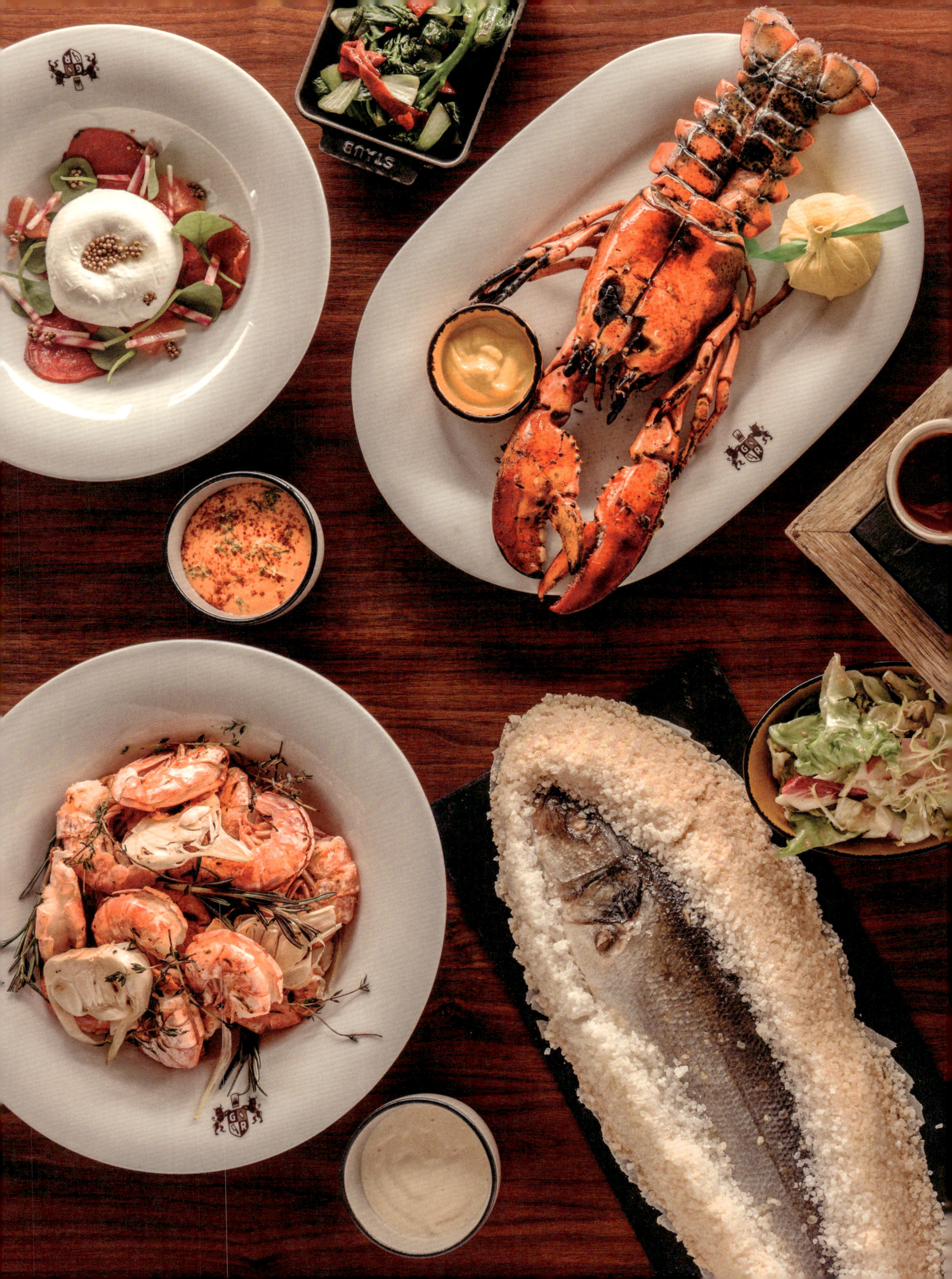

Grill Royal

Berlin's Hospitality
since the Nineteenth Century

Erwin Seitz

Prelude on the Stage

Berlin, December 2016. We go to Deutsches Theater in Berlin-Mitte, where Goethe's *Iphigenia* is playing this evening. We want to go out one last time before the end of the year for an inspiring evening—and we're counting on the fact that they usually show excellent theater there. And Goethe's *Iphigenia?* Well, we'll see; it's not an easy piece for the stage. There's a lot of talking, and not a lot happens on the surface.

The small stage is all in black—and Iphigenia, the first to appear, is wearing an all-white dress of light material, or maybe it's just a nightgown, without any jewelry and reduced to the existential: processes of the soul. The other actors join her; together they paint the stage area white. It's not a perfect white, though; here and there, black can be seen peeking through. It's not all that easy to transform the space we live in: from the black of the abyss into innocent white.

Iphigenia feels driven by the dark forces of fate. She seems to belong to a family that's been cursed by the gods, exiled to an island where King Thoas rules. He'd like to marry her, but she wants to return to her native land and find her brother Orestes. She distracts Thoas, while Orestes secretly lands on the island. They hatch out a plan to flee behind Thoas's back. But that would only mean more lying and deception, and that fate would repeat itself. Iphigenia senses this, contemplates it, imagines other possibilities for human interaction, calms down and becomes more judicious, decides to deal with Thoas in a more trusting, forthright manner, and counts on his understanding. Increasingly, as personified by Kathleen Morgeneyer, she adopts a casual, classical tone, entirely true to the poet's words, an enchanting parlando of the kind one seldom experiences in theater today. It's so quiet you could hear a pin drop in the theater; everyone is listening intently.

This works, you think. It doesn't always have to be a spectacle. Things can also be more refined, even in this hectic day and age. And maybe, when talking about this type of dramatic art, we shouldn't say that it "works one more time," but rather: "this works again now," after all the recent acrobatics and noise on the stage. Taking stock, recognizing oneself, finding a means for communication, learning a way to live—after all, these are the timeless elements of being human.

The visitor takes a look around in the theater where, in the past, around 1900, the bourgeois dramatic arts outstripped the Royal Theater on Gendarmenmarkt because they were closer to reality, more authentic—and where so many famous people directed, performed, and sat in the audience, among them Max Reinhardt, Alfred Kerr, and others. Where classics were performed as well as works by contemporaries; where tradition and modernism were woven together. Today, young, unchaperoned, elegantly dressed Muslim women in hijab once again sit in the audience in small groups and listen to what a female protagonist from the height of the European Enlightenment has to say. Everyone else in the theater is listening closely too, as though Goethe were still, to this day, one of us.

In Search of a Lost Center in Berlin

Once upon a time, the theory of Prussianness did not include evening entertainment following a visit to the theater. As subordinates, citizens should delight in noble sentiments and then redirect their efforts to their domestic tasks. Heinrich Heine, who studied in the Prussian capital in the 1820s, was outraged over this parsimony and escaped to Paris. Even after he became chancellor and prince, Bismarck, who had spent many years in Berlin as a high school and university student at that time, didn't like to think back to early Berlin. In a retrospective conversation in 1884, Julius von Eckardt noted: "Tales of old Berlin and of the limitations of his tailoring became an occasion on which it was considered wasteful when one (as the Prince said) dared dine on a beefsteak in the Café Royal for 'eight Jute' and to drive around the city center in a carriage."

Goethe, of course, didn't go in for Prussia's Spartanism. His motto was: Remember to live! Work hard and enjoy! For his part, he celebrated the art of hospitality in his house on Frauenplan in Weimar, and many ascetic Prussians who visited him from Berlin with their high-flown ideas were astonished that the prince of poets could so nonchalantly dedicate himself to sensual pleasures.

Nearly every other day, Goethe dined for two or three hours in the company of friends and acquaintances. The range of dishes went from simple home cooking to luxurious delicacies such as caviar and oysters. There was, of course, conversation at the table, quite a lot of conversation on artistic themes: fine arts, reading and travel experiences, things happening outside in the world. This style of living gradually caught on in Berlin, too. This was precisely what famous, open-minded writers of journals and memoirs of the late nineteenth and early twentieth centuries such as Marie von Bunsen and Harry Graf Kessler valued about Goethe and his writings: the art of communication, of intellectually stimulating small talk, of good manners toward people and things, a warm-hearted and convivial atmosphere and connoisseurship of pleasures.

We who come to see Goethe's theater this evening decide not to return home right away, but to allow the theater experience to resonate and to let the impressions it's left behind deepen elsewhere, in a place with a similarly stage-like atmosphere, enriched with a culinary dimension. We proceed on foot from the theater to Friedrichstrasse and see people streaming out of the Friedrichstadtpalast. Soon, just a stone's throw away from Friedrichstrasse station, we're standing on Weidendammer Bridge, in the middle of which an old cast-iron railing sports the Prussian eagle. During the time of the GDR, Wolf Biermann posed before this eagle, which fit with his ballad of the Prussian Icarus. It's a proud eagle, but with a wing down, a symbol for the authoritarian state that makes no headway and eventually fails, whether it be Prussia or the GDR. We lean over the railing, look down onto the Spree, and read the words "Capitalism Kills Love" written above an illuminated cellar space on the quay.

So this is how things are: it used to be dark submission to fate that destroyed love, then it was socialism, and now, it seems, it's capitalism. We don't necessarily believe in the phrase, we have some degree of trust in ourselves, and so we descend the broad steps to the quay. On the wall is the sign "Grill Royal," although—in contrast to the era of the Café Royal—the time of Prussian kings and courtly and aristocratic society is long since perdu, replaced first by a bourgeois class, then the National Socialist regime, later socialism, and finally capitalism. All kinds of contradictions here, breaks, ambiguities!

As we descend the steps, we know more or less what awaits us at the bottom, and we let ourselves be drawn in. We know the Grill Royal, which opened in 2007 in the cellar on the quay wall, in a tall residential and commercial building in finest pre-fab architecture from the final days of the GDR. The waterfront location is attractive, the subterranean situation a kind of underground, added to which is the ambiguity of the many monuments in the surroundings. In the background is the magnificent neo-baroque curved façade of the Bode Museum on Museum Island, which looks as though there had never been any breaks in Berlin's history or in the German past.

How to deal with it? Should we wear a sackcloth and ashes, should we complain about capitalism? The founders of the Grill Royal have other things on their minds. As the word "royal" suggests, they'd like to bring a sense of the wider world back to Berlin-Mitte, and the saying "Capitalism Kills Love," a work of art by the artist collective Claire Fontaine that's installed above the entrance, is a self-ironic gesture, because many of the guests are members of the group that profits from capitalism.

The owners dared to transform the place, to create something new and glamorous without whitewashing the old gray entirely. Berlin-Mitte, today a place for a civilian society that enjoys life, works hard, and has fun—in a princely fashion, but tailored to the contemporary bourgeoisie. It was originally three people who initiated the restaurant: Stephan Landwehr, Boris Radczun, and Thilo Wermke, although the latter soon bowed out. Landwehr and Radczun are the driving force behind the Grill Royal; both new to the restaurant business, they bring a fresh approach to the profession. In the meantime, the duo has once again become a trio: Moritz Estermann has joined them as managing director.

In the eighties, Landwehr studied business communication at the Hochschule der Künste in Berlin, but never completed his studies. He found his way into Berlin's art scene early on, worked in studios, opened a frame shop. In the nineties, Radczun studied architecture in Weimar and Berlin; he, too, failed to get a degree. What he missed in the architecture department was, as he says, a "feeling for materials." He took on jobs in the restaurant business, became a caterer and ran a club until he temporarily moved into Landwehr's apartment, where they cooked together for their many friends. The idea was born to furnish a place similar to a living room. At the same time, it should be an urbane location, large and spacious. Nothing nostalgic, no black and white coolness, but comfortable, with a warm atmosphere and first-class, no-frills food.

If you tell the story flatteringly, perhaps the two dropouts always had a kind of gastronomic mission that had to break out sooner or later. Maybe there's nothing more to the art of living than hospitality. In any case, it was a matter of finding a new feeling for living in Berlin-Mitte. One day, Landwehr walked over the Weidendammer Bridge, and behind a broad storefront window, he happened upon the empty cellar space on the quay and said to himself (with an instinct for genius loci): this is it. Radczun was also taken by it right away. The biographical background of the two, their connections to the art and architecture scenes, their experience in the restaurant business: all of it would come into play here. No more trash, no over-the-top design—and no hyper-creative cuisine! Rather, a happy medium: elegant and relaxed, natural and unpretentious, cozily German and cosmopolitan, and all at the same time.

Ethics of the Worldly

Ever since the founding of the Empire in 1871, Spartan Prussianness had been eroding away. Berlin became the capital of the Reich and as such sought to become a metropolis: urbane and internationally important. Germany's new political role at the heart of Europe should find its cultural expression, especially in the capital. A fixed point in the wide world, the "monde," was for a time the imperial-royal court. Even modern-minded historians such as Harry Graf Kessler in his reminiscences *Gesichter und Zeiten* (Faces and Times) portray the first emperor of the second German Empire, Wilhelm I, as a grandseigneur and the empress Augusta, a grande dame whose salon in the Altes Palais on the corner of Unter den Linden and Bebelplatz was not only open to aristocrats and nobility, but also to the bourgeoisie, particularly scientists.

The same went for the Kronprinzenpalais on Unter den Linden, near the palace where Crown Princess Victoria, daughter of the English Queen Victoria, also held an open aristocratic/bourgeois salon. The highlights of the season, which lasted roughly from November to April, were the receptions and court balls in the palace, where gentlemen arrived in full dress uniform or tuxedo and ladies in evening dress.

If one wished to claim a cultural rank for Berlin, then one had to be able to provide showcases for elegance: ballrooms in the palace, salons in the Palais, opera houses, concert halls, theaters, and museums for the fine arts. In Berlin, the larger part of these institutions was still under imperial-royal patronage around 1871.

Only the salons were chiefly noble-bourgeois establishments and a temporary substitute for the lack of highbrow gastronomy in the city. The salons of Jewish ladies here were a sensation already in the late eighteenth and early nineteenth centuries: for instance the salon of the enchanting Henriette Herz. During the course of the founding of the Empire, when after 1871 Berlin transformed from a puritan Prussian city into the more vivacious German capital, salon culture blossomed once again, always under the auspices of elegant ladies. Certain salons were only open to the nobility, while others were mixed, with both aristocrats and the bourgeois. The women who gave most thought to the ideal salon considered the socially mixed circle to be the true salon, where not only aristocrats grew bored in the most refined of ways, but where men and women of the world were joined by people from the sciences, the arts, industry, and high finance, as was the case in the salons of Marie von Schleinitz and Anna von Helmholtz.

In salons such as these, people met after dinner, arrived in fashionable clothing, displayed grace and taste, exhibited tactful manners, dexterity, and bearing, remained open to the ideas of the time and entertained liberal ideas, conversed, changed subjects, shone with esprit and tolerance—a kind of laboratory of modernism. People conversed over the paintings and engravings in the salon, played music, drank tea, and nibbled on baked goods. Sabine Lepsius, herself a Berlin salonière, reported on the soirees of Anna von Helmholtz: "With her excellent aesthetic sense and the instinctive aversion of a 'grande dame' to anything philistine, Mrs. von Helmholtz knew how to lend a dynamism and stature to her conviviality and to impose a certain style on even the most rebellious types."

One learned the art of leisure and idleness and had a certain amount of work to do to achieve it; it was a kind of worldly ethics that entailed a particular comfort of interior style, approach to art, fashion sense, reading, an individually acquired way of thinking, world knowledge, courtesy, generosity, and benevolence. While it was a question of distinction, connections, and personal advancement, the true salon radiated far more civilizing impulses and gave its members several pleasant hours of enjoyment and amusement, gallantry and flirting. The many journals, letters, memoirs, and writings of Berlin's salon ladies constitute a veritable treasure testifying to the fine way of living and private hospitality—even though today this literature can often only be obtained in second-hand bookstores. In his book *Das vornehme Berlin* (Genteel Berlin), however, Günter Erbe offers wonderful insight. In any case, no one falls for the cliché anymore that Berlin has no tradition of elegant manners and friendliness.

Restaurant Society

Until 1871, one could count the establishments for commercial gastronomy and the hotel industry on one hand. The fine hotel business emerged in fits and starts from the early nineteenth century on, along the city's representative boulevard, the Lindenkorso. In 1819, an older inn there in which Goethe had spent the night in 1778 was transformed into a gourmet restaurant in the new Parisian style: the Jagor, Unter den Linden, number 23. Guests no longer dined together at a common table, the table d'hôte, where all guests were served the same menu at a pre-arranged time, but were seated at individual tables and ordered à la carte.

New freedoms arrived with the French Revolution, not only in politics, but also in gastronomy. For Paris, the gastrosoph Brillat-Savarin documented this development in 1825 in his book *Physiology of Taste*. For Berlin, the young Heinrich Heine became the crown witness to such changes. In his *Briefe aus Berlin* (Letters from Berlin), he rejoiced: "Bow down, you modern Peruvians—Jagor lives here." With the "modern Peruvians," he was referring to the unsuspecting Prussian potato eaters, of course. This establishment, however, was a "gateway to paradise" where brilliant inventions such as truffle ice cream could be found. One surviving menu from the Jagor from the year 1830 offers exclusive appetizers including "small patés," "smoked Rhineland salmon," "omelette with juice," "fresh caviar," and "twelve oysters," which were the most expensive dish, presumably because they'd been delivered fresh from Hamburg in an express carriage. There were also peewit eggs, beef marrow, sweetbread croquettes, lamb cutlet, and finally beefsteaks, literally "beef-stakes."

Heine liked even more to go to the Café Royal at Unter den Linden, number 33, opened in 1820. "A meeting place for the elegant, educated world," he wrote in his *Briefe aus Berlin*. A pleasant reception greeted the guest: attentive, finely mannered, without fawning, and there were good things to eat and drink, besides. The talented and expert could be found here: composers, opera singers, theater directors, politicians, journalists. The young Otto von Bismarck also frequented the place, where he, somewhat audaciously, ordered his "beefsteak for eight Jute."

It was only during the course of the founding of the Empire in 1871 and Berlin's transformation from Prussian to German capital that elegant cafés, restaurants, hotels, and grand hotels popped up along the boulevards Unter den Linden and Friedrichstrasse as well as in the entire Dorotheen- and Friedrichstadt, bourgeois establishments with a conviviality akin to the salons. Parallel to court society, a bourgeois and upper-class smart set emerged which, to an extent, comprised the restaurant society. The expanding industry made the bourgeoisie rich; the railroad changed the tempo and rhythm of life, and, when Friedrichstrasse station was built, penetrated to the center of the city as more tourists than ever streamed to the metropolis. It was no longer only the high aristocracy who were connected across Europe; the bourgeois from industry, high finance, and art were as well: they knew Paris and London, as often as not New York, and they mastered a certain worldly air.

In 1875, the grand hotel Kaiserhof opened on Wilhelmplatz near the former chancellery, and it soon became the foremost address on the plaza, resembling as it did the Berlin Schloss in its four-winged layout. More importantly, its spatial design came close to that of a palace. While guests were previously restricted to amusing themselves at a princely accommodation's table d'hôte, the Kaiserhof offered a reception hall, restaurants, salons, and ballrooms.

The imperial-royal family didn't consider it beneath them to frequent the Kaiserhof, but some members of the nobility, such as Princess Marie Radziwiłł, found it frivolous to be seen here. There was always a risk that the doyenne of Berlin's elegant society might suddenly find herself seated next to a bourgeois parvenu. For Princess Marie, who led an exclusively noble salon on Pariser Platz, a luxury hotel of this kind was nothing more than a "tavern."

Yet she would find herself increasingly alone in her views. In the capital, the moneyed and educated aristocracy was gaining importance alongside the hereditary nobility: men of industry, bankers, scientists, professors, writers, publishers, editors, as well as members of the bohemia and the demimonde, as it was called—painters, musicians, actors, and beauties. Their rank was no longer decided at court, but in the newspapers.

Thus, it was a socially heterogeneous and illustrious group of aristocratic and bourgeois guests that met in the Kaiserhof. In 1909, Jules Huret described the scene in the grand hotel in his book on Berlin: "This time, I went to the Kaiserhof, which is situated in the city center near the embassies and ministries and is excellently managed and decorated. There are many rich foreigners to be found, while the fashionable Berliners hold their banquets and balls there. / Scar-covered officers, Jewish bankers and their wives, traveling envoys, young diplomats looking for rich heiresses brush up against recently arrived Yankees. Russian ladies dripping with costly baubles, elegant American women in huge feather boas, wearing flowing veils on their heads and gloves up to their elbows, laughing and talking loudly alongside their serious, cleanly shaven, bespectacled spouses."

Slowly, the Hohenzollern Court lost its power to set the tone, particularly with Kaiser Wilhelm II on the throne. He was erratic, bizarre, held speeches that were scandalously chauvinist, that frightened the nobility and the bourgeoisie alike, and that isolated Germany politically in Europe. In the 1890s, Princess Daisy von Pless declared: "The Emperor and the Empress have no notion of manners." Berliners gave him the nickname "William the Sudden" to mock him.

Be that as it may, Wilhelm II supported the opening of the grand hotel Adlon on Pariser Platz in 1907, just as his grandfather, Wilhelm I, had previously supported the Kaiserhof. Hotel founder Lorenz Adlon had long been managing the restaurant Hiller at Unter den Linden No. 62/63. In 1910 he sold the Hiller to Alfred Walterspiel, who was now both patron and chef. Both hotels, the Adlon and the Hiller, attained gastronomic fame far beyond the city limits. Much later, in 1952, after Walterspiel had long since moved to Munich to run the hotel Vier Jahreszeiten (Four Seasons), he wrote his book *Meine Kunst in Küche und Restaurant* (My Art in the Kitchen and Restaurant) and explained: "I gathered the larger part of the practical experience recorded in this book during the years I was owner of the Hiller restaurant in Berlin." Here, on the Lindenkorso and in the footsteps of Lorenz Adlon, he developed his culinary standards, which he recorded in a book that went on to become Germany's most influential reference for fine dining throughout the first decades following World War II, inspired by the Belle Époque in Berlin. The cookbooks of Eckart Witzigmann, published from the 1970s on, went further and introduced the nouvelle cuisine.

Walterspiel incorporated some of his impressions from the Berlin period into his work, and once again, they didn't portray Wilhelm II in the most flattering manner. Just as the emperor was unable to address himself for any length of time to anything serious, so too was he unable to develop any form of charming hospitality: "After dinner at the Imperial Court," Walterspiel wrote, "we could always look forward to some brisk business, because a large number of the guests weren't satiated due to the rapid service customary there. Often, a meal consisting of as many as seven courses had to be served within an hour. And when His Majesty deigned to engage one of the guests in conversation, he or she often got nothing at all to eat, because the lackeys had to stick to their appointed schedule and clear away even the untouched dishes."

The art of hospitality was no longer practiced at court, but rather in bourgeois-noble salons or bourgeois-upper-class cafés, restaurants, and grand hotels. In the Hiller, stars and famous people romped about, while the owner paid fervent attention to the individual wishes of his guests. "Many of the great singers," Walterspiel added, "came and went in my establishment. (...) I became acquainted with the idiosyncrasies of world-famous artists. Caruso, for instance, was always accompanied by his doctor and was only permitted to eat eggs over easy, cooked on both sides, as well as spinach, macaroni, and other Italian dishes. Sometimes he came alone, and then I was able to pamper him. (...) The great singer Melba had particularly good taste. It was always a joy to work for her, while Sarah Bernhardt, a slave to her moods, was difficult to please. We also had many worries with the unforgettable Eleonora Duse. In life as on the stage, she was a nervous wreck; she had fine taste, but she took too little time to eat. Emmy Destinn, the divinely gifted singer from Prague, had a magnificent appetite and an excellent sense of humor." Effectively the ideal guest!

Several small salons were attached to the restaurant, and things turned out rather libidinous there at times. It so happened that the headwaiter at the salon, in taking reservations, overlooked the fact that Privy Councilor X was having dinner with Mrs. So-and-so in one salon, while in the other his spouse was busy dining with the young actor Y. When "Madame," as Walterspiel called her, heard her husband's voice in the next room, she was gone within five minutes.

The mood was more proper in the Borchardt restaurant in Französische Strasse, near Gendarmenmarkt (today's Borchardt is situated next door to the former building, where the restaurant's specialty food shop was originally located). In this establishment, which was founded in 1855, something of an aristocratic conviviality remained intact that was less audacious and less intense in terms of abandonment to sensuous pleasures. This is how Helene von Nostitz recalls the time in her book *Aus dem alten Europa* (From Old Europe): "The conversations that took place in the breaks between meals were usually of a serious nature. Occasionally, a Berlin joke would make its way through the room, but there was no audacity in the atmosphere. An international courtesan would never wander in here by mistake and fill the room with noise. Parents gazed at their daughters, reassured that they wouldn't be subjected to any unwelcome surprises here."

The spectrum of lifestyles broadened; everyone could seek heaven according to their own fashion. On the intersection of the boulevard Unter den Linden and Friedrichstrasse, and soon around Potsdamer Platz as well, Berlin's city center transformed into a district of offices, shops, and entertainment, with grand hotels, restaurants, cafés, theaters, cabarets, department stores, and banks. Volker Wagner documented this urban growth process excellently in his study *Die Dorotheenstadt im 19. Jahrhundert* (Dorotheenstadt in the 19th Century). Some time later, the same development took place further westward, to the south of Bahnhof Zoo, on the axis Tauentzien and Kurfürstendamm. Berlin vied with Paris, London, New York, and Chicago. And indeed, to American observers it seemed as though Berlin were the German Chicago: it had rapid growth, industrial progress, and was a place of unlimited possibilities.

Some were happy about this, while others just shook their heads. Princess Marie Radziwiłł was horrified both at the speed of bourgeois industrialization and swagger and at the demise of the imperial-royal court; in a letter, she vent ed: "Because what has Berlin become? A gigantic city with tasteless decorations and unbelievably tall buildings. Nothing but banks and hotels. A real American city, without a court, without the equipage of the royal family, just automobiles that from time to time employ the strangest music to signal that a prince is traveling the road." But was this complaint justified? Wasn't she herself the best proof that there was still a considerable number of elegant salons in Berlin with European character? And weren't the great hoteliers and restaurateurs like Adlon and Walterspiel adopting some of the attention and friendliness the salons were famous for?

In his *Briefen aus der Reichshauptstadt 1895–1900* (Letters from the Imperial Capital 1895–1900), Alfred Kerr welcomed the new bourgeois arrivals, the educationally ambitious, the careerists, charlatans, adventurers, and economic parvenus that loved to blow their own horns. The journalist preferred them to the flunkeys and philistines. He liked the "Little City W," the new western section of Berlin along Kurfürstendamm and beyond. For him, it was a symbol of a political and cultural movement toward the West. Describing the villa colonies in Grunewald, he wrote: "Everything here comes close to a wealthy German Englishness." To him, this meant a less chauvinist, more sporting life; it meant a sphere of liberalism and a more tactful type of person. Kerr was referring to a bourgeois civilian society living in the here and now: "We, the new people, believe that existence here on Earth is the main thing."

Grill Room

Along with the gourmet type of restaurant that became popular in the late eighteenth century, primarily in Paris, over the course of the nineteenth century, the so-called grillroom came into being. While French grande cuisine prevailed in the finer restaurants, and its sauces and stews required a considerable amount of time to prepare, the grillroom hailed from the Anglo-American tradition and focused on beefsteak broiled on a hot iron grill: rare cuts of beef, especially rump steak and filet, but also rib-eye and French entrecôte, called Hohe Rippe in German.

Strictly speaking, the grillroom grew out of the combination between formal restaurant and simple steakhouse, in other words, it was a mixture of French and Anglo-American culinary practice. The steakhouse restricted itself to the beefsteak, while the grillroom offered other dishes from French grande cuisine along with the beefsteak. Conversely, restaurants also added beefsteak to their menu in addition to dishes of haute cuisine, as Berlin's Jagor had already done in 1830.

The beefsteak was a finer cut of steak; it didn't require much time to grill and it stood for a brisker era with its railroads and automobiles, while the glowing red grill was an apt emblem for the Industrial Revolution that had made the bourgeoisie rich. The steak could be cooked on the hot grill with a flick of the wrist; it was usually juicy and gave off a strong aroma with charred and smoky overtones. When they dined in the grillroom instead of the restaurant, grand hotel guests could feel like a real part of contemporary life.

In his book *Grandhotels*, Habbo Knoch writes that after 1850, luxury hotels in New York and London began setting up grillrooms alongside their classic restaurants. The most famous grand hotel of the Belle Époque, the Ritz in Paris—where the great Swiss hotelier Cäsar Ritz and the French master chef Auguste Escoffier had been working together since 1898—, also received a grillroom. And in her memoirs, Hedda Adlon, daughter-in-law of the hotelier Lorenz Adlon, testified that a grillroom existed in the legendary hotel at Brandenburg Gate from 1907 on. Along with grilled beef, oysters, caviar, lobster, sole, and dishes with Périgord truffles—all of which had prevailed as delicacies over a decades- or centuries-long selection process—were usually also served in the grillroom. The grillroom offered the most exclusive items, and sometimes enjoyed a higher status in the grand hotel than the restaurant opposite.

In 2007, the founders of Grill Royal on Weidendammer Bridge in Berlin didn't have to start at zero. There had been establishments with royal pretences on the Spree since 1820, when the Café Royal opened—and a noble grillroom already existed in 1907 in the Adlon. Delicacies of older Berlin cuisine disappeared at various times, however, whether it was during the phase of urban development prior to World War I or after the bombings of World War II. The Jagor, the Café Royal, the Kaiserhof, the Hiller, and the old Adlon all disappeared. At the very latest at the end of World War II, these showcases of elegance were reduced to rubble.

But their memory lived on. Following 1945, socialism in the eastern sector of the city showed no particular interest in bourgeois or upper-class entertainment culture, opting instead for simple domesticity, but in the western sector, a new Kempinski Hotel was built on Kurfürstendamm shortly after the war ended, and starting in 1952, guests could also dine there in a "grill." When members of the international jet set visited the city, they stopped by there. The Kempinski Grill exists to this day, even though the waiters have long since stopped serving in tuxedos.

It can't necessarily be claimed that a smart set existed in the city during the time the Berlin Wall existed, but there were a few establishments where the art scene came together, for instance Exil on Paul-Lincke-Ufer (where the restaurant Horváth is located today); the Paris Bar on Kantstrasse, or Café Einstein on Kurfürstenstrasse. After the Wall fell, similar places cropped up in Berlin-Mitte, where a few politicians with savoir vivre also lived: the new Borchardt on Französische Strasse; Café Einstein on Unter den Linden; and since 2000, the reception hall of the new Adlon could also be counted among the urbane showcases for Berlin hospitality. But for the time being, one searched in vain for the royal grill.

While planning his own place, Boris Radczun soon began dreaming of a grill. As he says, he knew the famous steakhouse Gene & Georgetti in Chicago: impressive in look, and with a touch of ganster life in the air—comfortable, but not too complicated. In addition, he was familiar with the brasserie La Coupole in Paris, a spacious restaurant from the Art deco era that still had something of a Paris atmosphere. He also knew what had been on the menu of the old Adlon, and he'd occasionally eaten at the grill in the Kempinski Hotel on Kurfürstendamm.

In addition to this, the time-honored grand hotels such as the Baur au Lac in Zurich, founded in 1844, were just rediscovering their former grillrooms. After some temporary trials and tribulations with Euro-Asian fusion food and patio furniture indoors, the Rive Gauche at the Baur au Lac was transformed back into a classic grill in 2005. Since that time, the deep brown, club-like Neo-Gothic wainscoting dating from 1890 once again matches nicely with the purist, comfortable furniture, the cream- and pistachio-colored chairs, upholstered settees, and lampshades. In terms of interior architecture, Radczun also admired the rooms in James Bond films, with motifs of space stations or luxurious yachts, often designed by Klaus Adam, who was born in Berlin and, as a Jew, was forced to flee the National Socialists with his parents.

Grill Royal
Berlin, December 2016, 10:30 p.m. We enter the Grill Royal in order to allow our theater experience to linger on and then slowly ebb away. Although the ceiling of the Grill Royal isn't all that high, a large room opens up that provides

ample space. At this time there are more than a hundred guests present, all of them eating, drinking, laughing, radiating energy. One feels immediately arrested by it all. The lighting is subdued, but not too dim. Warm colors glow; here and there one can see the light brown or grayish green of coarsely woven fabric on well-upholstered settees, and between them the white tablecloths, white plates, food, and filled glasses, contrasting with the orange-red of the small lampshades on the shelves between the seats and the matte glass of the supporting columns spread around the room. As a whole, it resembles a snug underwater station that has just surfaced from the River Spree.

We haven't made a reservation, and in the entrance area we ask if there's a table for two. We're asked to be patient for a few moments. The waiter has a look to see if a spot has opened up somewhere. "Yes, we have a table for you. Have a seat at the bar or couch while we prepare your table." Everything proceeds in an uncomplicated and friendly way, without too much ado on the part of the service. A few moments later we're seated at a pleasant table, not far from the window front and its view of Weidendammer Bridge and the buildings rising up behind it, lit up and twinkling in the night. It feels a little like being in New York, but in reality we're enjoying the Berlin Midtown feeling.

We order oysters, Sylter Royal, six of them, and we ask if we can have two plates with that, in order to share the dish. "Of course," the friendly waiter says. At this time of night, our hunger isn't all that great, but a few tasty delicacies are in order. The oysters are to be followed by a lobster bisque. We ask the waiter what wines he'd recommend, something by the glass. "A glass of champagne or Burgundian Chardonnay." This time we decide on the Chardonnay, because it has a bit more spice, balm for the soul in wintertime. If it were summer, it would have been champagne.

The six oysters are served on crushed ice. Although on the whole the light in the room is pleasantly subdued, small spotlights illuminate the center of the table, making the mother of pearl on the open shells glitter, as though their contents were endlessly precious. The Sylter Royal is a small oyster, and one could easily underestimate it. We slurp it into our mouths and press it against our gums. It tastes delicious: creamy and mineral, with a touch of ocean breeze and a startling freshness. For a few moments we're quiet; we enjoy the lark. The foamy lobster broth is no less fresh and light, and it has a fabulously fine spicy taste derived from the roasted lobster carcass and cognac. Presumably, a bisque like this is the best you can have from the lobster. We resume talking and look around.

Among other things, one goes to the Grill Royal to watch people—to see and be seen. The guest is both participant and observer. There are longer paths between the niches, and they're like runways at a fashion show. One path leads to the smoker's lounge, a smaller adjacent salon where large photographs of topless women are displayed. Shamed be he who thinks evil of it. Of course it happens that a man and a woman who don't yet know one another become acquainted amidst the cigarette smoke—as was once the case in the adjacent salons of the Hiller.

In the restaurant, stars and famous people appear, and it's quite possible that a Hollywood star suddenly takes a seat at the next table, for instance the enchanting Scarlett Johansson or the bloody good-looking George Clooney. Berlin gallerists and their painters come here, as do fashion designers, actors, soccer stars, and now and again a politician with a sense of style. The head of the restaurant, Andrea Kauk, keeps an eye out to prevent groups from forming and to ensure that there's a pleasant mixture of guests from different social backgrounds—one might say sound Berlin salon culture. In any case, for Radczun, the Grill Royal should be a kind of "people's restaurant" where anyone who can foot the bill feels at home.

Be that as it may, the cult around famous guests is limited. When they happen to arrive, they're greeted by the head of the restaurant or the owner, but it all happens without too much ado. The hosts prefer to chat longer with their regular guests, who are frequently personal friends or close acquaintances. Landwehr and Radczun always have a witty comment ready for the waiters and cooks. It's like a big family: the guests, the waiters, the owners.

Sometimes the owners eat with their families or friends at the staff table across from the bar, right at the entrance. It's delightful how much they enjoy the food and drink and entertainment. At some point, it seems as though they were infecting the restaurant with their good mood and their down-to-earth manner. Guests looking mainly for distinction in their choice of restaurant are not necessarily in the right place. Of course one can network here, because quite a few of the guests know one another and introduce their friends. What's practiced here is a kind of Berlin restaurant society, mixed with visitors to the city. But many are simply here to enjoy themselves and to savor a few pleasant hours.

Beef culture

In the foreground is the culinary experience itself. Everything plays a role: the location of the place, the interior design, the atmosphere, the guests, the service, the cuisine. And the cooking here is of course subjected to a clear structure through the term "grill." You can't escape beef culture. Displayed in refrigerators with glass fronts, guests see meat aging on bones: at least this applies to American beef, which is always delivered on the bone and then left to age for two or three weeks, after which it spends another week or two in the glass refrigerator.

American beef is the most reliable for the gourmet taste, because it's subjected to strict federal regulation. In no other country in the world do cattle farming, steakhouse, diner, and hamburger play such a big role as in the USA. This is where the cowboy became a national icon, a figure that reinforces American identity: an image of freedom and adventure. Cattle invoke power and force, and so does their meat, beef. And the guests in a Berlin grillroom would also like to find a bit of inspiration in this.

It was no accident that the American tradition of cattle breeding developed. In the plains of the North American continent, the needed land could be found: the Great Plains, stretches of prairie in the Midwest, at the heart of which are Nebraska and South Dakota. In the western parts of these regions, toward the Rocky Mountains, it's mostly grassland unsuited to agriculture, and hence it's used for cattle farming; in the eastern regions, where there's more rainfall, chiefly wheat and corn are grown.

The majority of the time, the animals don't live in the stalls, but in the pasture; in the summer they eat grass and herbs, and in the winter hay. Before they're slaughtered, they spend at least three months outside, in an enclosure; they're not only fed hay, but also wheat and corn, so that their meat acquires the desired marbling effect.

The American FDA introduced specifically defined quality grades to measure the degree of marbling, the strands of fat in lean meat. The highest is "Prime Grade," with a fat content of over ten percent, followed by "Choice Grade," with five to ten percent. But it's become apparent that the degree of marbling alone does not decide whether or not a cut of meat is above-average quality.

Other factors come into play. The right breed is required for the meat to develop optimally. In the Midwest, the majority of cattle out to pasture are Angus and Hereford, traditional thoroughbreds originally bred in Scotland and England. For meat, only the heifer, the grown cow that has not yet calved, is used, and the ox, the castrated bull. Older milking cows and bulls are largely unable to produce a rich marbling. American beef has both texture and tenderness; it's juicy and full-bodied, with an intense taste—pure pleasure.

One would think that two main culinary movements of our time—the trend toward vegetarianism and beef culture—would have nothing to do with one another. But in many places, people are turning away from large-scale industrial livestock farming, sometimes with, sometimes without meat. Beef culture means meat from species-appropriate animal farming for special occasions—the steaks are now better matured and tenderer than before the invention of sophisticated cooling systems. There's also been progress in the way animals are kept and meat is consumed.

On the menu in the Grill Royal, there are other kinds of beef beside the American brands, and they are among the best that can be had today: from the Japanese Wagyū beef from Kobe, sometimes just called Kobe beef, to Australian Wagyū beef, to Temmener Queen, an organic grass-fed beef from the Mark Brandenburg. The latter feeds primarily on grass and hay and is not fattened in any particular way. The meat is not quite as heavily marbled as American or Kobe beef, and for this reason it's not always reliably tender. But now and again, the Temmener Queen outshines all other kinds with its uncommon mineral depth and spice.

On the carte du jour one can occasionally find steaks from older birthing cows kept in pasture. These cows are not as lean as those from the dairy industry, and their meat is well marbled. A steak from one of these animals can taste marvelous. In any case, in Germany one would like farmers, ministries, dealers, and cooks to improve their cooperation and develop a fine beef culture comparable to the USA.

In the Grill Royal, each steak is cooked in two steps: first it's quickly charred on the hot grill, beneath a gas flame, and then it's gently cooked another minute or two in the oven. Urim Bytyci has been the experienced grill master there for several years, occasionally substituted by one of the two sous-chefs in the kitchen, Christian Lorenz or Enrico Melillo. The following order is probably not a bad recommendation for the guest: oysters, lobster bisque, entrecôte from American beef, Béarnaise sauce.

Roel Lintermans has been the new chef since November 2016. The native Belgian spent his learning and wandering years at the elbows of cooks who count among the most famous of our time: Alain Ducasse and Pierre Gagnaire, part of the time in Paris, a part in London, a part in Berlin. He also has experience at one of the legendary grand hotels in the French capital, the Crillon. Of course he can't just turn the menu at the Grill Royal upside down; that's not how he does things. First he shows respect for what has already been achieved. And the grill should remain a grill, of course. Grill master Bytyci remains one of the chef's main supports, but he likes to do things a tiny bit better. The oysters are opened and handled a little bit differently, the lobster bisque feels a touch lighter and more fresh, the "Plateau de fruits de mer" is gradually taking on a stronger Atlantic character, with periwinkles, razor clams, and crabmeat. Salad and vegetables seem more in season, while the alternating antipasti of the carte du jour taste pure and fresh.

Maître Andrea Kauk, who has been at the Grill Royal almost from the very beginning, is also the sommelière, supported by the acting restaurant head Stephan Schubert and the assistant sommeliers Nikolaus Laurentius and Torben Gottwald. As was the case in the grillroom during the days of the

Belle Époque, the Grill Royal also maintains a classical focus in wine: Mosel, Rheingau, Champagne, Burgundy, Bordeaux, Piemonte. The great names can be found on the wine menu, but also lesser known winemakers that offer fine wines for reasonable prices.

Departure
It's midnight, and the Grill Royal is gradually thinning out. We ask for the bill and leave a decent tip. It's midweek, and we don't want to overdo it with our little escapade. Only now, toward the end, as the room slowly empties out, do certain contemplative or provocative artworks stand out. I see a pair of figures, two invalid soldiers, evidently in Prussian uniform, while elsewhere a female vulva glows in neon light; and then a huge ear appears, as though there were much to listen to here. Allusions everywhere, without any of it seeming obtrusive. A world of different ideas and proposals—echoes of postmodernism and irony, but in a place with a genuine gastronomic core, perhaps altogether a kind of romantic late modernism, a space for self-realization, for living well. We leave the restaurant, happy from an inspiring evening: Iphigenia, Sylter Royal, and wonderful conversation.

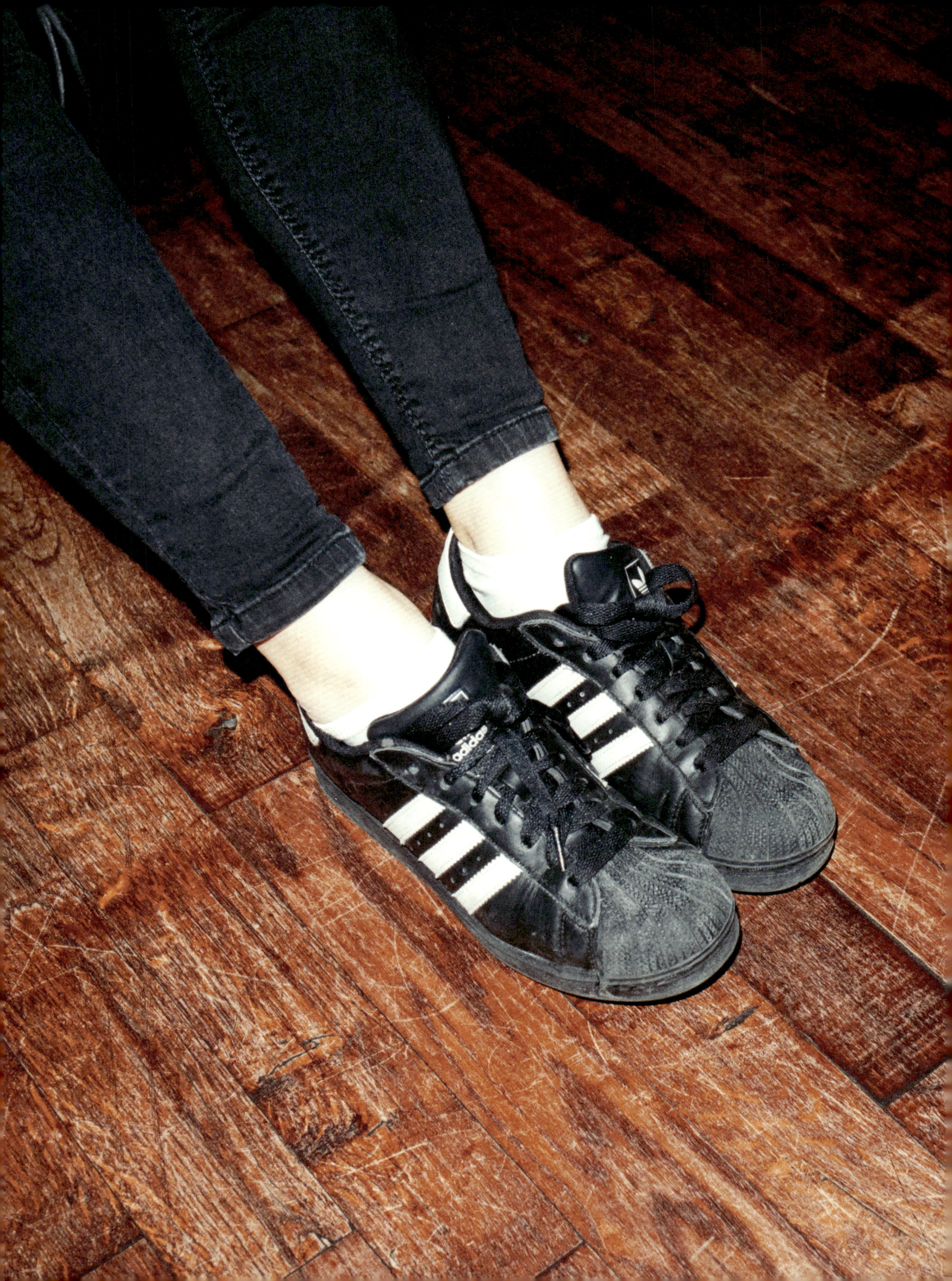

One Night

Maxime Ballesteros

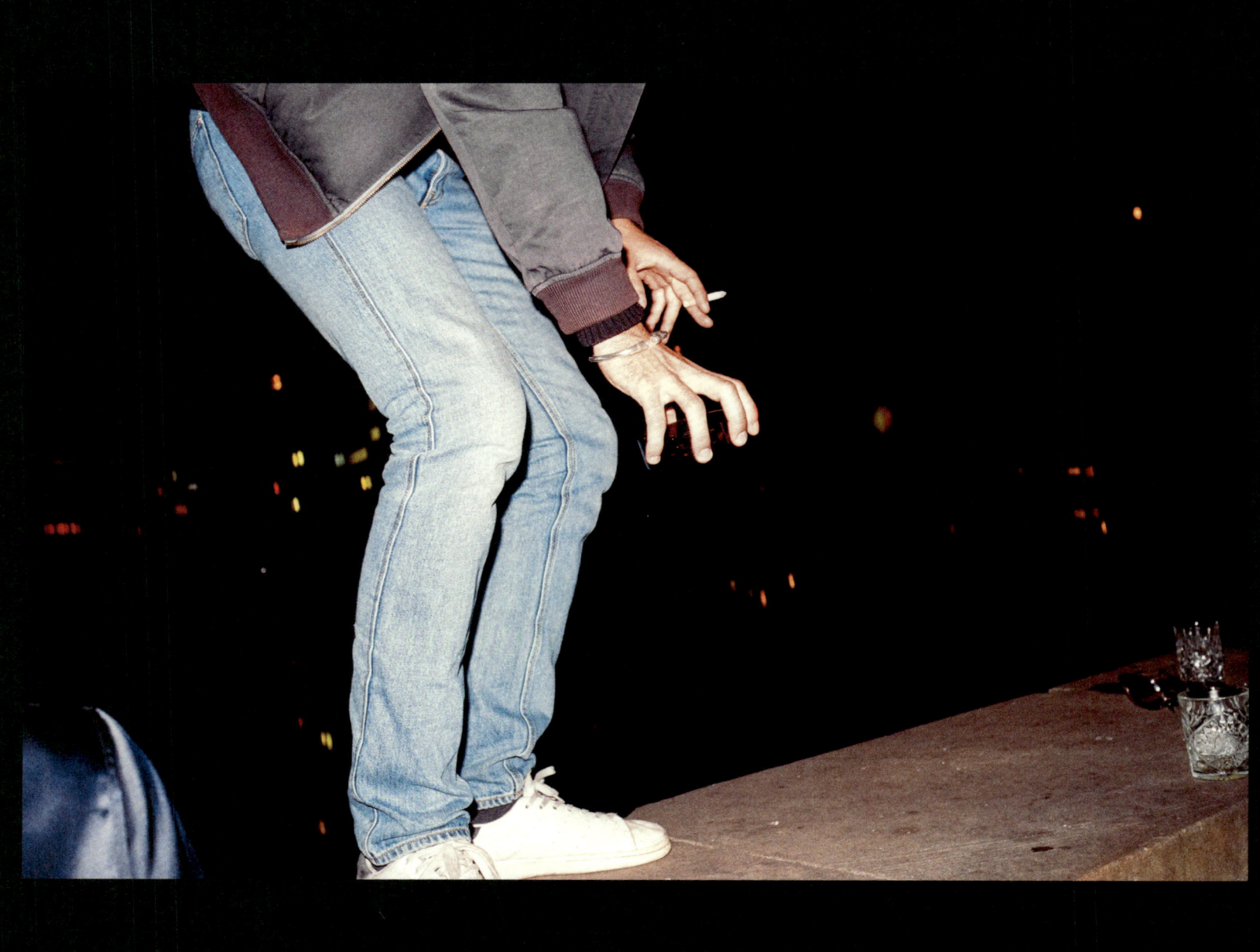

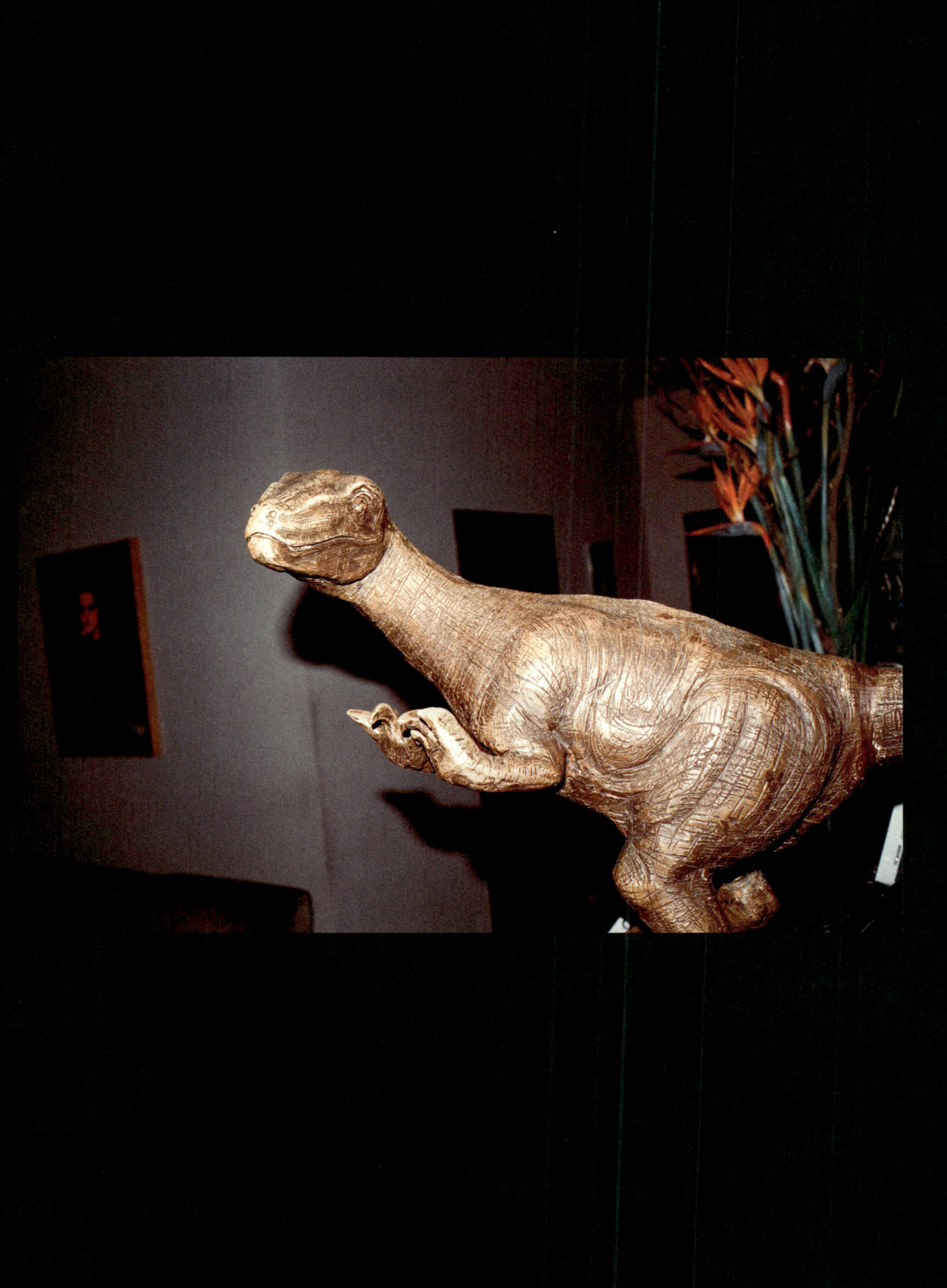

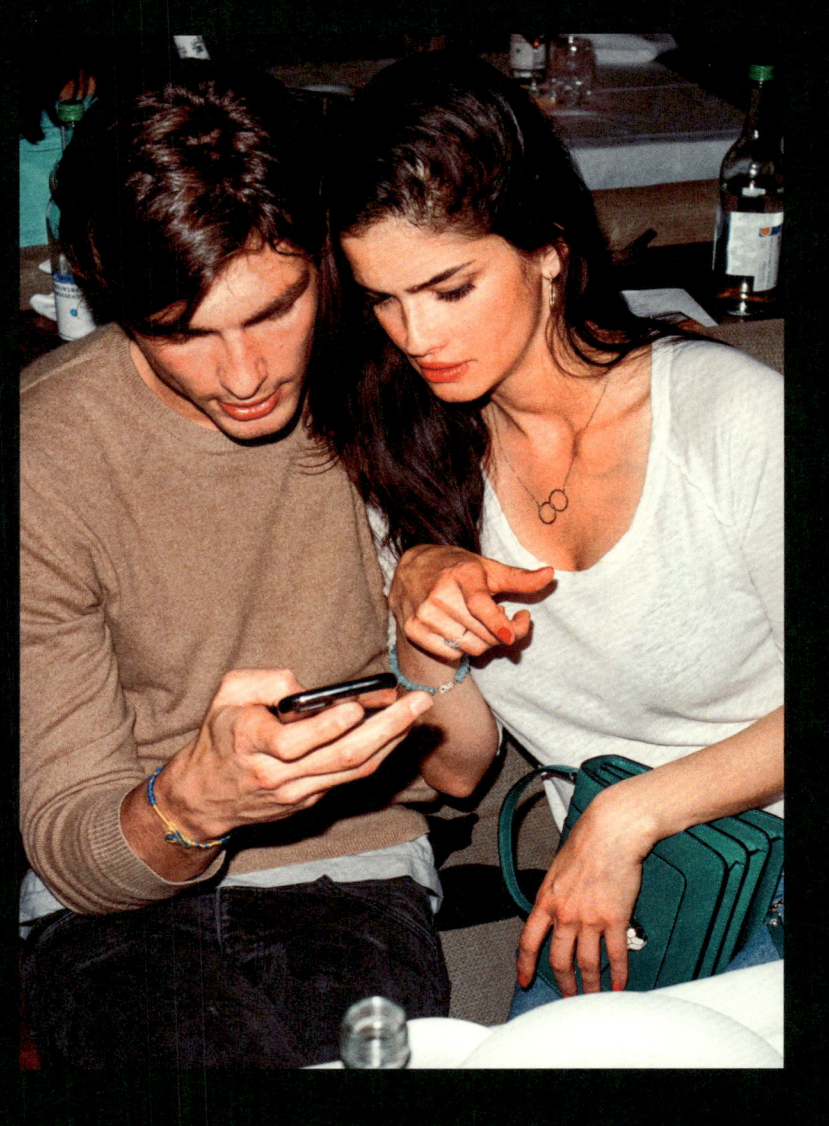
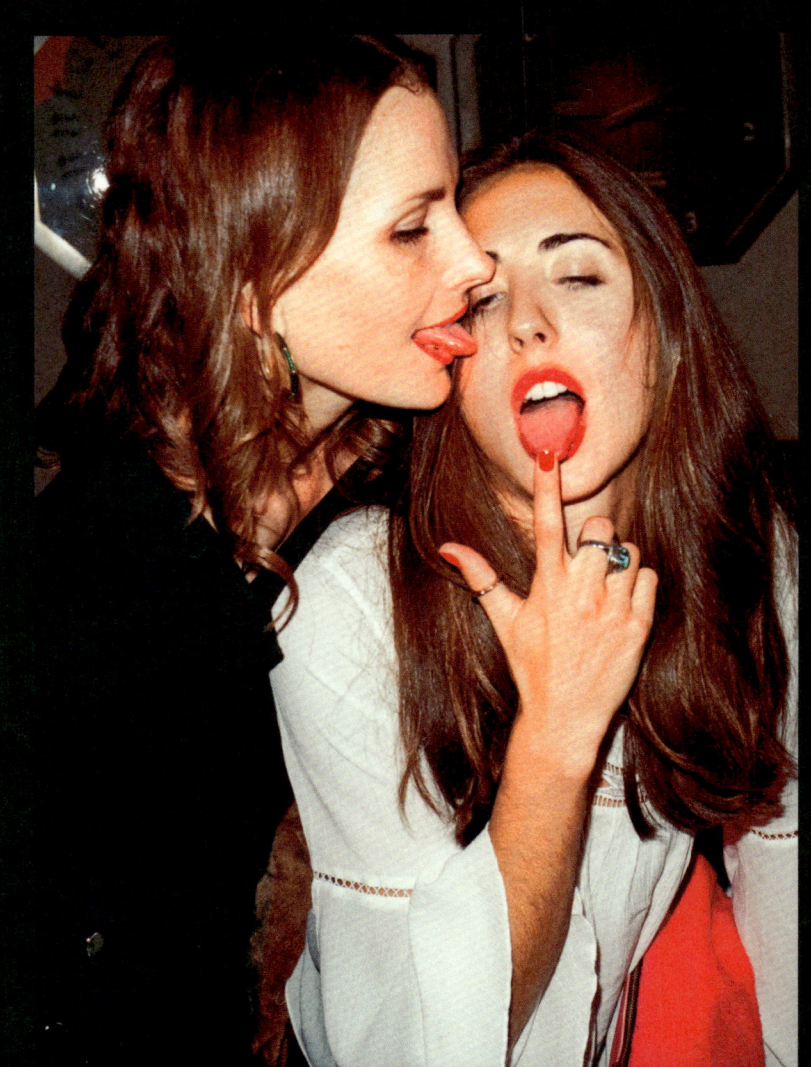

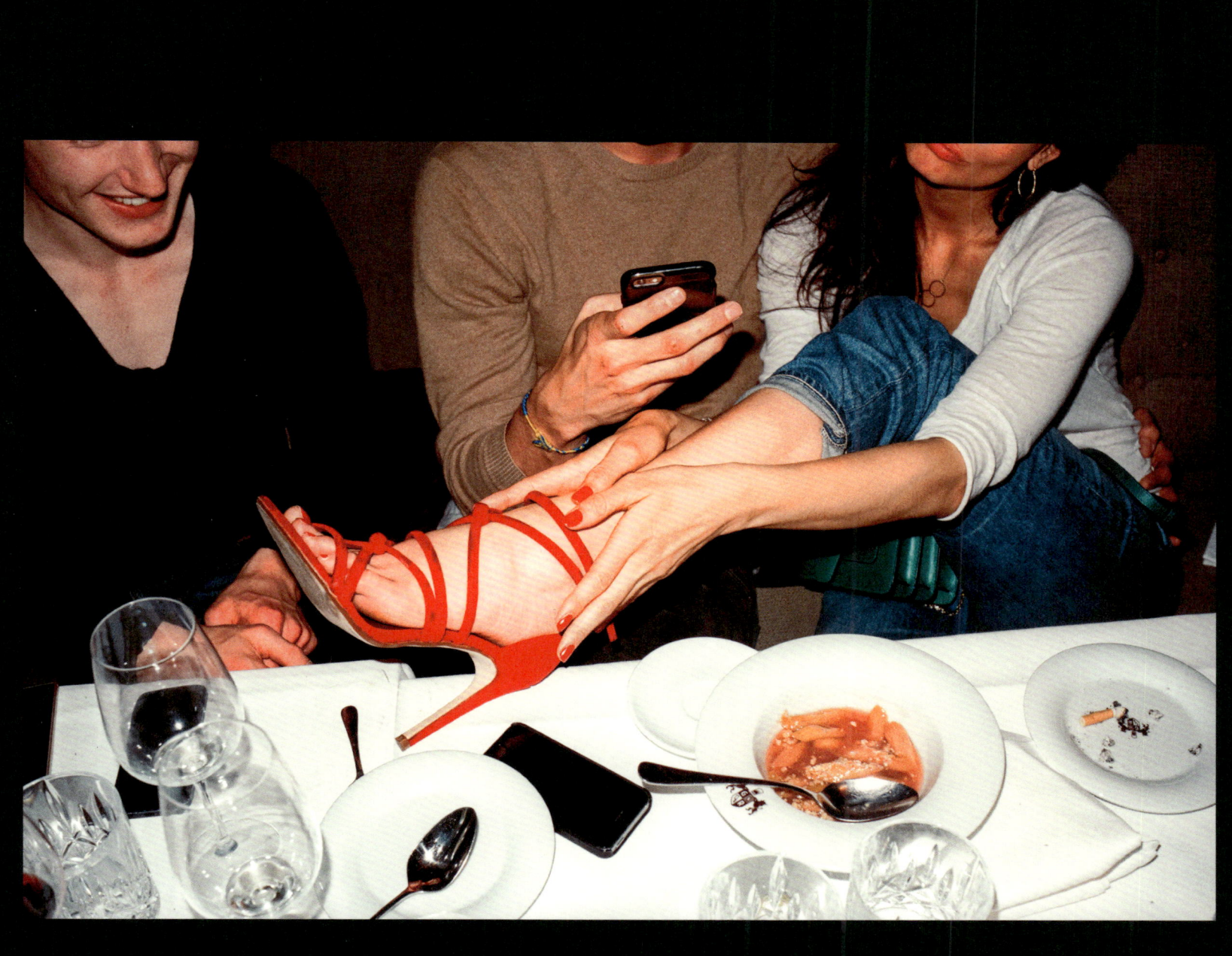

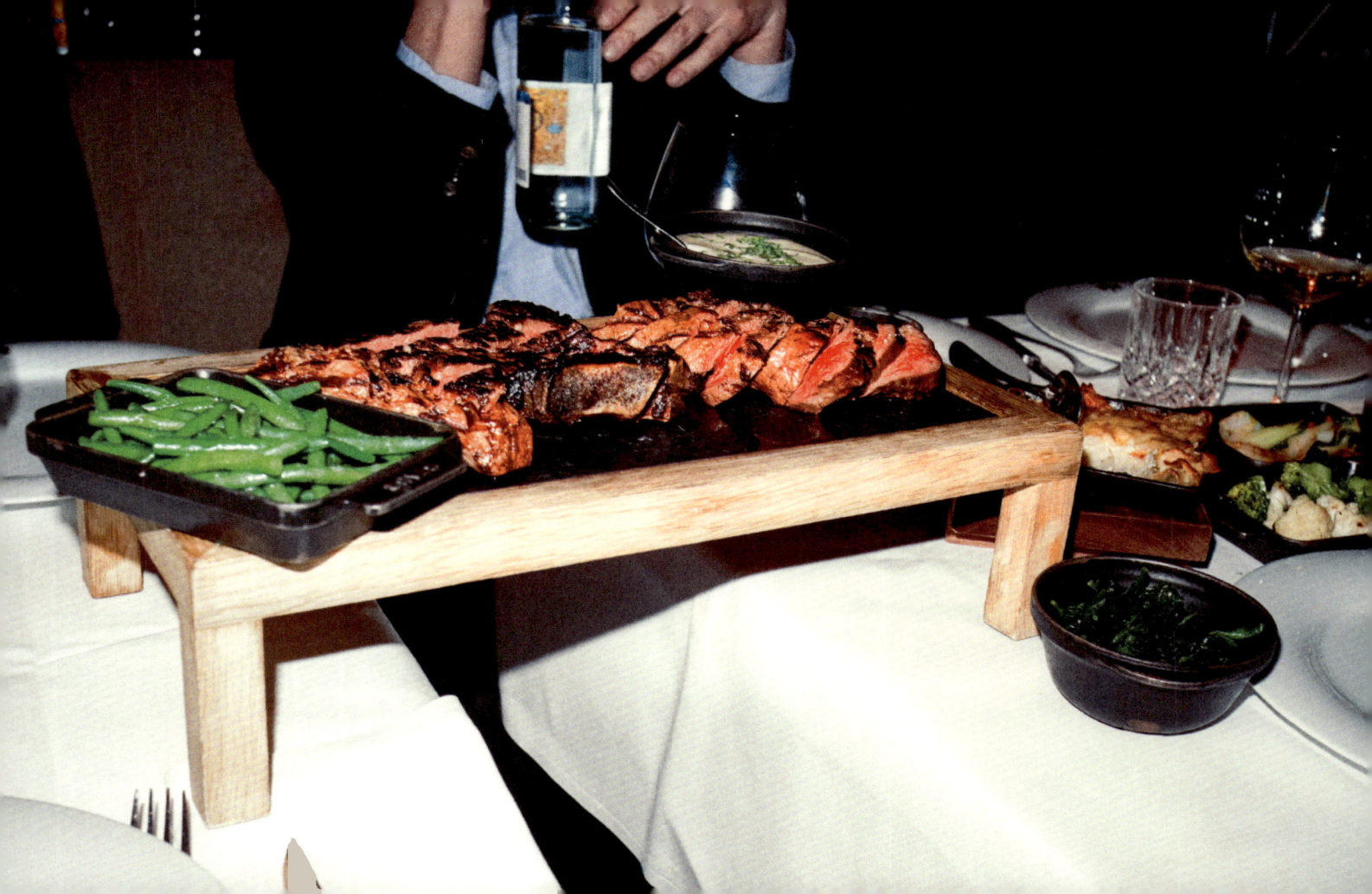

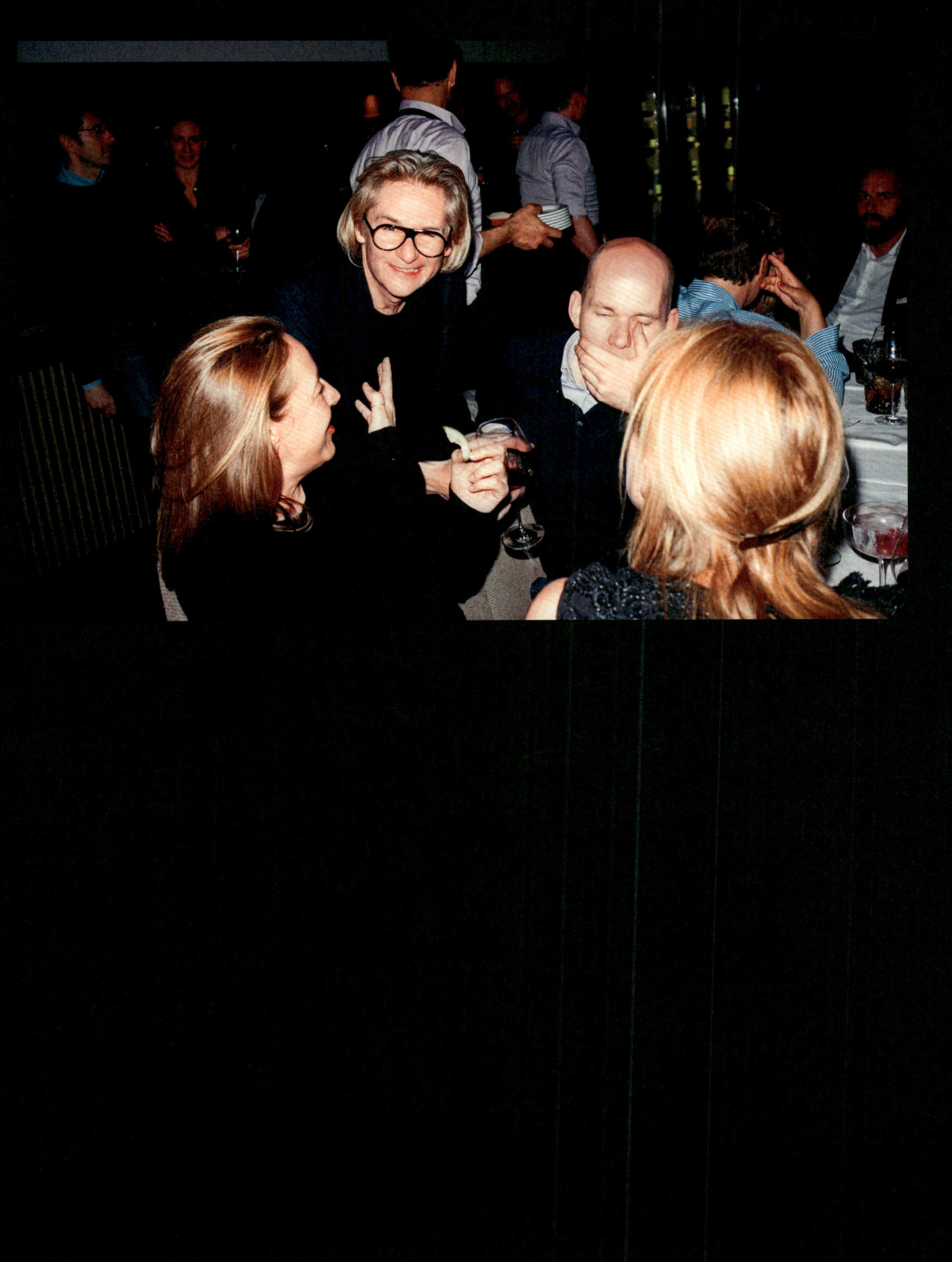

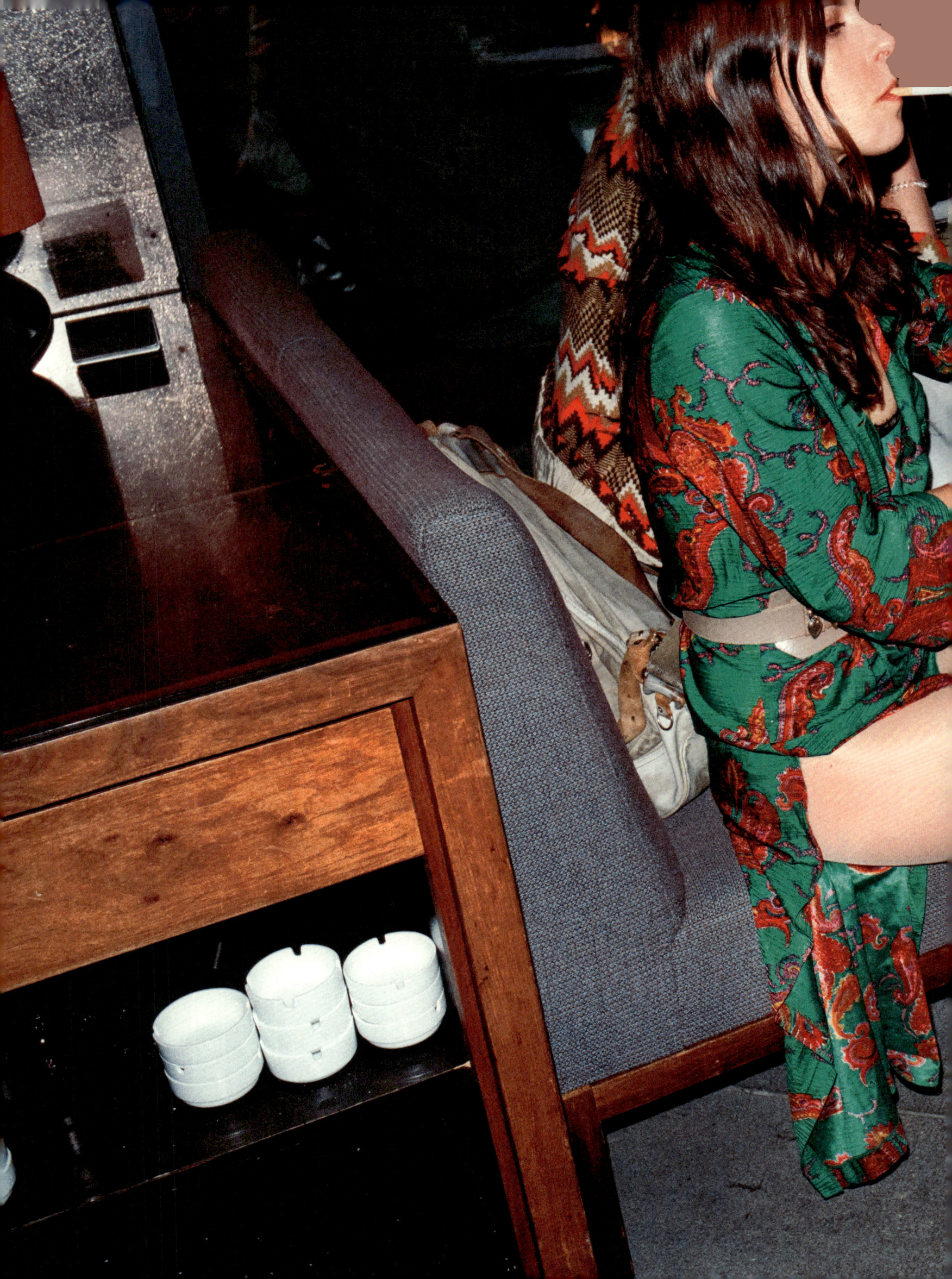

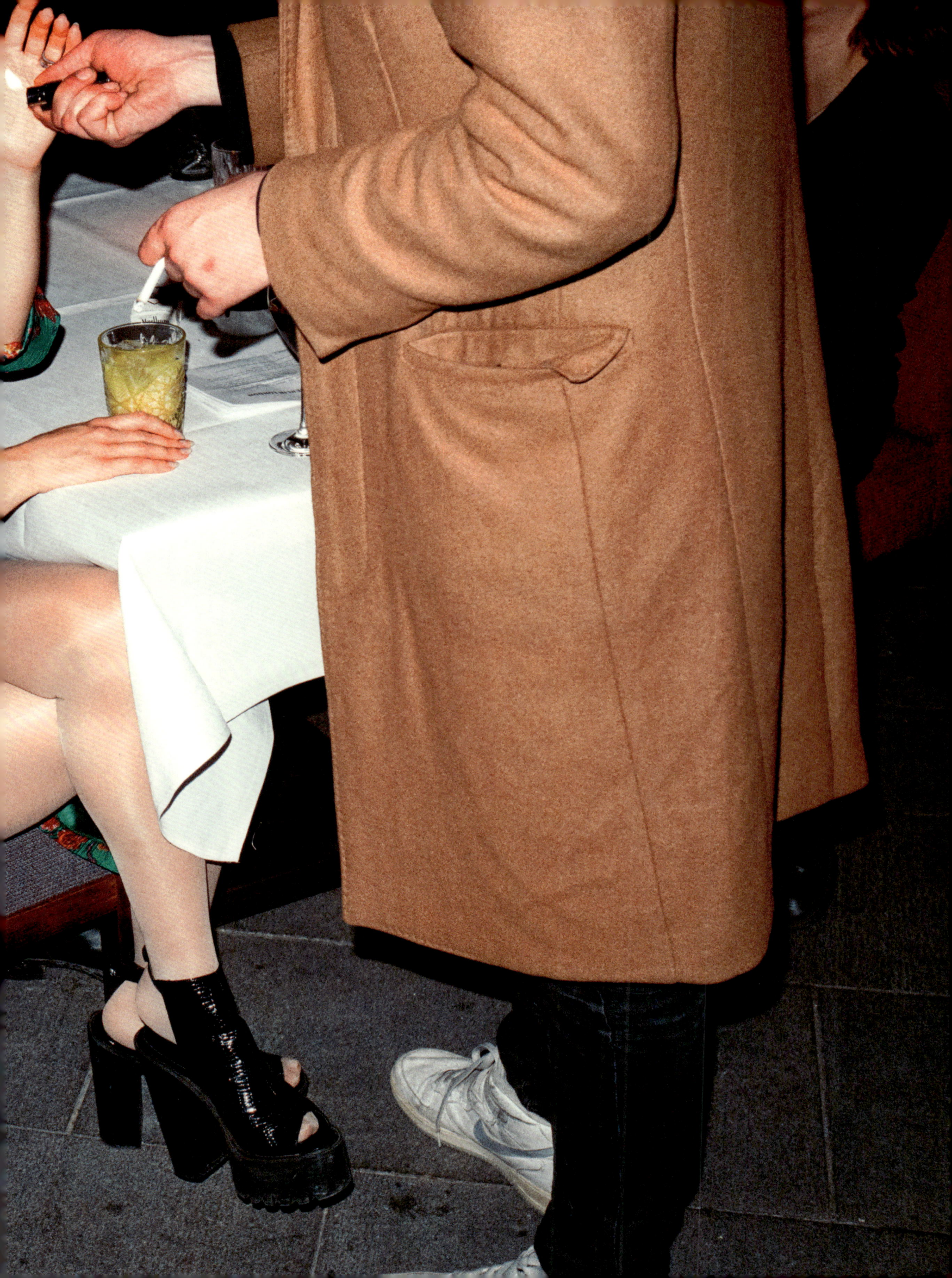

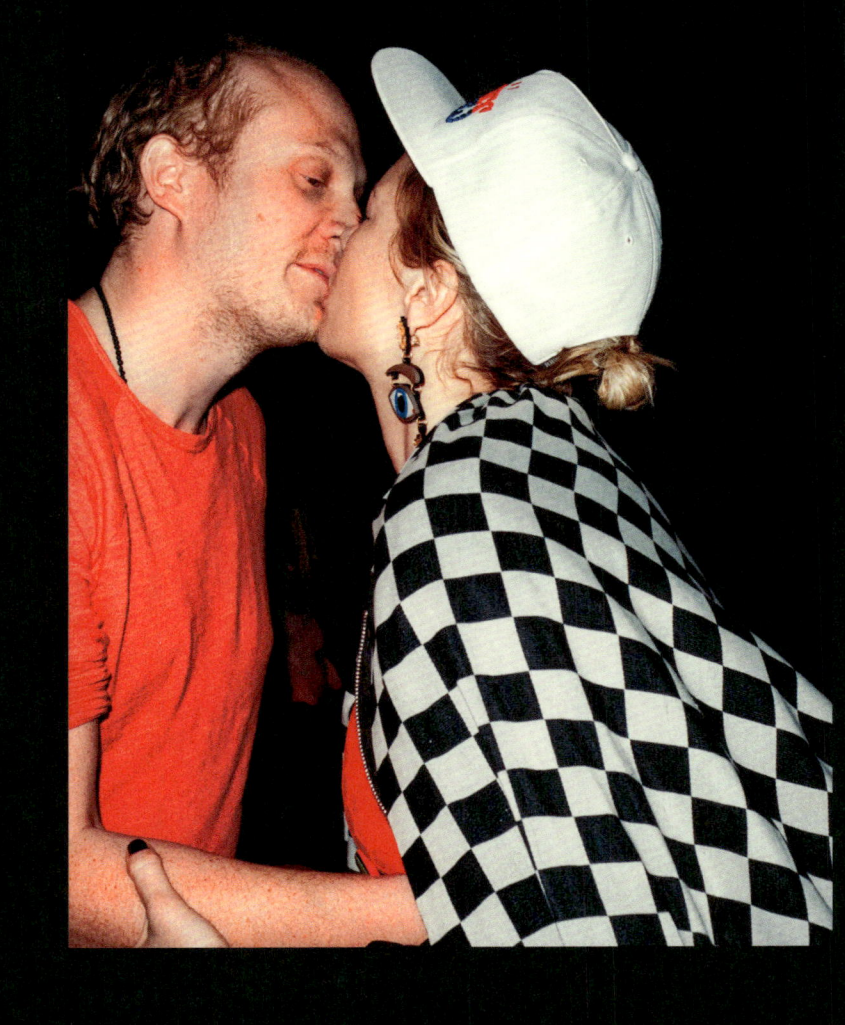

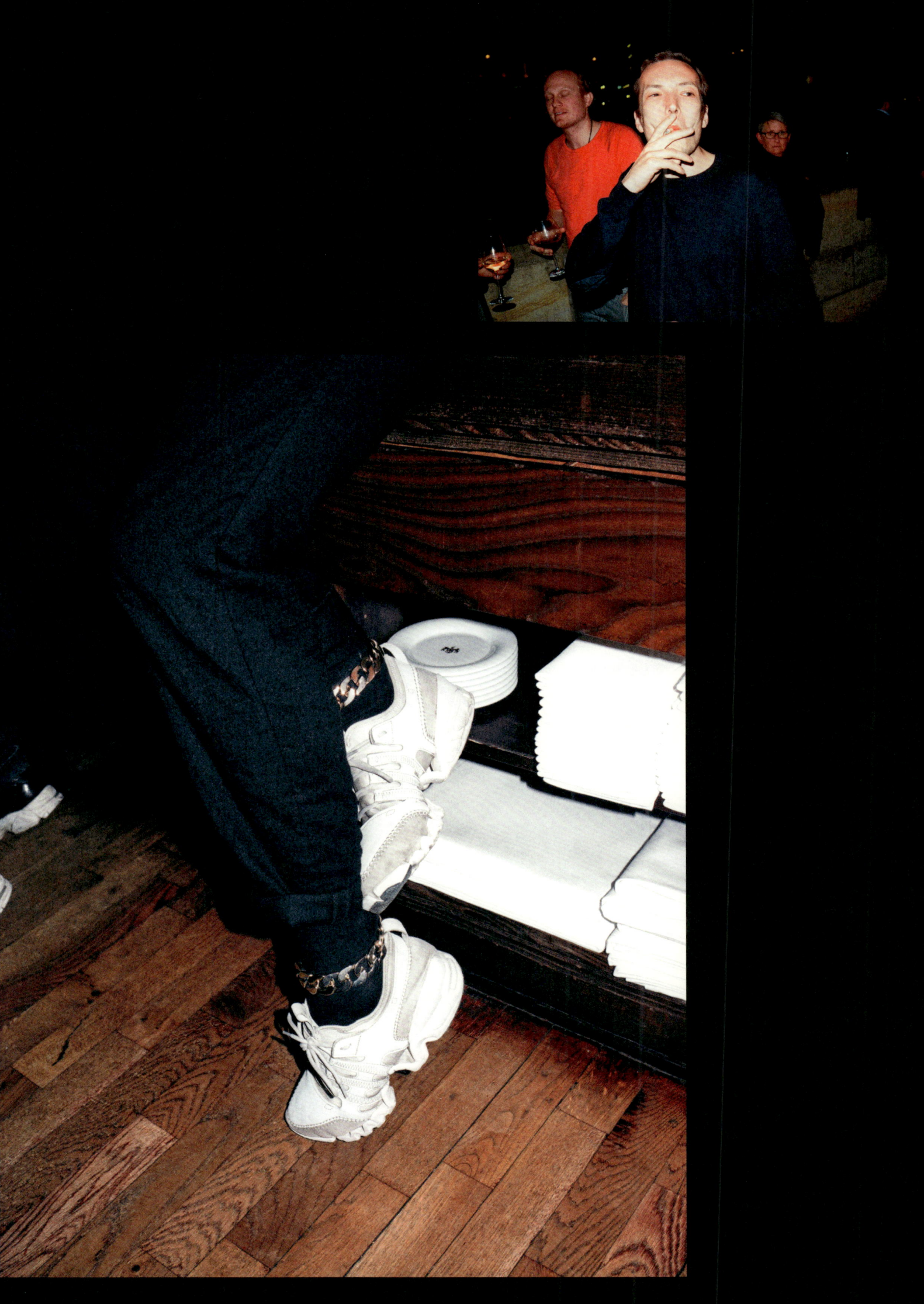

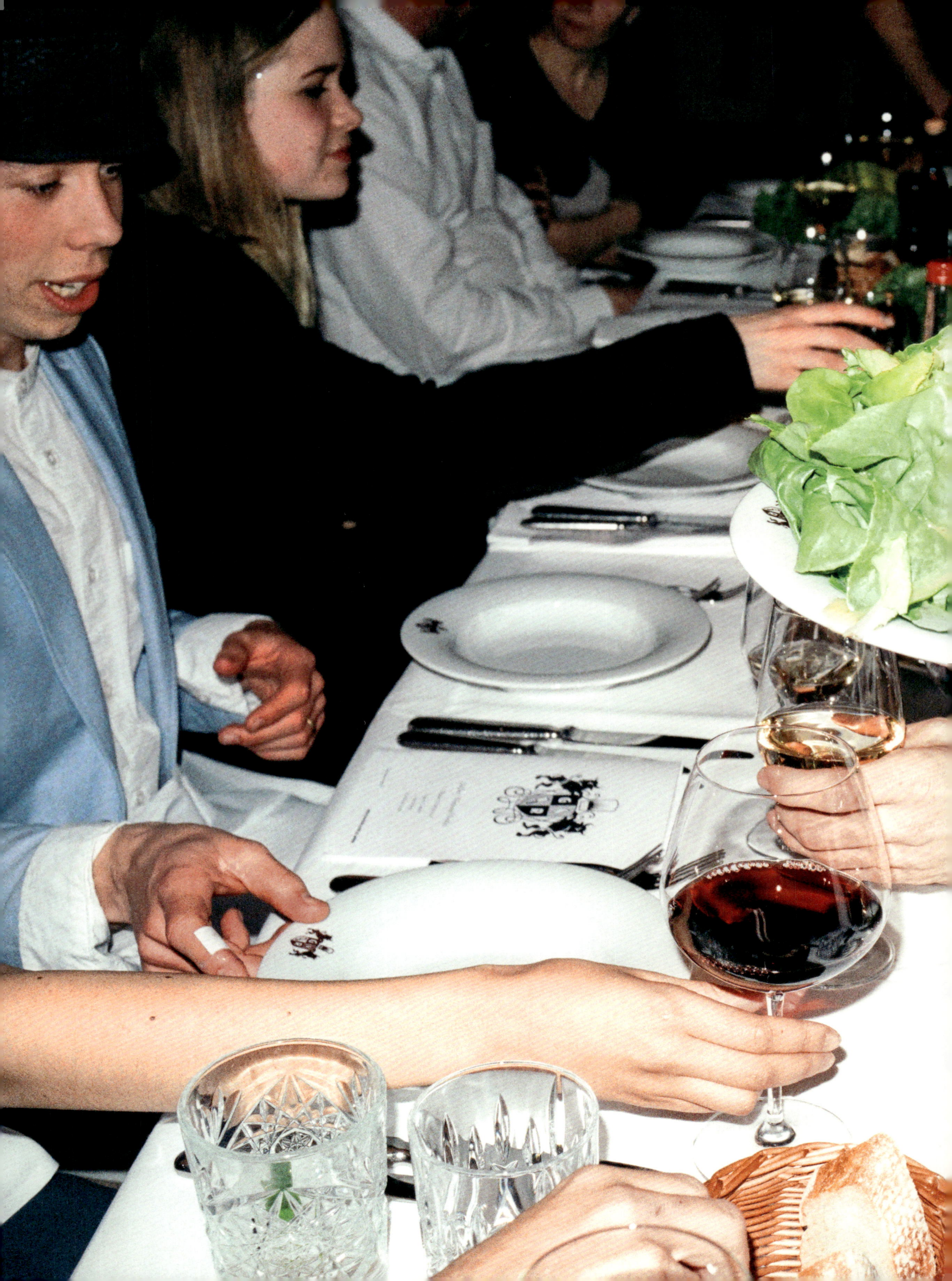

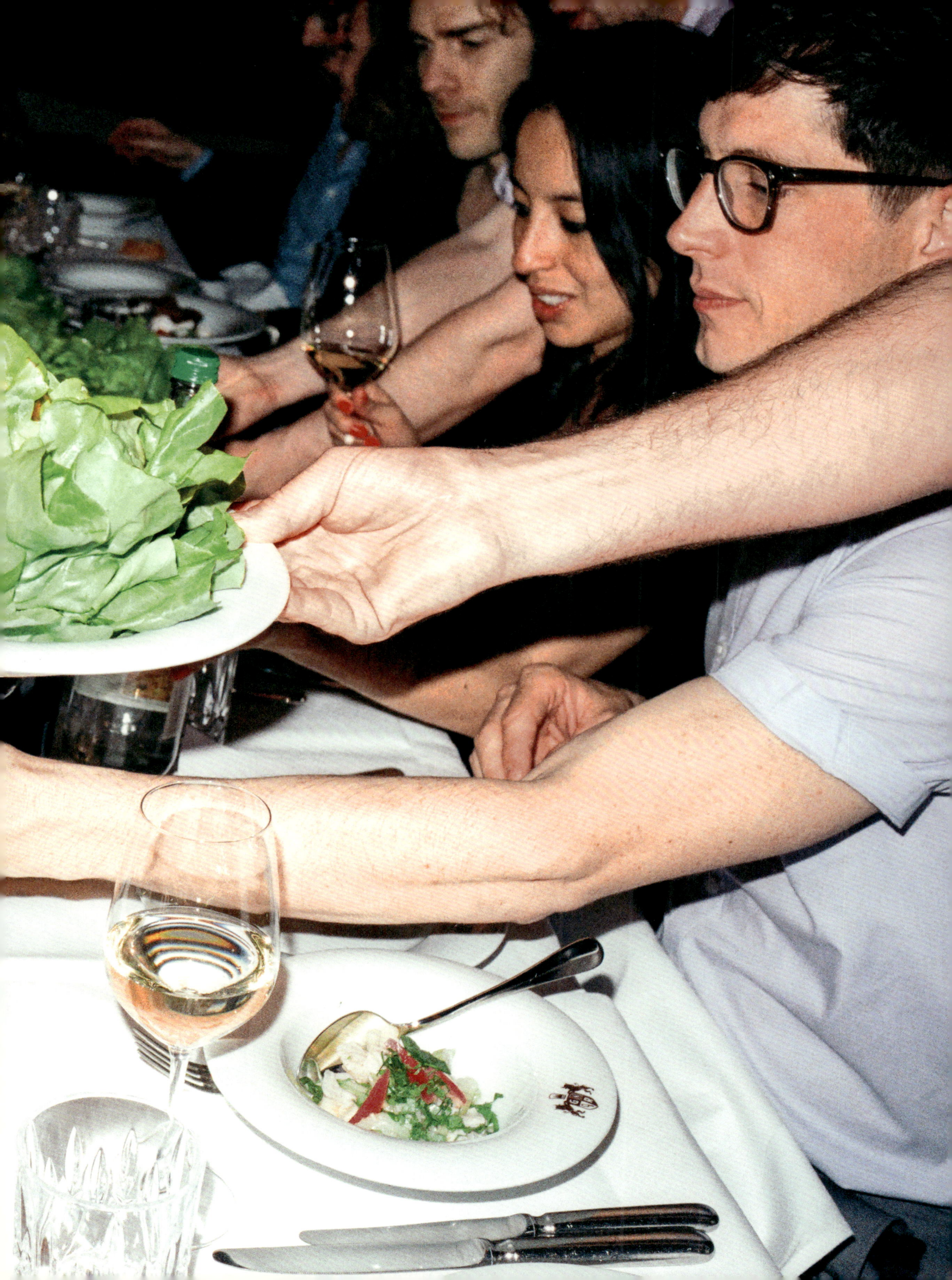

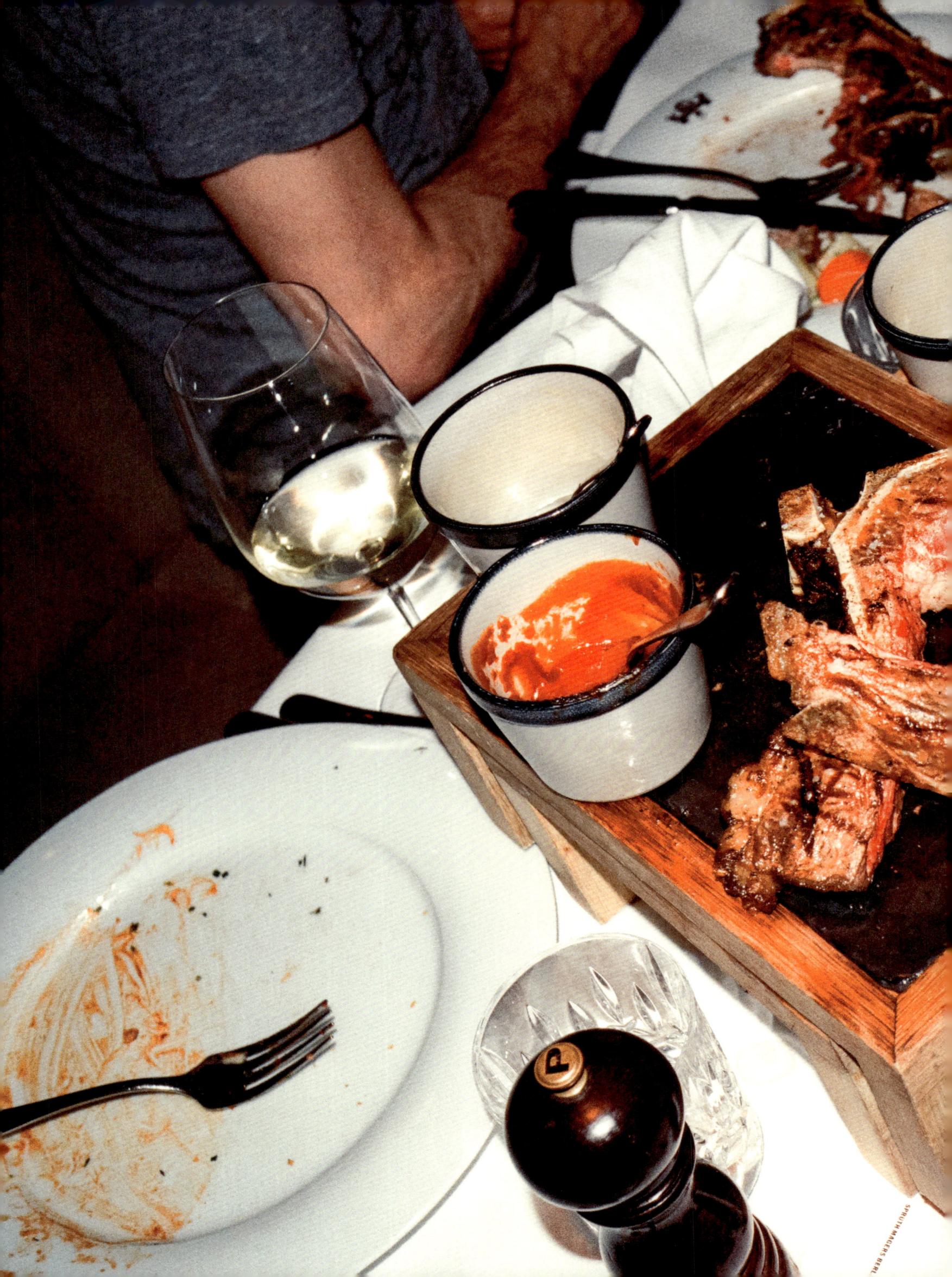

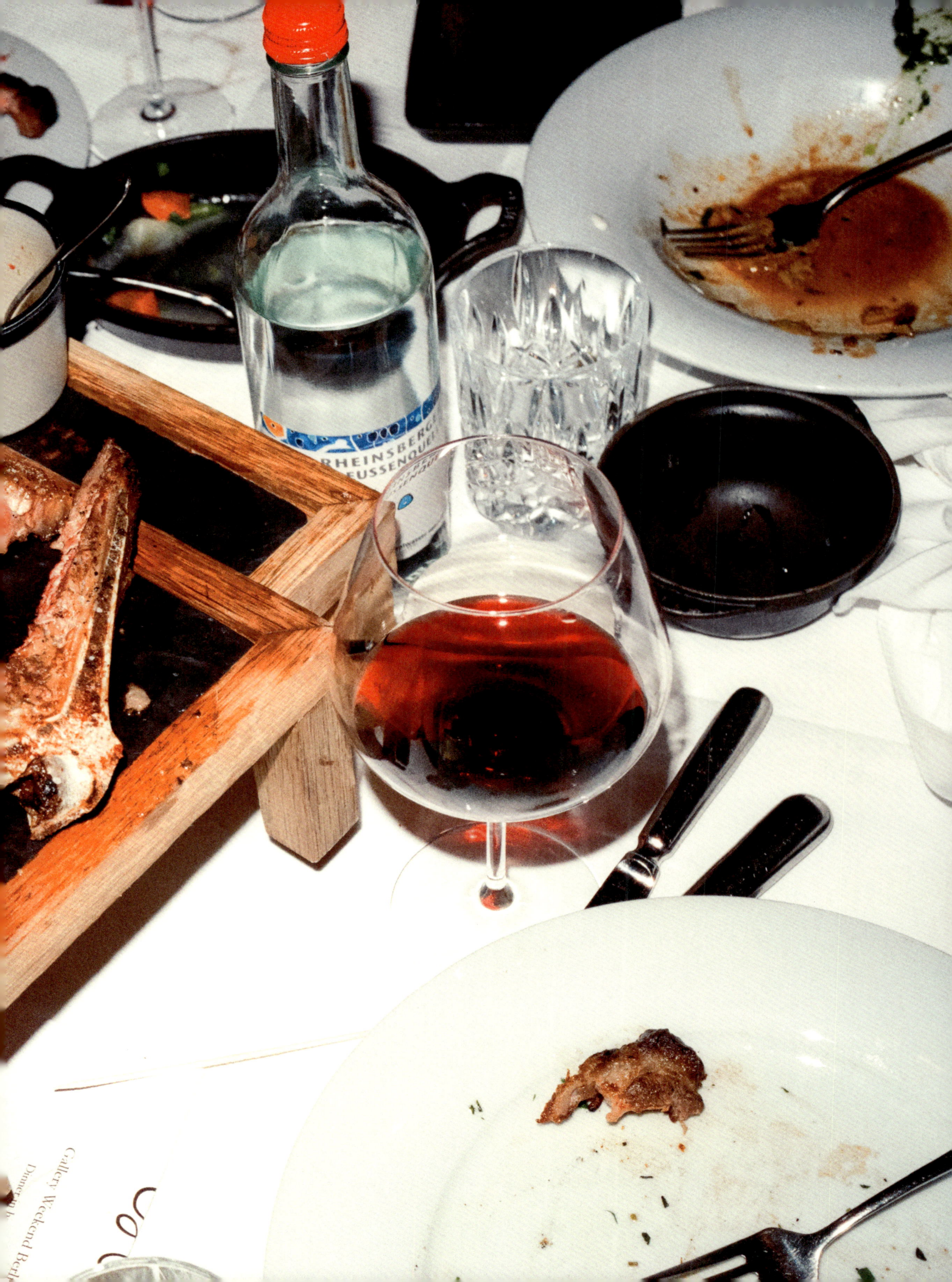

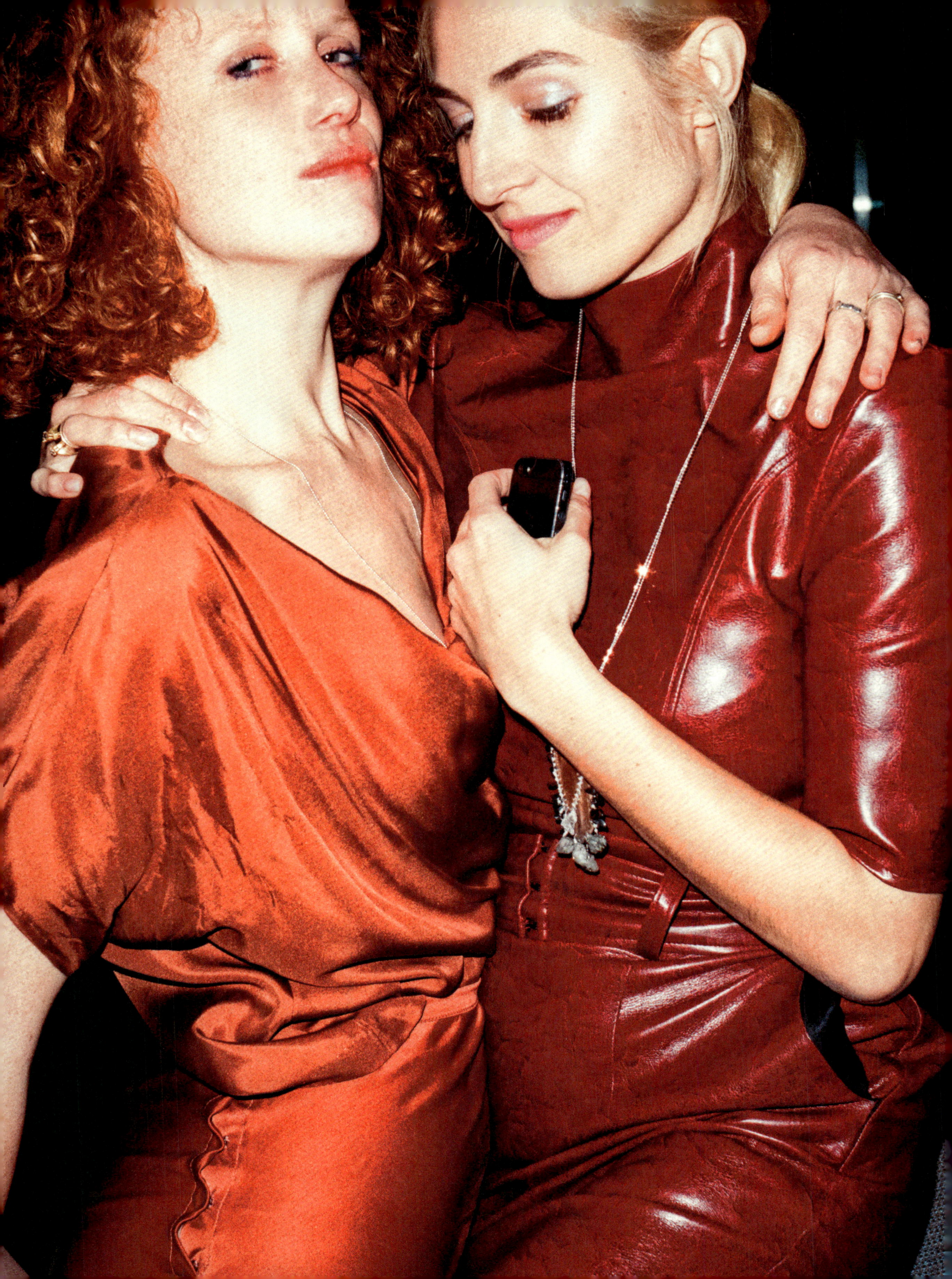

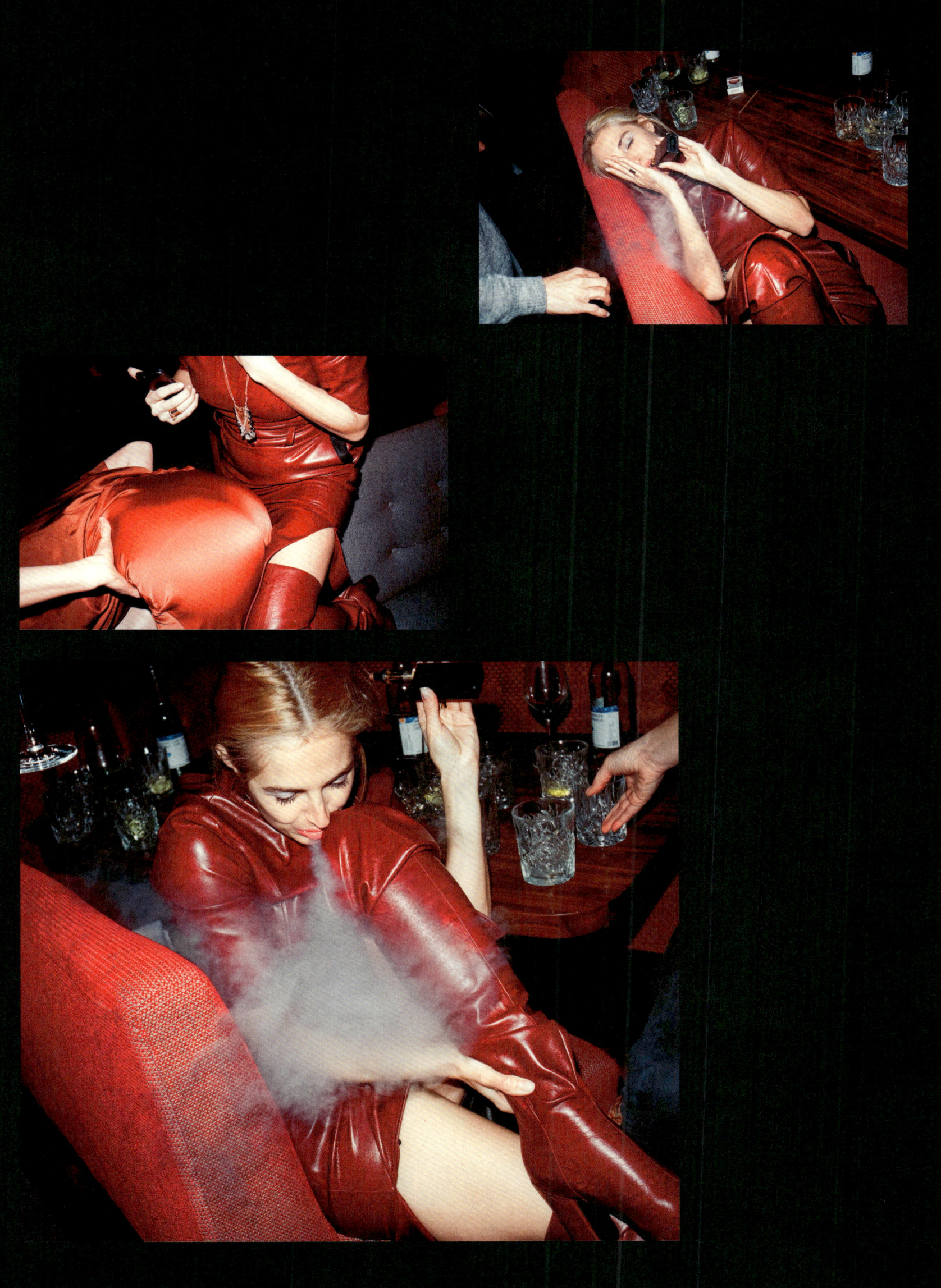

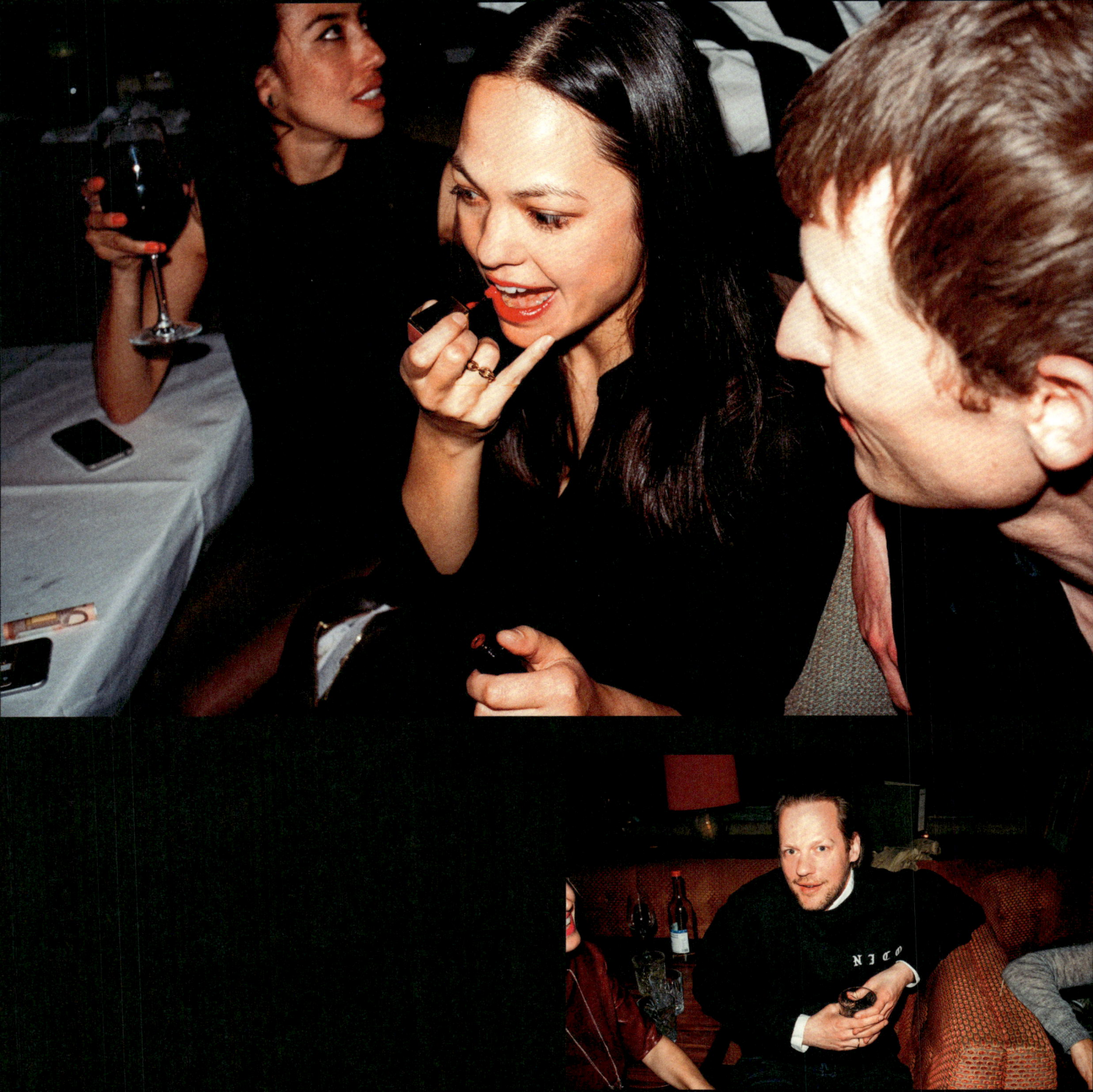

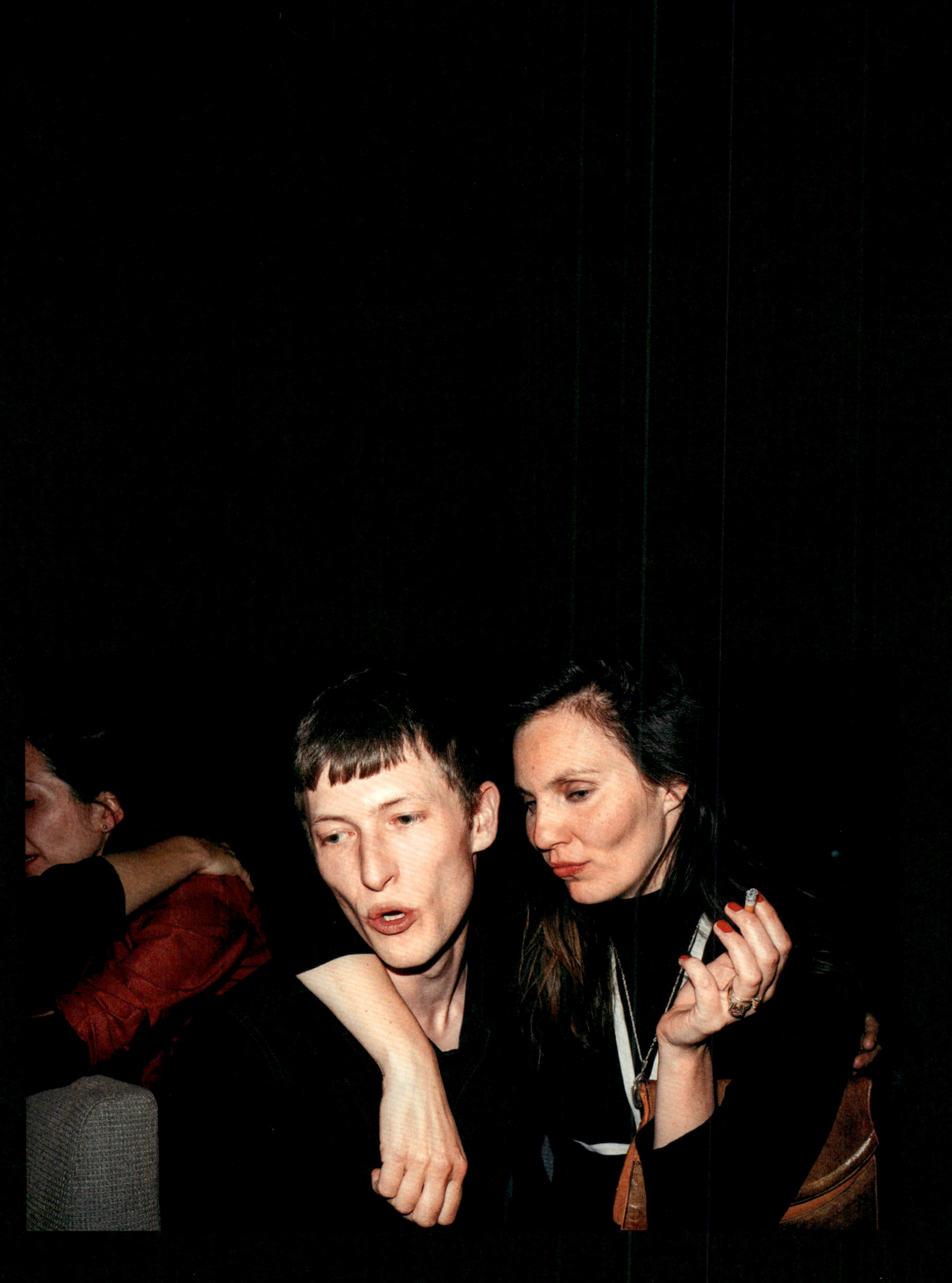

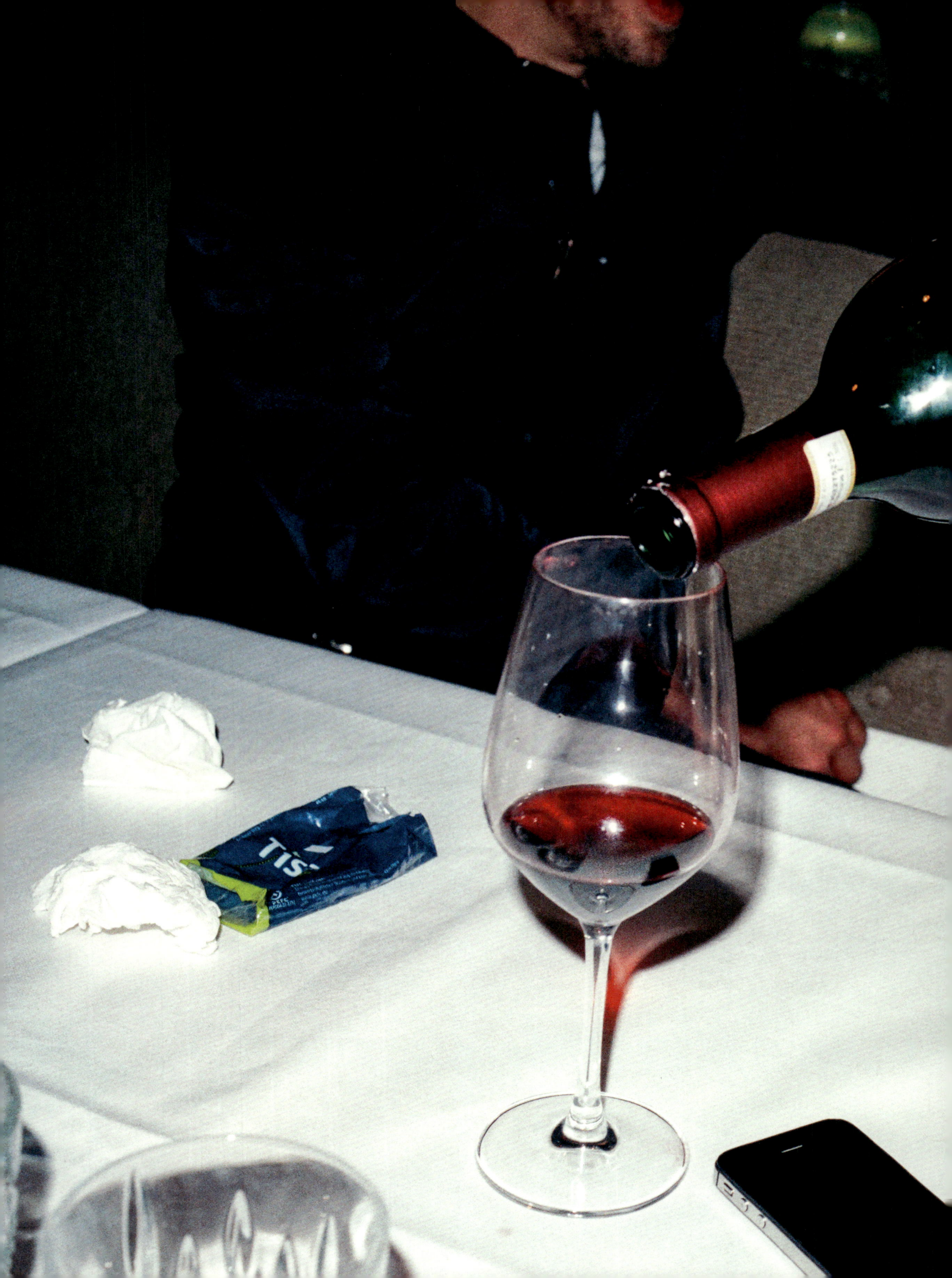

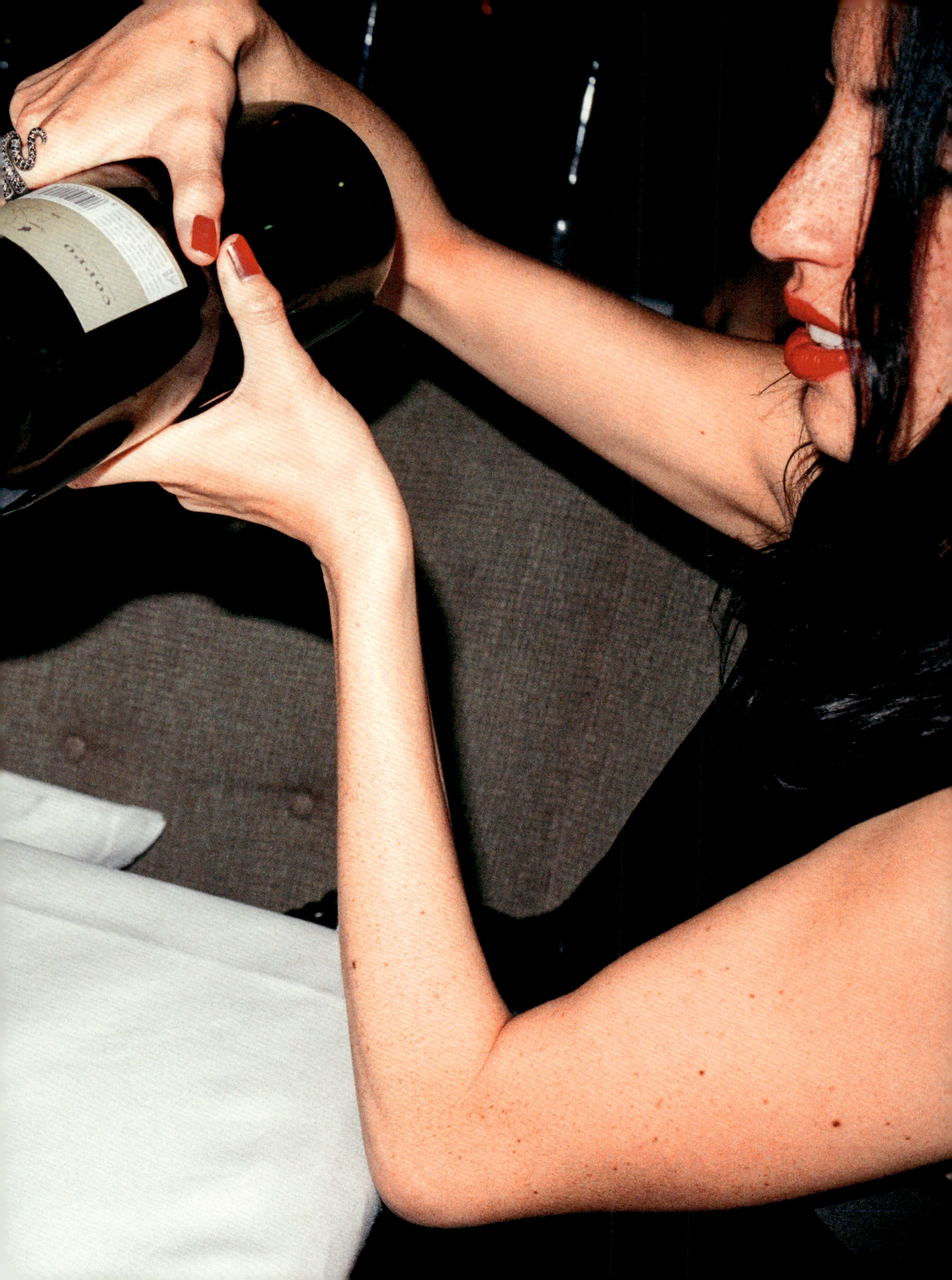

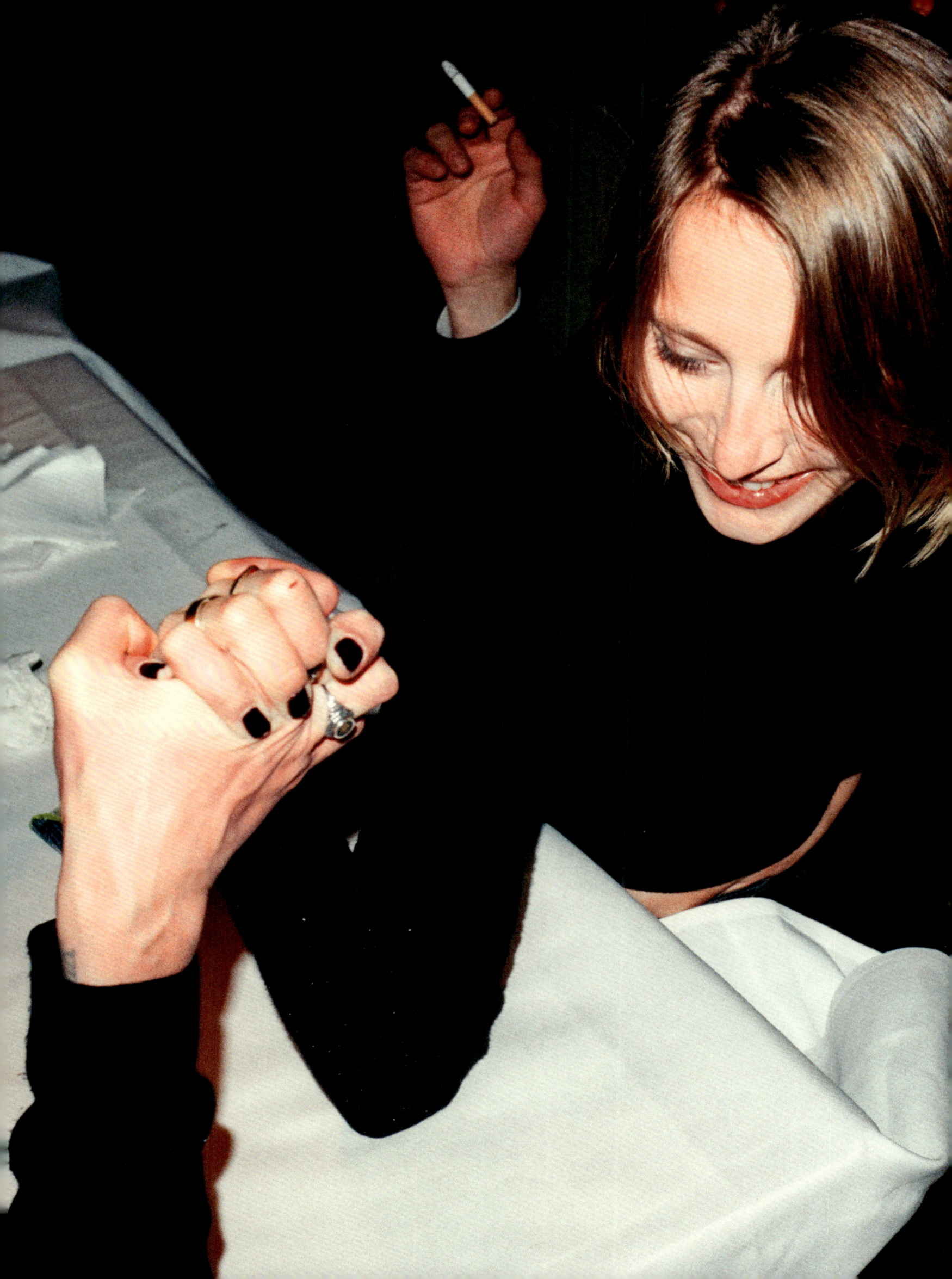

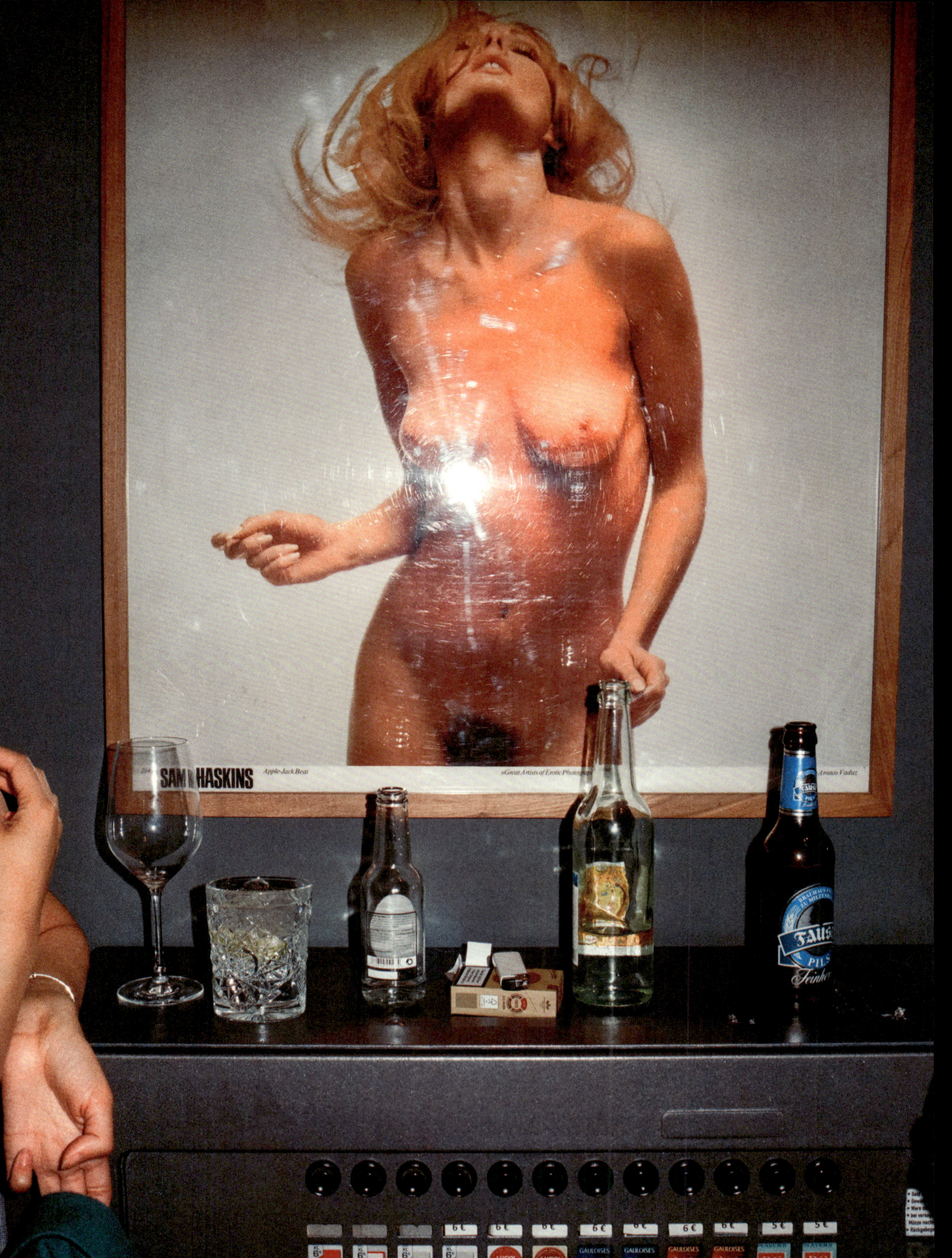

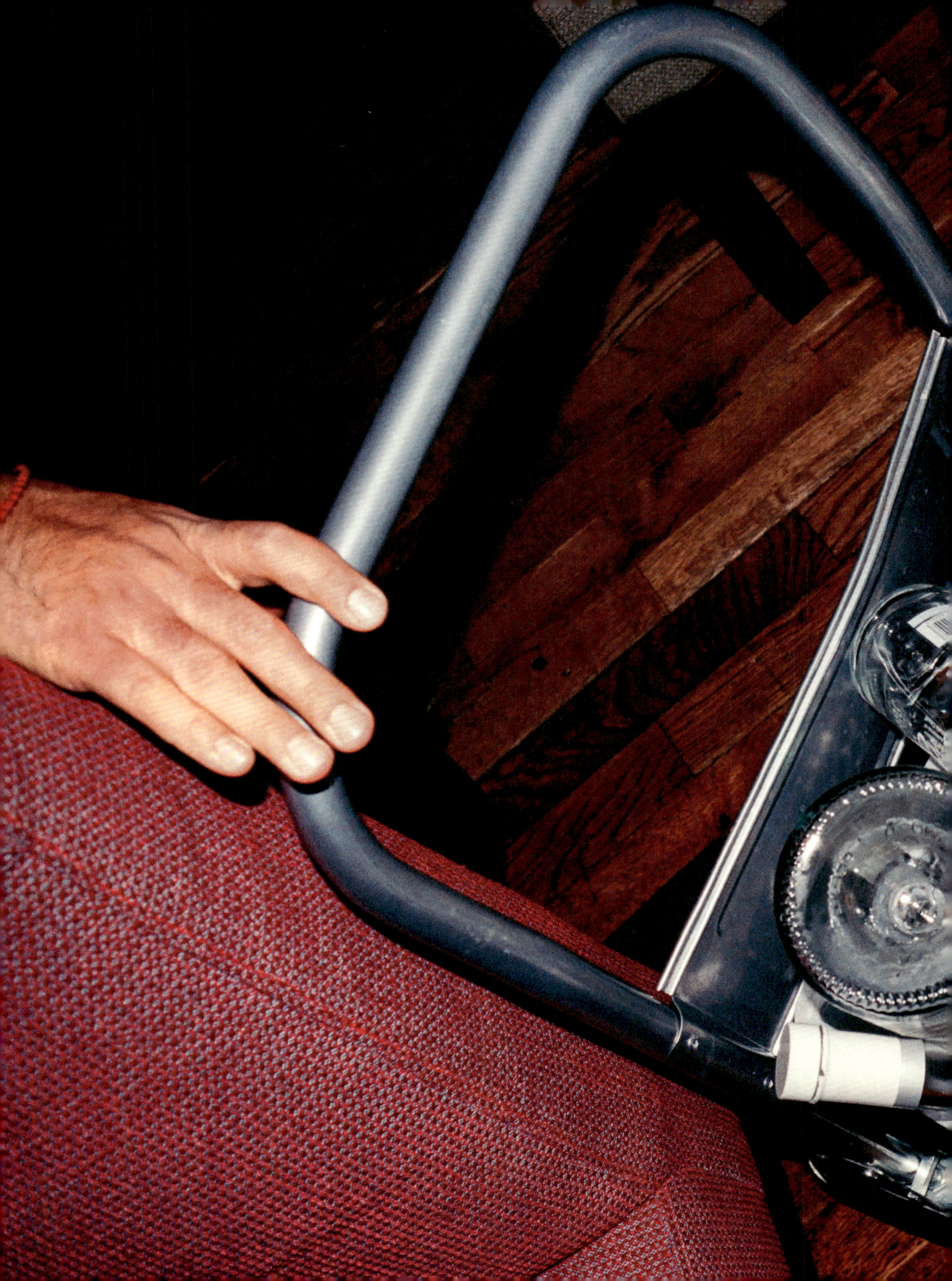

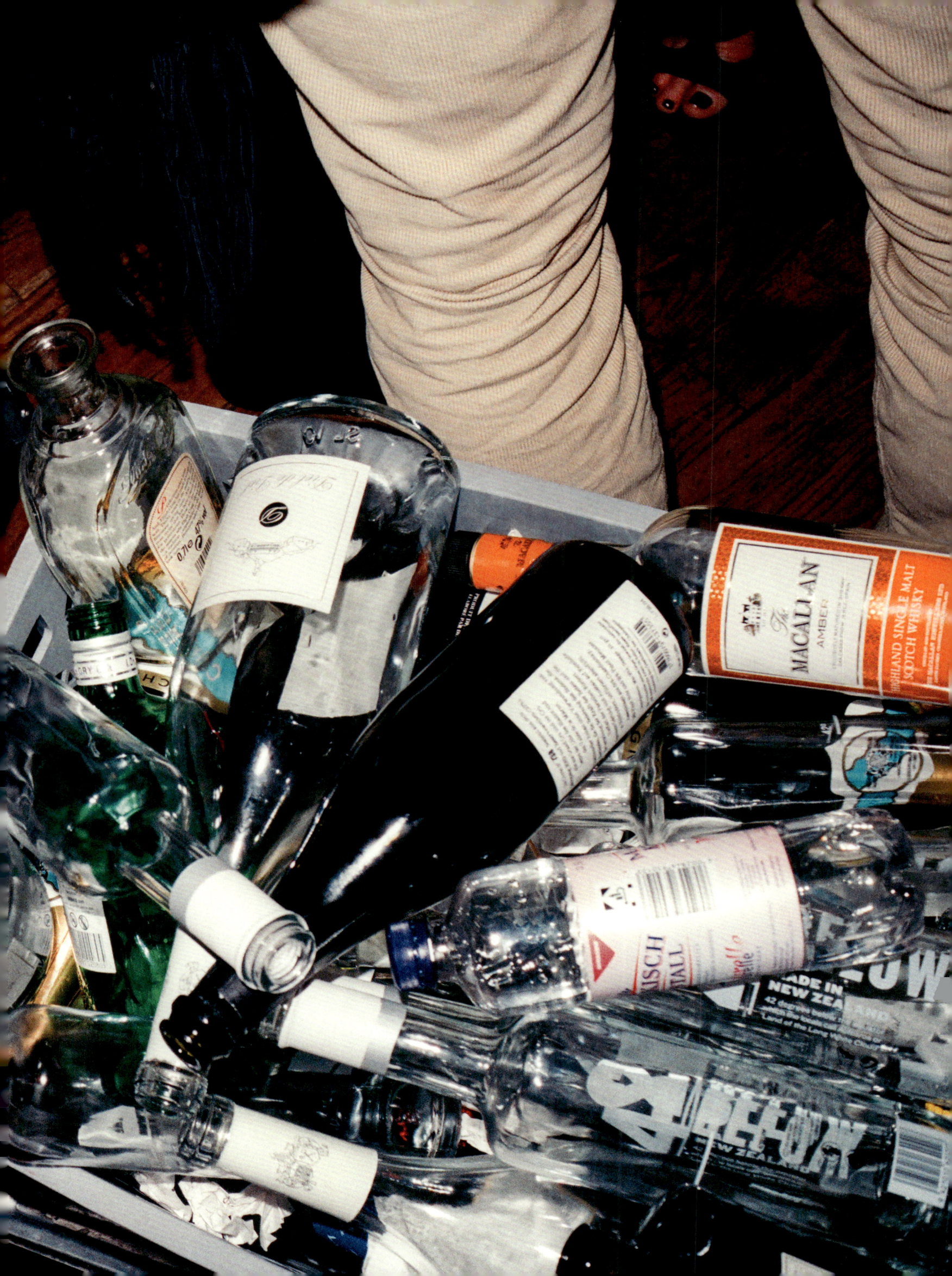

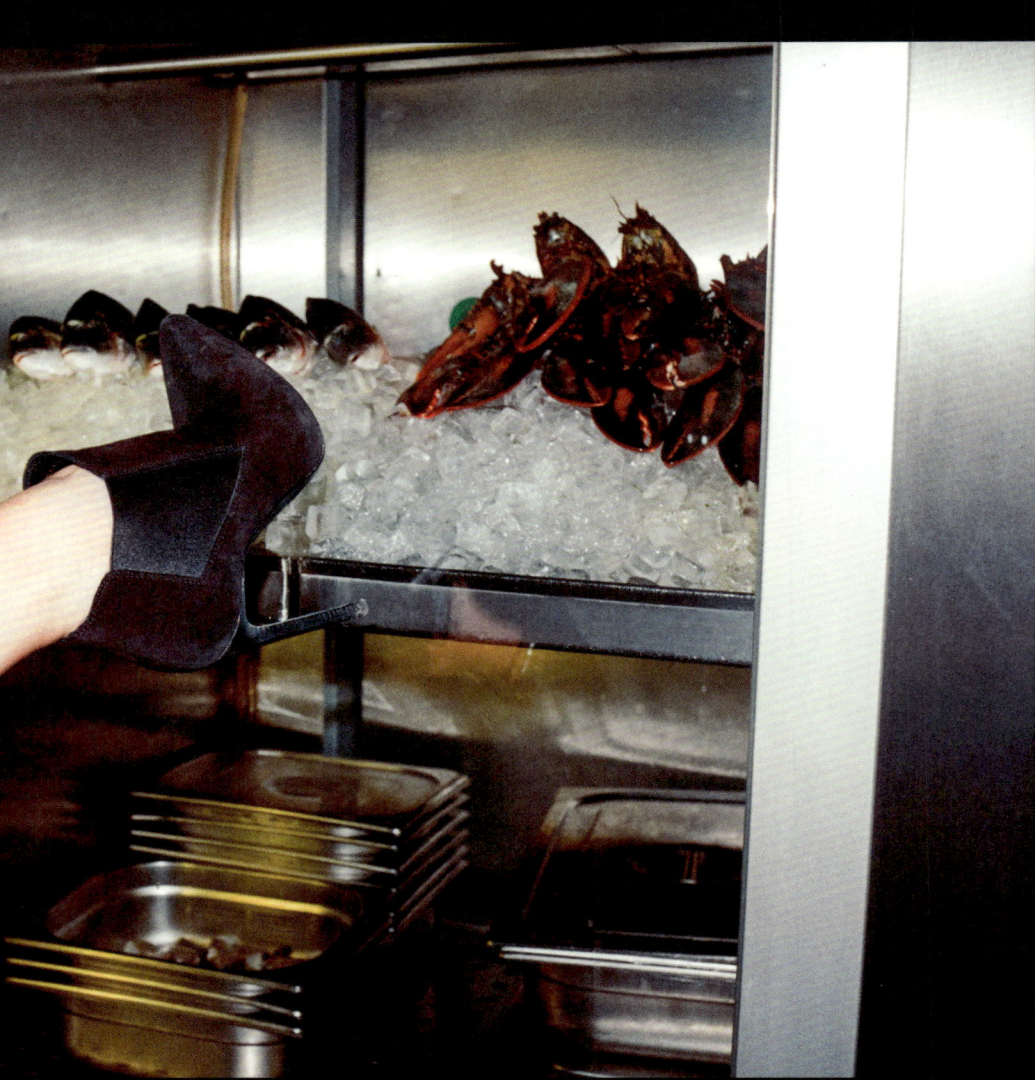

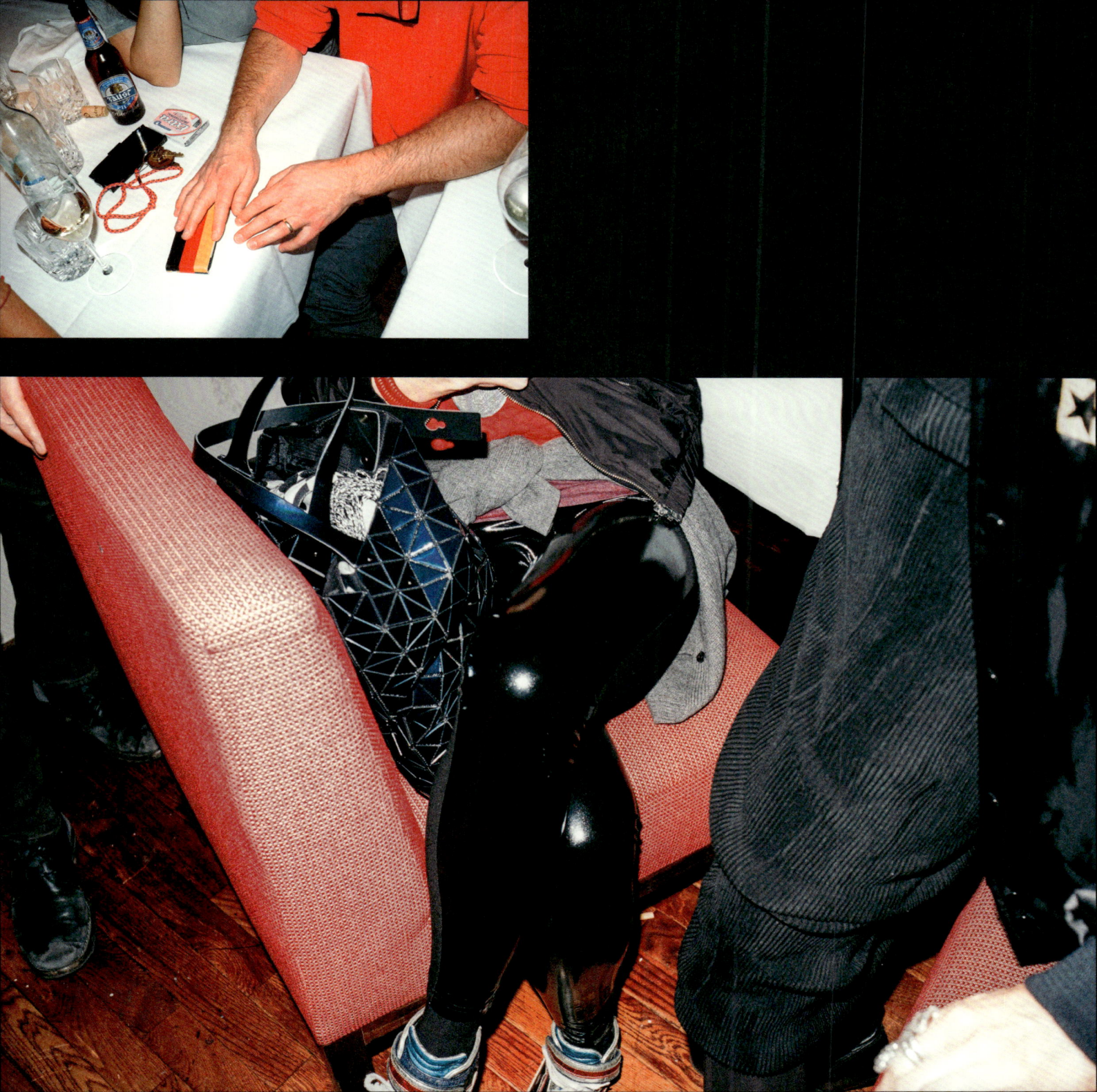

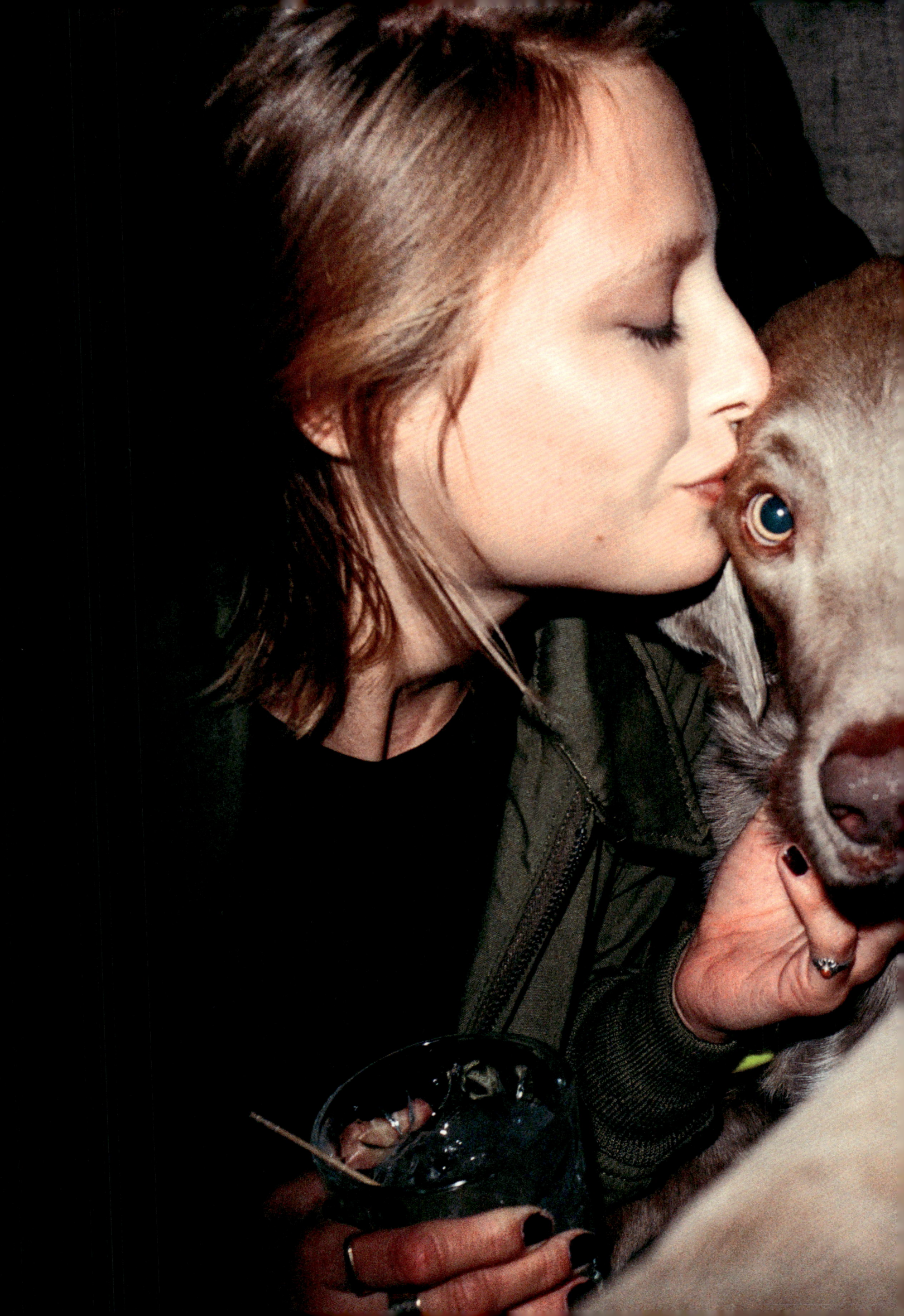

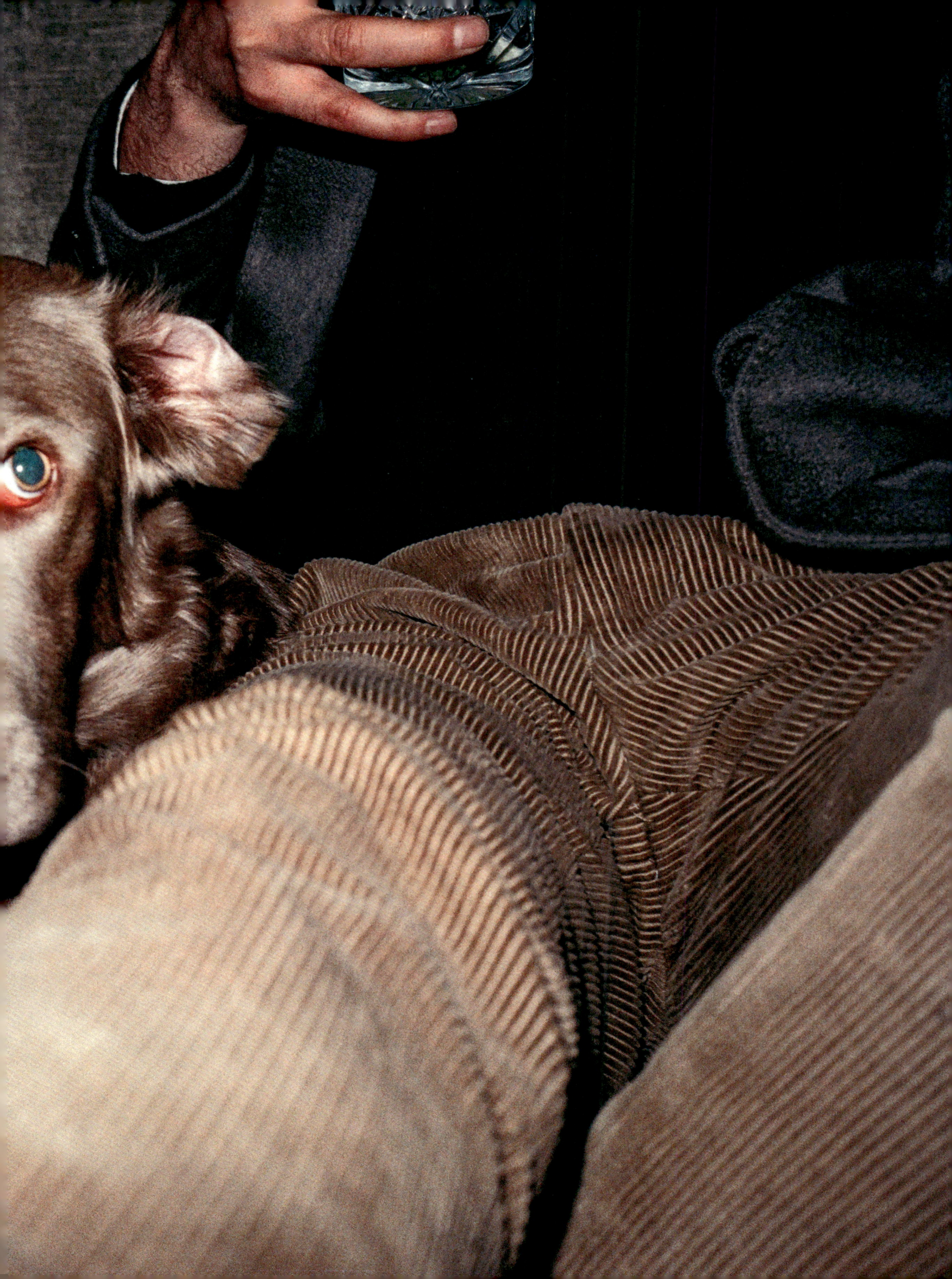

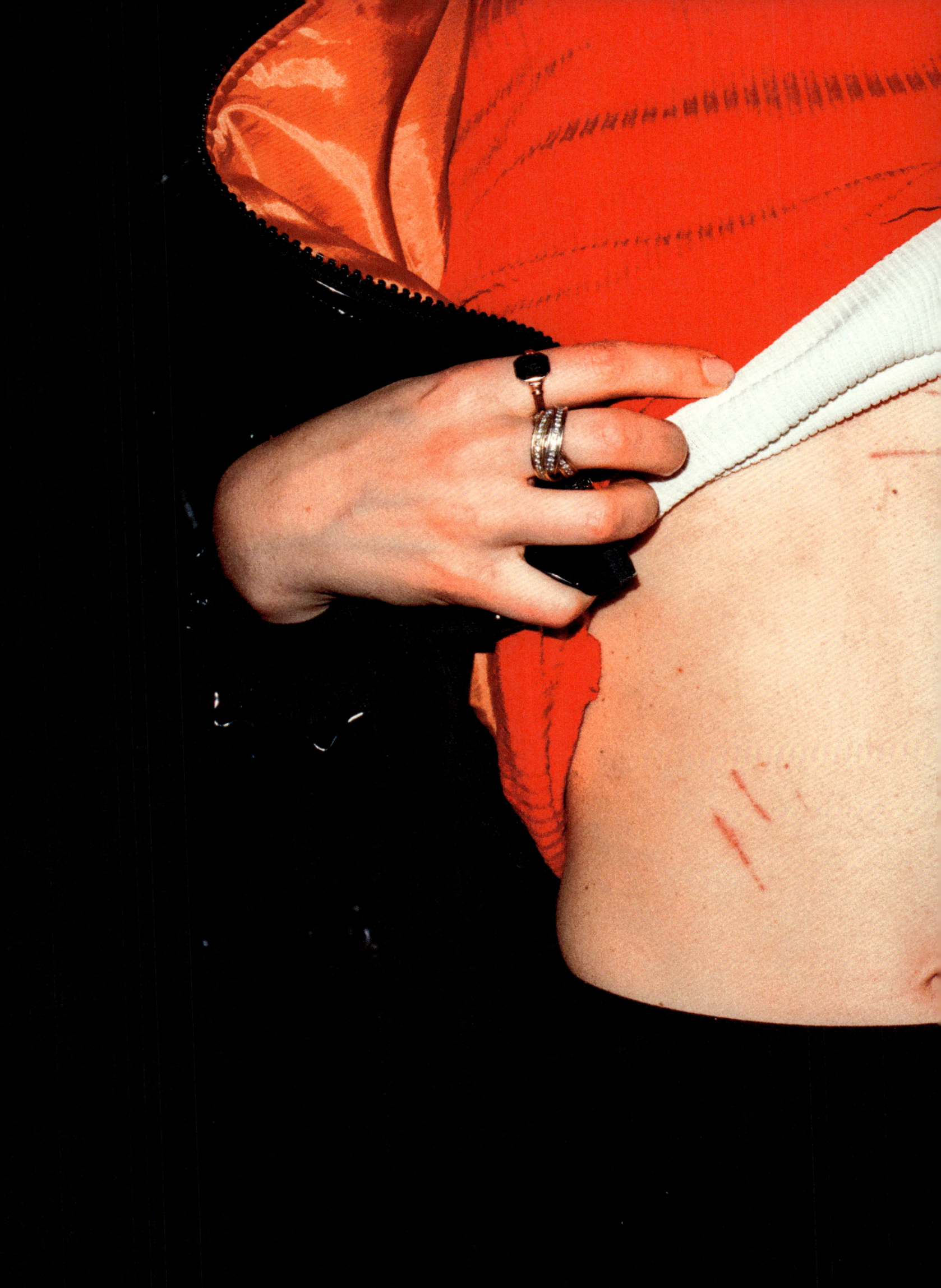

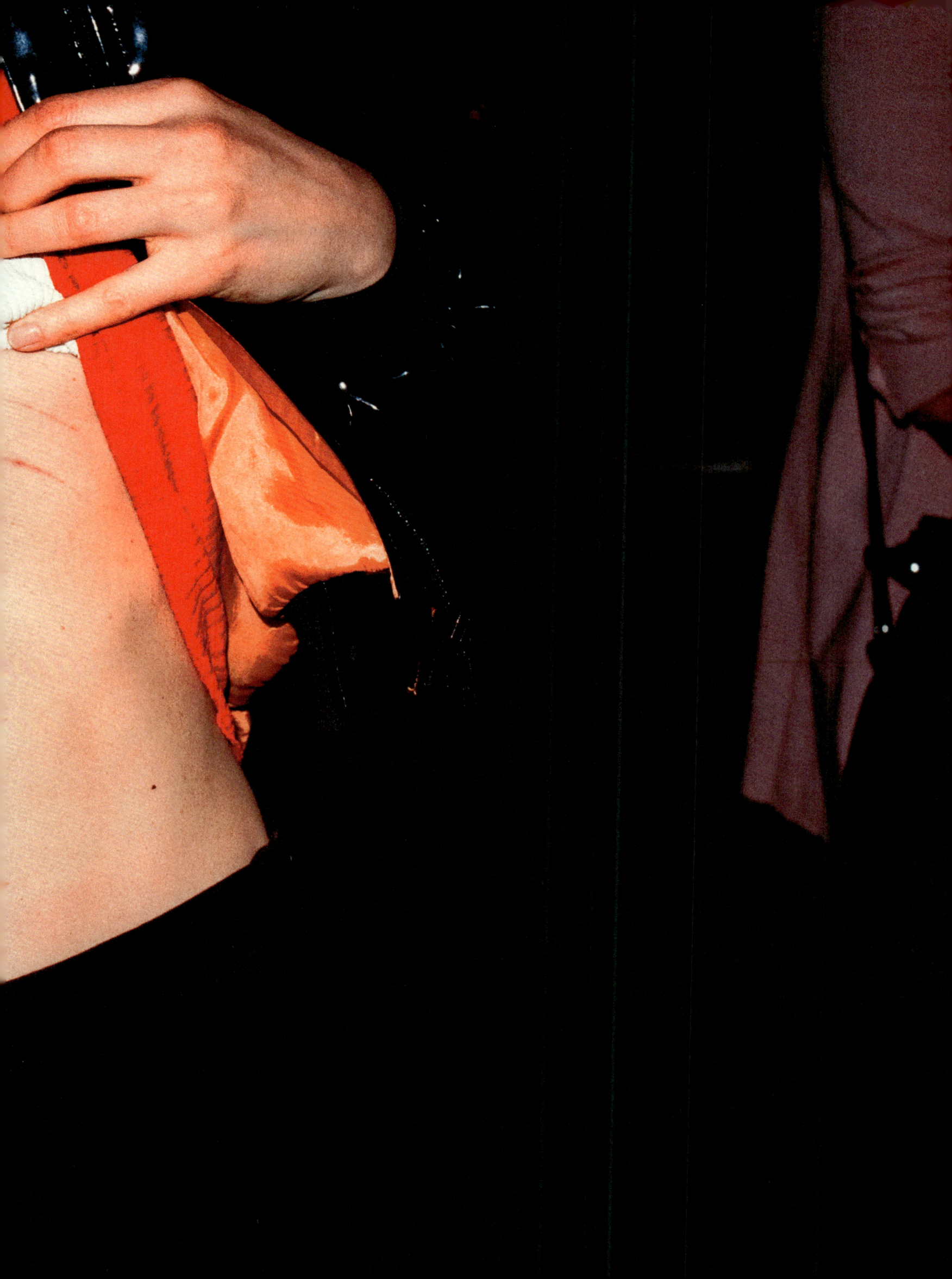

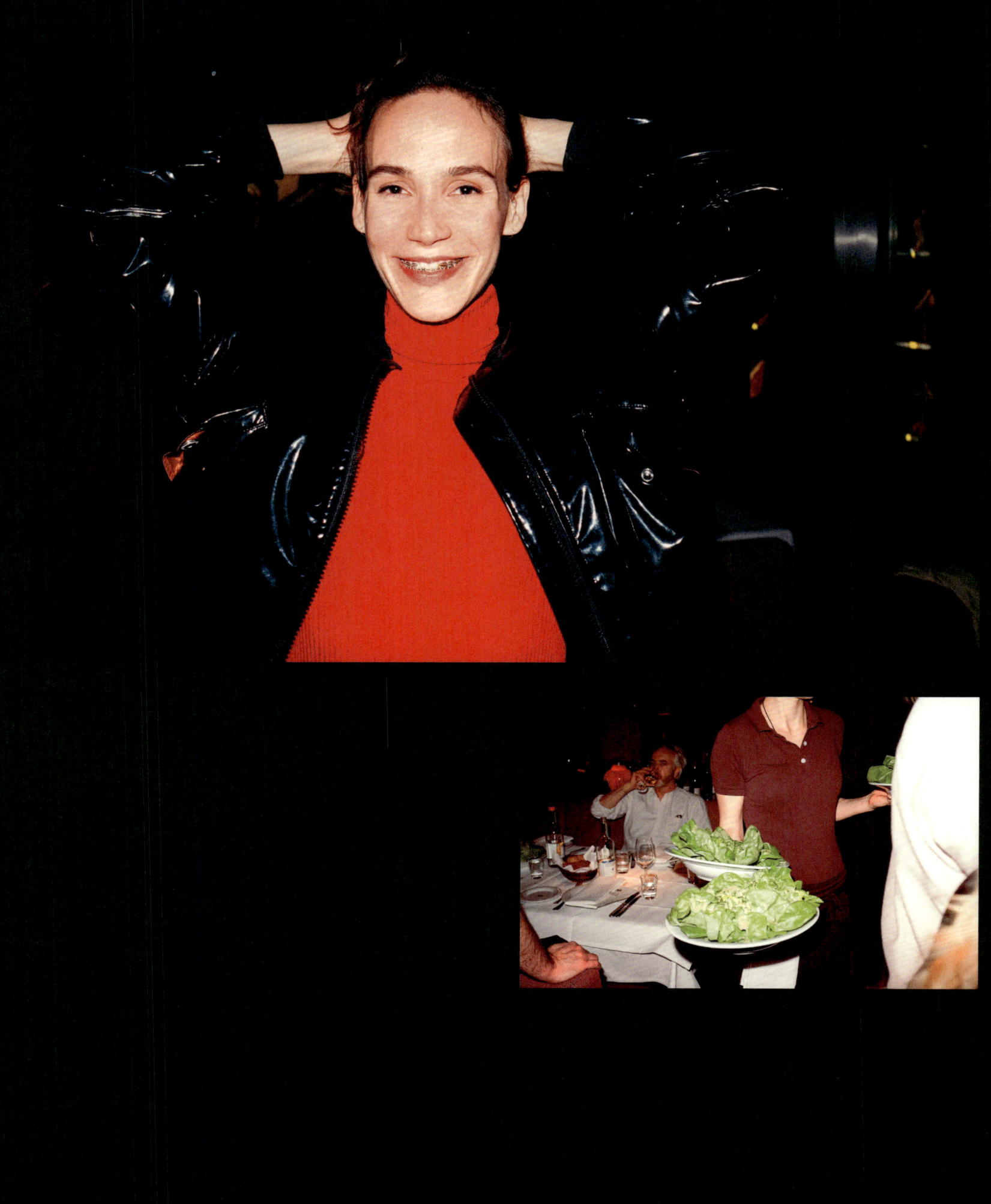

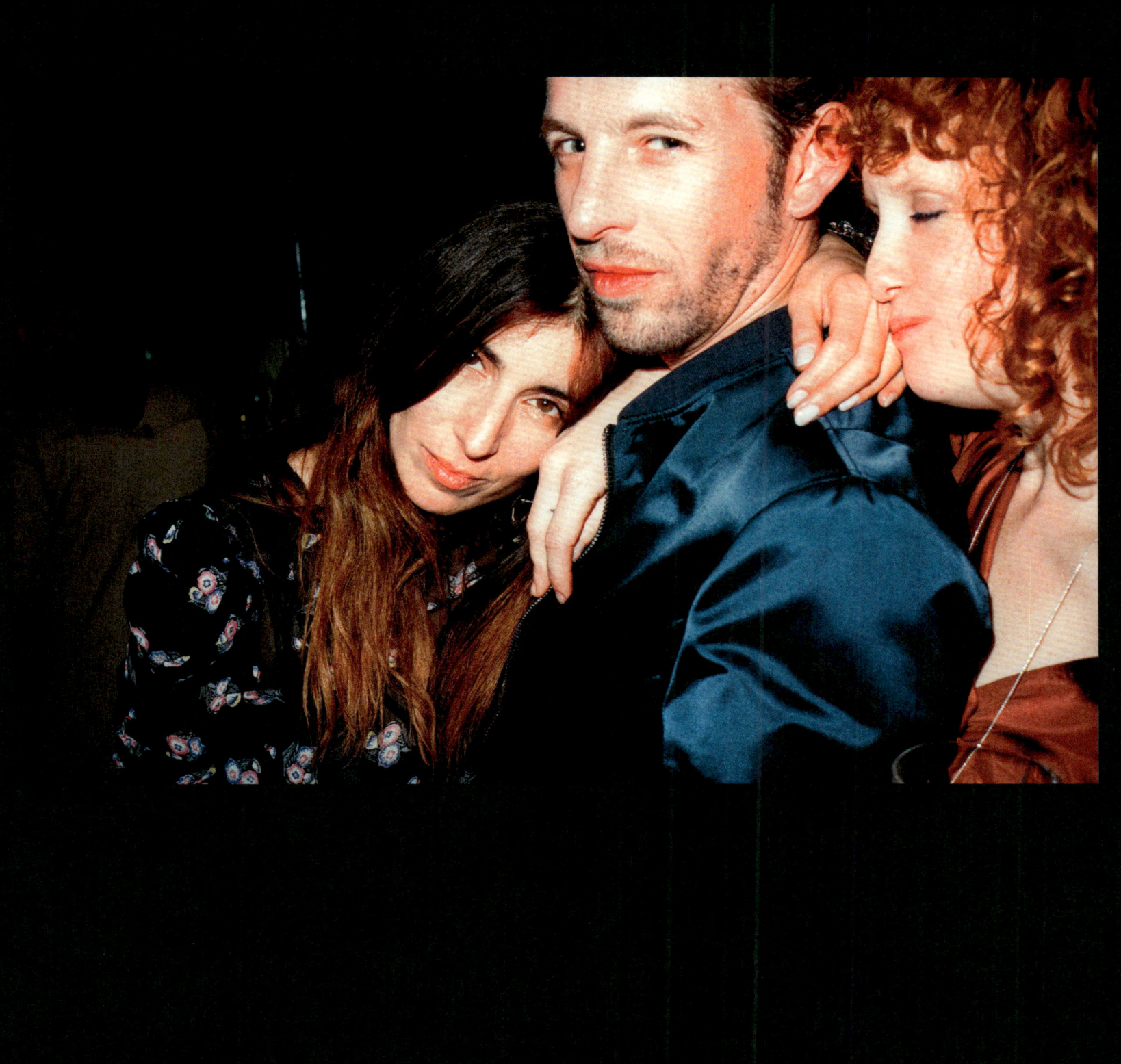

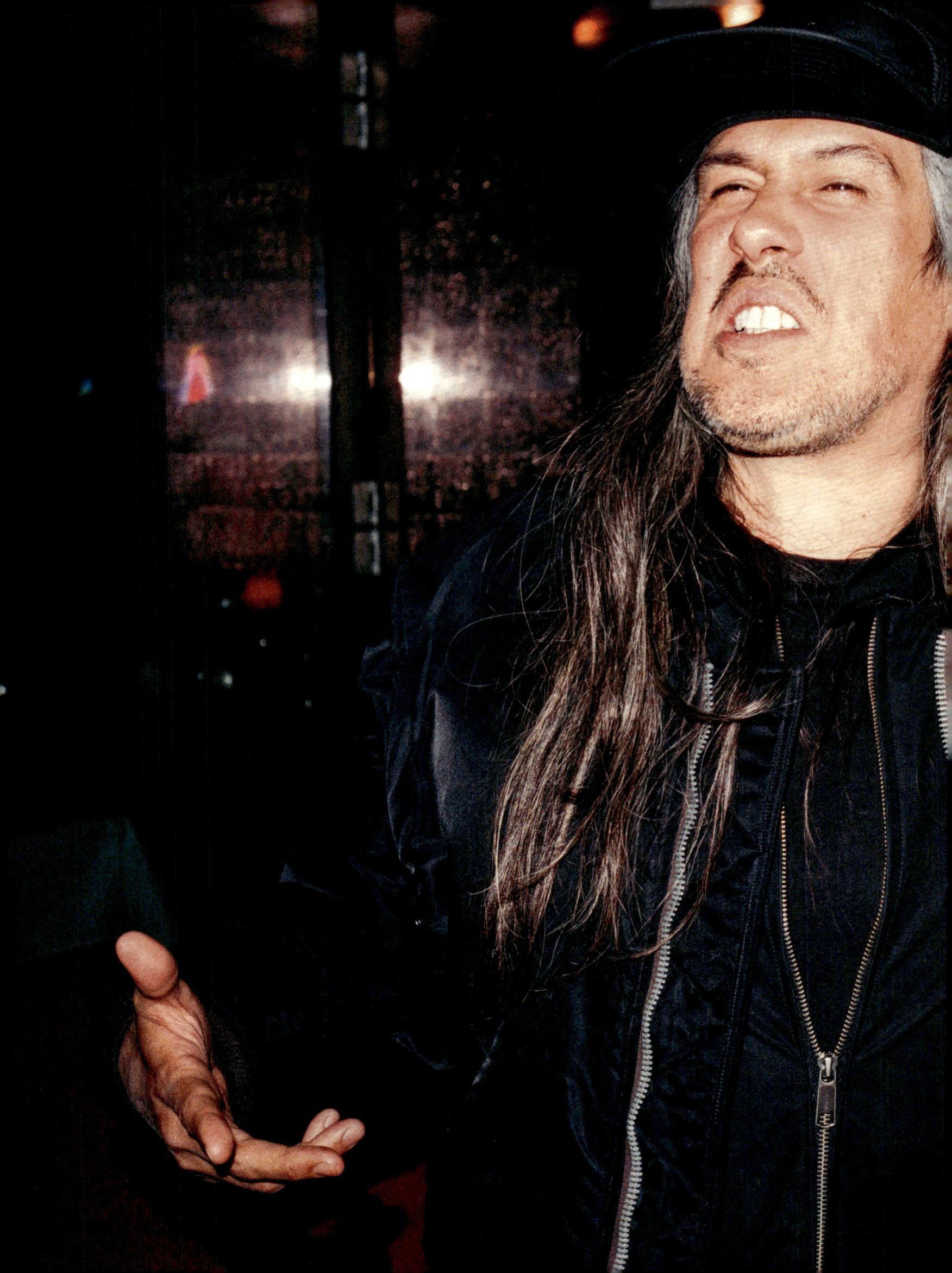

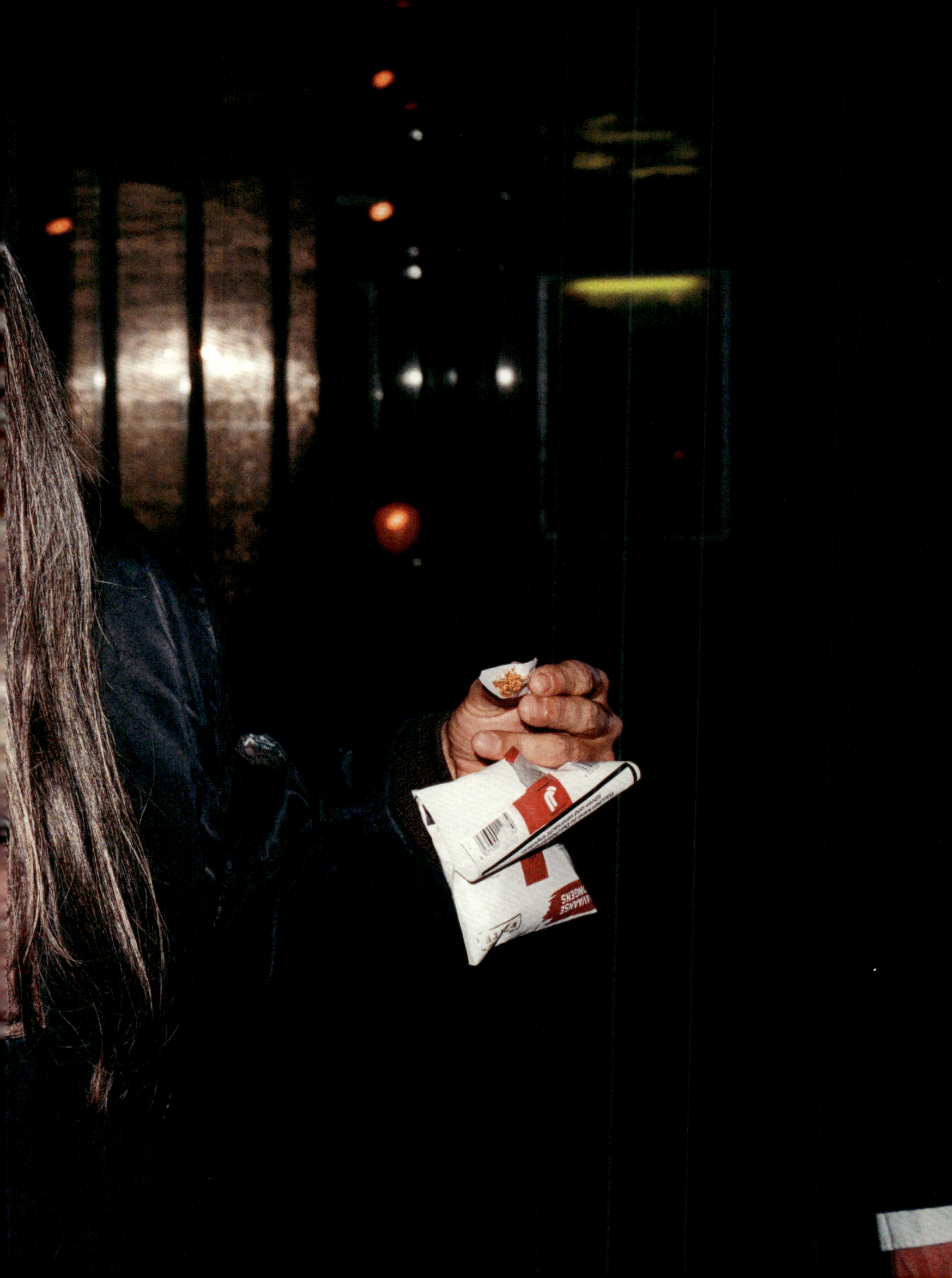

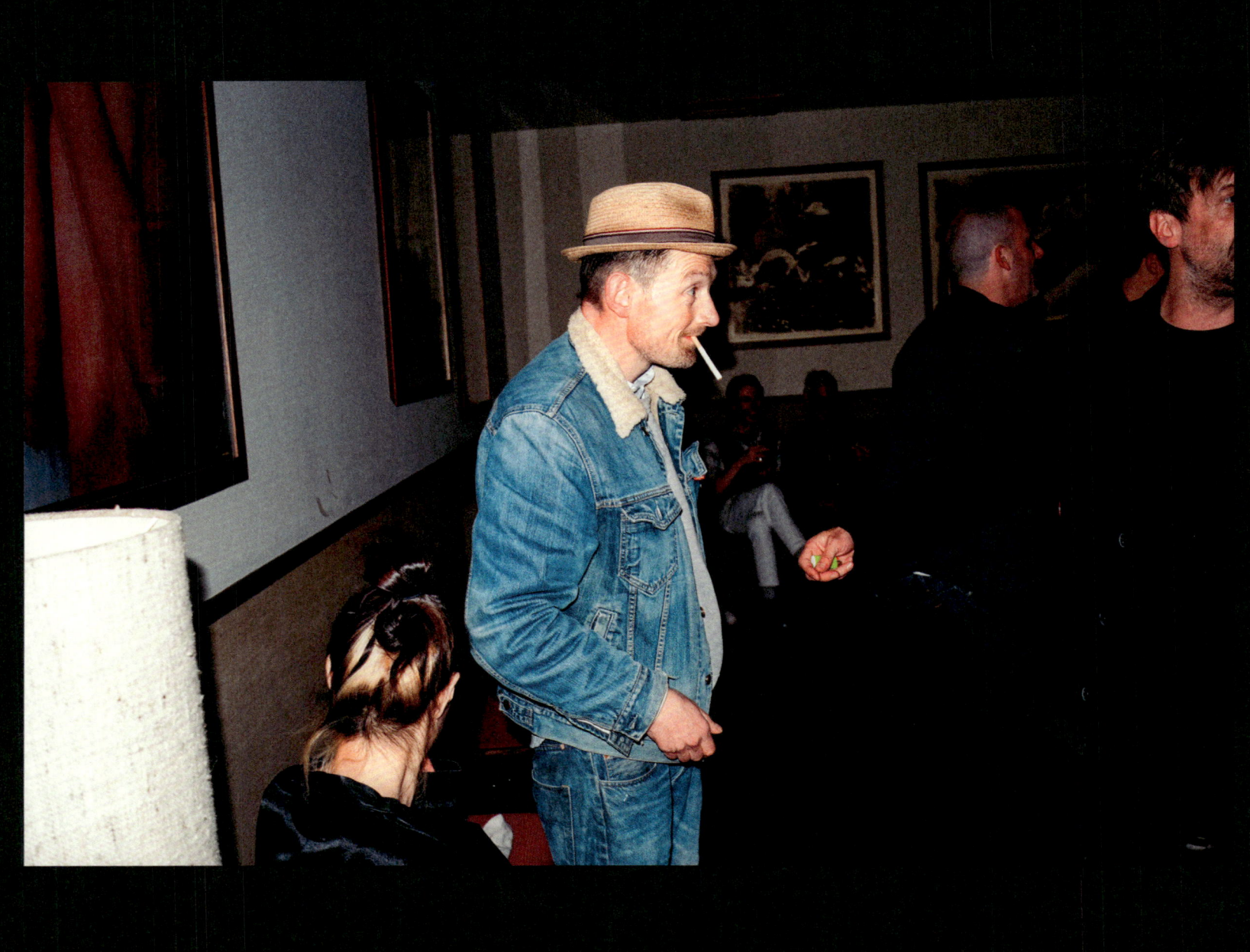

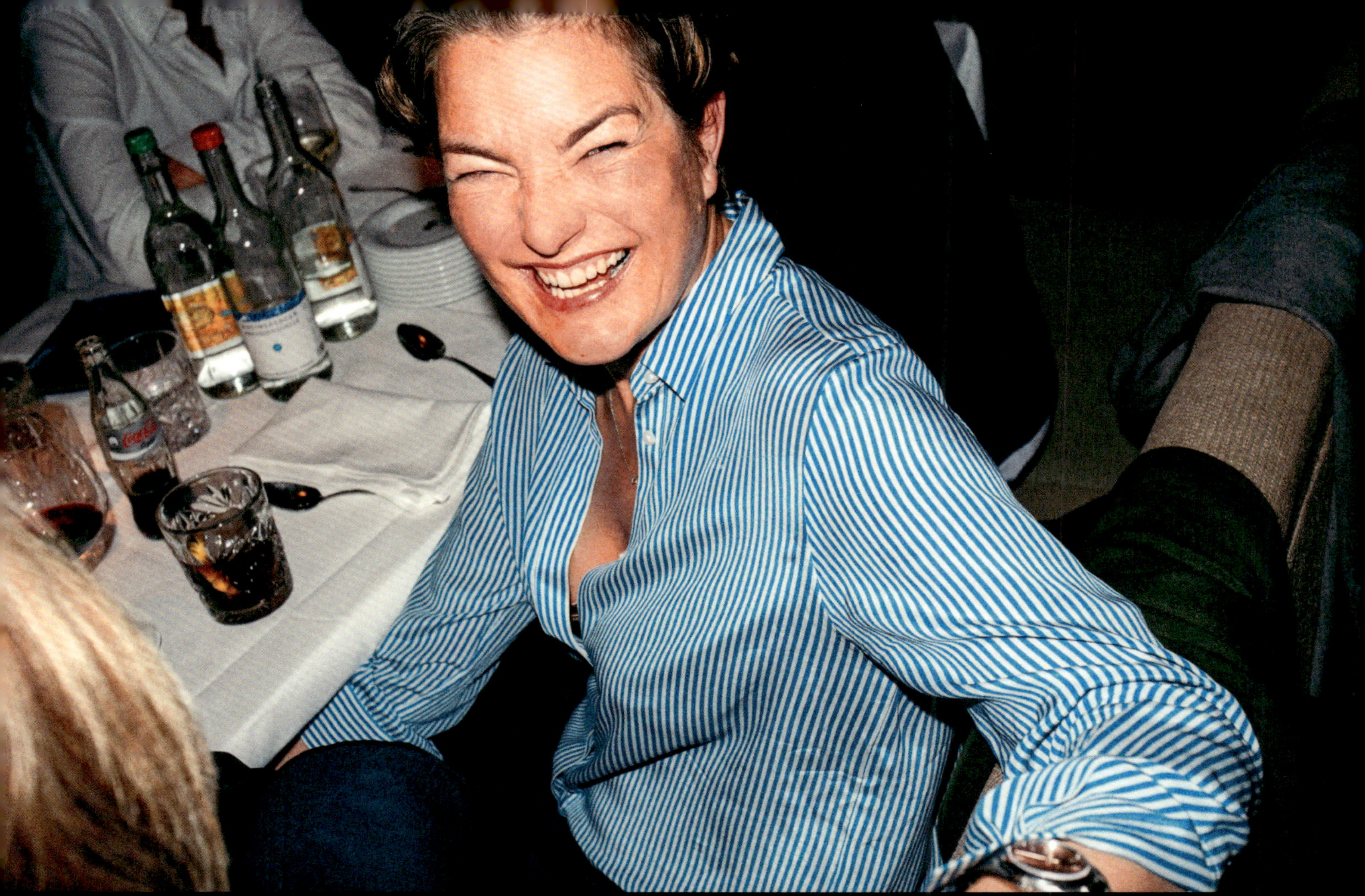

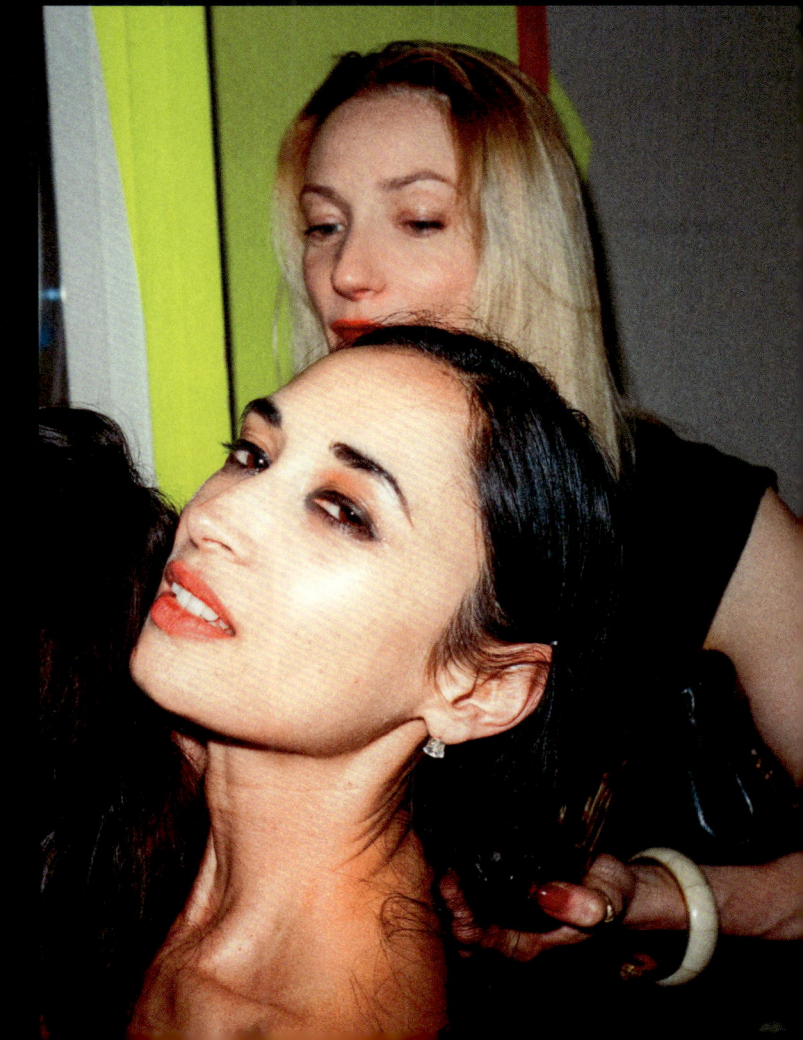

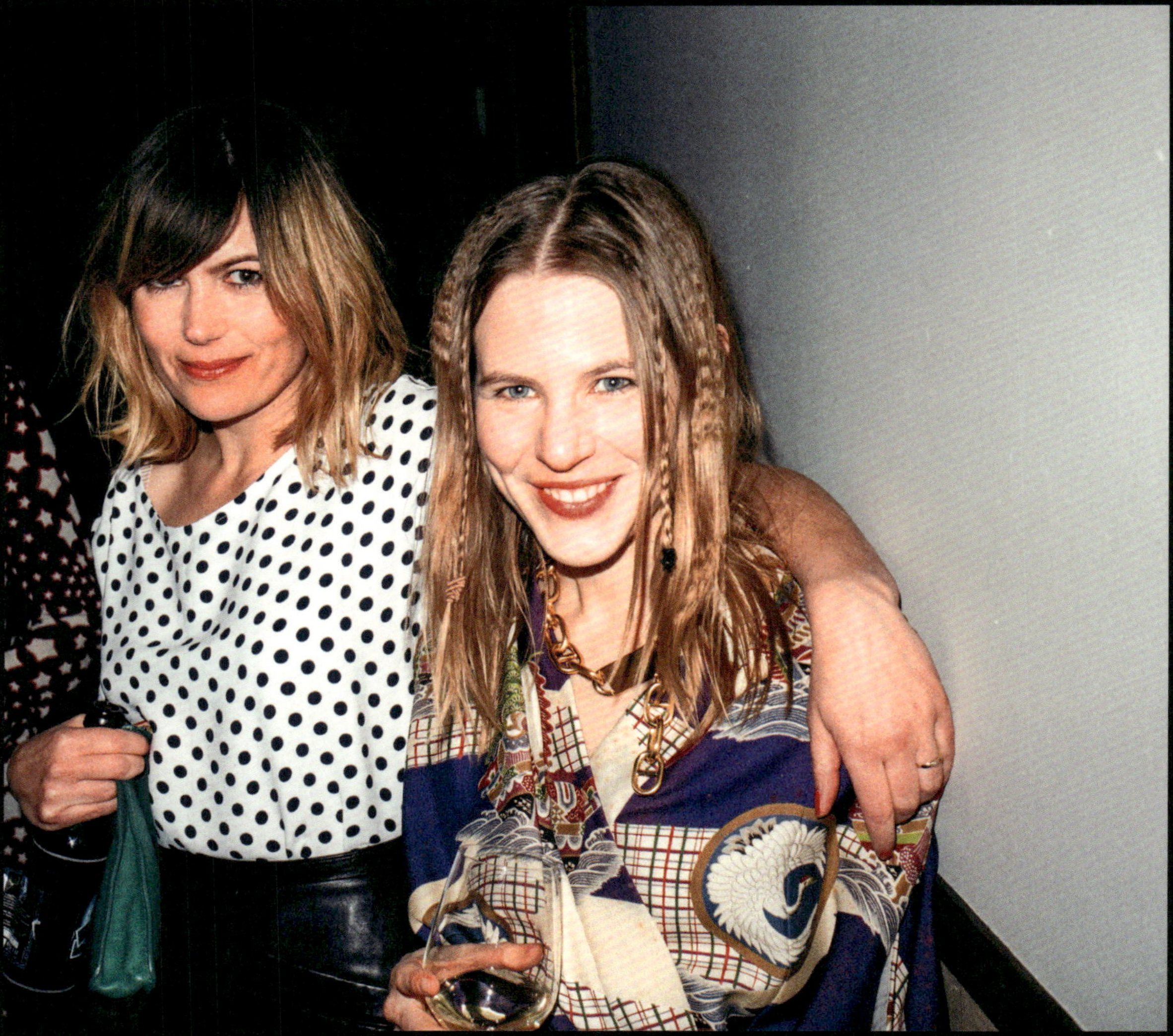

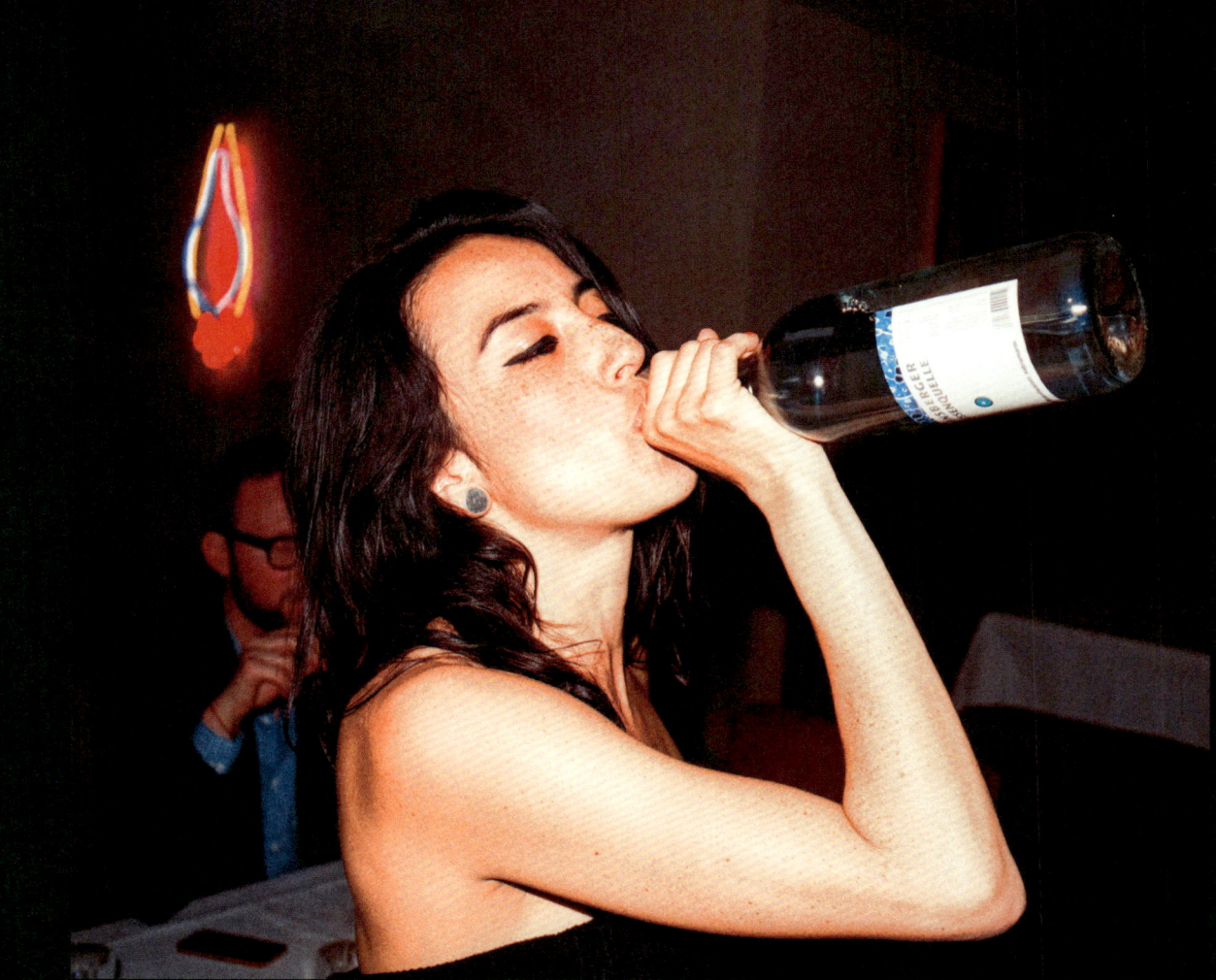

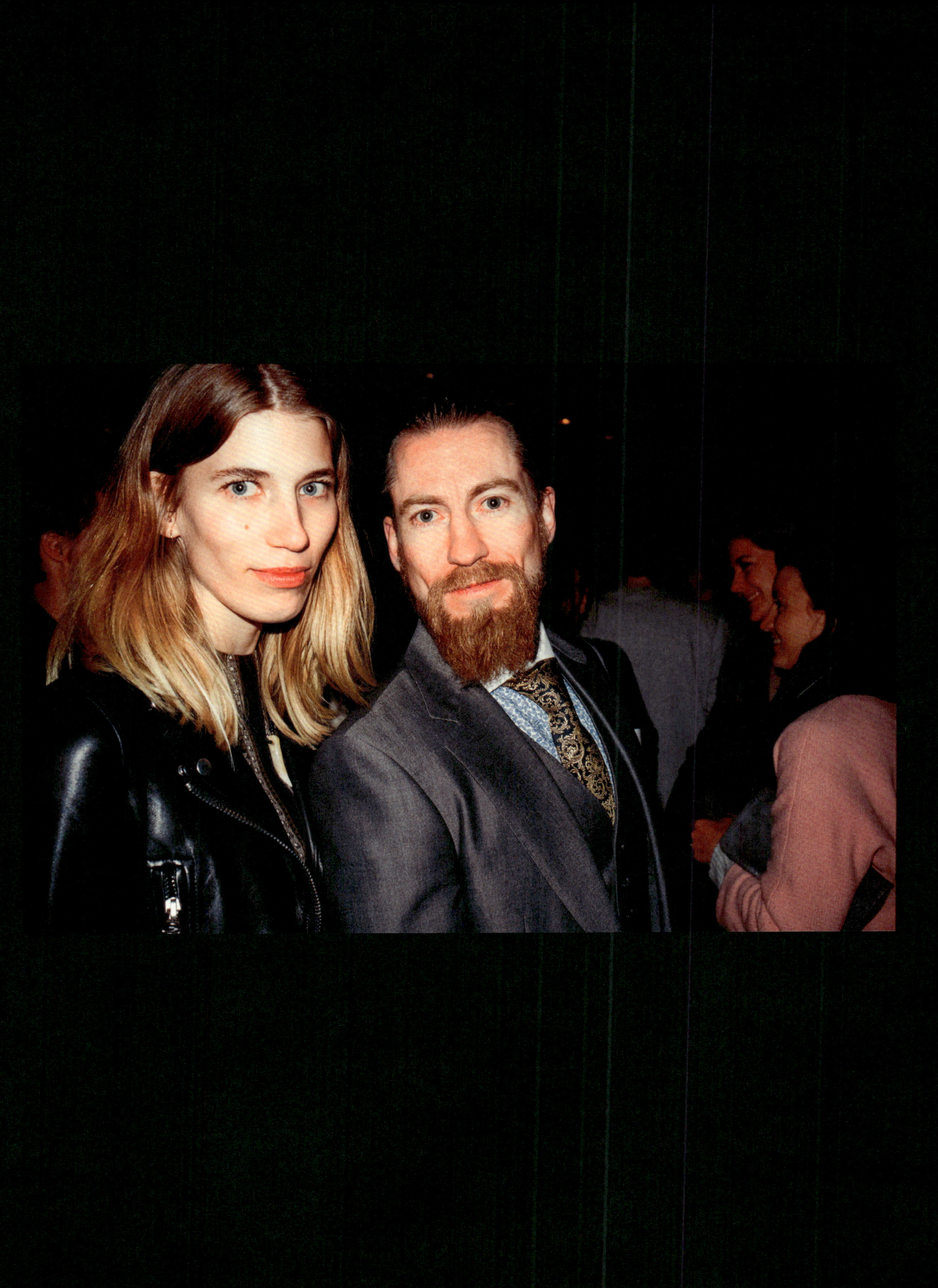

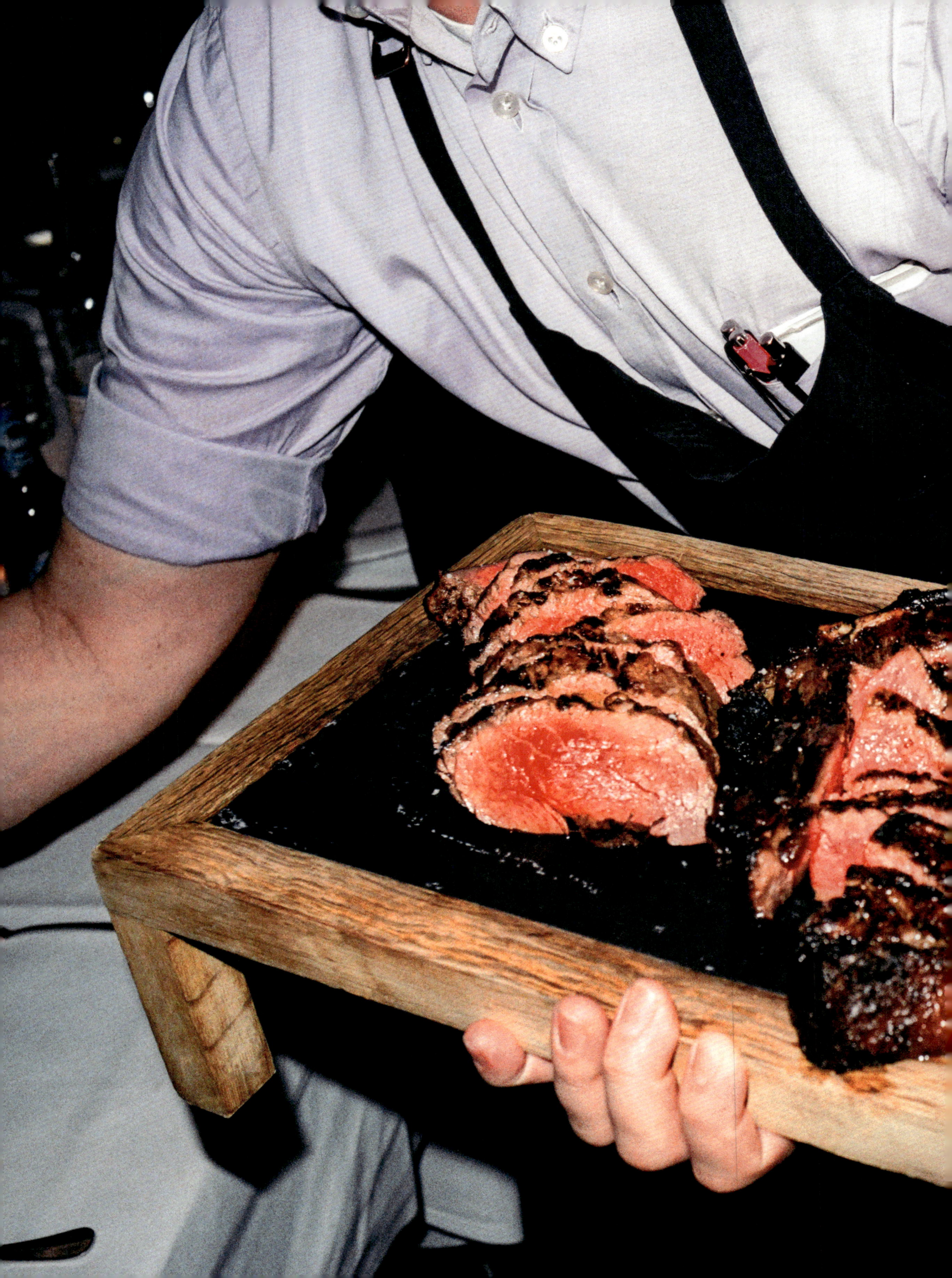

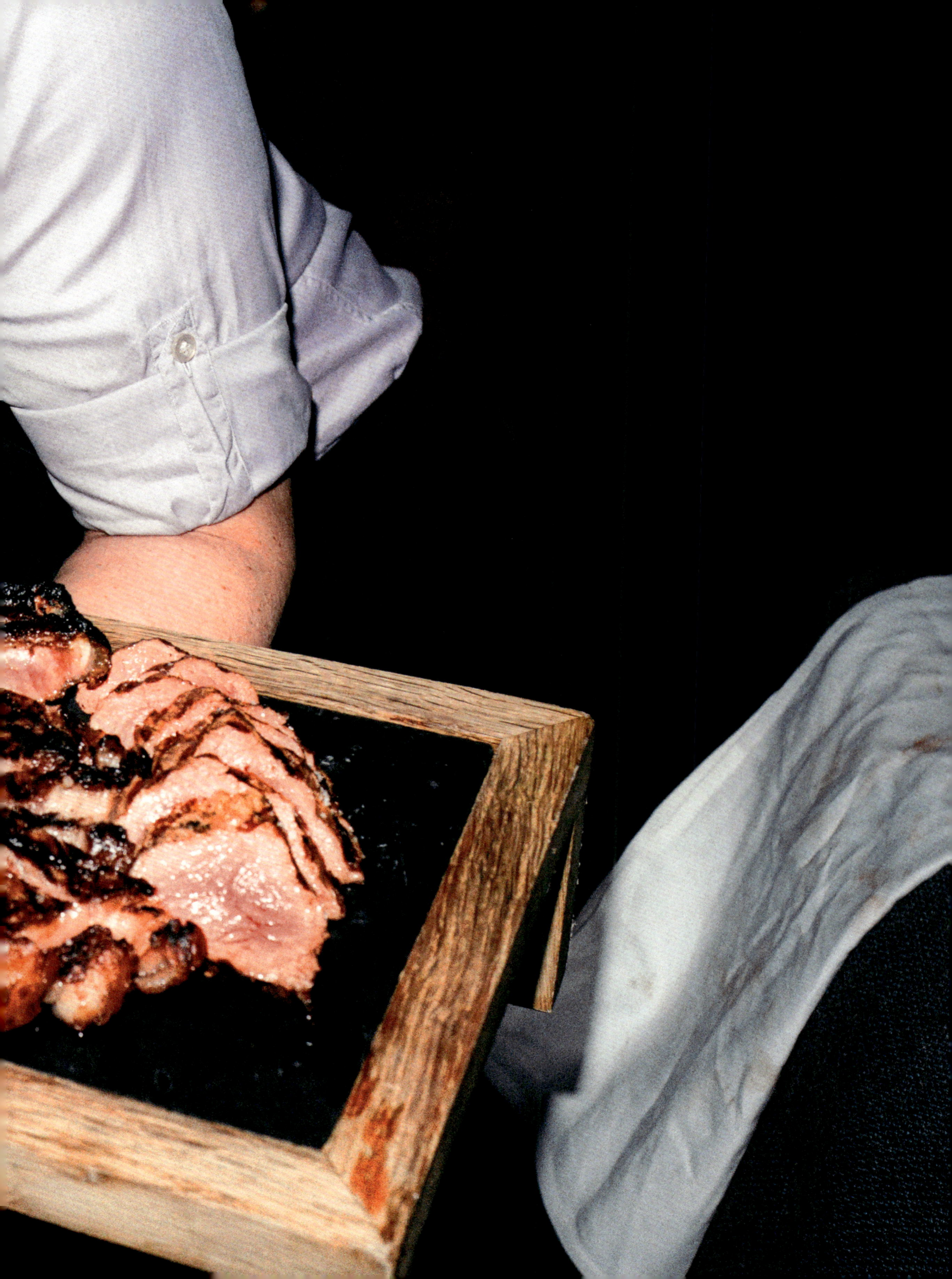

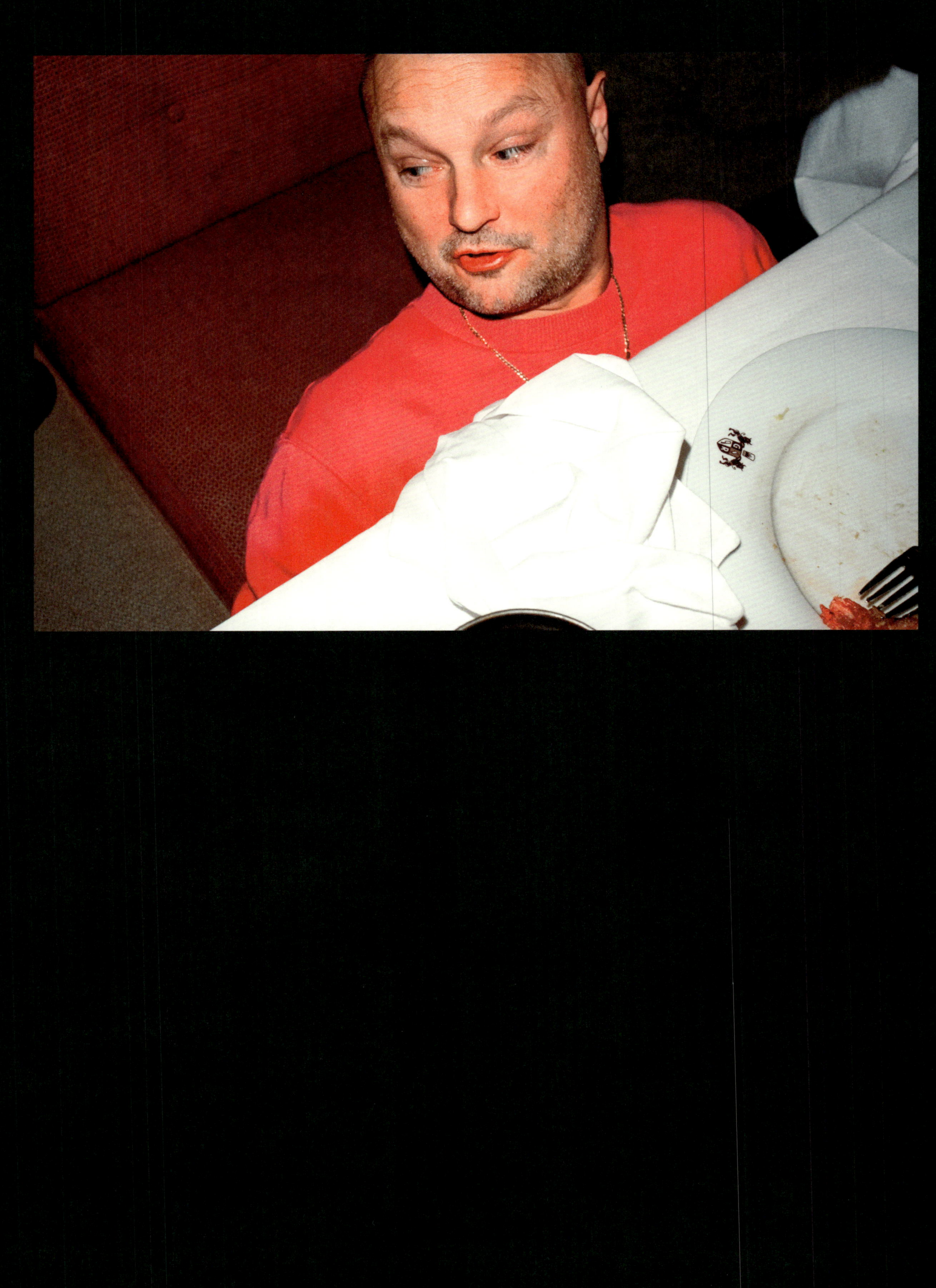

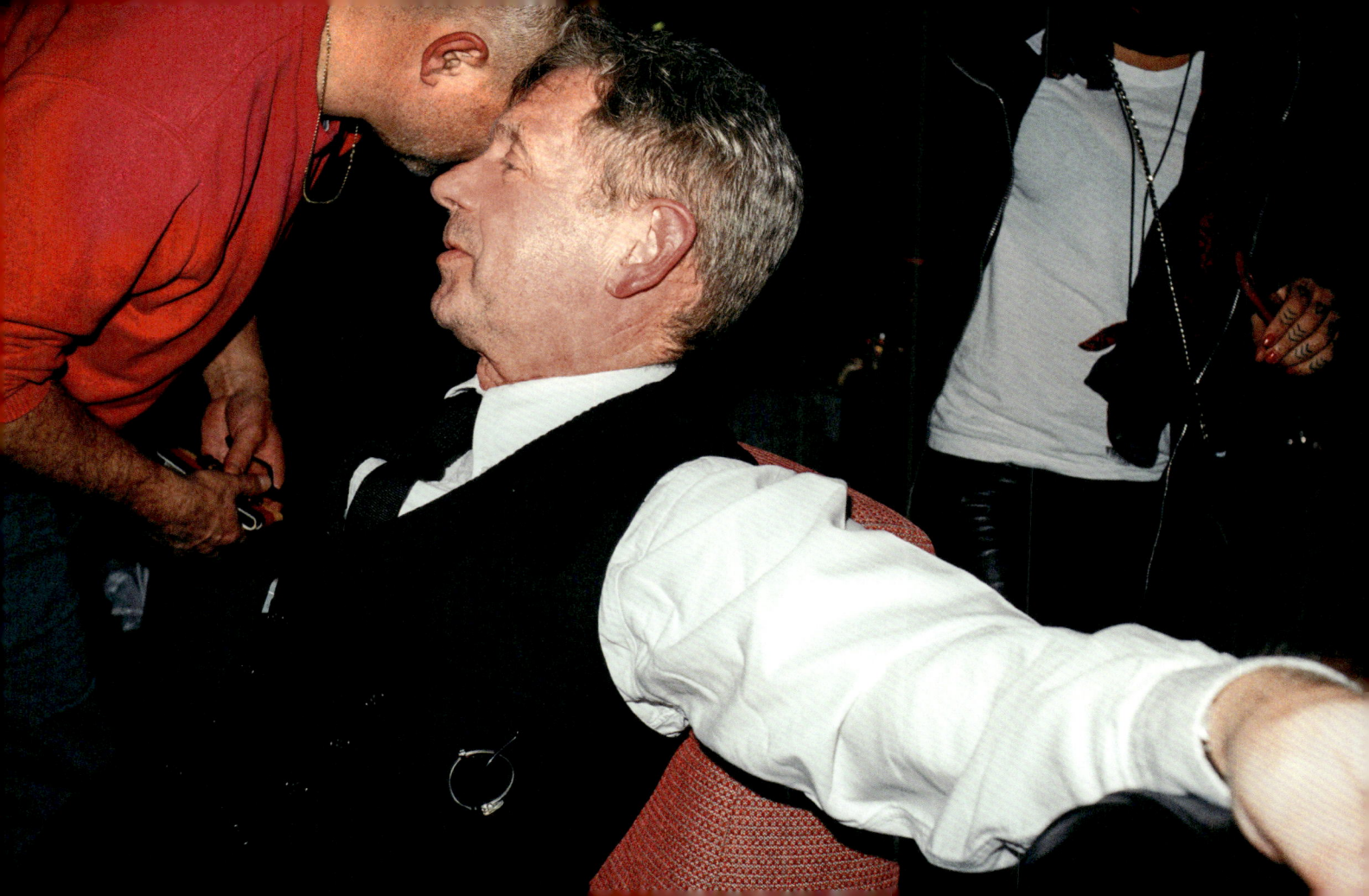

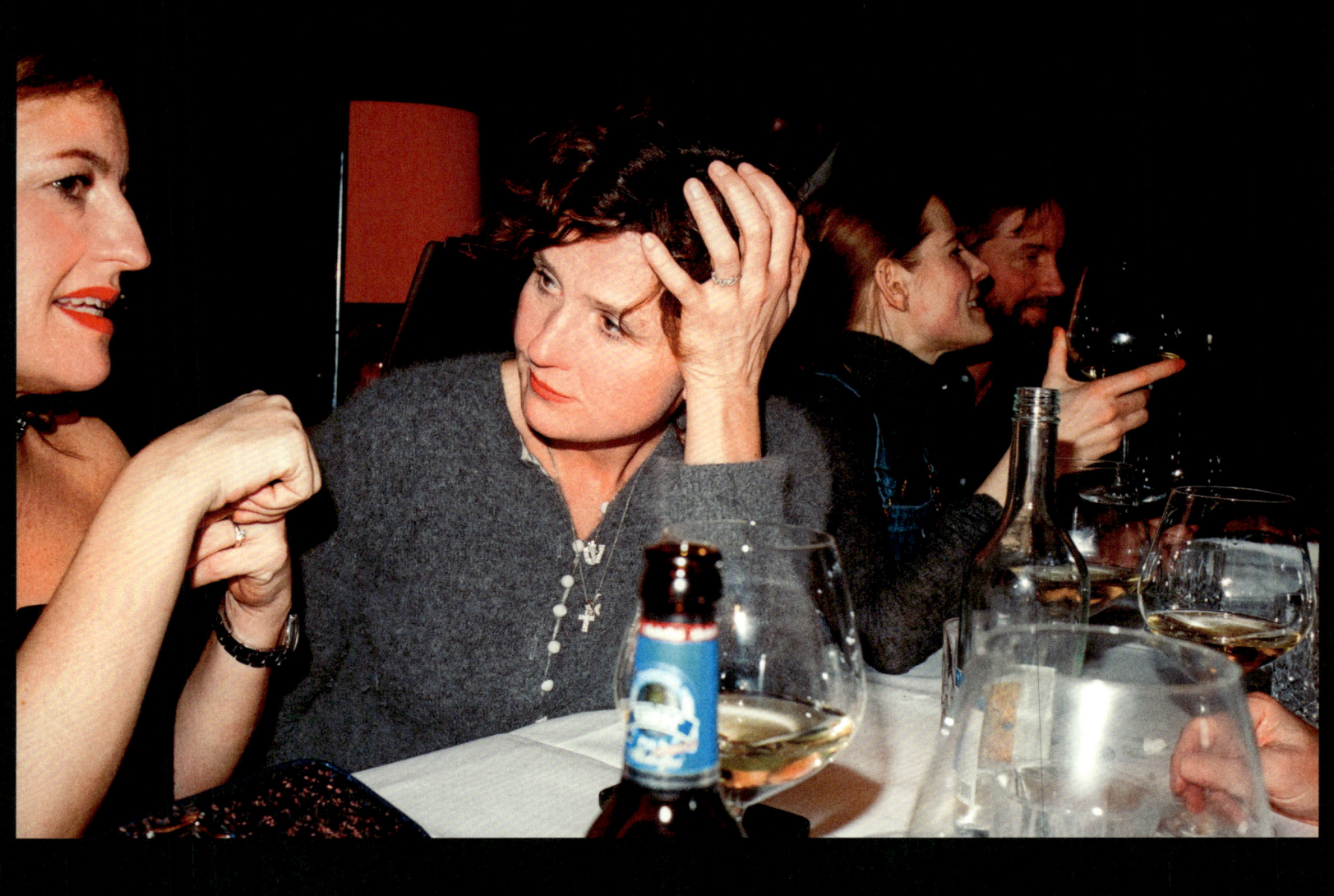

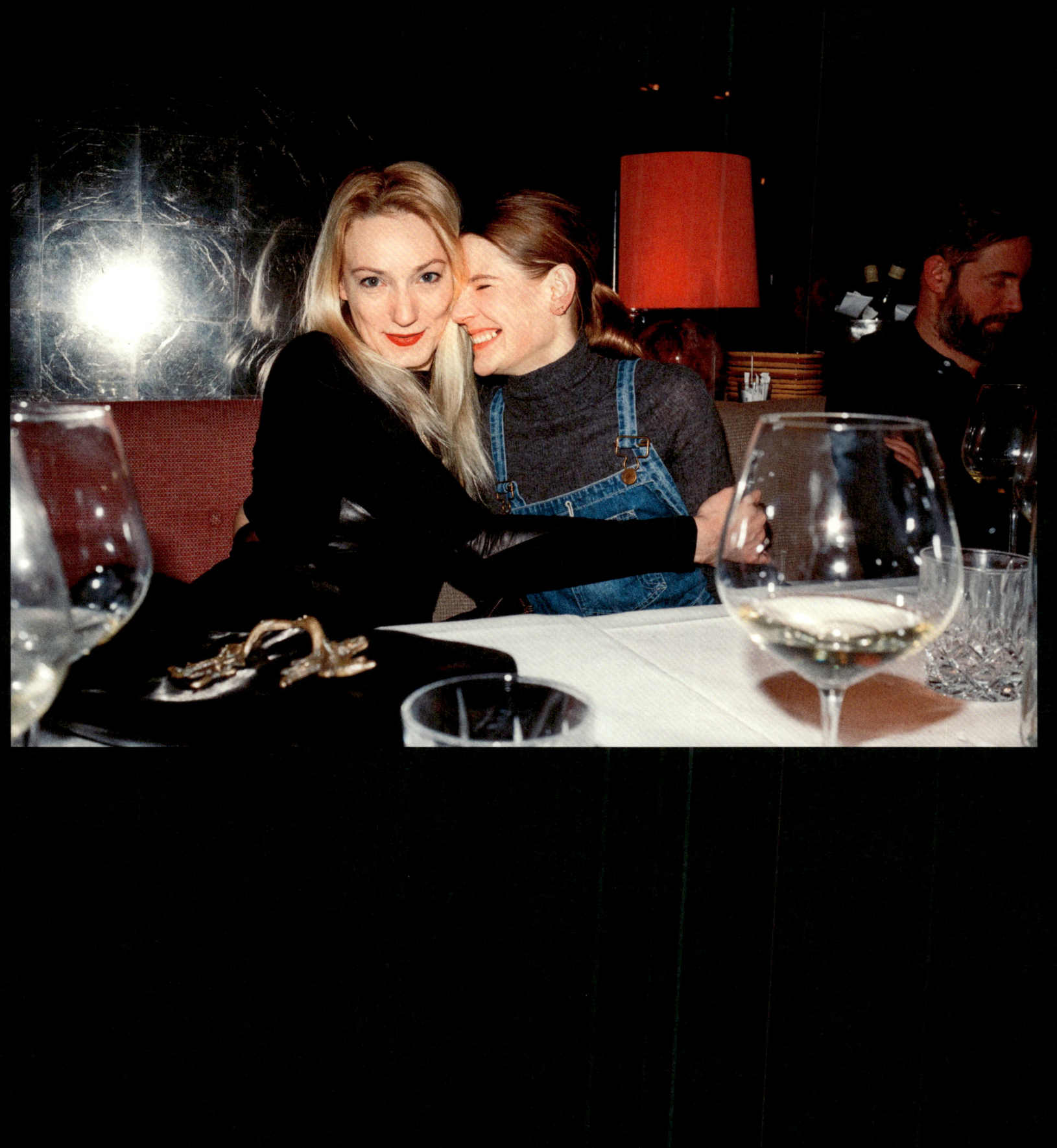

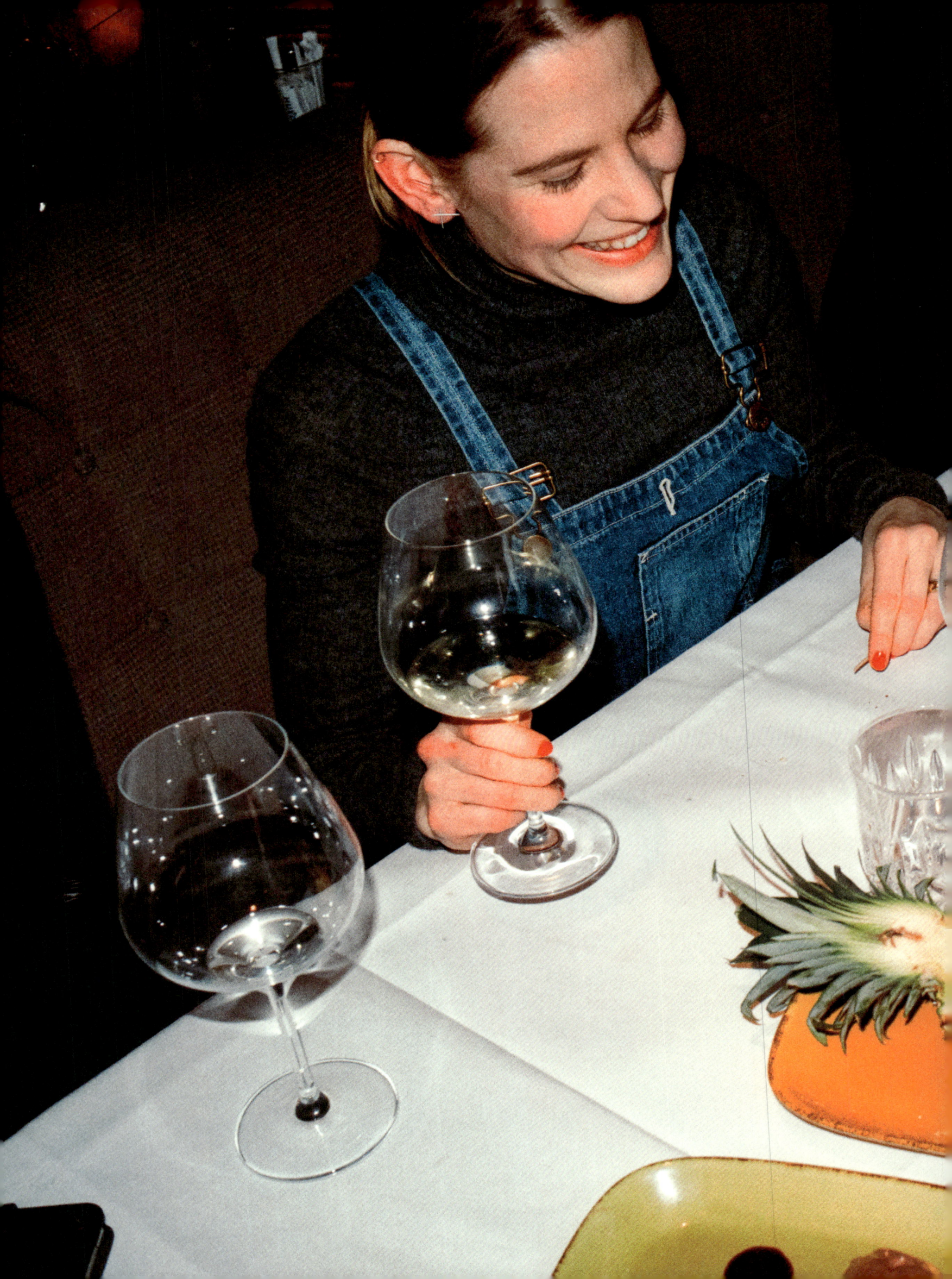

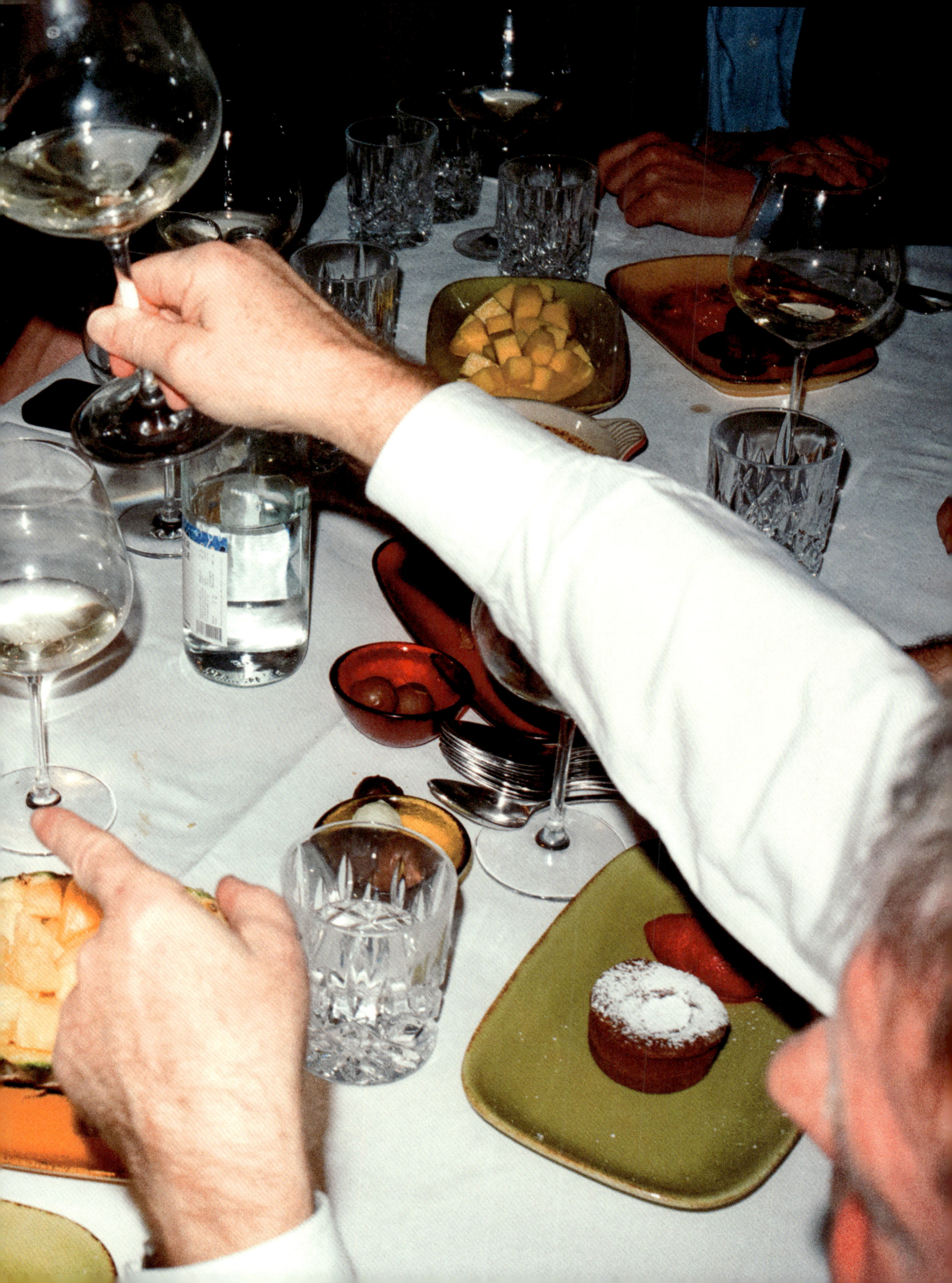

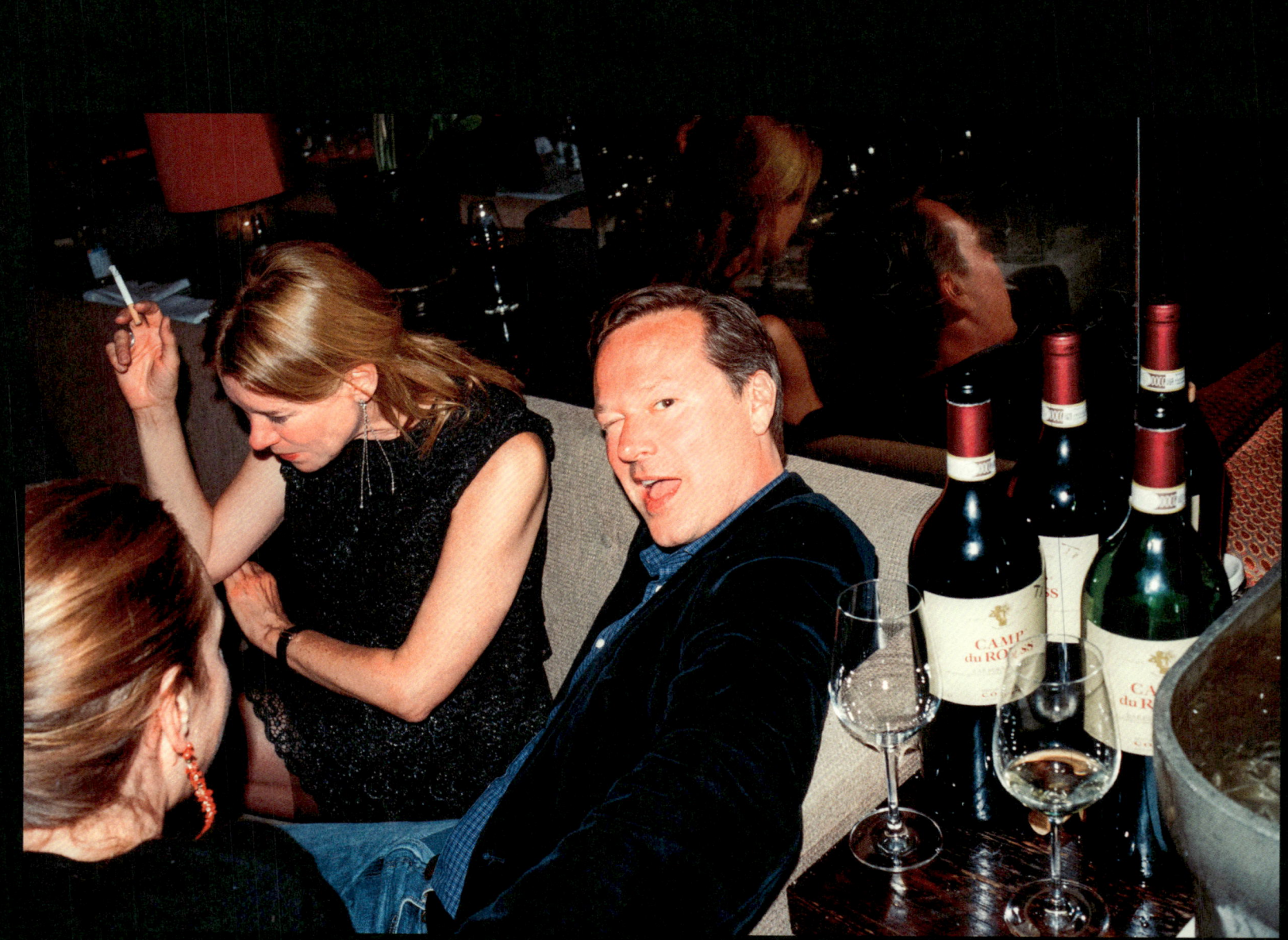

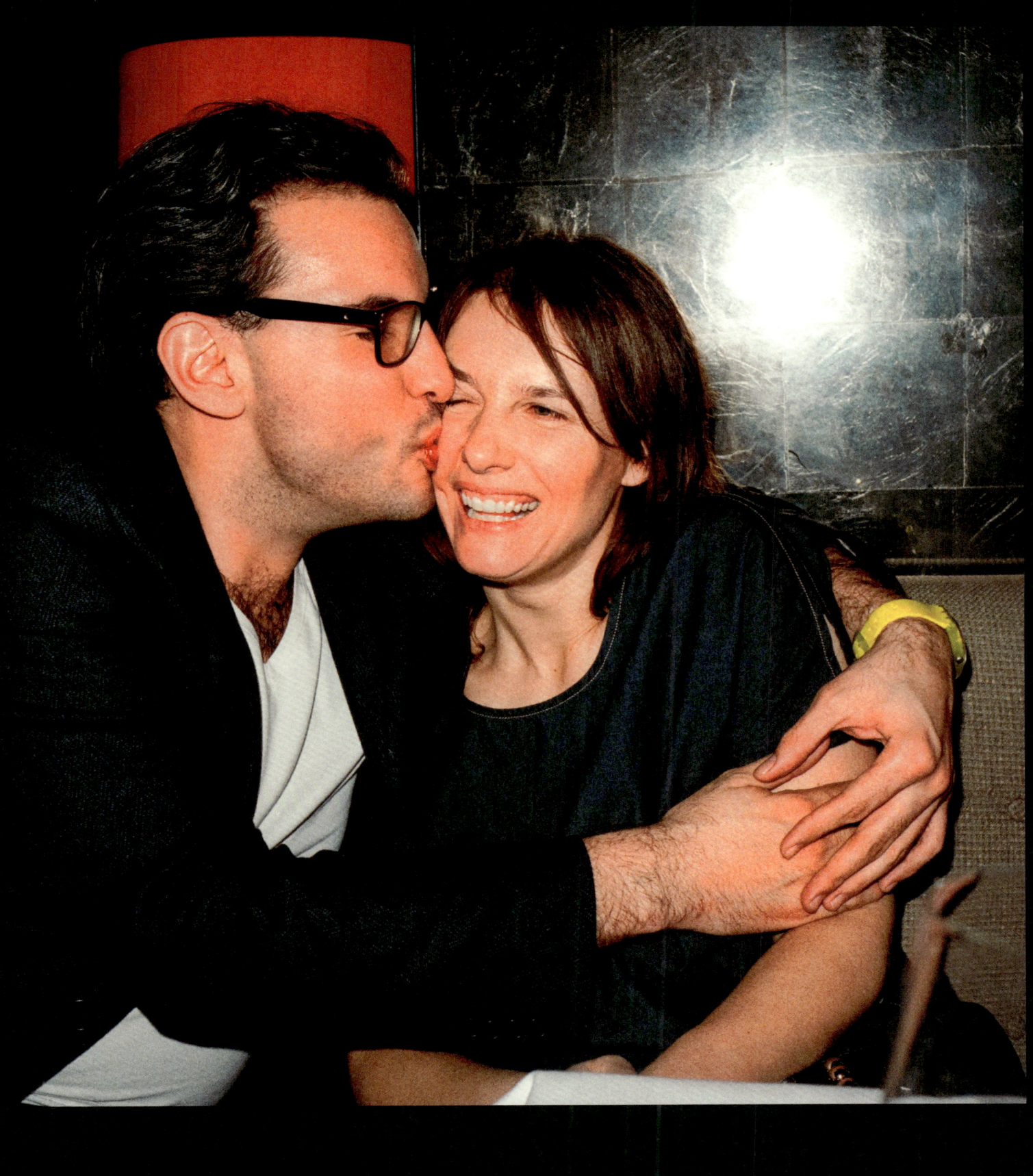

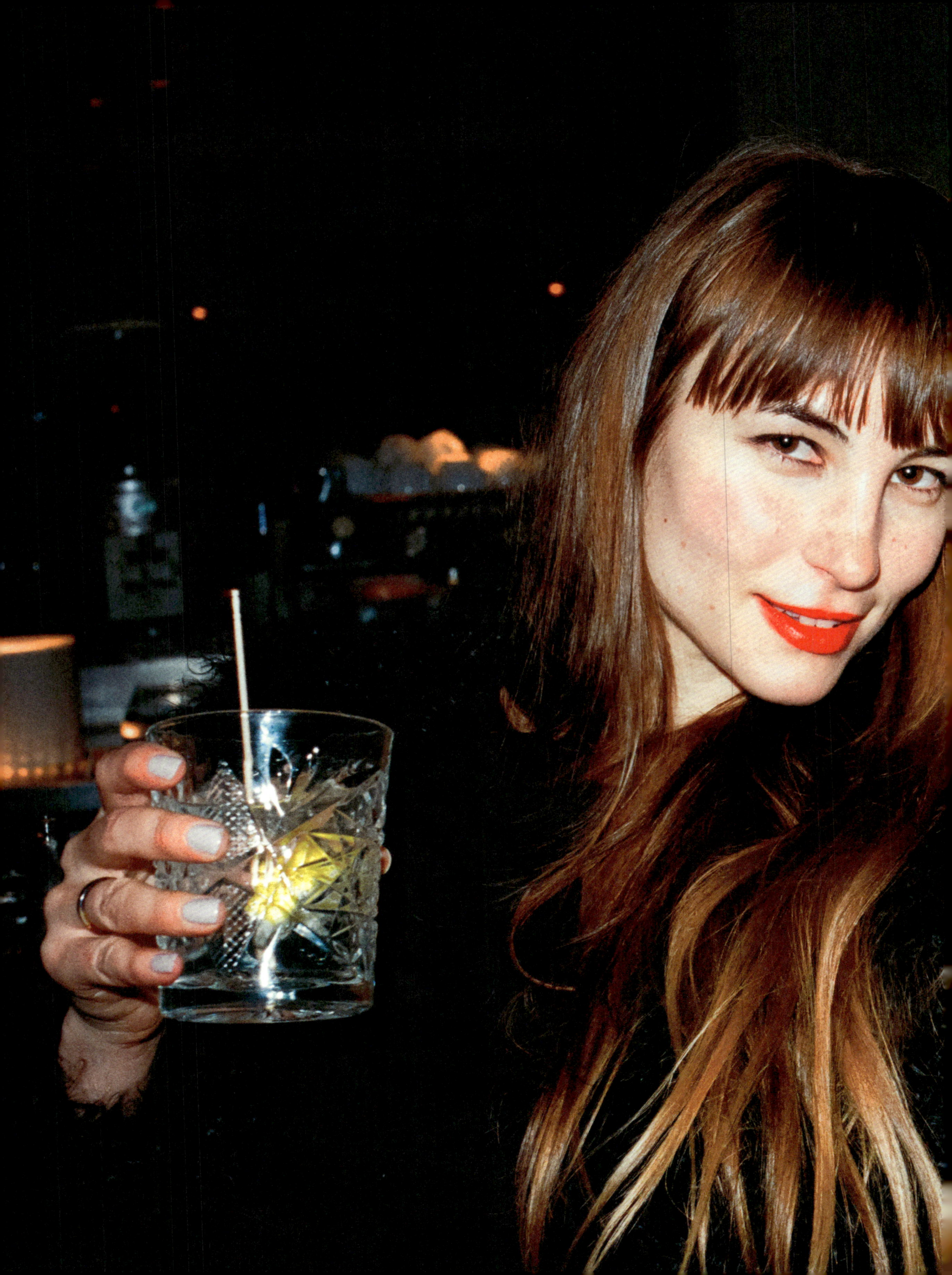

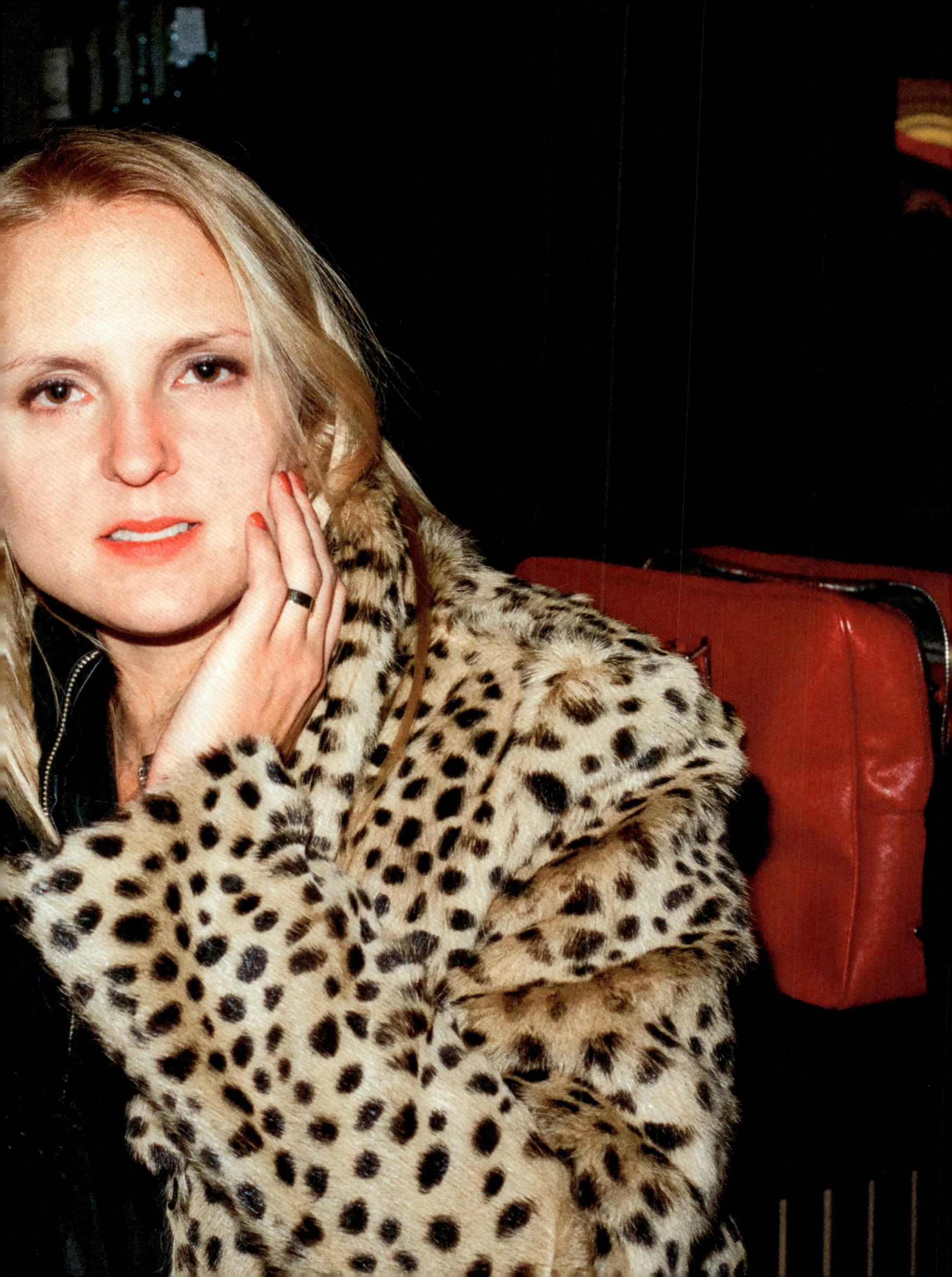

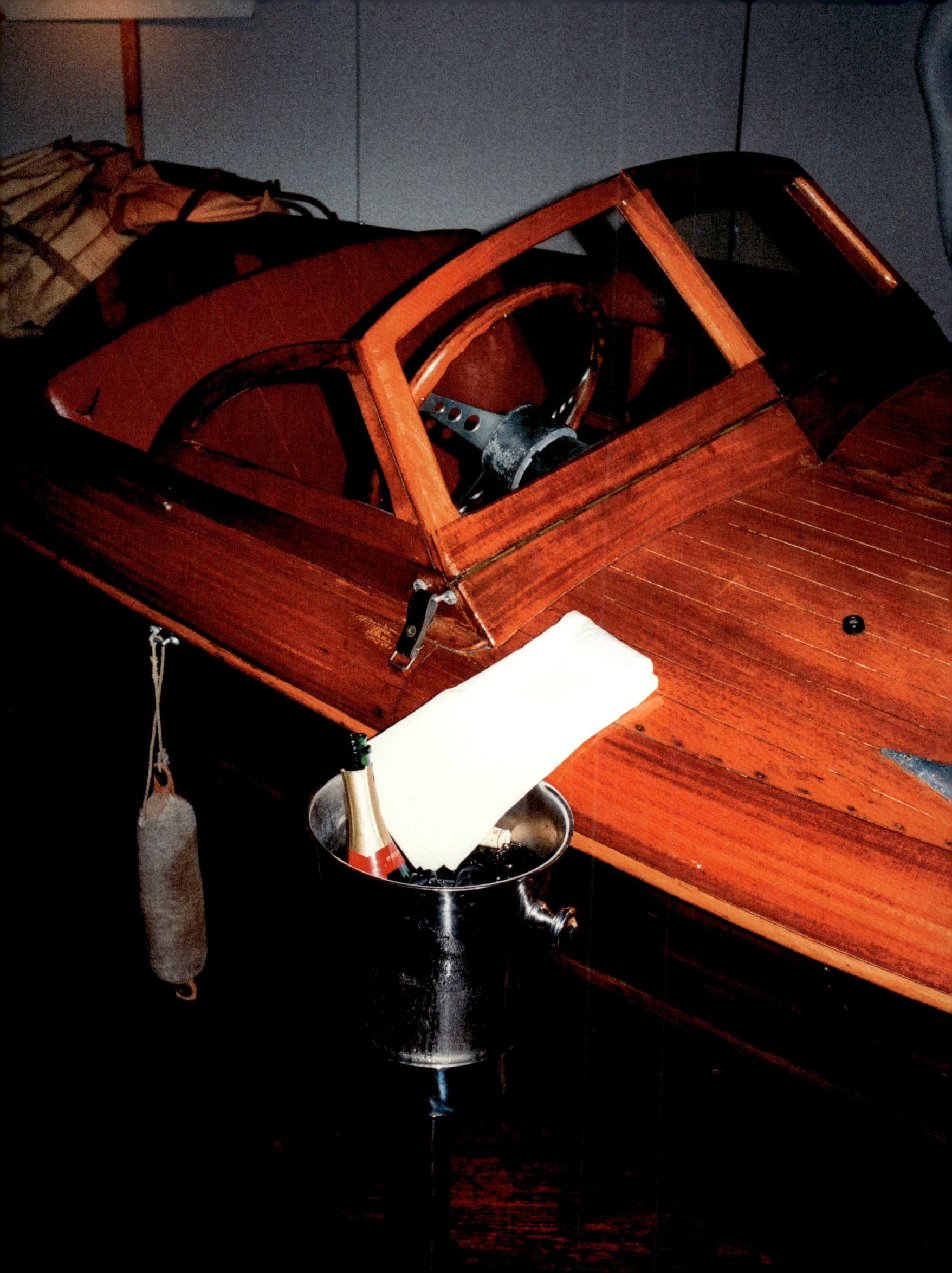

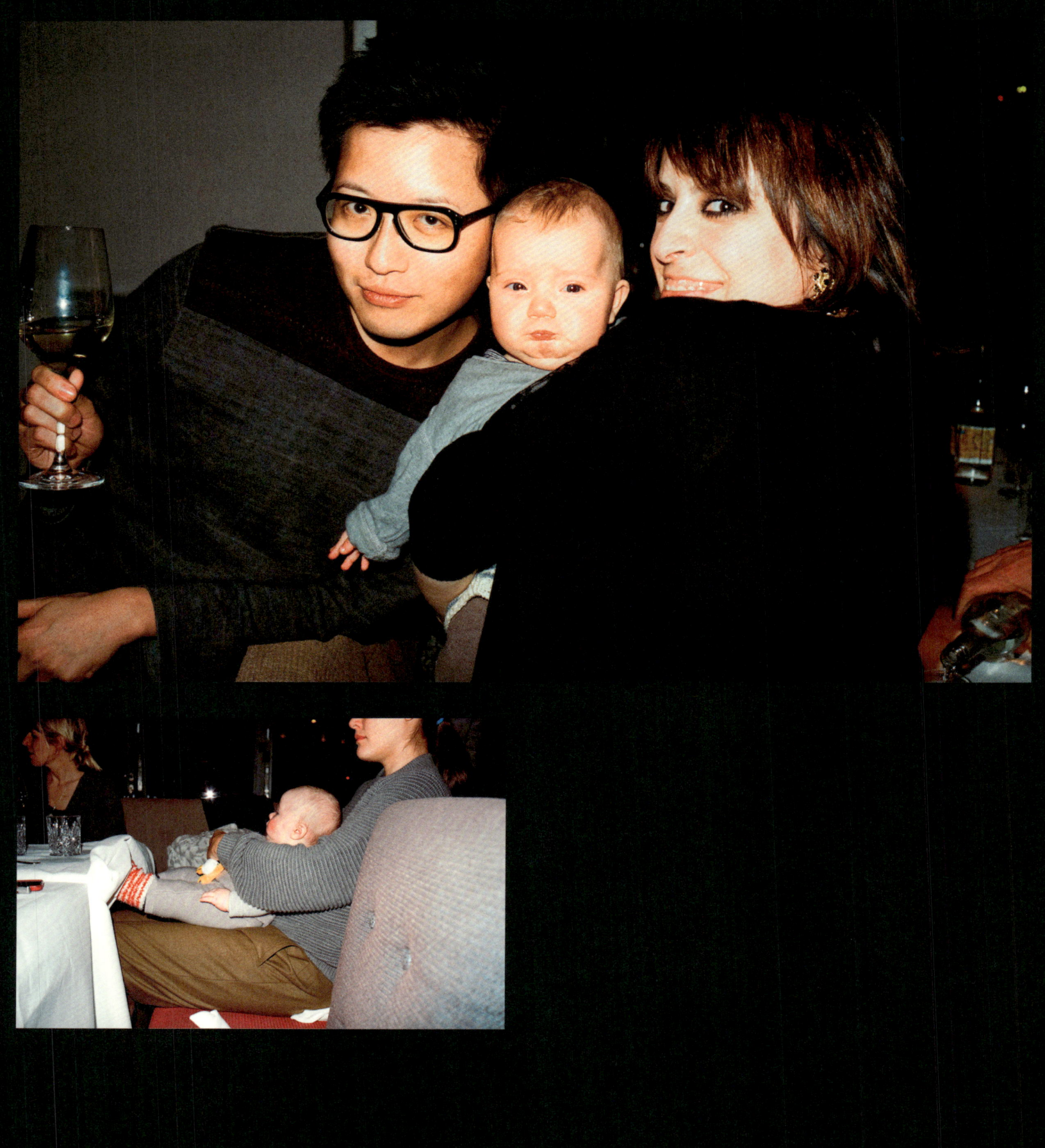

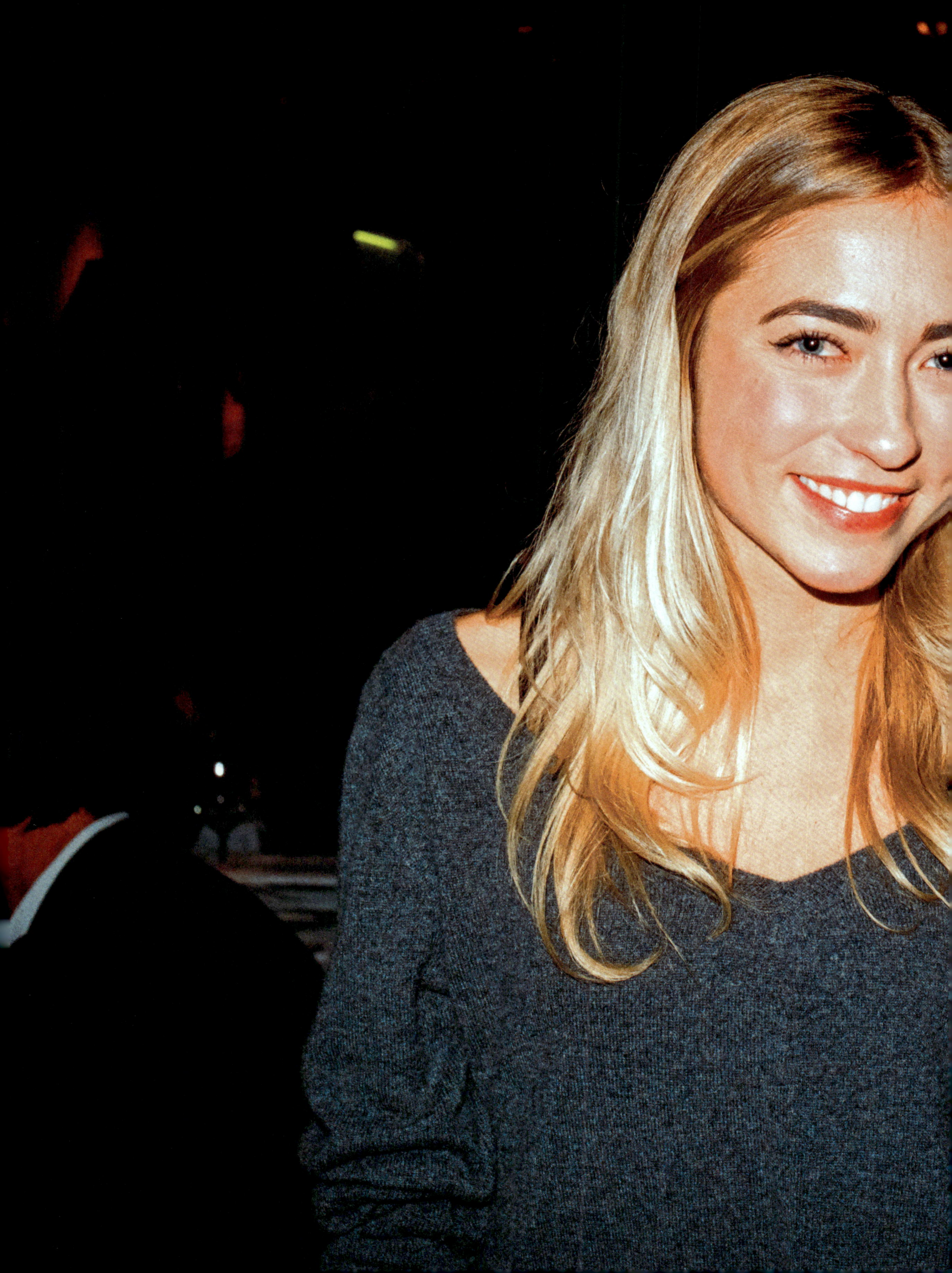

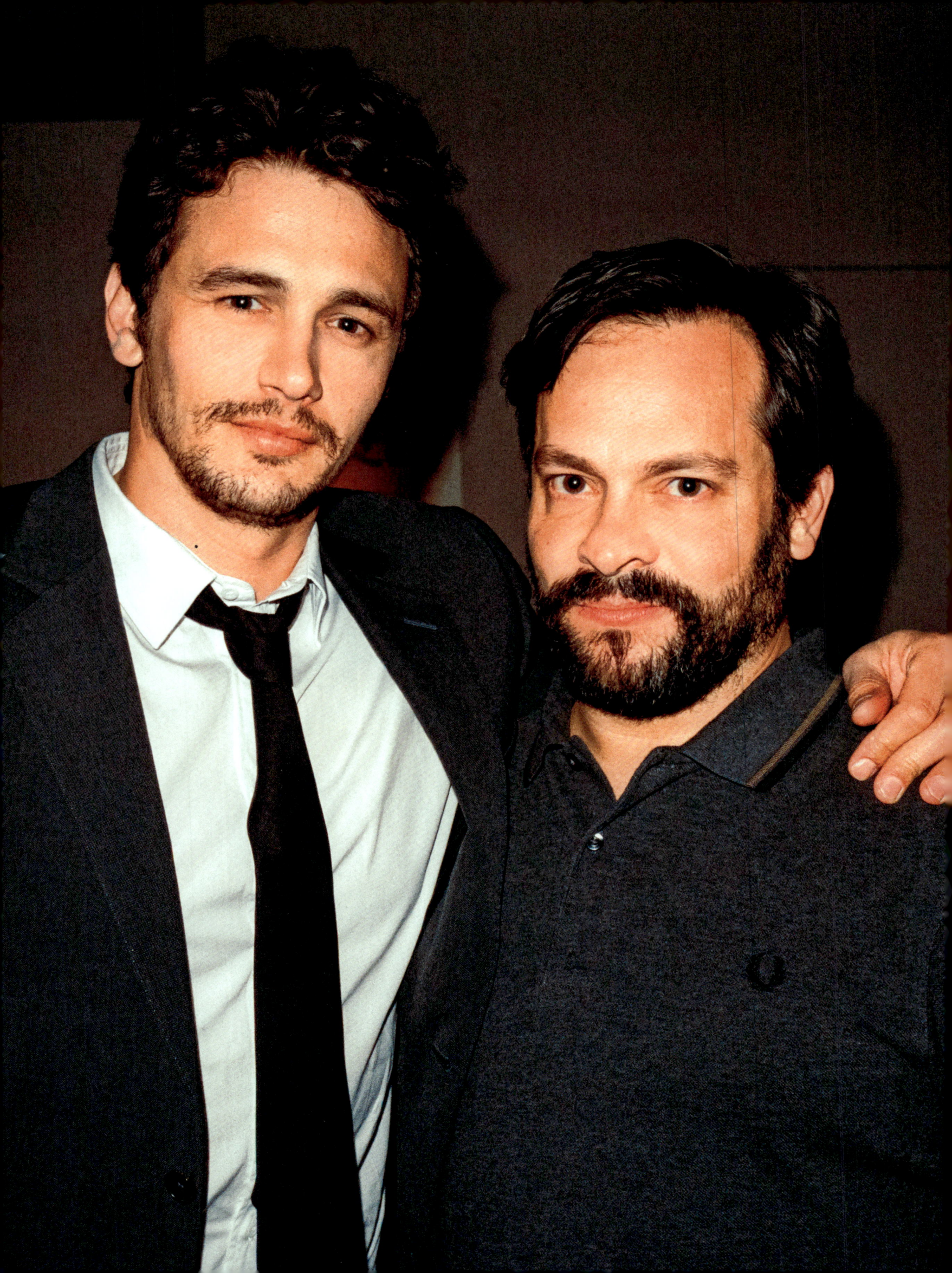

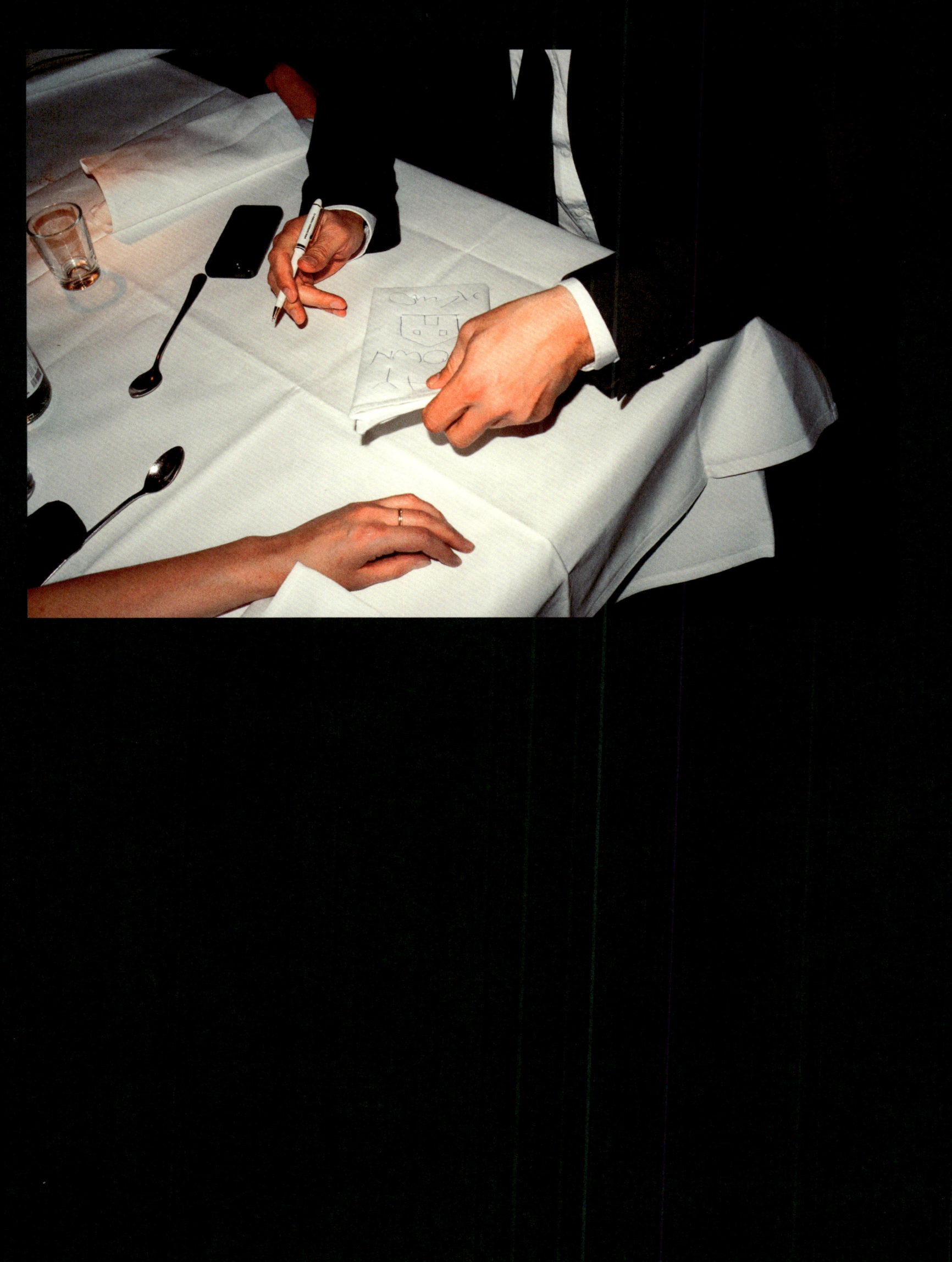

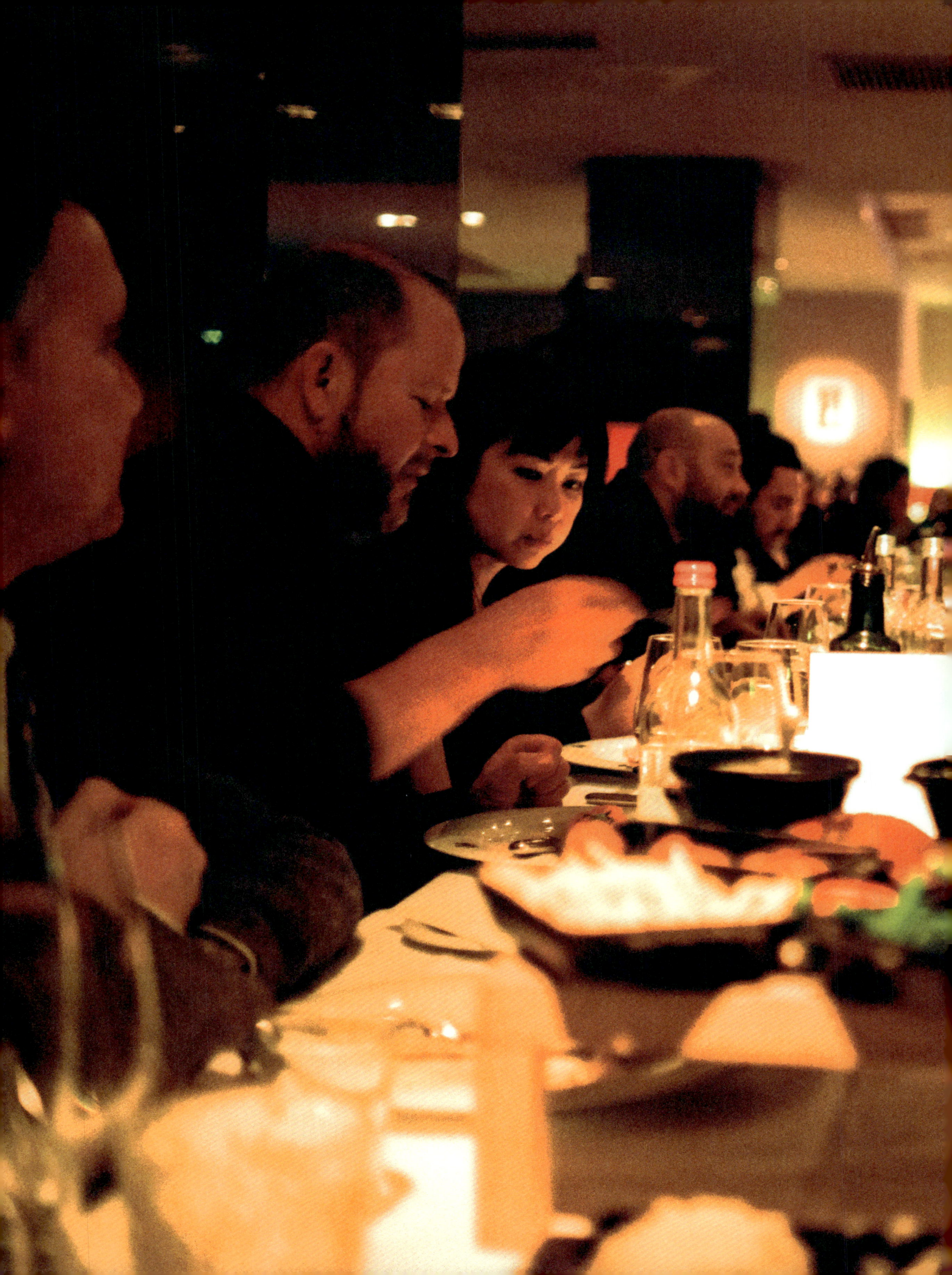

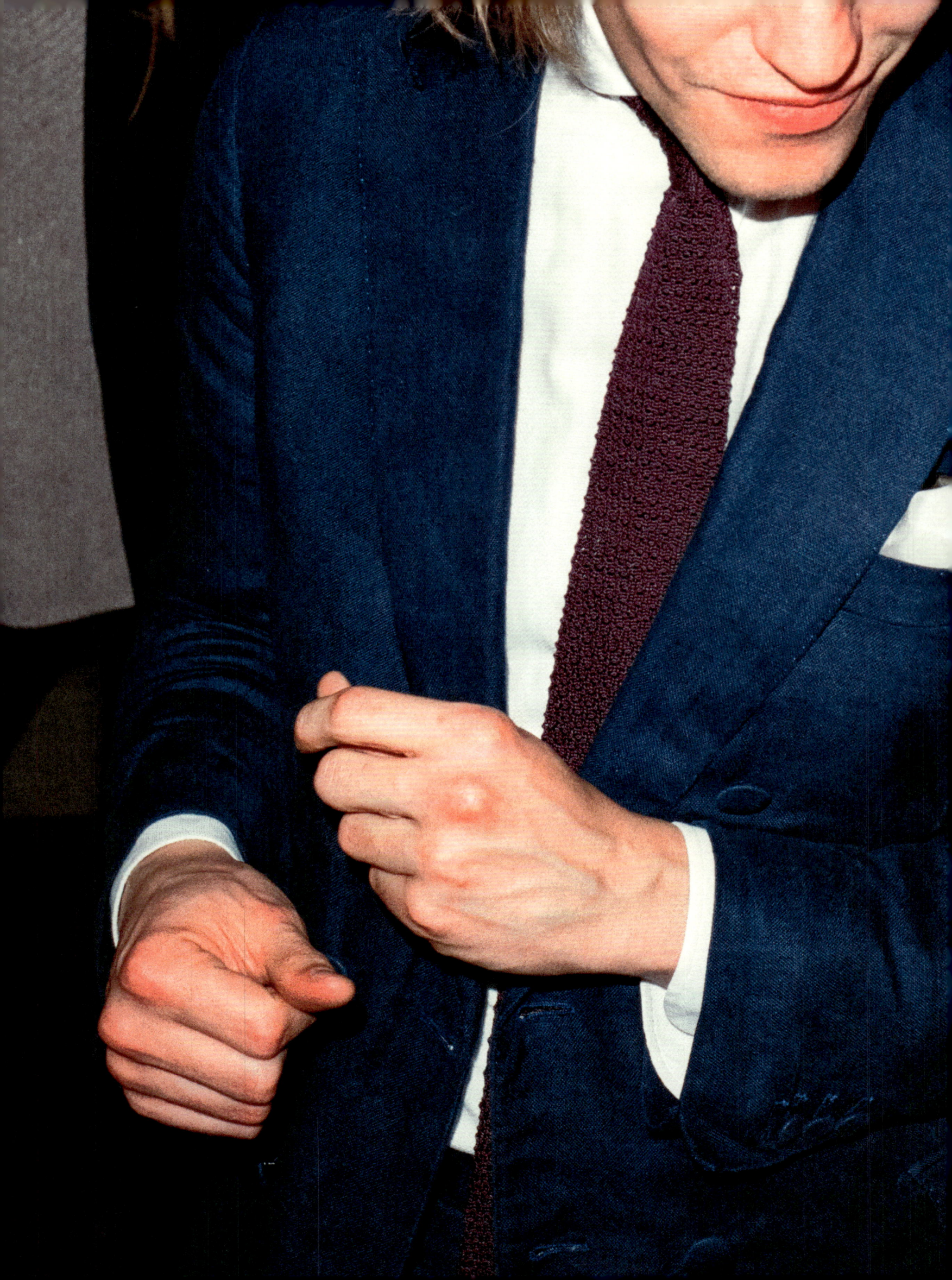

Der Dandy, der Fälscher und die Kurtisane

René Pollesch

Weißt du, ich sah einmal eine berühmte Schauspielerin, in deren Vorstellung ich gehen wollte, Fiona Shaw, kurz vor ihrem Auftritt, vor dem Bühneneingang des Theaters aus ihrem Taxi steigen. Sie war zu spät, aber überhaupt nicht in Eile. Sie stieg aus, mit mindestens zehn Einkaufstüten, auf denen Chanel und Vuitton stand, sehr elegant, äußerst mondän. Ich selbst war der Meinung, dass für die Zigarette, die ich rauchte, schon kaum mehr Zeit war. Ich rauchte äußerst hektisch und so, aber wusste eben *auch,* was ich der Straße schuldig war. So wie sie eben. Ich wusste nicht, ob es sich überhaupt noch lohnte, ins Theater zu gehen. Würde ich sie da genauso erleben können, in totaler Geberlaune? Dazu ist man ja nicht immer in der Lage. Oder wann ist man überhaupt in der Lage, etwas zu geben? Doch nicht um Punkt acht Uhr abends, wenn der Vorhang hochgeht. Ich bin natürlich trotzdem rein, und da saßen jetzt alle, gespannt auf ihren Auftritt. Und der Vorhang ging auf, in so übertriebenen Pendelbewegungen, die sich wahrscheinlich dieser völlig überschätzte Stephen Daldry ausgedacht hatte, selbst wenn es nicht seine Inszenierung war. Und da stand sie nun: Fiona Shaw. Nackt, mit hängenden Schultern und nassen Haaren, stieß sie einen markerschütternden Schrei aus. Und natürlich stand sie jetzt da und war überhaupt aufgetreten, um nun das größte Unheil vor uns aufzuführen, dass sich überhaupt denken lässt. Aber ich war natürlich vor allem beeindruckt von der Schnelligkeit ihrer Verwandlung. Über die Verwandlung, die sie beim Wechsel von der einen Bühne auf die andere vollzogen hatte. Ich möchte gar nicht wissen, wie schnell das gegangen wäre, wenn sie sich verspätet hätte, wenn sie ihren Auftritt beinahe verschlafen hätte, die Zeit, die sie gebraucht hätte, um zu Hause aus dem Bett zu fallen und dann auf der Bühne zu stehen. Natürlich wäre beides gar nicht so unähnlich. Im Bett wäre sie wahrscheinlich genauso nackt gewesen wie später auf der Bühne. Und ich hätte mich nicht weiter um den Unterschied gekümmert. Aber was so ähnlich aussieht – einen Anruf zu kriegen, zu wissen, dass man zu spät ist und dann in beinahe derselben Aufmachung auf der Bühne zu stehen –, ist hier natürlich etwas völlig anderes. Und was so grundverschieden aussah, die Art wie sie aus dem Taxi ausstieg und wie sie dann auf der Bühne stand, war natürlich das gleiche. Die Lust an der Verkleidung. Sie spielte. Es war der Versuch, an eine Kommunikation heranzukommen über das Außen. Alle auf der Straße hatten ihr insgeheim gehuldigt. Natürlich formierte sich auf der Straße keine Zuschauergruppe um sie herum, aber alle sahen, von welcher Größe dieser Taxiauftritt war. Von welchem Respekt gegenüber den Passanten er erfüllt war. Wäre sie in einem Jutesack zum Bühneneingang gegangen, um sich im Austausch die nackte Haut überzustreifen, natürlich wären dann die Zuschauer, die nichts davon mitbekommen hatten, wie sie ihr Taxi verlassen hatte, ebenso von ihrer Darstellung einer nackten antiken Frau beeindruckt gewesen.

Warum auch nicht. Ihr standen ja die Mittel dafür zur Verfügung. Niemand erwartete im Theater von ihr, dass sie sie selbst war. Aber leider auf der Straße ... Und obwohl sie auf der Bühne aussah wie eine nasse Katze, die auf der Ölspur der Antike in ihre Antigone-Tragödie stürzte, wusste ich doch, sie kam nicht in einem Hemd zu ihrem Auftritt.

Wenn sich Schauspieler noch heulend verbeugen, weil sie annehmen, sie wären noch in der Rolle, oder was die mit ihnen gemacht hat, da kann man nur sagen: Nein, die waren in der Rolle auch schon nur sie selbst.

Das ist das Missverständnis: dass immer die Frage ist, was die Rolle mit einem macht und nicht, was man mit der Rolle gemacht hat. Diese trostlose Leidenschaft, beim Schlussapplaus noch immer erfüllt von der Rolle aufzutreten. Warum nicht die eine Rolle ausziehen und sich überschwänglich in einer anderen verbeugen?

Weißt du, ich war auch einmal zu spät und hätte natürlich ungeschminkt vor dir auftauchen können, aber da ich ja weiß, dass du die Wahrheit nicht so schätzt wie die anderen, nutzte ich den Weg und eine irgendwie verregnete oder verspiegelte Straße dazu, mich aufzudonnern. Es kam mir vor wie im Traum, denn warum sollten Straßen plötzlich verspiegelt sein.

Der Spiegel war in der Tat groß genug. Ich sah aus wie Maria Magdalena beim Textlernen. „Das Bett war nicht benutzt. Hingestreckt lag das arme Geschöpf, das im Herzen von tödlicher Wunde getroffen war. Sie zeigte die Aufrichtigkeit dieser Reue einer Magdalena, deren klassische Haltung die der gottlosen Kurtisane war." Ich war so schön. Jemand wollte etwas sagen, aber ihm fehlten die Worte. „Sie arbeitet an der Schönheit der Geste. Das ist eine mondäne Geste, das ist keine Innerlichkeit." Weißt du, wie würde denn so ein Auftritt vor einem Theater aussehen, wenn sich alle nur mit sich selbst beschäftigten? Da wäre nichts. Nichts Mondänes. Keine Eleganz vor einem Taxi. Nur man selbst. Oder bei einem sexuellen Akt im Schlafzimmer. Man erwartet Ungeheures und stößt nur auf sich selbst. Selbstverwirklichung im Schlafzimmer, das ist doch das Letzte. Zuhause herrscht eine Bekenntnismentalität, die recht niedrige Umgangsformen mit sich bringt, die wenig Lebensfreude und Eleganz zulässt. In der alles wegfällt, was uns stört. Worum geht's denn hier eigentlich? Es geht um die Schönheit einer Geste im öffentlichen Raum. Das ist ein Missverständnis, dass du meine Höflichkeit, meine Inszenierung und meinen Gebrauch mondäner Genussmittel hier als Übertretung missverstehst. Es ist zivilisiertes Verhalten. Begegnen wir uns doch endlich einmal zivilisiert. Das hier ist keine Übertretung. Es sieht gut aus, und ich will, dass du dich wohlfühlst. Ich versuche, eine Beziehung zu dir herzustellen. Ich will ein Verhältnis mit dir eingehen, deshalb rauche ich. Das hier mache ich doch für dich. Siehst du das nicht!

Hier scheint es das totale Missverständnis zu geben. Zwei Menschen treffen sich auf einem öffentlichen Platz und verstehen die Schönheit ihrer Gesten nicht mehr. Wie kommt es, dass man alles, was sie tun, für einen Ausdruck ihres Selbst hält?

Weißt du, das ist doch genau das, woran man die Komplizen des Kapitals erkennt. Daran, dass sie einem das Rauchen verbieten. Sie halten jede Inszenierung für den brutalen Ausbruch eines Selbst. Das ist so ein Missverständnis. Wie konnte es dazu kommen, dass das Selbst vor allem Ruhe braucht? Warum diese Stille? In der Öffentlichkeit? Im Zuschauerraum eines Theaters! Warum spielen die denn nicht? Woher kommt die Stille im Zuschauerraum? Was ist denn da los?

Wenn etwas gespielt wird, ist das im Moment eine ziemliche Herabsetzung. Man solle doch die Fiktion lassen und wieder zur Wirklichkeit zurückkehren, sagt man. So als hätte das Spiel keine Wirklichkeit. Es ist im Moment kaum mehr zu verstehen, dass es einmal eine Zeit gab, in der man nicht wusste, wen man vor sich hatte. Natürlich ist das dann irgendwann gekippt, man hat es nicht mehr ausgehalten und mit der ganzen Identifizierung angefangen, die Polizei, Lee Strasberg. So sah einmal der öffentliche Raum aus, dass man nicht wusste, wen man vor sich hatte. Weil da gespielt wurde. Jetzt weiß man aus ganz anderen Gründen nicht mehr, wen man vor sich hat. Es ist so schwer, jemandem den Unterschied zwischen einem aufstiegssüchtigen Talent und einem verbissenen Karrieristen zu erklären. Es gibt oft für zwei Sachen, die vollkommen unterschiedlich sind, nur ähnliche Begriffe. Alles gibt sich der allgemeinen Äquivalenz anheim. Es gibt nur noch die Kreisligisten der Liebe, und ihre Filme, und es ist immer das gleiche, man sieht nur Schritt – Schritt – Stolper.

Weißt du, wenn du dich verstellst und etwas für mich inszenierst, dann muss ich nicht an dich glauben. Ich bin ja nur mit dem Glauben belästigt, wenn du das nicht tust. Und wenn du, wie man so sagt, „pur" vor mir stehst. Aber du weißt das immer noch nicht. Du kommst mir vor wie ein Spieler, der an das glaubt, was er macht. Nur ich, dein Zuschauer, den hast du durch alle Haken, die du geschlagen hast, trainiert, anders auf dich zu sehen. Darauf, dass man eben nicht glauben muss, wenn man liebt. Godard hat leider einmal einen Film gemacht, bei dem steht am Ende so in der Gegend herum: „Wer liebt, der muss glauben." Ja leider, könnte man dem jungen Joseph da sagen. Und vielleicht meinte Godard auch, fragt ihn lieber nicht. Der ist kein unaufgeklärter Gottesdienstbesucher. Der weiß, man kann auch niederknien und die Hände falten und die Lippen bewegen wie zu einem Gebet, und dann glaubt man.

F: Weißt du zum Beispiel, wovor ich total Angst habe vor der Kamera? Es gibt immer sozusagen diese Momente ...
B: Ja.

F: Ja? Wo ... so ... man merkt so ... das Gesicht ..., man kann gar nichts dagegen tun oder so.
B: Ja!?

F: Aber das Gesicht schwappt in so 'ne allzu bekannte Coolness rein. Oder so ...
B: Ja, ja, ja!

F: Weißt du, was ich meine?

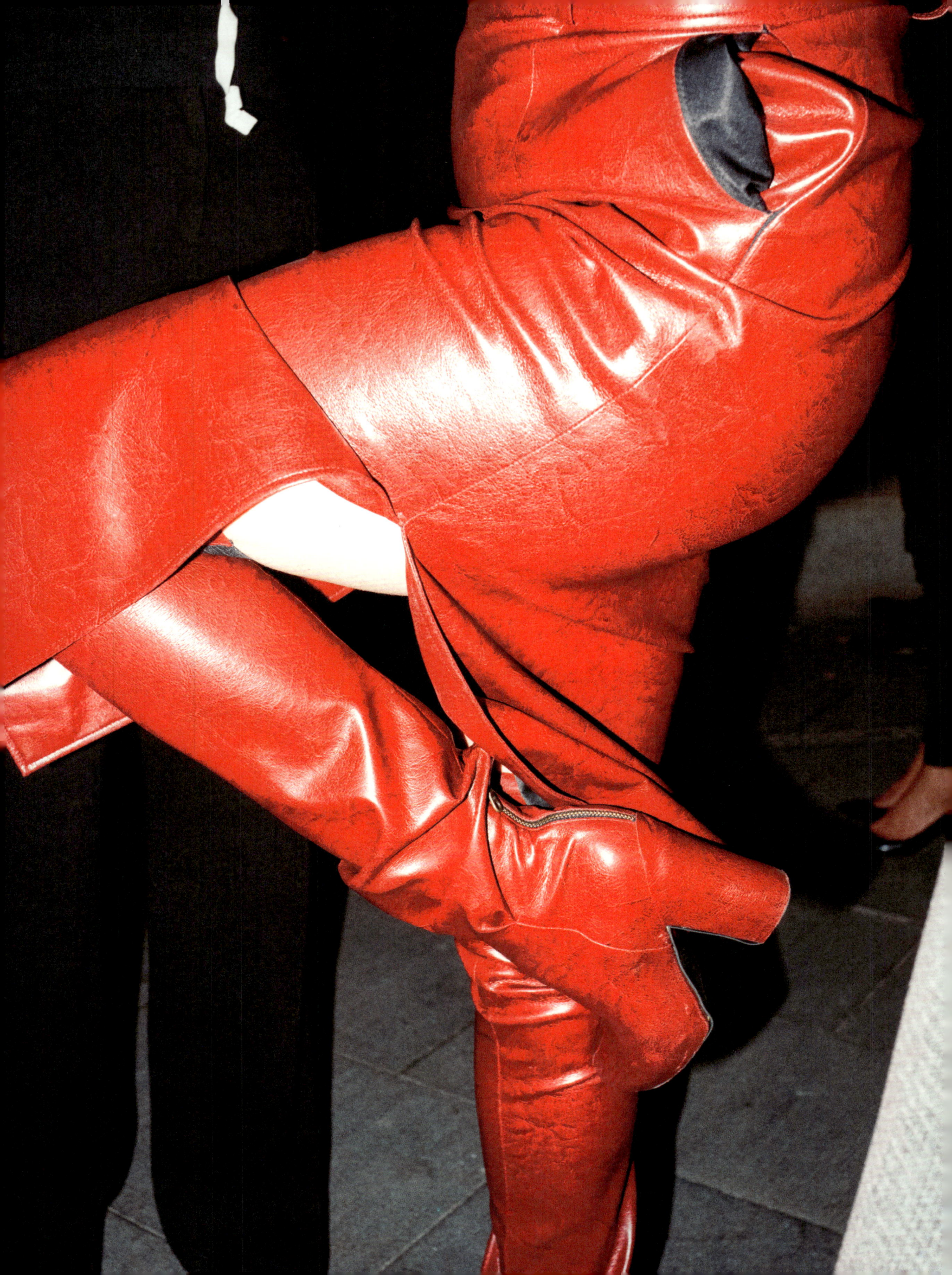

The Dandy,
the Faker,
and the Courtesan

René Pollesch

You know, I once spotted a famous actress whose show I was going to see, Fiona Shaw, getting out of a cab by the theater's stage door just in time for her performance. She was running late but in no hurry at all. She stepped out of the car toting at least ten shopping bags emblazoned with brands like Chanel and Vuitton, very elegant, a very classy chic. And there I was thinking that I almost didn't have time to smoke my cigarette. I puffed frantically and all that, but then I *also* knew what I owed to the street. And so did she. I wasn't sure seeing the show was even worth it anymore. Would I experience her in there just as I'd experienced her out here, giving freely of herself? Few people are capable of such generosity at all times. Or when is one actually capable of giving of oneself at all? Certainly not at 8 p.m. sharp when the curtain rises. Of course I did go in, and there they all sat, eagerly expecting her entrance. And the curtain went up, with an extravagant swinging motion that was probably the brainchild of that vastly overrated Stephen Daldry, even though he hadn't directed the production. And then she stood before us: Fiona Shaw. Naked, her shoulders slumped, her hair wet, she let out a bloodcurdling scream. And of course she now stood there and the whole point of her being onstage was to perform for us the most calamitous misery conceivable. But of course what impressed me more than anything else was the speed of her metamorphosis. The metamorphosis she'd undergone as she'd switched from one stage to the other. I don't even want to know how quickly she would've done it if she'd been late, if she'd almost overslept, how long it would've taken her to fall out of bed at home and walk out onto the stage. Of course, the two wouldn't even be all that dissimilar. She'd presumably have been just as naked in bed as then, later, on the stage. And the difference wouldn't have mattered much to me. But of course what looks so similar—getting a call, knowing you're late, and then walking out onto the stage in virtually the same getup—is at bottom something very different. And of course what looked so fundamentally different, the way she got out of the cab and how she then stood on the stage, was really the same thing. The pleasure of being in disguise. She was acting. It was the attempt to approach an act of communication by way of its outside. In the street, everyone had secretly worshipped her. No group of spectators had thronged around her in the street, of course, but everyone had seen how grand this appearance by cab was. How much respect for the passersby was in it. If she'd walked to the stage door in a jute sack she'd then taken off to slip into her naked skin, the spectators, who obviously wouldn't have noticed her getting out of the cab, would've been no less blown away by her portrayal of a naked woman from antiquity. And why shouldn't they have been. After all, she had what it took. No one in the theater expected her to be herself. But unfortunately, in the street ... And although on the stage she looked like a wet cat careening down the ancient oil-slick road into her tragedy of Antigone, I still knew she hadn't arrived for her performance in shirtsleeves.

When actors keep blubbering through the curtain call, persuaded that they're still inside their role or whatever it did with them, all one can say is: no, they were just being themselves even when they were inside their role.

That's the misconception: that the question is always what the role does with you and not what you did with the role. That dismal zeal with which actors try to seem possessed by their roles through the final applause. Why not take off the one role and bow, effusively, in another?

You know, I was late once myself, and of course I could've shown up in front of you without makeup, but since I know that you don't appreciate the truth the way the others do, I used the opportunity of some rain-slick or mirror-clad street along the way to gussy myself up. It was like in a dream, because why would streets suddenly be mirror-clad.

The mirror was in fact large enough. I looked like Mary Magdalene memorizing her lines. "The bed was unused. Stretched out upon it was the poor creature struck in the heart by a fatal wound. She expressed the sincere contrition of a Magdalene whose classical posture was that of the Godless courtesan." I was so beautiful. Someone wanted to say something but didn't have the words. "She's working on the beauty of the gesture. It's a fashionable gesture, not inwardness." You know, what would that sort of appearance in front of a theater look like if everyone were concerned only with themselves? There would be nothing to it. No chic. No elegance beside a cab. Only you yourself. Or during a sexual act in the bedroom. People expect some enormity and encounter only themselves. Self-fulfillment in the bedroom, now that's bullshit. There's a confessional mentality that prevails in the home, and the fairly uncouth manners that go with it leave little room for joie de vivre and elegance. It eliminates everything that stops us in our tracks. What's this really about? It's about the beauty of a gesture in public. You're making a mistake when you construe my politeness, my performing and indulging in fashionable pleasures as a transgression. It's civilized behavior. Let's encounter each other in a civilized manner for once. This here is not a transgression. It looks good, and I want you to be comfortable. I'm trying to establish a rapport with you. I want to build a relationship with you, that's why I'm smoking. I'm doing this here for you. Can't you see that!

This would seem to be an instance of complete misunderstanding. Two people meet in a public square and no longer understand the beauty of each other's gestures. How is it that everything they do is taken to be an expression of their selves?

You know, that's exactly how you recognize capital's accomplices. By the fact that they prohibit smoking. They take all theatricality for a brutal eruption of a self. That's such a misconception. How did we get to a point where the self needs quiet above all? Why this silence? In public? In a theater auditorium! Why aren't they acting? Whence that silence in the auditorium? What's going on here?

When something's a performance, that is, at that moment, pretty degrading. Time to drop the fiction and get back to reality, people say. As though the acting were without reality. It's become almost incomprehensible today that there was a time when people didn't know who they were dealing with. Of course, there came a tipping point, people could no longer stand it and the whole identification thing started, the police, Lee Strasberg. The public space was once a place where people didn't know who they were dealing with. Because it was a place where people acted. Now, for completely different reasons, people no longer know who they're dealing with. It's so difficult to explain the distinction between a ruthlessly ambitious talent and a grimly determined careerist. There are often things that are utterly different and the only terms we have for them are similar. Everyone and everything is adrift in universal equivalence. All that's left are the minor leaguers of love, and their films, and it's forever the same thing, all you see is step — step — stumble.

You know, when you fake it and perform something for me, then I don't have to believe in you. I'm only importuned by the need to believe when you don't do that. And when, as they say, you stand before me "just as you are." But you still don't get that. To my mind you're like an actor who believes in what she does. It's just that, with all your sudden twists and turns, you've trained me, your spectator, to see you from a different angle. To recognize that to love doesn't necessarily mean to believe. Godard, unfortunately, once made a film where in the end the message is kind of: "To love is necessarily to believe." Sadly, that's true, one might tell young Joseph. And perhaps Godard also meant to signal, better don't ask him. He's not a naïve churchgoer. He knows you can kneel and fold your hands and move your lips as though you're praying, and that's to believe.

F: You know, for instance, one thing I'm totally scared of in front of the camera? There are always these moments when, like ...
B: Yes.

F: Yes? When ... like ... you realize that ... the face ..., it's like there's nothing you can do about it.
B: Yes!?

F: But the face spills into some sort of cool that's all too familiar. Or like ...
B: Yes, yes, yes!

F: You know what I mean?

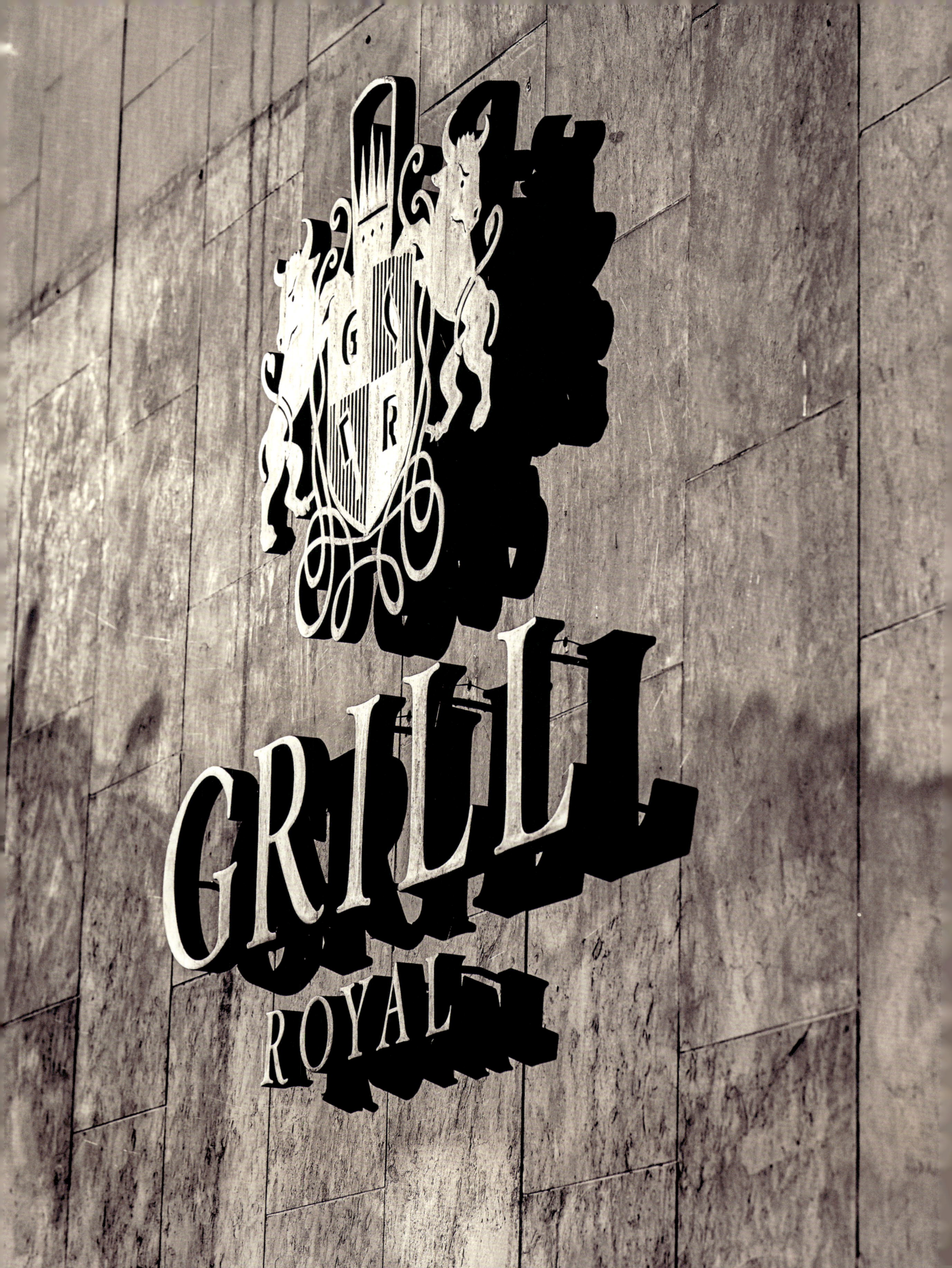

A Day

Peter Langer

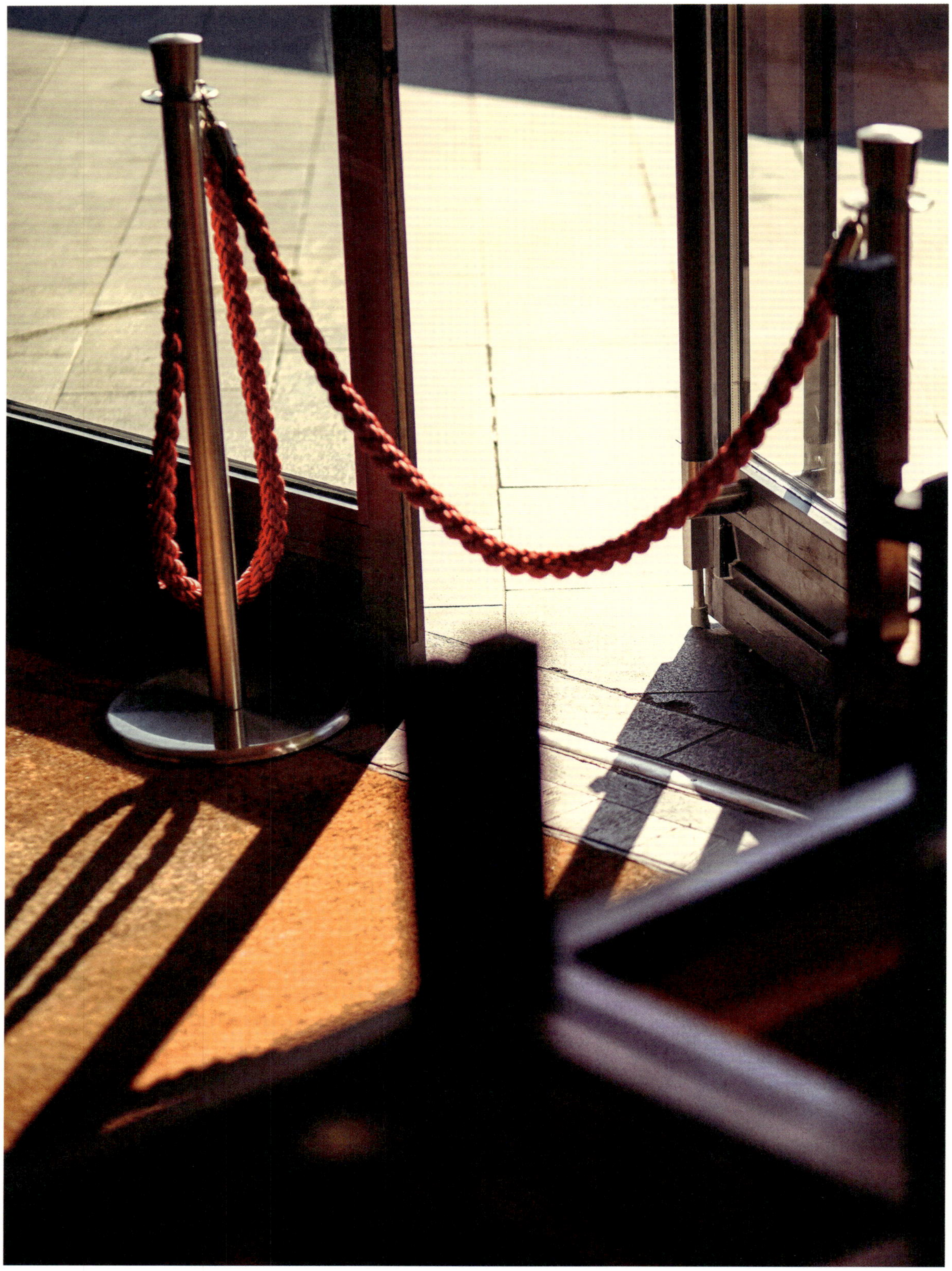

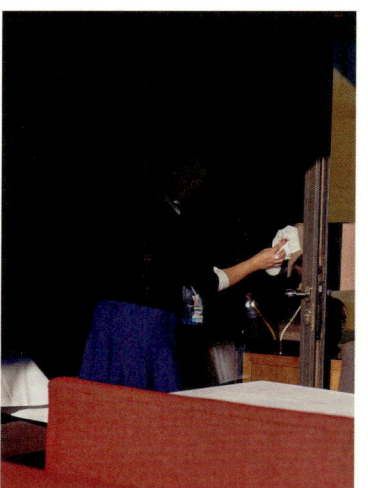
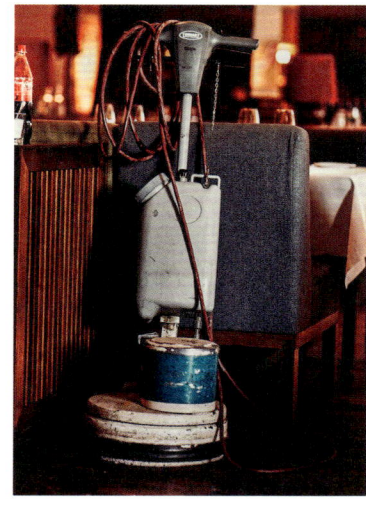

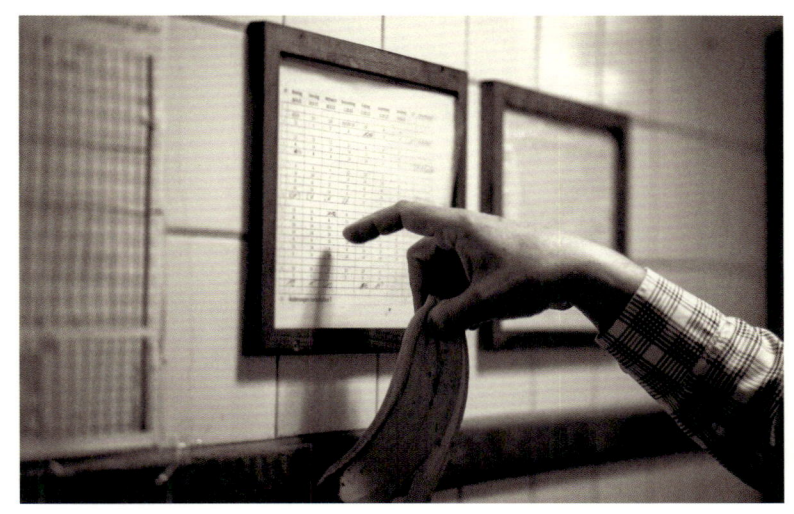

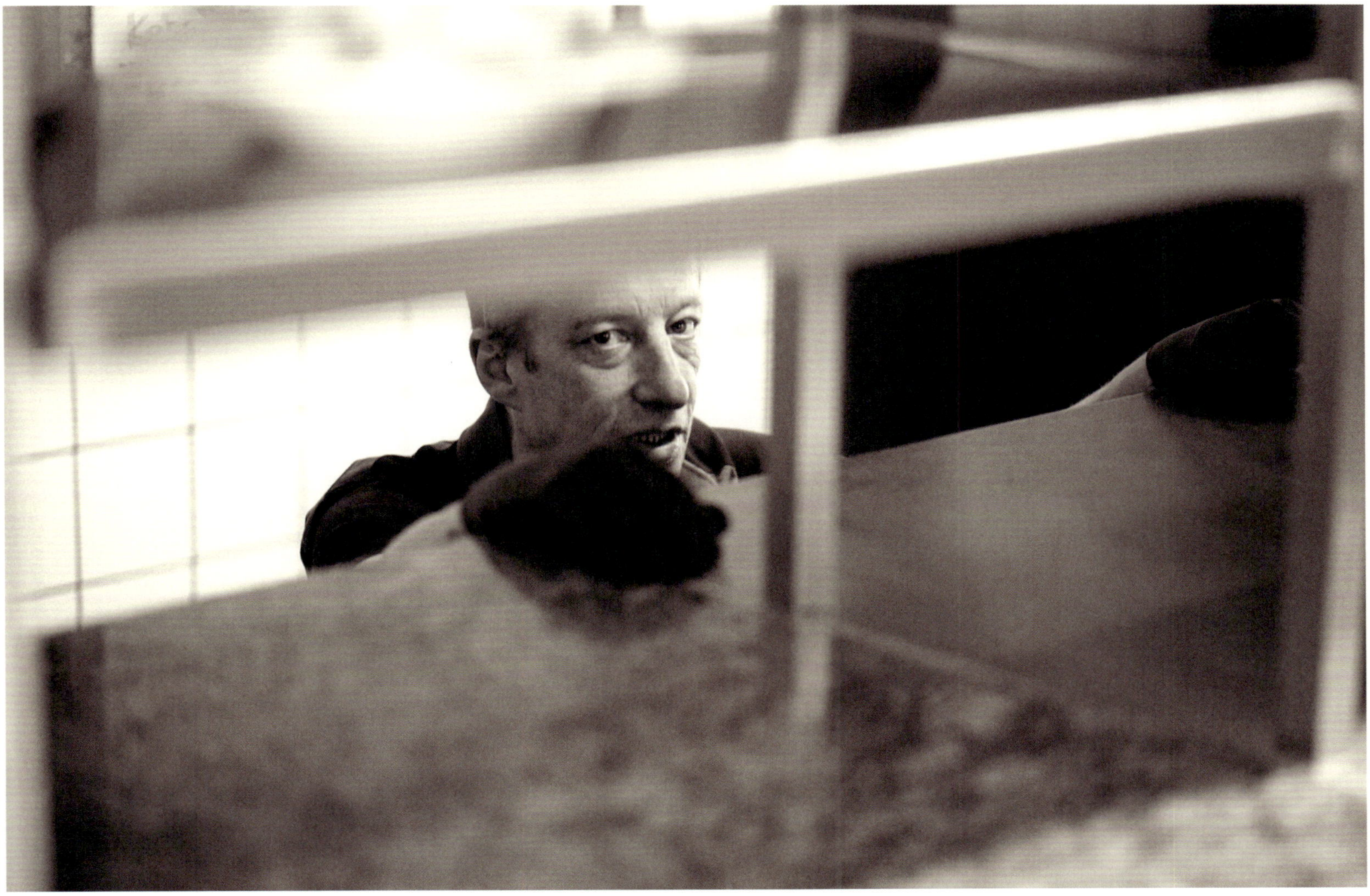

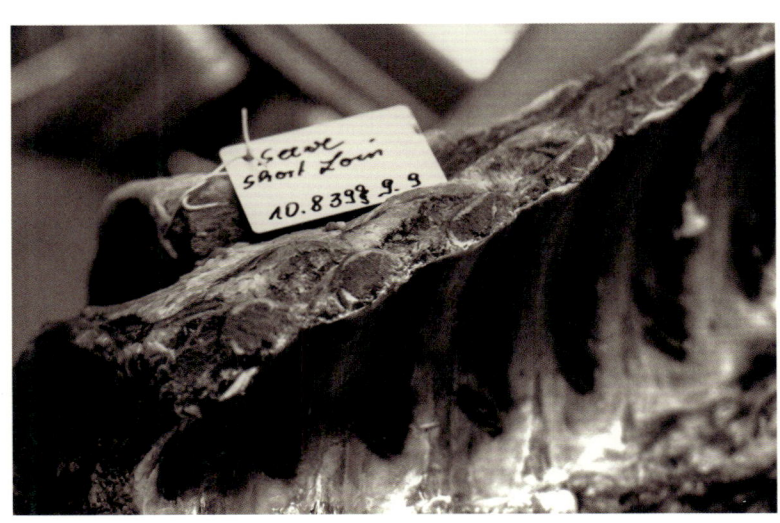

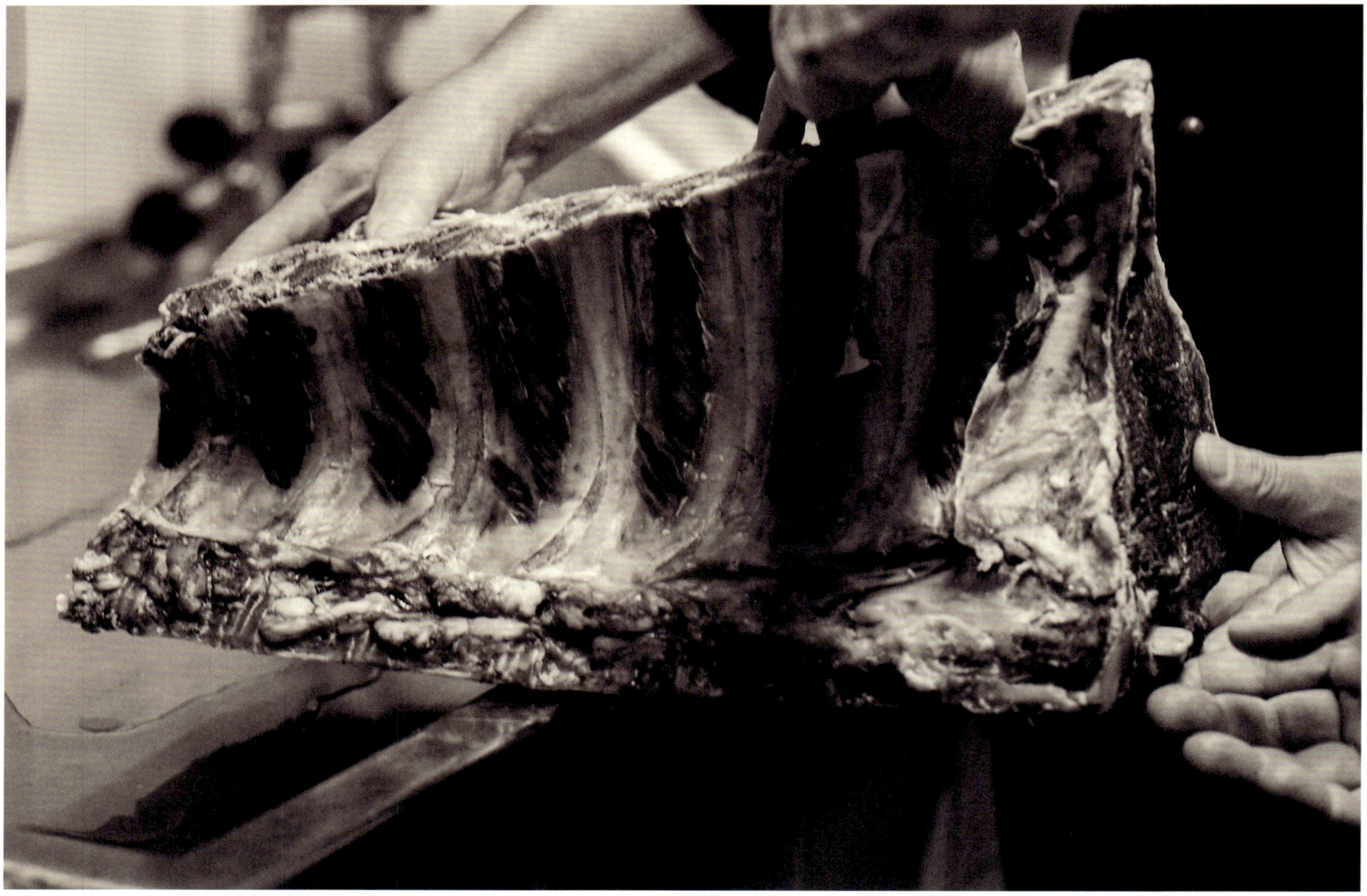

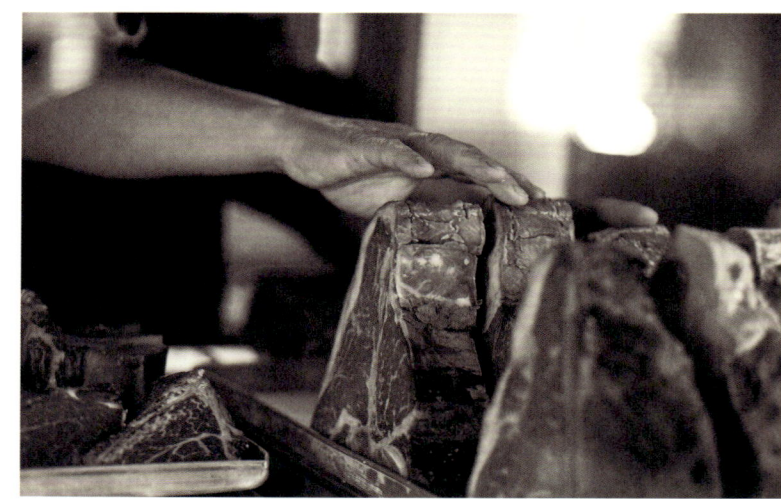

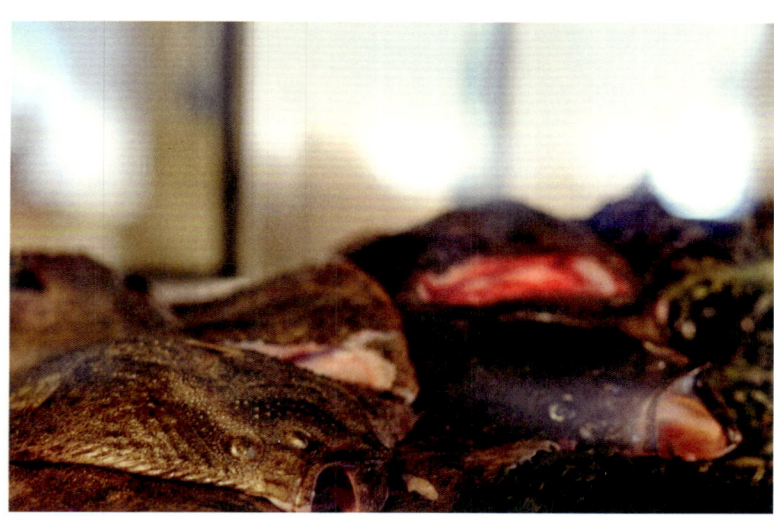

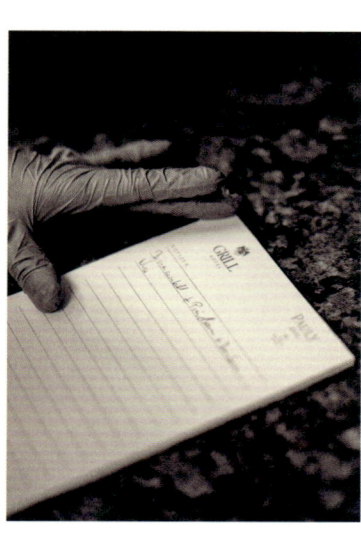

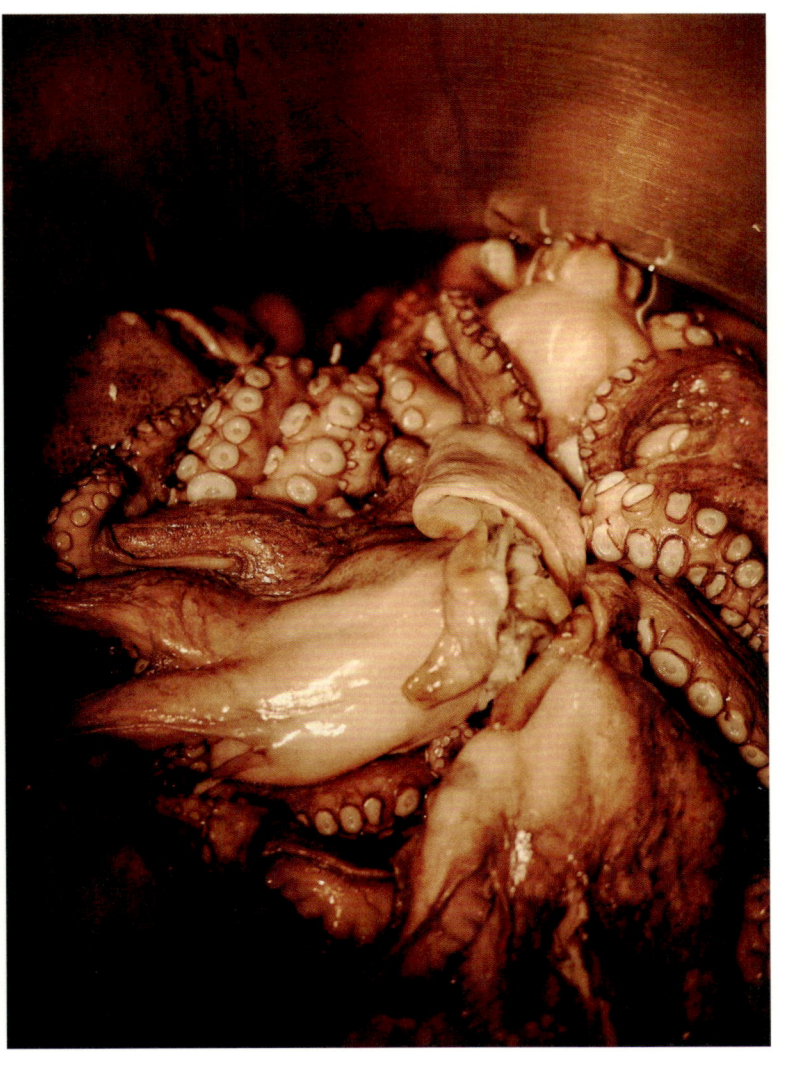
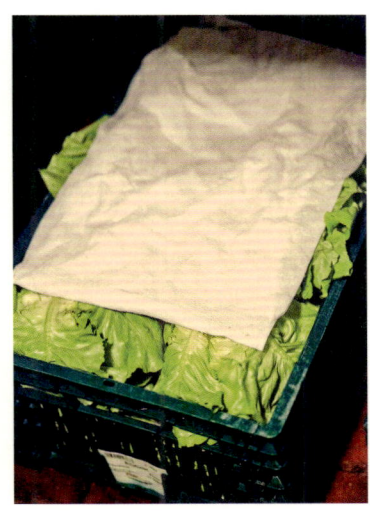
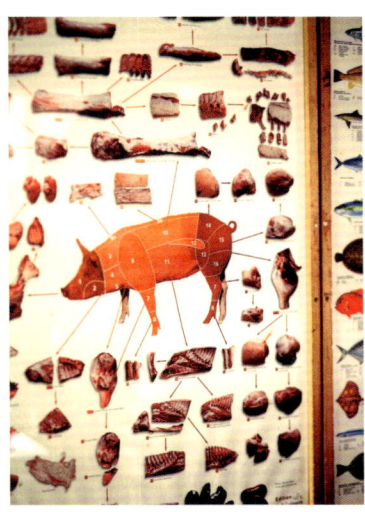
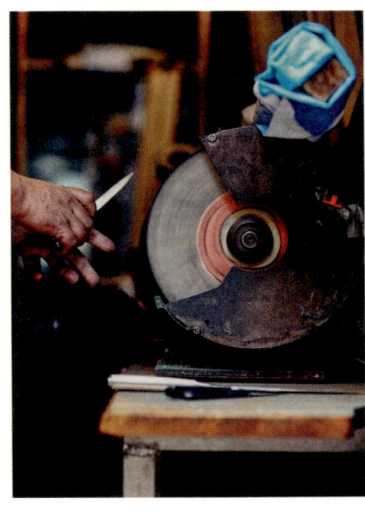
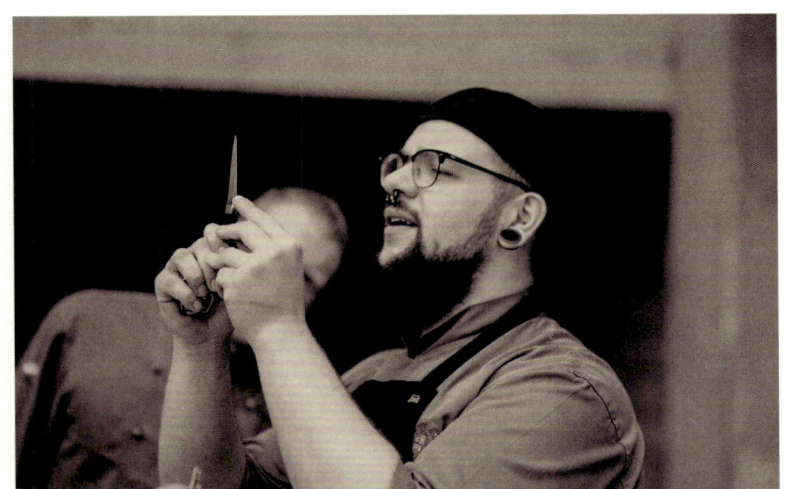
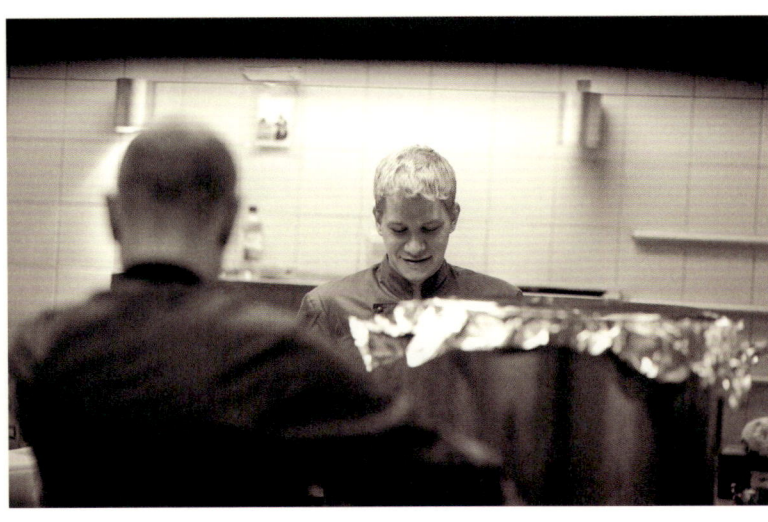
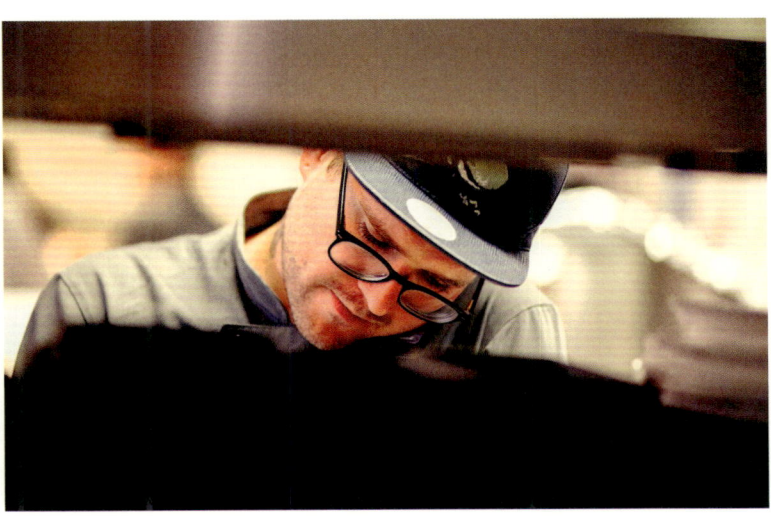

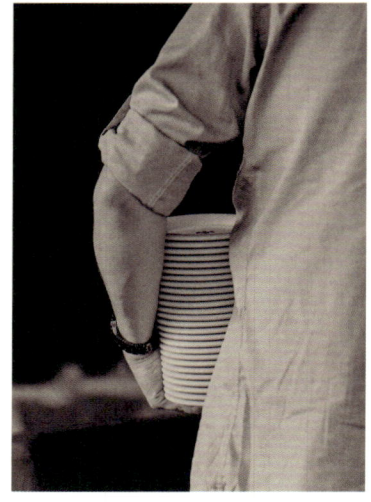

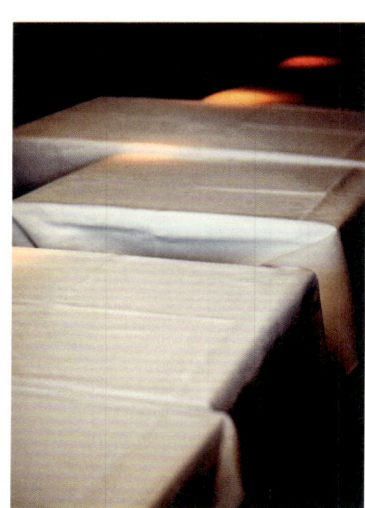

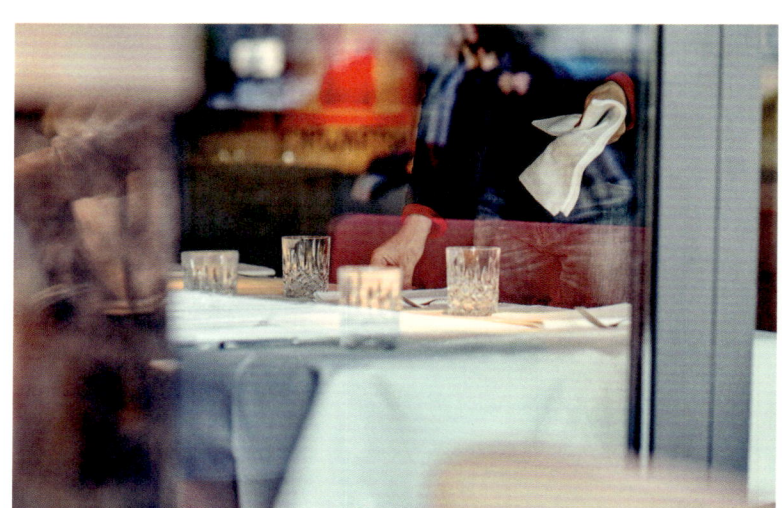

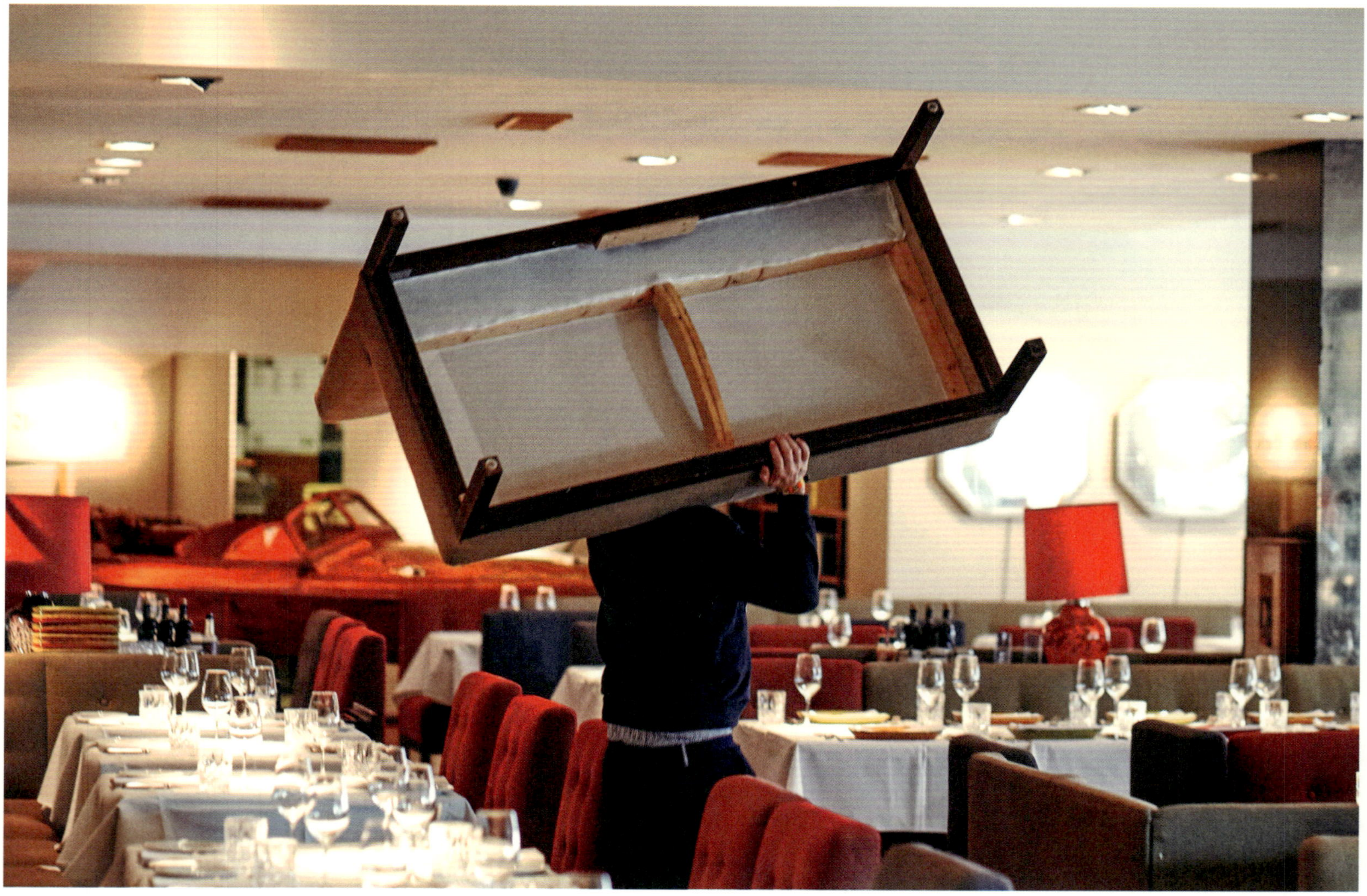

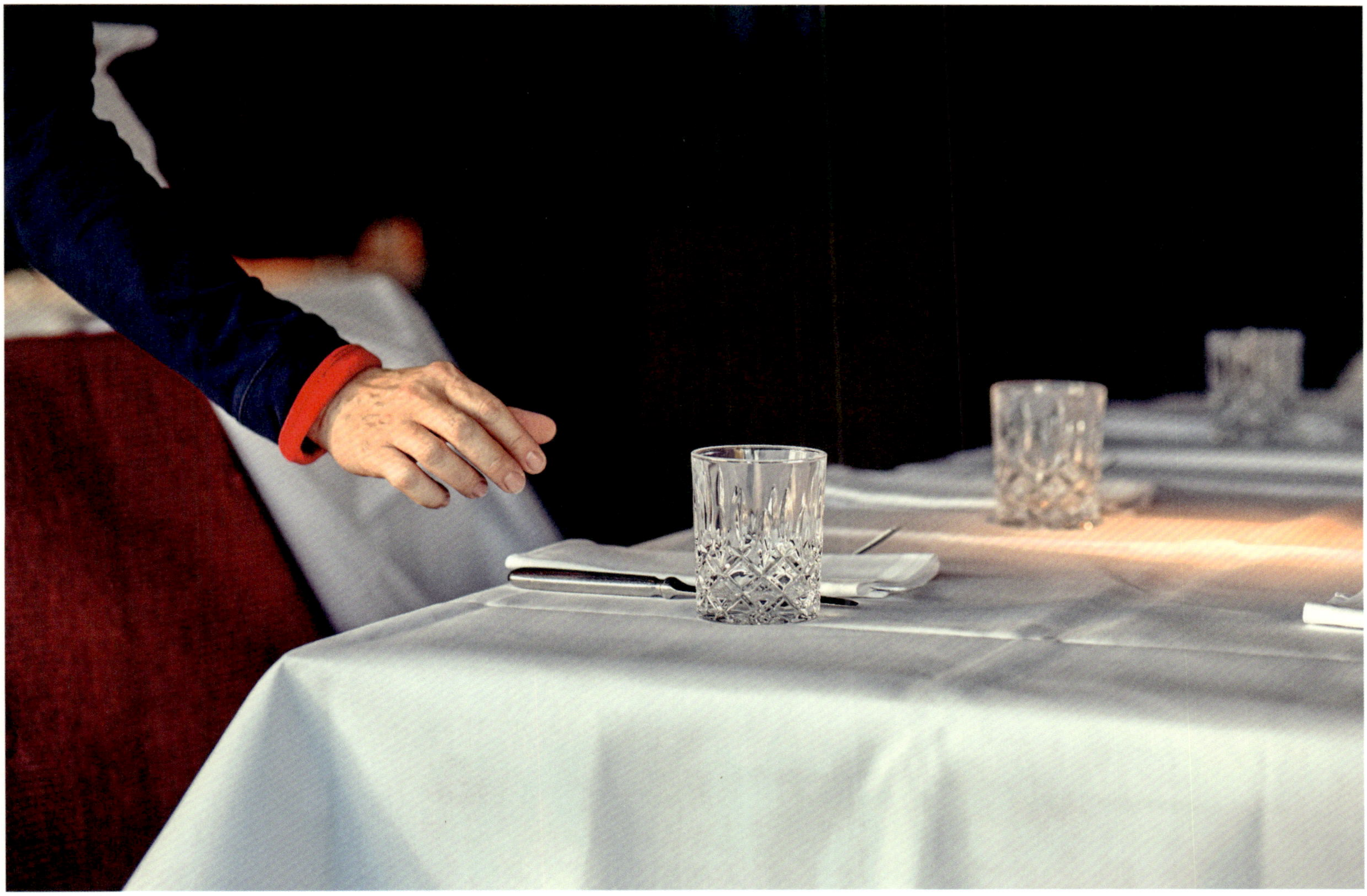

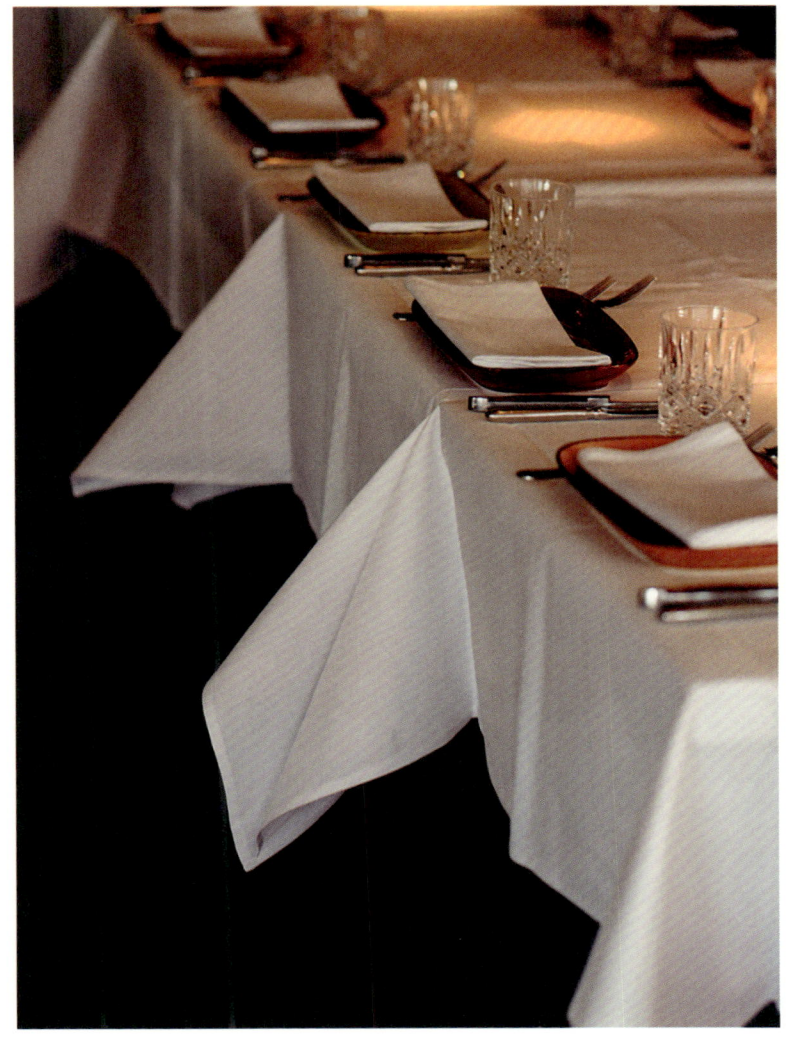

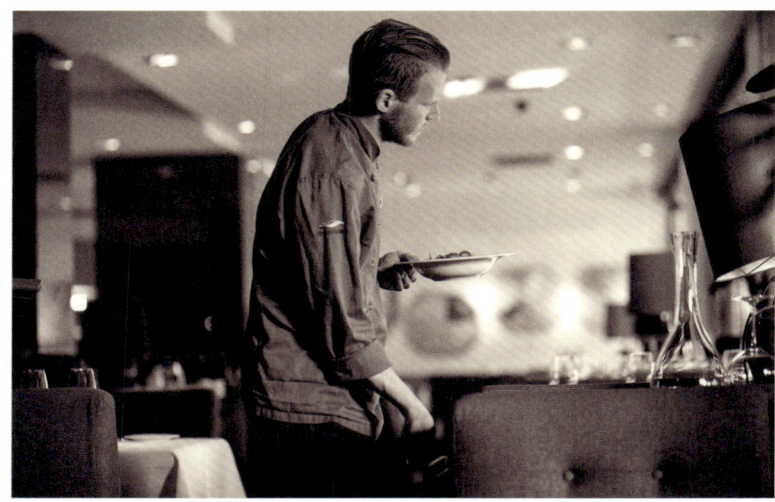
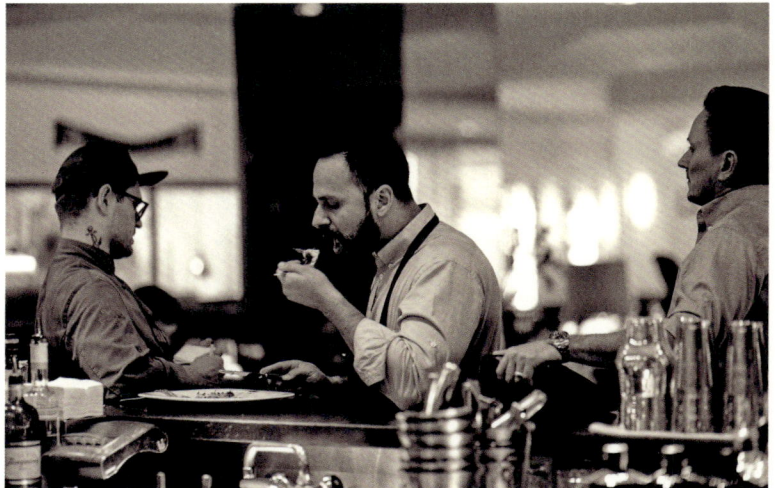

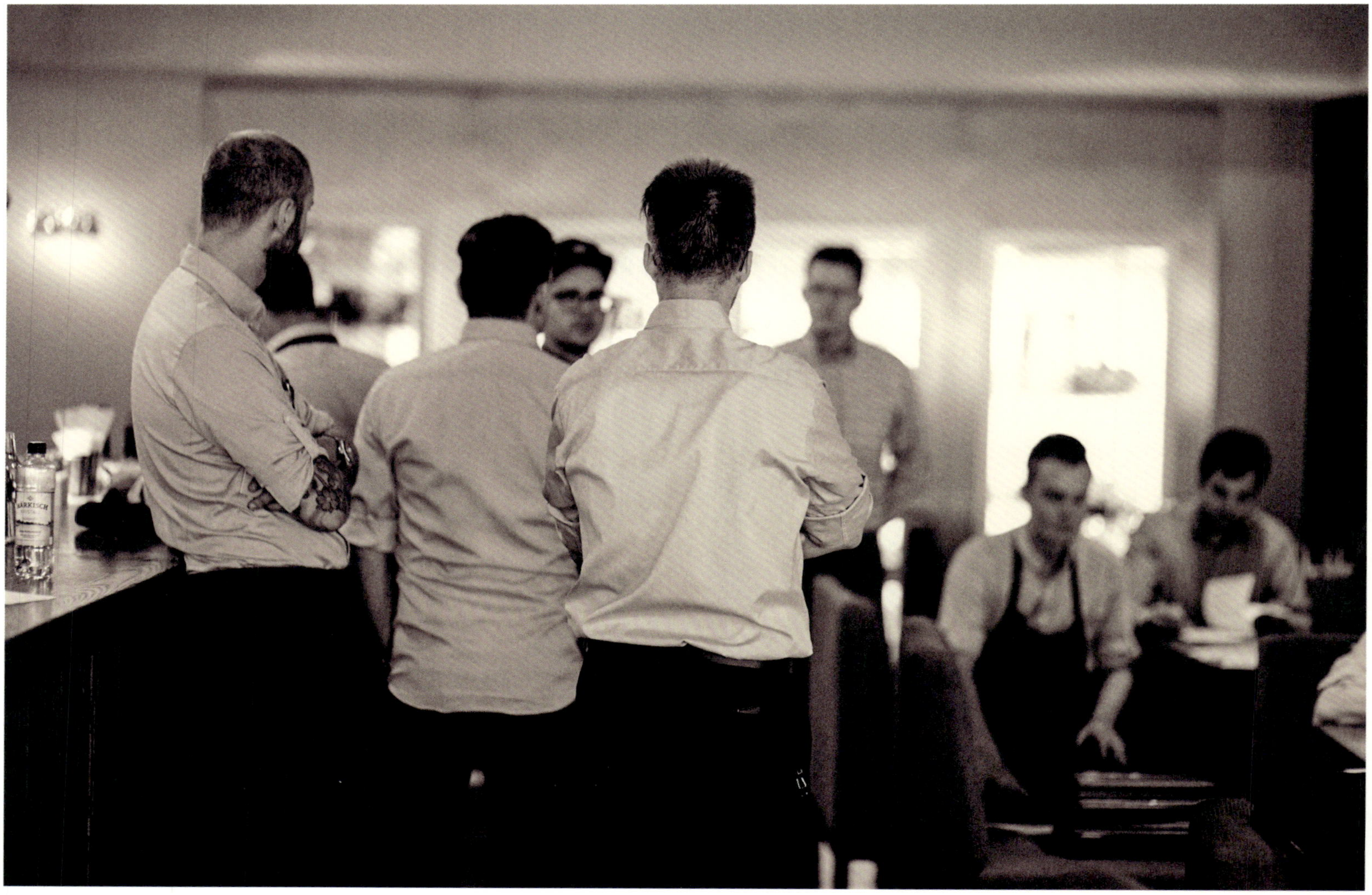

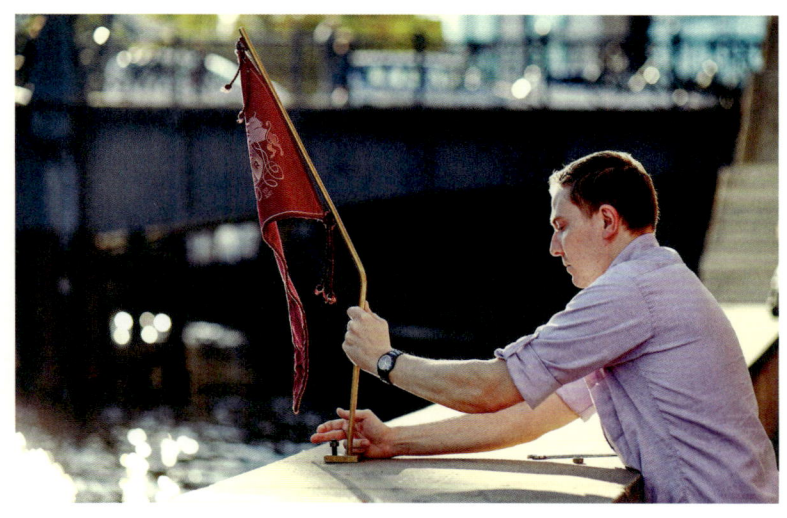

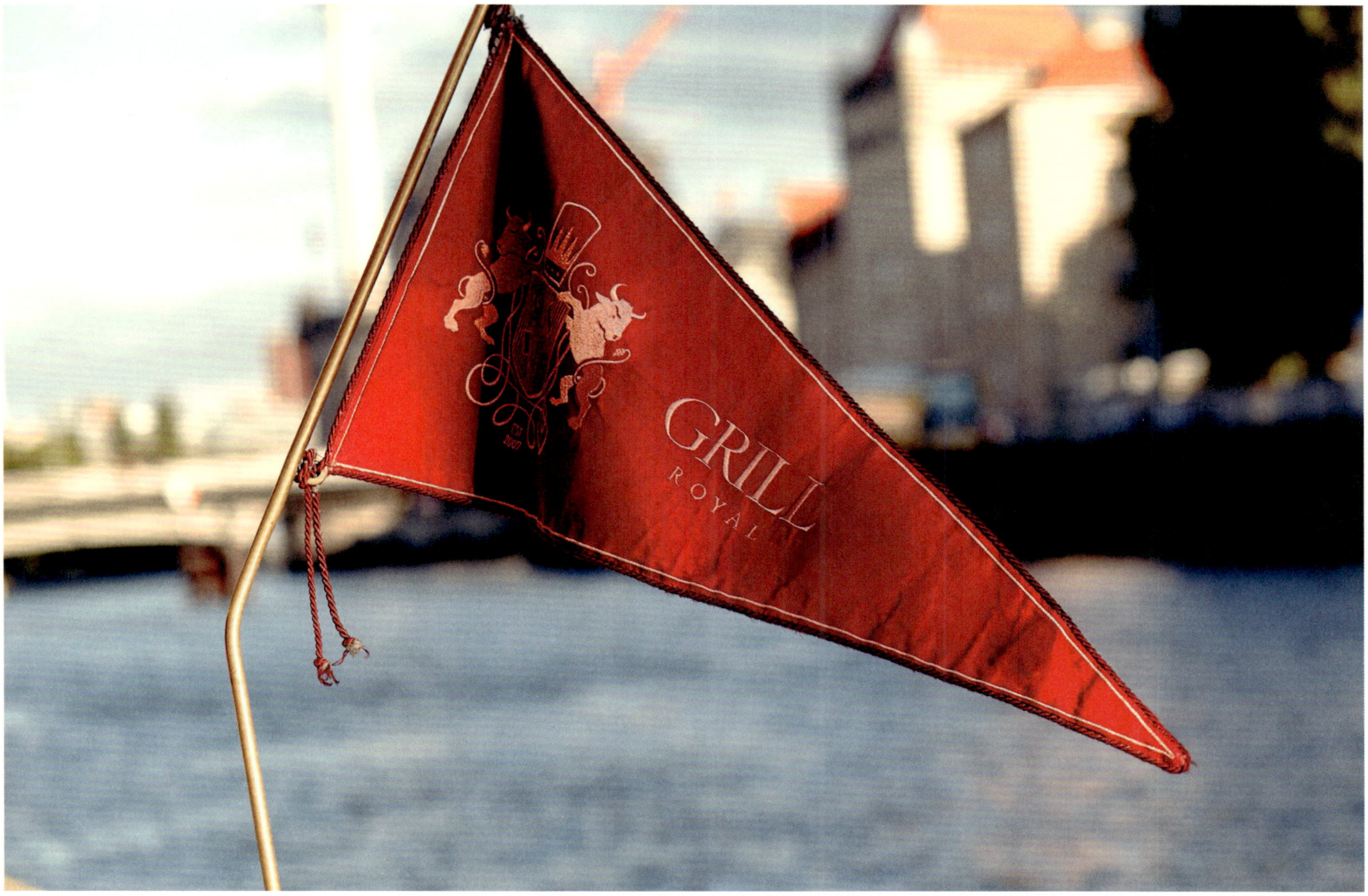

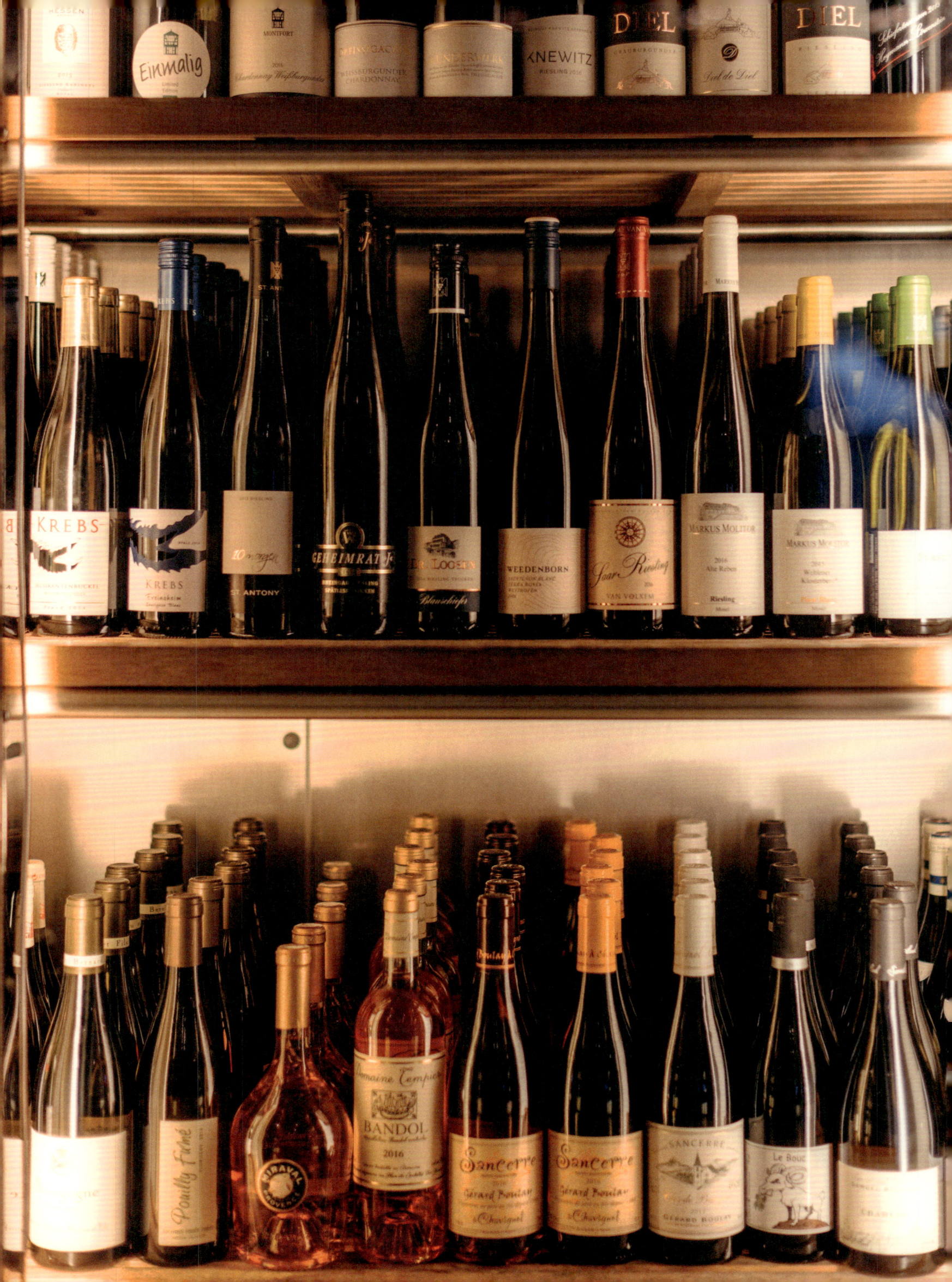

Ein Gespräch über Wein

mit Andrea Kauk und Moritz Estermann

Stuart Pigott

Es ist 17 Uhr an einem Mittwochnachmittag, als ich das Restaurant Grill Royal auf der Suche nach der Wahrheit im Wein betrete. Noch herrscht Ruhe vor dem abendlichen Sturm. Moritz Estermann entschuldigt sich, dass wir etwas auf die langjährige Sommelière des Hauses, Andrea Kauk, warten müssen, weil sie in einer Besprechung mit der Service-Mannschaft ist. Zuerst führt er mich hinter die Kulissen, wo ich noch nie war, obwohl ich seit kurz nach der Eröffnung 2007 Gast im Grill Royal bin. Dann setzen wir uns in eine Ecke, fangen an zu reden, und bald kommt auch Andrea Kauk dazu.

STUART PIGOTT (SP): *Wir waren gerade im Weinkeller vom Grill Royal, wo ich nüchterne Holzregale und lauter Flaschen, meistens stehend, gesehen habe. Das mache ich auch so, denn Wissenschaftler haben bewiesen, dass es für die Lagerung egal ist, ob die Flasche liegt oder steht.*

MORITZ ESTERMANN (ME): Wir sind kein Museum, und alle Flaschen müssen sich verkaufen, auch die teuren Flaschen drehen sich innerhalb von eineinhalb, maximal zwei Jahren. Keine Flasche liegt länger bei uns. Wir haben Weine, die wir reifen lassen, von denen wir sagen, dass sie besonders sind und an die wir nicht mehr rankommen. Aber diese Flaschen liegen nicht hier.

SP: *Was ist für einen Wein hier im Grill Royal teuer?*

ANDREA KAUK (AK): Richtig teuer sind natürlich die großen Bordeaux und die großen Burgunder.

SP: *Mit einem vierstelligen Preis?*

ME: Ja. Auch.

SP: *Wer trinkt im Grill Royal eine Flasche Wein für eine vierstellige Summe?*

AK: Ganz verschiedene Leute. Oft kosten diese Flaschen bei uns weniger als im Weinladen. Es gibt Gäste, die das honorieren und sagen: „Kaufe ich mir!" Wir haben letztes Jahr hier vorne einen wunderbaren Tisch gehabt. Champagner Clos du Mesnil von Krug und 1990er Château Latour aus dem Bordeaux wurden getrunken. Der Kellner hat dann vorsichtig nach dem Grund gefragt und bekam zur Antwort: „Wir trinken auf meine Scheidung ..."

SP: *Hier im Grill Royal addieren sich manche Sachen nicht nur auf der Rechnung schneller zusammen. Ich gehe manchmal rein und sage zu mir selbst:*

„Heute werde ich nur Weißwein trinken, um nicht zu spät im Bett zu landen!"
Aber in meinem Innersten weiß ich, dass noch eine Flasche Rotwein dazu
kommen wird, und dann noch ein paar Drinks an der Bar!
Was wäre im Grill Royal eine günstige Flasche Wein?

AK: Preiswert wäre bei den Rotweinen eine Flasche unter 40 Euro, zum
Beispiel ein einfacher deutscher Spätburgunder oder auch unser günstigster
Wein aus Tasca d'Almerita auf Sizilien.

SP: *Und in Weiß, was ist da günstig und gut im Grill Royal?*

AK: Günstig und gut ist zum Beispiel ein Wein vom Schlossgut Diel an
der Nahe, mit dem arbeiten wir direkt zusammen. Auch der Grauburgunder
von Fritz Keller in Baden ist mit Sicherheit eine saubere Sache und vom
Preis-Leistungs-Verhältnis her perfekt.

SP: *Schon diese Beispiele deuten auf die Vielfältigkeit des Weinprogramms*
im Grill Royal hin. Viele Leute denken ja, dass es hier nur teure Bordeaux und
Prestige-Champagner gibt. Das ist aber überhaupt nicht der Fall.

AK: Unser Herz schlägt seit vielen Jahren schon für die Burgunder. Wenn
man Wein liebt und relativ viel trinkt, dann geben einem die Weine aus bestimmten Traubensorten wie Pinot Noir einfach mehr. Viele vertragen sie
auch besser.

SP: *Hier im Grill Royal ist mir Pinot Noir oft sehr leicht die Kehle hinunter-*
geflossen, gelegentlich mit einer durchaus gefährlichen Geschwindigkeit.

AK: Das stimmt. Für mich können die Weine auch gerne aus Deutschland
stammen. Das ist für uns vor zehn Jahren die große Entdeckung gewesen,
wie gut die deutschen Weine sind, oder die österreichischen. Wir finden es
spannend, dass es auch Weine aus ganz weit entfernten Gebieten wie etwa aus
Kanada in guter Qualität gibt. Da wir aber ein klassisches Restaurant sind,
haben wir zum Beispiel nicht so viele spanische Weine. Die Schwerpunkte
liegen eher in Frankreich oder Deutschland.

SP: *Meine ersten Erinnerungen an den Grill Royal sind stark von Champagner*
geprägt.

AK: Als Sommelière weiß man, dass ein Champagnerrausch nach wie vor etwas Besonderes ist. Es gab hier einige große Feiern, da wurde Champagner aus 6- und 9-Liter-Flaschen serviert. Die Gäste wollten die leeren Flaschen nicht mehr hergeben: „Nein, nein, die ist mein Baby!" Das ist typisch für Champagner, dass die Leute damit so fröhlich sind.

SP: *Ich finde es toll, wenn manche Leute den Grill Royal mit einem Baby verlassen, ich meine, mit einem Baby, das sie nicht mitgebracht haben. Zu einem großartigen Restaurant gehören große Emotionen. Für mich ist gute Gastronomie auch immer ein Theaterstück, aber der Grill Royal wurde bewusst wie eine Bühne gestaltet, oder?*

ME: Ja, wir wollten es zu einem Ort machen für Menschen, die kommunikativ sind und aus sich rausgehen. Bei der klassischen Gourmetküche der 1980er und 1990er Jahre war der Gast zur totalen Passivität verurteilt. Er musste nur „ja, toll" sagen, aber durfte nicht fragen, ob ein Fenster aufgemacht werden könnte oder nach Salz verlangen. Wir wollten die guten Produkte und Weine davon befreien. Man kann ohne Voranmeldung und ohne sich dafür chic anzuziehen in den Grill Royal kommen, Austern essen oder eine Flasche Krug-Champagner trinken. Das ist die Freiheit, die es hier gibt.

SP: *Viele Menschen wissen, dass der Grill Royal eine besondere Location mit einem besonderen Profil ist. Viele denken an Fleisch, an die Steaks oder an das menschliche Fleisch, das hier zu sehen ist. Aber was ist das Wein-Profil vom Grill Royal?*

AK: Ich glaube, dieses Profil ist klassisch, aber auch cool.

SP: *Ist nicht eigentlich die Art und Weise des Weinkonsums im Grill Royal das Besondere und nicht die Vielfalt der Weinkarte?*

AK: Das stimmt, aber es ist erstaunlich, wie sehr unsere Weinkarte den alten Weinkarten vom Anfang des 20. Jahrhunderts wie beispielsweise der des Hotel Adlon ähnelt. Klassische Weine machen auch besonders glücklich.

SP: *Auch wenn es hier unkompliziert ist, läuft trotzdem keine Musik, es ist keine Party?*

ME: Nein, es ist ein Restaurant! Ein eigenes Kontinuum, bei dem es um Essen und Weine geht. Manche Leute kommen in den Grill und bleiben sechs Stunden. Wenn ein Kinofilm nicht gut ist, gehe ich nach dreißig Minuten raus.

Sechs Stunden sind ja drei oder vier Kinofilme. Die Zeit verfliegt hier. Man verkauft keine guten Weine, wenn im Hintergrund Musik läuft.

SP: *Saß jemals ein Gast im Grill Royal mit einem Glas Wein vor sich und einem Kopfhörer auf dem Kopf?*

ME: Nein! Wenn du Musik hörst, dann ist der Song nach drei Minuten zu Ende, und du weißt, wie lange du sitzt. Du sollst aber die Zeit komplett vergessen. Du kannst herumwandern, an die Bar, in den Raucherraum, und dann gehst du, wann du möchtest.

SP: *Wenn Du heute Abend Gast im Grill Royal sein würdest, was würdest Du trinken?*

ME: Einen weißen Bourgogne, am liebsten eine tolle Lage aus dem Mersault, und bloß nicht zu kalt! Stephan zieht da meistens mit, Boris mag lieber Amarone. Der erzählt immer noch von dem wunderschönen Abend mit den „It was just the Amarone" singenden Pet Shop Boys.

SP: *Wie habt Ihr die fantastischen Produkte entdeckt? Ich meine nicht nur den Wein, sondern auch das Fleisch von lokalen Anbietern?*

ME: Wir haben uns natürlich umgehört, aber am Ende finden auch eine ganze Menge Dinge den Weg zu einem. Man fährt raus und guckt sich einen Bauernhof an. Dabei merkten wir, dass wir zu Beginn gar nicht viel über Fleisch wussten. Wir haben zum Beispiel gelernt, dass wenn das Tier, zum Beispiel draußen in der Uckermark, eine Vielzahl von verschiedenen Pflanzen frisst statt nur einer Sorte Gras, ist das Fleisch bissfest und kriegt einen wahnsinnig guten Geschmack, der tiefer und grüner ist. Man kann sich entscheiden, ob man ein butterweiches Fleisch essen will oder eines mit solch einem Geschmack.

SP: *Die Parallele zum Wein ist da ganz offensichtlich. Es gibt fruchtbetonte, leicht verständliche Weine und andere, die viel Charakter haben, aber nicht so charmant sind. Was hat sich in den letzten zehn Jahren in puncto Wein im Grill Royal geändert?*

AK: Wir sind viel professioneller geworden.

ME: Ihr seid viel lockerer geworden!

AK: Am Anfang bestand die Weinkarte aus einer DIN-A4-Seite für Weißweine und einer DIN-A4-Seite für Rotweine. Jetzt stehen über 1800 Weine auf ihr.

SP: *Wie ist es für Dich, wenn der Laden pickepacke voll ist, zum Beispiel während der Berlinale, wenn hier die Hölle los ist? Jeder Gast hält sich für wichtiger als der andere, jede Schönheit glaubt, die Schönste im Restaurant zu sein.*

AK: Super! Das ist die beste Zeit, man wird gefordert, aber es macht auch tierischen Spaß.

SP: *Was sind die spannendsten Weine, die momentan auf der Karte stehen?*

AK: Auf jeden Fall die großen Weißweine von Niepoort & Kettern, weil sie komplett anders schmecken als alle anderen Weine, die man von der Mosel kennt. Bei den Rotweinen der 1964er Barolo von Bersano und auch alte Burgunder, obwohl alle sagen, dass man sie jung trinken soll. Burgund ist inzwischen eines der ganz großen Themen.

ME: Es ist ein Lebensthema, das Lebensthema für den Grill Royal!

SP: *Und wie sieht es beim Champagner aus?*

AK: Bei Champagner Egly-Ouriet und auch, aber der ist eigentlich unbezahlbar, der Clos d'Ambonnay von Krug.

ME: Oh ja ...

SP: *Wie laufen die edelsüßen Weine im Grill Royal?*

AK: Sie gehen ganz gut, am besten glasweise. Zum Beispiel eine gute Riesling-Auslese zum Käse oder manchmal auch eine Flasche Château d'Yquem.

SP: *Verhalten sich junge Gäste in Sachen Wein anders als ältere Gäste?*

AK: Die jungen Gäste sind offener, sie lassen sich mehr beraten und sie lassen sich auf Weine ein, die sie nicht kennen. Sie experimentieren und sagen auch, wenn ihnen ein Wein nicht gefällt.

SP: *Stell Dir vor, Du hast frei und ich lade Dich in den Grill Royal ein. Dann* sage ich, dass Geld keine Rolle spielt. Welche Flasche bestellst Du? Es darf ruhig dekadent sein.

AK: Das bin ich aber nicht! Ein Château Rayas 1994 von Châteauneuf-du-Pape.

SP: *Das ist eine sehr gute Wahl. Leider kann ich Dich heute Abend nicht in den Grill Royal einladen. Aber wenn ich das nächste Mal hier zum Abendessen bin, werde ich diesen Wein bestellen.*

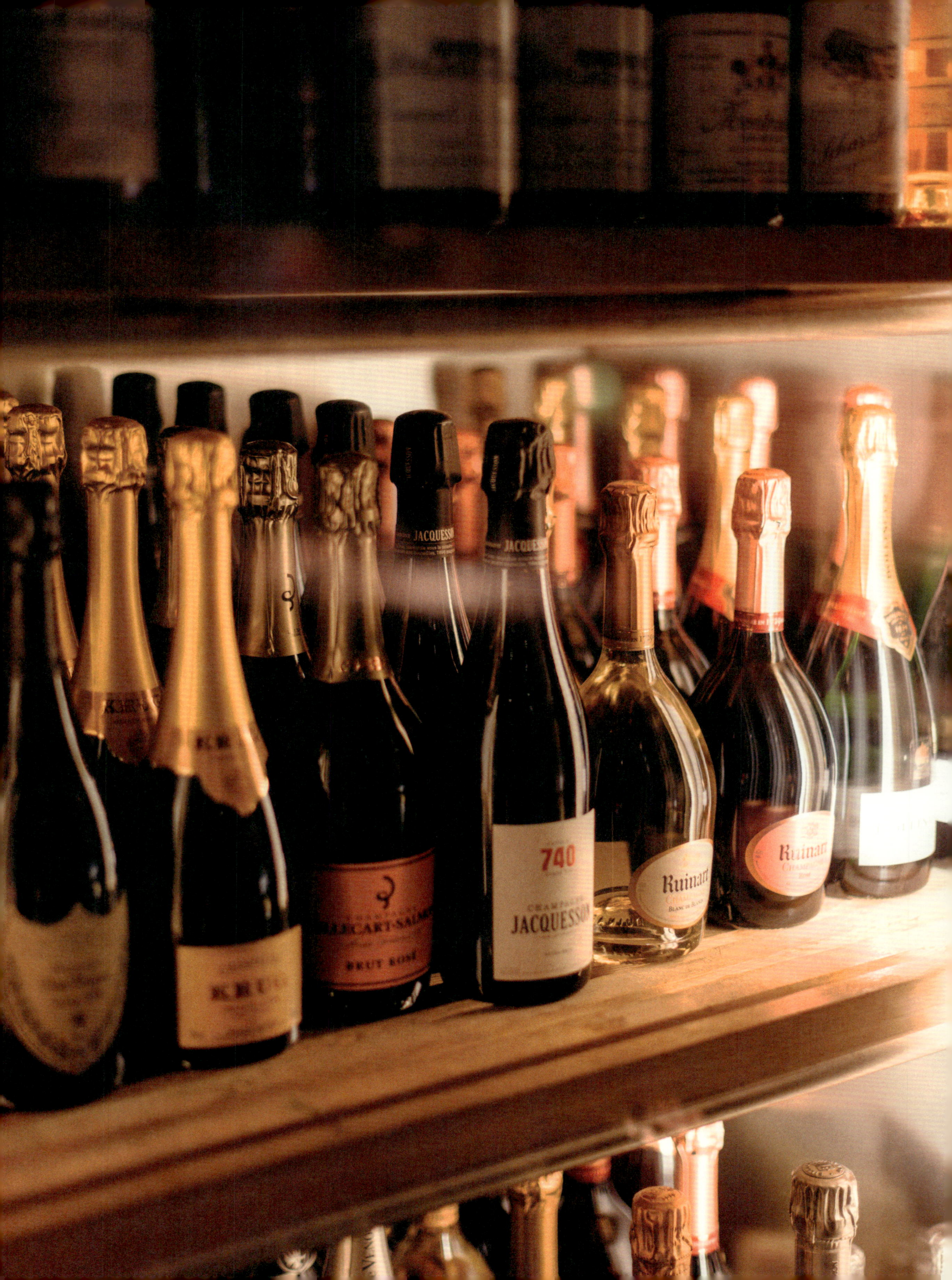

A Conversation About Wine

with Andrea Kauk and Moritz Estermann

Stuart Pigott

It's 5 p.m. on a Wednesday afternoon when I enter the Grill Royal restaurant in search of the truth about wine. It's quiet still, the calm before the evening storm. Moritz Estermann apologizes that we have to wait for the restaurant's long-time sommelière, Andrea Kauk, who's still in a meeting with the service staff. He leads me backstage, where I've never been before, although I've been going to the Grill Royal since shortly after it opened its doors in 2007. We take a seat in a corner, start to talk, and soon Andrea joins us.

STUART PIGOTT (SP): *We were just in Grill Royal's wine cellar, where I saw sober wooden shelves and a lot of bottles, most of them standing. That's how I do it too, because scientists have proven that it doesn't matter if wine is stored standing or lying on its side.*

MORITZ ESTERMANN (ME): We're not a museum, and so all the bottles have to be sold; even the expensive wines turn around in one and a half, at the very most two years. None of the bottles stay with us longer than that. We have wines that we let mature, the ones we say are special, and that we can't get near. But these bottles aren't here.

SP: *What's considered expensive for a wine here at Grill Royal?*

ANDREA KAUK (AK): Well, it's the great Bordeaux and Burgundy wines that are really expensive, of course.

SP: *A four-figure price?*

ME: Yes, that too.

SP: *Who drinks a bottle of wine at Grill Royal for a four-figure price?*

AK: Different kinds of people. The bottles often cost them less here than in a wine store. We have guests who value this and say "I'll buy it!" Last year, we had a wonderful table here at the front. They were drinking Clos du Mesnil champagne by Krug and a 1990 Château Latour from Bordeaux. Cautiously, the waiter asked them the reason, and the answer was: "We're drinking to my divorce ..."

SP: *Here at the Grill Royal, some things add up quickly, not only on the bill. Sometimes I come here and say to myself: "I'm only going to drink white wine to-night, and not go to bed too late!" But deep down I know that there will be another bottle of red wine, and then a few drinks at the bar! What would be a good price for a bottle of wine at Grill Royal?*

AK: A good price for a red wine would be under 40 Euros, for instance a simple German Pinot Noir, or our least expensive wine, from Tasca d'Almerita in Sicily.

SP: *And the whites? What would be a good bargain at Grill Royal?*

AK: We have a wine from the Schlossgut Diel in the lower Nahe region that's inexpensive and very good—we work with them directly. And the Pinot Gris from Fritz Keller in Baden is certainly a very solid thing, and perfect in terms of the price-quality ratio.

SP: *The examples already indicate the broad range of Grill Royal's wine program. People tend to think that there are only expensive Bordeaux wines and prestige champagnes here. But that's not the case at all.*

AK: Burgundy has been in our hearts for many years already. If you love wine, and drink quite a bit, then you just tend to get more out of certain types of grapes, such as the Pinot Noir. And many people tolerate them better.

SP: *Here at the Grill Royal, it's often happened that a Pinot Noir has slipped lightly down my throat, occasionally at a fairly dangerous speed.*

AK: That's true. As for me, I like the wines from Germany. That was a major discovery for us ten years ago: to learn how good the German wines really were, or the Austrian wines. We were also fascinated to learn that there were high-quality wines coming from very distant regions, for instance Canada. But because we're a classic restaurant, we don't carry very many Spanish wines. The focus is more on France and Germany.

SP: *Champagne figures strongly in my first memories of Grill Royal.*

AK: As a sommelière, I know that a champagne high is something very special. We had some large celebrations here, where champagne was served from six- and nine-liter bottles. The guests didn't want to give the empty bottles back: "No, no, that's my baby!" This is typical for champagne, that it makes people so happy.

SP: *I think it's great that you can leave Grill Royal with a baby, I mean, a baby you didn't bring with you. Great emotions are part and parcel of a great restaurant. For me, good gastronomy is always theatrical, but Grill Royal was deliberately designed as a stage, wasn't it?*

ME: Yes, we wanted to turn it into a place for people who are communicative, who can let themselves go. In the classical gourmet cuisine of the 1980s and 1990s, the guest was sentenced to complete passivity. All he or she could say was "it's great." They weren't allowed to ask if a window could be opened or if the waiter could please bring the salt. We wanted to liberate the good products and wines from this. You can turn up at Grill Royal without a reservation and without being dressed fancily and order oysters and a bottle of Krug champagne. That's the freedom we offer here.

SP: *Many people know that Grill Royal is a special place with a special image. Many think of meat, of steaks and of the human flesh that can be seen here. But what's Grill Royal's wine image?*

AK: I believe it's classic, but also cool.

SP: *But the special thing at the Grill Royal is the way wine is consumed, isn't it—and not the variety of the wine list?*

AK: That's true, but it's amazing how similar our wine list is to the old lists from the early twentieth century, for instance at the Hotel Adlon. Classic wines make people especially happy.

SP: *Even though the atmosphere is uncomplicated here, you still don't play music, so it's not a party?*

ME: No, it's a restaurant! It forms its own continuum, and it's all about food and wine. Some people come to the Grill Royal and stay for six hours. If I don't like a movie, I leave after half an hour. Six hours are three of four movies. Time flies here. You don't sell good wine when there's music playing in the background.

SP: *Have you ever had a guest in the Grill Royal who sat with a glass of wine in front of them while wearing headphones?*

ME: No! When you listen to music, the song is over after three minutes, and so you know how long you've been sitting there. But you're supposed to forget time completely. You can wander around, to the bar, the smokers' room, and you can leave when you wish.

SP: *If you were a guest this evening at Grill Royal, what would you drink?*

ME: A white Bourgogne, preferably from a great area in Mersault, and not too cold! Stephan usually plays along, but Boris prefers Amarone. He still tells the story of the wonderful evening with the Pet Shop Boys singing "It was just the Amarone."

SP: *How did you discover all these fantastic products? I don't only mean the wine, but also the locally produced meats?*

ME: We definitely asked around, but in the end, a lot of things really just came to us. And then we traveled to have a look at the farm in question. The first thing we realized is that we didn't know a lot about meat in the beginning. We learned, for instance, that when an animal, as is the case out in the Uckermark, eats a large number of different plants instead of only one kind of grass, then the meat is firm to the bite and takes on a really good taste that's deeper, greener. You can decide if you want it very tender, or if you prefer to have this other taste.

SP: *The parallels to wine are obvious. There are fruity, light-bodied wines, and others with a lot of character that are not quite as charming. What has changed over the past several years at Grill Royal in terms of wine?*

AK: We've become much more professional.

ME: You've gotten far more relaxed!

AK: In the beginning, the wine list consisted of an A4-sized page for white wines and another for reds. Now we have over 1,800 kinds.

SP: *How is it for you when the place is bursting at the seams, for instance during the Berlinale, when all hell breaks loose? Every guest thinks they're more important than the next, every beauty thinks she's the fairest in the land.*

AK: Great! That's the best time, it's a challenge, but it's an incredible amount of fun.

SP: *What are the most interesting wines currently on the list?*

AK: Definitely the great white wines from Niepoort & Kettern, because they taste completely different from every other wine we know from the Mosel. Among the red wines, the 1964 Barolo from Bersano and a few old Burgundies as well, although everyone says you have to drink them young. Burgundy has turned out to be a major theme.

ME: It's a life theme, the life theme for Grill Royal!

SP: *And what about champagne?*

AK: Among the champagnes there's Egly-Ouriet, and also Clos d'Ambonnay from Krug, but it's unaffordable.

ME: Oh yes ...

SP: *How do the sweet wines do at Grill Royal?*

AK: They sell pretty well, particularly by the glass. For example a good Riesling Auslese (selection) with cheese, or sometimes a bottle of Château d'Yquem.

SP: *Do the younger guests behave differently than others in regards to wine?*

AK: The younger guests are more open, they tend to accept advice, and they'll try a wine they don't know. They experiment, and they have no problem saying when they don't like a wine.

SP: *Imagine you have some time off and I invite you to the Grill Royal. And then I say that money's no object. What bottle would you order? It's OK if it's decadent.*

AK: But I'm not! A Château Rayas 1994 from Châteauneuf-du-Pape.

SP: *That's a very good choice. Unfortunately, I can't invite you to Grill Royal this evening. But the next time I'm here for dinner, that's the wine I'll order.*

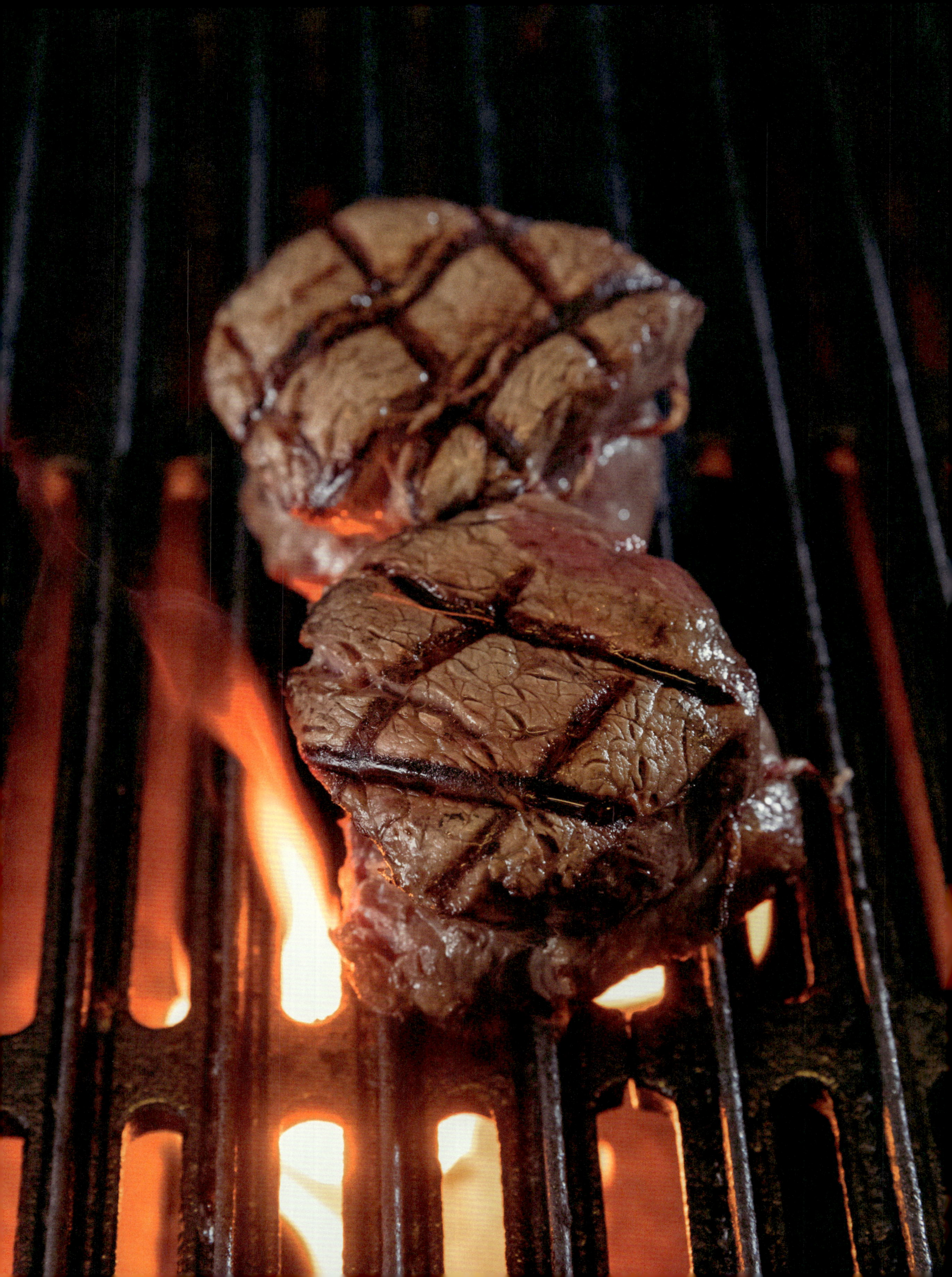

Fleisch – mehr als nur ein Stück Lebenskraft

Thomas Vilgis

Fleisch – von der Weide in die Küche

Ganz abgesehen von vielen Diskussionen um Tierwohl, Ethik und Veganismus, Kochtechniken und Gemüsevielfalt, bleibt Fleisch ein wesentliches „Genussmittel" in der Gastronomie. Fleisch verdient weit mehr Aufmerksamkeit als ihm in gedankenlosen Fressorgien am einen oder ideologischen Diskussionen am anderen Ende entgegengebracht wird. Weitab von solchen Fragen ist Fleisch ein einzigartig strukturiertes „Biomaterial". Sein Aufbau und seine Struktur lassen aus einer ganz nüchternen, naturwissenschaftlichen Sichtweise selbst abgebrühte Gourmets vor Ehrfurcht erstarren. In der Welt der Mikro- und Nanometer zählen ausschließlich klare physikalisch-chemische Gesetze. Grund genug für eine sanfte Annäherung an tief zwischen Proteinstrukturen verborgene biophysikalische Geheimnisse, wie sie sich beim einfachen Braten (Abb. 1) bereits offenbaren.

Bevor das Fleisch in die Küche kommt, war es Teil eines lebenden Tieres. Je nach zugewiesener biologischer Aufgabe sind vollkommen verschiedene Stücke für den Verzehr verfügbar: schieres Muskelfleisch, etwa Herz oder Rücken, oder mit Bindegewebe durchwachsene Stücke aus Bein und Schulter. Allein diese sichtbaren Unterschiede in Farbe, „Durchwachsenheit" oder Gewebestruktur lassen sich auf die unterschiedlichen Anforderungen zurückführen. Muskelfleisch, etwa in der Lende, ist für das Feintuning der Bewegungen der Wirbelsäule zuständig, der Bindegewebsanteil ist gering. Auf den Muskeln der Beine und Schultern ruht das ganze Gewicht des Tieres. Diese Muskeln sind hohen Belastungen ausgesetzt, weshalb ein hoher Bindegewebsanteil (Sehnen) eingelagert wird; die Kollagenfasern verfügen über höchste Zug- und Reißfestigkeit. Sie sind daher schwer (bis gar nicht) zu kauen – und erfordern, anders als Steaks, längere Garzeiten, etwa durch Schmoren.

Vom Fett ganz zu schweigen: Das intramuskuläre Fett (IMF) ist ein wesentlicher „Genussparameter". Bereits mit dem bloßen Auge ist der sensorische Unterschied eines stark marmorierten Stückes japanischen Wagyūs und einer fettarmen Rinderlende zu erkennen. Aber was bedeuten diese sichtbaren Fakten konkret? Das Ziel dieses Beitrags ist, Fleisch objektiver zu verstehen. Dazu ist es notwendig, tief in das Fleisch hineinzublicken, denn nur auf molekularer Ebene lassen sich Fakten erkennen, ohne in Spekulationen zu verfallen oder unklare Aussagen zu treffen.

Vom Muskel zum Fleisch

Bereits die Vorgeschichte des gewählten Stück Fleisches ist von großer Relevanz und zwar weitab von leicht zu beantwortenden Fragen etwa nach Zucht, Vorleben, Rasse oder Fütterung. Fleisch war zu Lebzeiten des Tieres ein aktiver Muskel und wurde während eines langwierigen und komplizierten Prozesses zum gereiften Stück Fleisch. Der streng hierarchische Aufbau von Muskelfleisch, vereinfacht in Abb. 2 dargestellt, ermöglicht das Zusammenspiel vielzähliger Proteine während der Bewegung. Jeder Muskel setzt sich aus Muskelfaserbündeln zusammen, diese wiederum aus Muskelfasern. Muskelfaserbündel und Muskelfasern sind jeweils von einer Bindegewebsschicht umgeben. Muskelfasern bestehen aus Myofibrillen. Dann erst, bei wenigen Mikrometern Länge, lassen sich die fibrillären Proteine Aktin und Myosin „erkennen".

Fleisch enthält etwa 75 Prozent Wasser und 20 Prozent Proteine. Diese lassen sich grob in drei Gruppen unterteilen: Den größten Anteil bestreiten mit etwa 50–60 Prozent die myofibrillären Proteine, die das Grundgerüst des Muskels bilden. Die zweitgrößte Gruppe von Proteinen ist größtenteils wasserlöslich und befindet sich im Sarkoplasma, in der Membran, im Inhalt der Muskelzellen, aber auch im farbgebenden Myoglobin sowie in einer Vielzahl von Enzymen, die zum Beispiel Transport- oder Reparaturaufgaben im lebenden Muskel erfüllen. Die Bindegewebsproteine, zu denen in erster Linie das in Form einer Tripelhelix vorliegende Kollagen gehört, sind in dieser nativen Form unlöslich. Das Wasser (die Fleischsäfte) befindet sich größtenteils in den intermyofibrillären Zwischenräumen, ein geringer Anteil (unter 10 Prozent) ist direkt mit den Proteinen assoziiert und daher sehr stark gebunden.

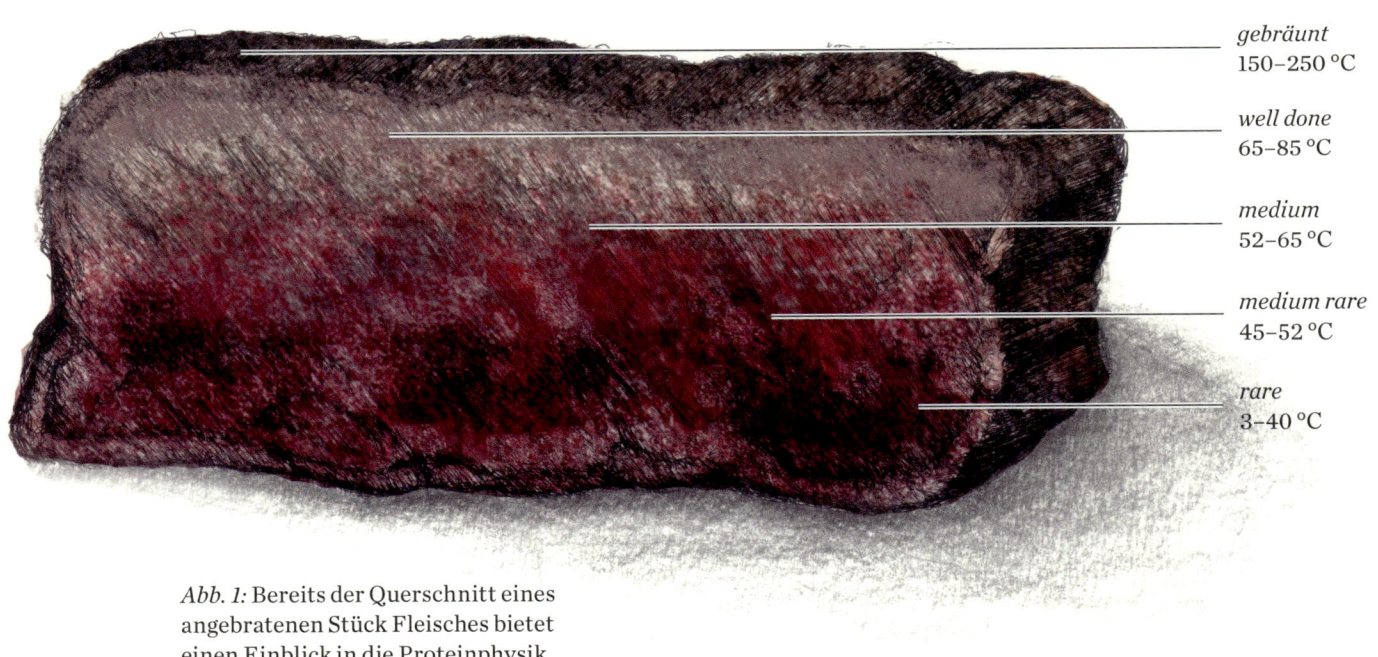

gebräunt
150–250 °C

well done
65–85 °C

medium
52–65 °C

medium rare
45–52 °C

rare
3–40 °C

Abb. 1: Bereits der Querschnitt eines angebratenen Stück Fleisches bietet einen Einblick in die Proteinphysik und die Welt der Aromen.

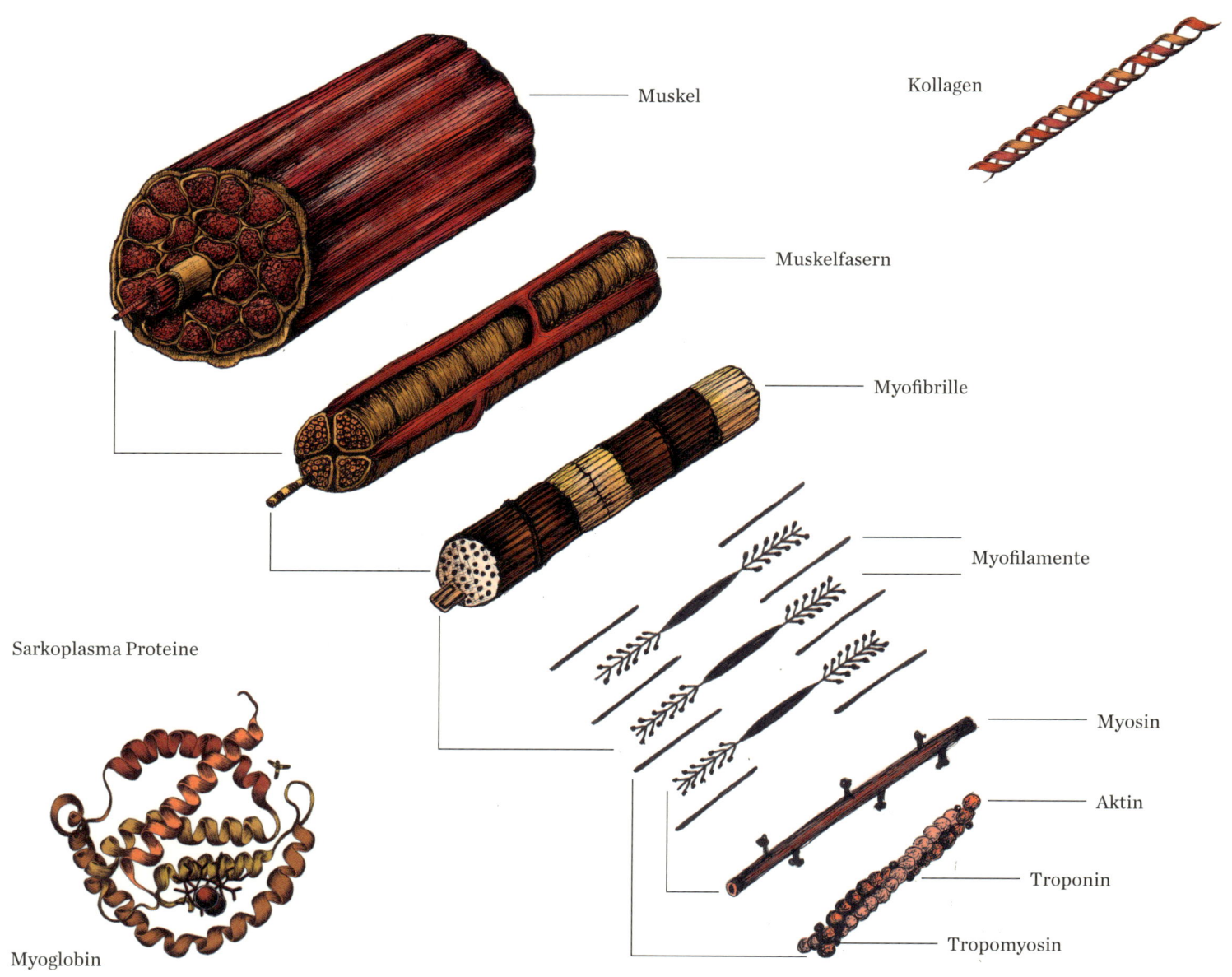

Muskel

Kollagen

Muskelfasern

Myofibrille

Myofilamente

Sarkoplasma Proteine

Myosin

Aktin

Troponin

Myoglobin

Tropomyosin

Abb. 2: Die Hierarchie der Proteine im Muskelfleisch
Im makroskopisch sichtbaren Bereich erkennt man Muskeln auf der Längenskala von 1 Zentimeter;
einzelne Muskelfasern haben die typische Größe von 1 Millimeter, ummantelt von einer dünnen,
aber stabilen Kollagenschicht. Strukturierte mikrometerlange Myofilamente (einzelne Proteine)
regeln das Geschehen auf Nanometerskalen. Diese Muskelzellen sind von der Zellmembran umgeben.
Das Zusammenspiel der Proteine Aktin, Myosin, Tropomyosin und Troponin in den Myofilamenten
bildet die Grundeinheit des Bewegungsapparats im lebenden Muskel.

Prozesse nach der Schlachtung

Eine wichtige Rolle für den Geschmack des Fleisches, insbesondere nach dem Reifen, spielt das Schaltmolekül Adenosintriphosphat (ATP), ein vierfach geladenes Molekül (Abb. 3), denn es speist und schaltet die Energie der Verschiebung in den Muskelfilamenten ein. Dadurch wird Muskelkontraktion und -entspannung überhaupt erst möglich. ATP ist also ein natürliches Phosphat, das aus einer organischen Adeningruppe, dem Zucker namens Ribose, und dem ionischen Teil, der Triphosphorsäure, besteht.

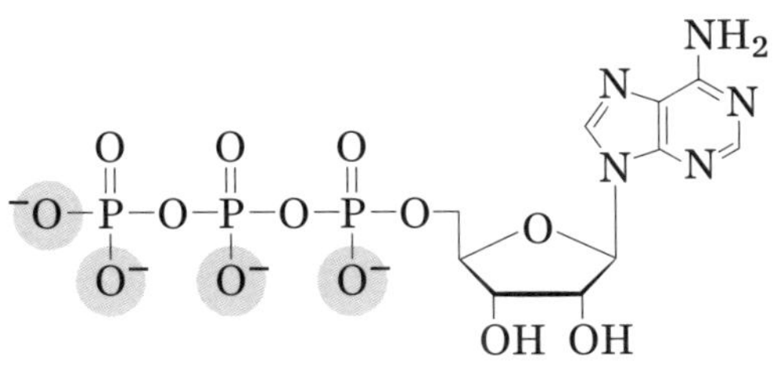

Abb. 3: Die Struktur des Adenosintriphosphat (ATP). Die Triphosphorsäure (P = Phosphor, O = Sauerstoff, N = Stickstoff, H = Wasserstoff) ist vierfach (!) elektrisch geladen.

Die enzymatische Spaltung des ATP setzt dabei entsprechende Konzentrationen von dreifach geladenen Monophosphationen frei (Abb. 4). Es entsteht beim ATP-Zerfall auf ganz natürliche Weise eine hohe Konzentration von dreifach geladenen Monophosphatonen. Diese „harte Chemie" ist beileibe keine blanke Theorie, denn die Überbleibsel des ATP sind für die Intensität des herzhaften Fleischgeschmacks, umami, für alle Fleischzubereitungen – egal ob Tatar, kurzgebraten oder geschmort – von entscheidender Bedeutung. Doch dazu später mehr.

Nach dem Schlachten der Tiere wird die Sauerstoffzufuhr im Muskel unterbunden, und ATP baut sich ab, ohne erneuert zu werden. Das hat, stark vereinfacht gesprochen, mehrere Konsequenzen: Nach dem Ab-

ATP: Ein Grundbaustein für die „Geschmackschemie"

Die Triphosphorsäure ist unter physiologischen Bedingungen vierfach negativ geladen. Diese ungewöhnlich hohe negative Ladung tritt während der Muskelbewegung mit den zweifach positiven Calciumionen Ca2+ in eine Wechselwirkung. Sie kann diese binden, behält dabei aber eine zweifache negative Ladung. Gleichzeitig korreliert das ATP mit den geladenen Aminosäuren des Myosins und kann an entsprechende Aminosäuren des das Aktin umgebenden Tropomyosins und des Aktins in Interaktion treten und somit die Verschiebung von Myosin gegenüber dem Aktin als „Elementarschritt" der Muskelkontraktion bewirken. Dazu wird ATP sukzessive in Adenosindiphosphat (ADP) und Adenomonophosphat (AMP) unter Abspaltung je einer Phosphatgruppe umgewandelt. Durch die sich dabei abschwächende Ladung ändert sich die Wirkungsweise: Myosin kann gebunden werden, Aktin und Myosin übertragen während der Bindungsphase Muskelkräfte und können durch die Bindung eines neuen ATPs an den Myosinkopf den Vorgang aufs Neue in Gang bringen: Muskelarbeit ist nur mit ATP und dessen enzymatischer Hydrolyse unter Energiefreisetzung möglich.

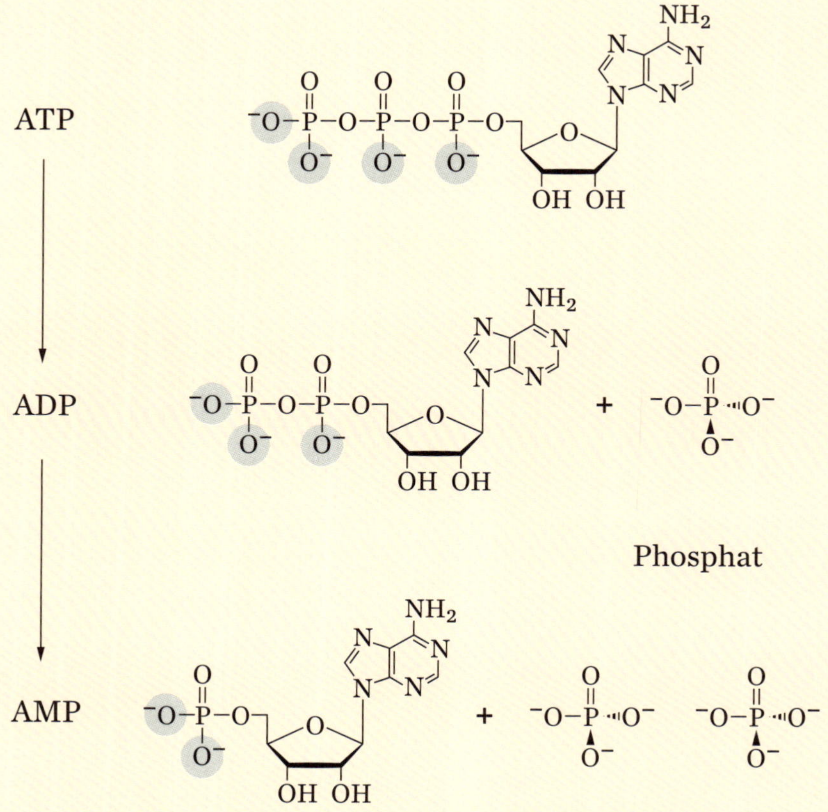

Abb. 4:
Der Abbau des ATP zu ADP und AMP setzt dreifach geladenes Monophosphat frei, während die Ladung von ADP und AMP abnimmt. Aus AMP werden letztendlich enzymatisch die „Geschmacksverstärker" Inosinmonophosphat (IMP) und Guanosinmonophosphat (GMP) erzeugt.

bau des hoch geladenen ATP fehlen entsprechende Abstoßungskräfte, um Aktin und Myosinköpfchen auf Abstand zu halten (Abb. 5). Folglich bilden Aktin und Myosin nach und nach stark gebundene, starre, unauflösbare Komplexe: Die Totenstarre tritt ein. Auch während der Fleischreifung können die stark gebundenen Aktin-Myosin-Komplexe nicht mehr gelöst werden. Die dabei ablaufenden biophysikalischen Prozesse enzymatischer Natur, die Fleisch zarter machen, betreffen nicht den Aktin-Myosin-Komplex, sondern die Veränderung von Proteinen in der Muskelzelle.

ATP bewirkt die Freischaltung von Bindestellen, an die sich das Myosinköpfchen kurzzeitig haften und die Muskelbewegung bewirken kann. Myosin selbst besteht im Wesentlichen aus zwei Helices, die wiederum zu Helices mit größerer Windungslänge gewunden sind. Sie enden in den Myosinköpfchen.

Ein Grundverständnis der postmortalen Vorgänge während der Transformation von aktivem Muskel zu Fleisch ist für das Verständnis des Wurstens von großer Bedeutung. In Abb. 5 sind sie daher noch einmal grob zusammenfasst.

Die Umwandlung des Glykogens zu Milchsäure senkt den pH-Wert des Fleisches auf etwa 5. Dies verändert nicht nur den Geschmack von süßlich in Richtung sauer, sondern hat direkte Auswirkungen auf die Struktur von Proteinen. Deren Bausteine, die Aminosäuren, sind sogenannte Zwitterionen, deren Ladung vom pH-Wert abhängt. Säure wird über Protonen, also positive Ladungen („Wasserstoffkerne") vermittelt. Diese positiven Ladungen schirmen negativ geladene Aminosäuren ab und „neutralisieren" sie. Negative OH-Gruppen überwiegen im alkalischen, basischen Zustand (pH geringer als 7) und schwächen positiv geladene Aminosäuren ab. Daher gibt es für die meisten Proteine einen bestimmten pH-Wert, bei dem alle Ladungen des Proteins „neutralisiert" werden. Das Protein hat an diesem „isoelektrischen Punkt" quasi die Gesamtladung Null und ist elektrisch neutral. Dabei ist der Zusammenhalt der Proteingestalt am schwächsten: Sie gibt ihre native Gestalt auf und denaturiert teilweise. Dies gilt auch für das Myosin, dessen isoelektrischer Punkt etwa bei pH-Wert 5 liegt. Die Myosinköpfchen denaturieren partiell, aber der feste Aktin-Myosin-Komplex bleibt bestehen.

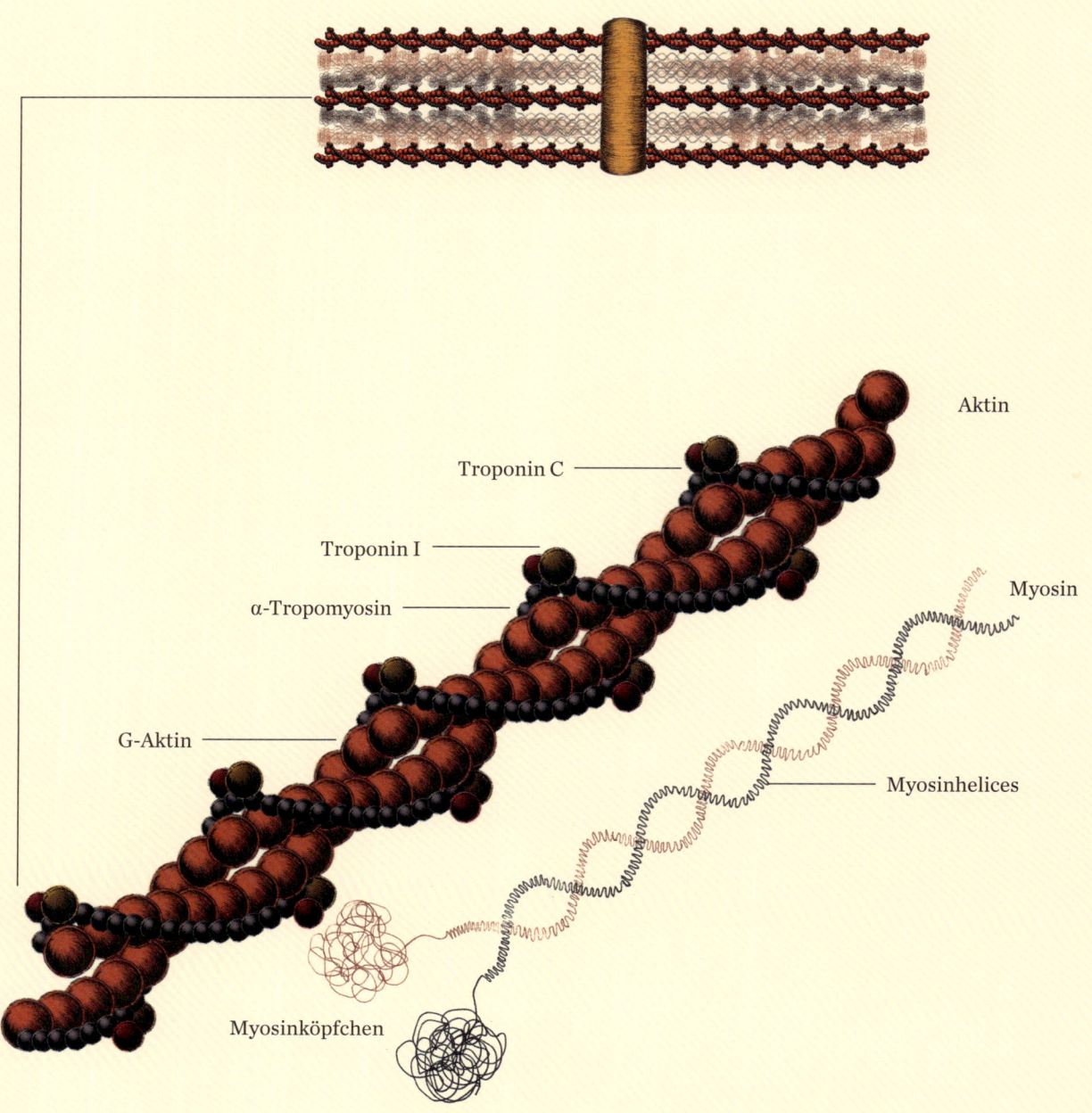

Aktin

Troponin C

Troponin I

α-Tropomyosin

Myosin

G-Aktin

Myosinhelices

Myosinköpfchen

Abb. 5: Stark vereinfachte Darstellung des Aktin-Myosinkomplexes in der Myofibrille einer Muskelzelle
Fibrilläres Aktin besteht aus helixförmig aneinandergereihten globulären F-Aktin Proteinen
(hellgraue Kugeln), die von α-Tropomyosin umgeben sind.

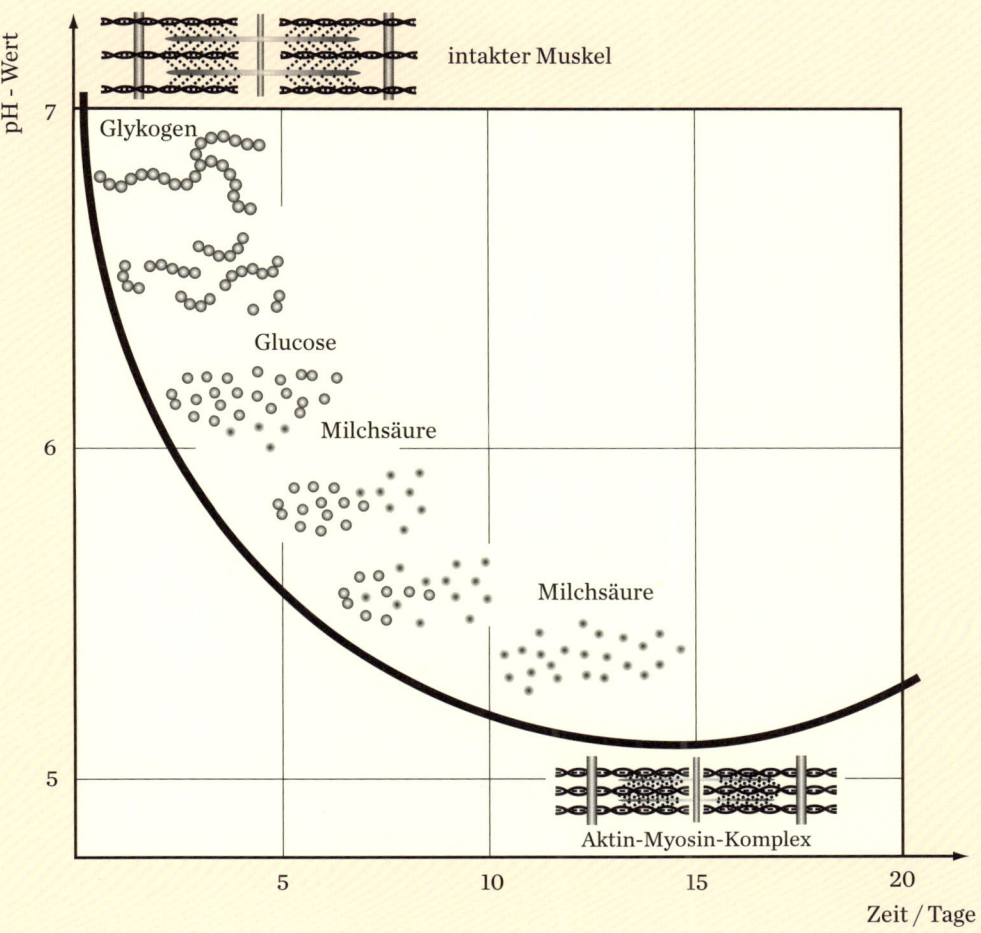

Abb. 6: Vereinfachte Darstellung der postmortalen Vorgänge
Zum Zeitpunkt des Schlachtens sind die Muskeln intakt, ATP ist vorhanden, ebenso wie das
Speicherkohlenhydrat Glykogen („tierische Stärke"). Glykogen wird enzymatisch zu Glucose
gespalten, das wiederum von Milchsäurebakterien anaerob zu Milchsäure fermentiert, sodass
der pH-Wert sinkt. ATP baut sich rasch ab, stark gebundene Aktin-Myosin-Komplexe bilden
sich vollständig aus.

Fleisch: thermische Veränderungen von Biomolekülen

Das thermische Verhalten der einzelnen Proteinklassen ist für das Verständnis der molekularen Vorgänge von immanenter Bedeutung. Die verschiedenen Proteine denaturieren, sprich „kochen", bei unterschiedlichen Temperaturen im Bereich von 48 °C bis 75 °C. Die einzelnen „Kugeln" im (fibrillären) Aktin sind G-Aktin, also globuläre Proteine. Perfektes Garen wird durch das Verändern der genau „richtigen" Proteine erreicht.

Je nach nativer Gestalt des Proteins hat eine Temperaturerhöhung unterschiedliche Auswirkungen: Bei globulären Proteinen, wie sie zum Beispiel im Sarkoplasma vorkommen, führt sie zur Entfaltung und damit zu einer Exposition hydrophober Aminosäuren. Diese können aggregieren und unter günstigen Umständen ein Gel mit hoher Wasserbindung bilden. Auch extrahiertes Myosin bildet unter Erhitzung Gele. Bei gestreckten Molekülen wie dem Kollagen kann der durch die Erwärmung hervorgerufene Wegfall von stabilisierenden Wasserstoffbrückenbindungen aber auch dazu führen, dass das Molekül sich aus entropischen Gründen, wie von gestreckten Polymerkonformationen bekannt, zusammenzieht. Daher schrumpft Kollagen in einem ersten Schritt der Denaturierung, bevor es bei höheren Temperaturen und längeren Zeiten in Lösung geht und damit zu Gelatine wird.

Mit Hilfe der dynamischen Differenzkalorimetrie (DSC für *Differential Scanning Calorimetry*) ist es möglich, die Denaturierungsprozesse im Labor zu verfolgen, wie es in Abb. 7 zu erkennen ist. Wird die Temperatur langsam erhöht, beginnt die Denaturierung der Proteine. Dies „kostet" Energie, die über Wärmeströme in empfindlichen Kalorimetern gemessen werden kann. Sie zeigen sich in charakteristischen „Vertiefungen".

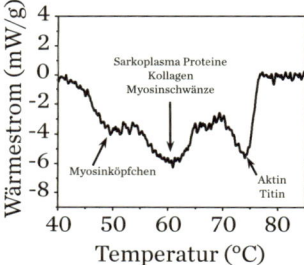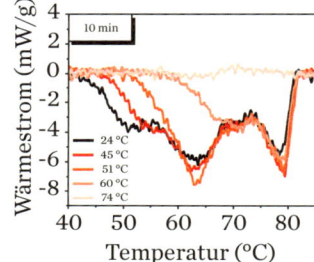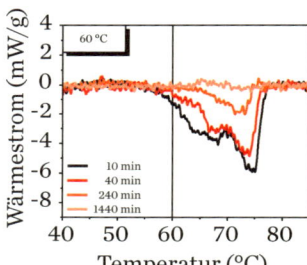

Abb. 7: Proteindenaturierung bei Schweinefleisch
a) Bei Temperaturerhöhung zeigen sich verschiedene „Vertiefungen" (Peaks), die durch den zugehörigen Energieverbrauch ausgelöst werden. Die Proteingruppen sind an den entsprechenden Peaks genannt. b) Mit zunehmender Temperatur einer Vorgarung (z. B. Sous-vide) müssen immer weniger Proteintypen denaturieren. Die Peaks verschwinden daher. c) Auch die Zeit spielt eine große Rolle. Wird das Fleisch bei 60 °C unterschiedlich lang gegart, verschwinden bei langen Zeiten selbst die Peaks, die zu hohen Denaturierungstemperaturen gehören. Die weitverbreitete Ansicht, es spiele keine Rolle, wie lange das Fleisch sous-vide gart, erweist sich daher als grundlegend falsch.

Aufgrund der Vielzahl der vorhandenen Proteine, die teilweise in ähnlichen Temperaturbereichen denaturieren, ist es nicht möglich, diesen Vertiefungen bestimmte Proteine zuzuordnen. Dennoch ergibt sich ein grobes Bild: Zuerst denaturieren die globulären Anteile des Myosins, die sogenannten Myosinköpfchen, bereits bei 48 °C. Um 60 °C liegen die Denaturierungstemperaturen der sarkoplasmischen Proteine und des Kollagens. Auch die helikalen Myosinschwänze entfalten sich in diesem Temperaturbereich. Am temperaturstabilsten sind Aktin und Titin, die erst zwischen 70 °C und 75 °C denaturieren. Selbst das Garen einzelner Proteine wie des Myosins geschieht in verschiedenen Temperaturbereichen, wie es anschaulich in Abb. 8 dargestellt ist.

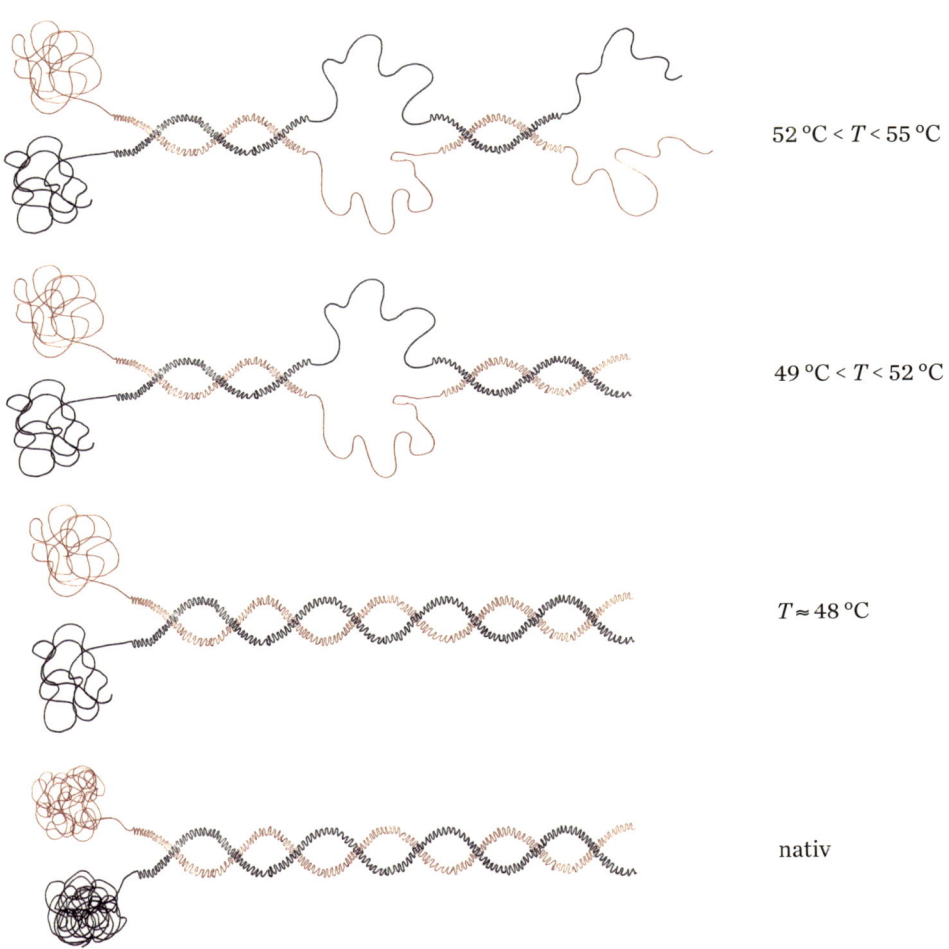

52 °C < T < 55 °C

49 °C < T < 52 °C

$T \approx$ 48 °C

nativ

Abb. 8: Die wichtigsten Denaturierungsstufen eines Myosins
Zunächst denaturieren die Köpfchen, die ihre ursprüngliche Gestalt und ihre angestammte biologische Funktion verlieren. Danach denaturieren die helixförmigen „Schwänze". Die einzelnen Proteine (schwarz und braun dargestellt), sind selbst von verschraubter (helicaler) Struktur, die sich wiederum zu einer „Superhelix" verwinden, deren Entfaltung und Entwindung höhere Energien, also höhere Temperaturen, benötigen.

Dry Aging vs. Nassreifung

Noch vor wenigen Jahrzehnten sprach niemand von „Dry Aging", sondern schlicht von Abhängen oder Reifen. Es war die Methode der Wahl, zartes Rindfleisch mit entsprechend feinen aromatischen Nuancen von Pilzen, einem Hauch Camembert sowie den würzigen Duft zu erhalten. Bereits während der Fleischreifung bilden sich Aroma und Geschmack. Erst mit der Unsitte, einzelne Stücke im Vakuum verpackt „reifen" zu lassen, gewöhnten sich Konsumenten an feuchtes Fleisch mit einer säuerlichen Note, geschuldet der anaeroben Milchsäuregärung unter niedrigen Temperaturen. Dies ist zwar vordergründig ein Vorteil für die Enzymaktivität, allerdings beginnt auch bei niedrigen Temperaturen eine langsame Milchsäuregärung unter anaeroben Bedingungen. Stets vorhandene Milchsäurebakterien bilden aus Zuckern (z. B. aus vorhandenen Glykogen oder Glykoproteinen aus den Zellwänden) Milchsäure und typische Aromaverbindungen. Das Fleisch und der sich langsam im Vakuumbeutel sammelnde Fleischsaft riechen typisch „säuerlich".

Dabei ist jede Nassreifung, auch wenn sie wegen des sinkenden pH-Wertes einen gewissen zartmachenden Effekt hat, ein spürbarer Nachteil beim Braten: Der Wassergehalt im Fleisch ist hoch, die Wasserhaltekapazität des Fleisches zu niedrig. Die Folge ist, dass durch die fortschreitende Temperaturerhöhung und Proteinveränderung während des Garens eine relativ große Menge an Fleischsaft freigegeben wird. Beim Sous-Vide-Garen sammelt er sich im Beutel (und dient bestenfalls der Sauce). Beim Braten in Pfannen, auf Planchas oder Grills, ist das freiwerdende Wasser von Nachteil: Es verdampft. Dabei ist Verdampfungswärme vonnöten, die der Umgebung und der Pfanne fehlt. Die Maillardreaktion, also die Bräunung, verzögert sich, das Fleisch „dämpft", solange Fleischsäfte freigegeben werden.

Beim abgehangenen Fleisch treten diese Probleme nicht auf, da der Wassergehalt des Fleisches in zweierlei Hinsicht minimiert wird: Bei Reifungstemperaturen zwischen 0 °C und 3 °C und einer Luftfeuchtigkeit um 80 Prozent „verdampft" Wasser aus dem Fleisch. Der Wassergehalt sinkt dabei von 75 auf ca. 65–67 Prozent. Beim Nass- oder Vakuumreifen sind lediglich Absenkungen von 1–2 Prozent zu verzeichnen.

Beim Dry Aging stellt sich daher ein niedriger, aber perfekter Wassergehalt ein: Im Fleisch verbleibt lediglich das Wasser (Fleischsaft), das bei herrschenden Temperaturen und Luftfeuchtigkeit verbleiben kann. Das Fleisch ist nach langen Reifezeiten jeweils im „thermodynamischen Gleichgewicht". Der so im Fleisch stärker gebundene Saft ist während des Bratens nur schwer zu verdampfen und bleibt neben dem intramuskulären Fett als ein wichtiger „Zartmacher" bei den Garungen *bleu, english* und *à point* erhalten.

Ganz abgesehen von Geschmack und Aroma ist das Bratverhalten des lange abgehangenen Stücks ausgezeichnet: In der Pfanne brät das Fleisch ohne große Verdampfungsschwaden, die Garung ist über die Wärmeleitfähigkeit der Proteine und des Fettes (unter Berücksichtigung von deren Umwandlungen) gegeben, die Bräunung geschieht rasch und gleichmäßig.

Aus wirtschaftlicher Sicht mag das Wet Aging ein Vorteil sein. Der Gewichtsverlust ist gering. Beim Dry Aging ist zwar der Gewichtsverlust erheblich, aber die positiven Effekte bei der Geschmacks- und Aromabildung überwiegen. Aus den ungesättigten Fettsäuren des intramuskulären Fettes und bei der Reifung freiwerdenden Aminosäuren bilden sich erdige, pilzartige Aromaverbindungen, Fruchtester und nussig-würzig duftende Pyrazine.

Einzelstücke lassen sich mittlerweile auch ohne spezielle Reifeschränke „agen". Mittels Reifebeuteln (sie bestehen aus semipermeablen, nach außen wasserdurchlässigen Schichten) kann Fleisch darin eingeschweißt werden. Das Fleisch „trocknet" dann langsam. Diese Methode ist sehr sicher, es kann sich kein Schimmel von außen bilden, und das stetige Absenken der Wassermenge verhindert eine dramatische Milchsäuregärung.

Im Übrigen eignen sich die semipermeablen Reifebeutel auch für das Herstellen einer Art von „Bündner Fleisch": Stark vakuumiertes, eventuell leicht in Meersalz gepökeltes, schieres Muskelfleisch aus der Lende von Rassen mit wenig intramuskulärem Fett ist nach zwei, drei Wochen „trocken" und entspricht von Textur und Farbe her dem Bündner Fleisch (wenngleich dort die Aromabildung anders abläuft).

Der Geschmack umami: herzhaft, fleischig
Der typische Fleischgeschmack ist von der Grundgeschmacksrichtung „umami" (japanisch für herzhaft, fleischig, wohlschmeckend) geprägt. Tatsächlich lässt sich „umami" sehr anschaulich auf die molekularen Details zurückführen. Umami prägt neben süß, sauer, salzig und bitter das Geschmacksprofil aller Lebensmittel auf der Zunge. Umami wird vor allem durch die Stimulation der Geschmacksknospen mit Glutamat ausgelöst. Glutamat wird eher mit „Geschmacksverstärker" und dem „Chinasyndrom" verbunden und weniger mit exquisitem Fleisch. Allerdings sind die weißen Kriställchen, (Natrium-)Glutamat, das Salz der Glutaminsäure, wiederum eine wichtige (aber wohlweißlich keine essenzielle) Aminosäure und somit fester und reichlicher Bestandteil jedes Proteins, egal ob tierisch oder pflanzlich. Ist die Glutaminsäure in die Proteinkette gebunden, löst sie keinen Geschmacksreiz aus. Wird sie aus dem Protein herausgetrennt und somit frei, triggert sie die Geschmacksknospen und signalisiert umami, eben jenen herzhaften Reiz auf der Zunge, wie er von Sojasaucen, Misopasten oder

lang gesimmerten Brühen und Fonds bekannt ist. All diese Verfahren dienen dazu, Glutaminsäure aus den Proteinen durch Spaltprozesse herauszulösen. Freie Glutaminsäure kommt im Fleisch ebenfalls bereits vor dem Reifen in geringen Mengen vor und sorgt damit für einen Hauch an umami im rohen Fleisch.

Die Glutaminsäure ist nicht der alleinige intensitätsbestimmende Faktor für umami. Vor allem die Abbauprodukte und chemischen Reaktionsprodukte des Muskelschaltmoleküls ATP liefern den eigentlichen Geschmacksverstärker für umami, das Inosinmonophosphat (IMP), das sich nach dem Abbau des ATPs nach dem Schlachten in großen Mengen im Fleisch bildet.

Aus Sicht der Geschmacksphysiologie ist dies mehr als spannend: Glutaminsäure löst direkt umami aus. Wirkt es zusammen mit dem Inosinmonophosphat, verstärkt sich der Umamigeschmack um ein Mehrfaches, wie etwa der japanische Wissenschaftler Kenzo Kurihara es dargestellt hat (Abb. 9).

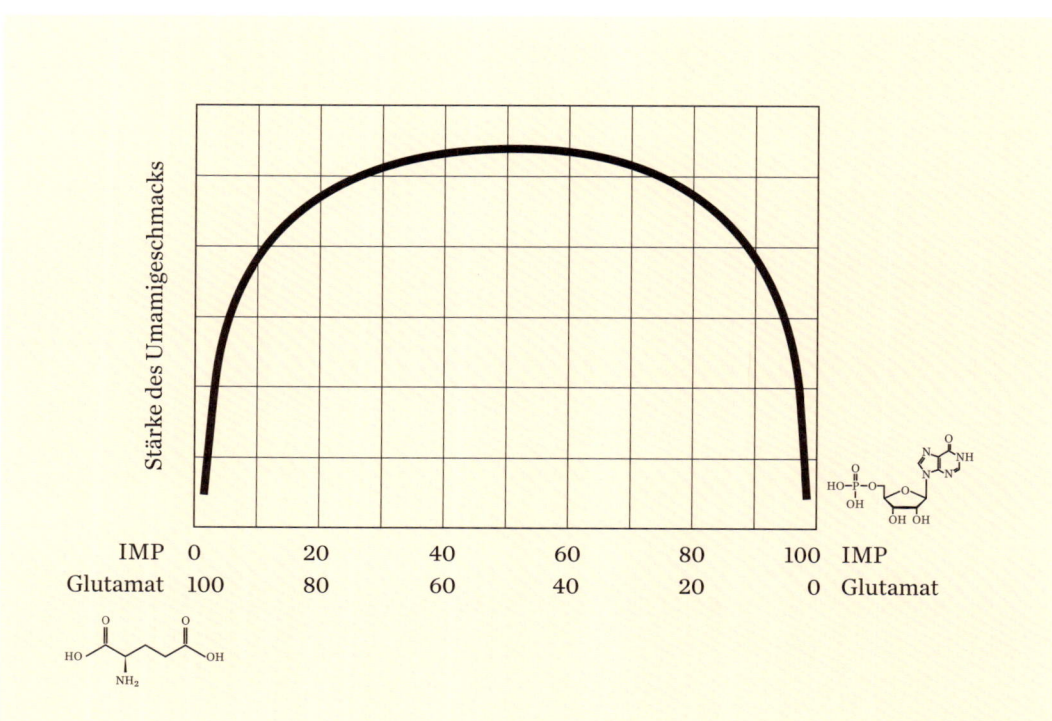

| IMP | 0 | 20 | 40 | 60 | 80 | 100 | IMP |
| Glutamat | 100 | 80 | 60 | 40 | 20 | 0 | Glutamat |

Abb. 9: Verstärkerwirkung und Synergieeffekt von Glutaminsäure (links) und Inosinmonophosphat (auch Inosinat, IMP genannt) verstärken sich. Beide für sich schmecken ein wenig umami, wirken sie aber zusammen, steigt die herzhafte Wahrnehmung stark an. Die Stärke des Umamigeschmacks lässt sich als Glockenkurve darstellen. Im Verhältnis 10 zu 90 und 90 zu 10 ist das Geschmacksempfinden daher stark, bei 50 zu 50 sogar maximal.

Prinzipiell lässt sich Fleisch, gemäß seinem Bindegewebsanteil, kurz braten oder lang schmoren. In beiden Fällen zeigt sich der Umamigeschmack auf unterschiedliche Weise, das Zusammenspiel zwischen Glutaminsäure und Inosinmonophosphat ist dabei vollkommen verschieden. Dabei spielt vor allem das Abhängen für Kurzbratfleisch eine wichtige Rolle.

Abgehangenes: umami I
Bei genauerem Hinschmecken erweist sich die eine Reifung über 20 Tage noch aus anderen Gründen als vorteilhaft. Enzyme spalten während der Reifung Proteine in Aminosäuren, wie es auch bei langem Schmoren und der Fermentation der Fall ist. Dabei erhöht sich die Anzahl der freien Aminosäuren. Beim Reifen bildet sich freie Glutaminsäure, die den Umamigeschmack erzeugt.

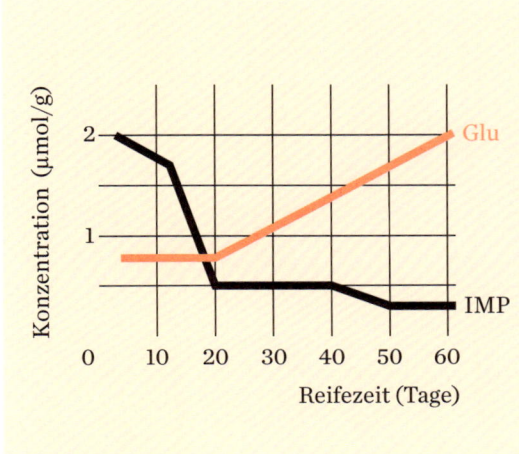

Abb. 10: Während der Fleischreifung nimmt die Konzentration des IMP in den ersten 20 Tagen ab und verharrt dann auf einem konstanten Wert, bis nach 40 Tagen Reifung wieder eine Abnahme erfolgt. Die Konzentration der freien Glutaminsäure (Glu) bleibt anfangs konstant. Nach 20 Tagen steigt sie an. Bei einer Reifung zwischen 35 und 40 Tagen ist die Umamiintensität am höchsten ausgeprägt.

In vielen Fällen nimmt trotz der beim Reifen steigenden freien Glutaminsäure aufgrund des Abbaus des Umamiverstärkers IMP die Umamiintensität ab, der „Flavour" – das Zusammenspiel von Aroma- und Geschmackswahrnehmung – aber zu, da während der Reifung über 20 Tage die Zahl und Konzentration von neuen Aromastoffen deutlich ansteigt.

Außerdem bilden sich durch das lange Reifen über enzymatische Prozesse „Vorläufer" von Aromastoffen, die in diesem Zustand noch nicht besonders riechen, allerdings bei der anschließenden Garung rasch eine Vielzahl von Aromen bilden, die bei der Nassreifung oder kürzeren Reifezeiten fehlen.

In Abb. 10 zeigt sich der grobe Verlauf während des Abbaus von IMP bei gleichzeitigem Anstieg freier Glutaminsäure. Dadurch wird der Abbau des „Geschmacksverstärkers" IMP nach langer Reifezeit für den empfundenen Umamigeschmack nach einer Reifezeit von 20 Tagen wettgemacht. Die üblichen Reifezeiten unter 20 Tagen haben einen eher nachteiligen Effekt, da IMP abgebaut wird, aber die Erhöhung der Glutaminsäure erst danach deutlich schmeckbar wird. Eine längere Reifung als 40 Tage ist allerdings kontraproduktiv. Zwar bildet sich noch mehr Glutaminsäure, aber das IMP baut sich weiter ab, was gemäß Abb. 10 den Gesamt-Umamieindruck verringert.

Des Weiteren bilden sich beim Reifen nicht nur freie Glutaminsäure, sondern auch weitere freie Aminosäuren, die an der Maillardreaktion beteiligt sind und neue Aromen freisetzen. Im Gegensatz dazu die Glutaminsäure: Sie sorgt auch in gebratenen Krusten für einen Umamireiz, denn sie wird nicht zu Aromen umgebaut. Das gegarte und zuvor lang gereifte Fleisch (egal ob gebraten, pochiert oder sous-vide behandelt) weist daher im Vergleich zum Nassgereiften eine überdurchschnittlich hohe Aromadichte auf.

Geschmortes: umami II
Auch beim Schmoren und Kochen von Fleisch wird durch die Hitzeeinwirkung über lange Zeit Glutaminsäure aus Proteinen freigesetzt. Durch das lange Köcheln spalten sich Proteine zu immer kleineren Bruchstücken. Auch „schmeckbare" Glutaminsäure entsteht, sowie kurzkettige Peptide, die zur Mundfülle (kokumi) beitragen. Dieses Phänomen ist hinlänglich bekannt. Eine klare Rinderbrühe „schmeckt" nach 20 Minuten Kochzeit immer noch fade – nach zwei, drei Stunden Simmern jedoch stark umami mit einer unglaublichen Mundfülle, trotz ihrer wässrigen Eigenschaften.

Beim „realen" Schmoren, wie z. B. bei einem Bœuf Bourguignon, genügt es allerdings nicht, lediglich auf die Umamierzeugung aus dem Fleisch zu achten. Natürlich tragen alle Gemüsezutaten, die schon traditionell dem Schmorprozess beigefügt werden, zum Umamigeschmack und zur Geschmacksverstärkung bei: Tomaten, Zwiebeln, Pilze und in manch mediterranen Ländern auch ein bis zwei Sardellen. Vor allem manche Pilze sind dabei erwähnenswert, denn Shitake, Morcheln und Steinpilze steuern nicht nur Glutaminsäure bei, sondern auch einen weiteren Geschmacksverstärker, Guanosinmonophosphat (GMP). Dies ist ein weiteres Phosphat aus dem Zelltreibstoff ATP, der sich dem IMP gegenüber lediglich in der Adeningruppe unterscheidet.

Dabei lässt sich aus physiochemischer Sicht der Begriff „Geschmacksverstärkung" jetzt klar definieren: Die Glutaminsäure (Glu) wirkt (neben der schwächeren Asparaginsäure) als Auslöser, während die beiden ATP-Abkömmlinge GMP und IMP als eigentliche Geschmacksverstärker wirken. Wie bereits ausgeführt wurde, wird IMP hauptsächlich über die Muskelarbeit bereitgestellt. Daher sind die besten Lieferanten für diesen „Geschmacksverstärker" auch Fleisch von allen Tieren, auch Fisch, die sich durch rotes Fleisch auszeichnen: Bonito-Flocken (die fermentierten, getrockneten und geräucherten) werden viel in Japan und Sardinen und Sardellen gern in der Mittelmeerküche verwendet. Getrocknete Steinpilze, Morcheln und andere Pilze, deren Mikroorganismen Sporen sind, und vor allem Shitake liefern beachtliche Mengen an GMP.

Die Glutaminsäure kommt, wie hinlänglich bekannt, vorwiegend in Kombualgen, Tomaten, Zwiebeln, Champignons, in Hülsenfrüchten und vielen Wurzelgemüsesorten vor – oft verwendete und kulturell verankerte Schmorzutaten. Daher erschließt sich das beliebte Dashi (japanischer Fischsud) sofort: Die Kombination aus Kombu (Glu) und Bonito (IMP) schmeckt „umami pur".

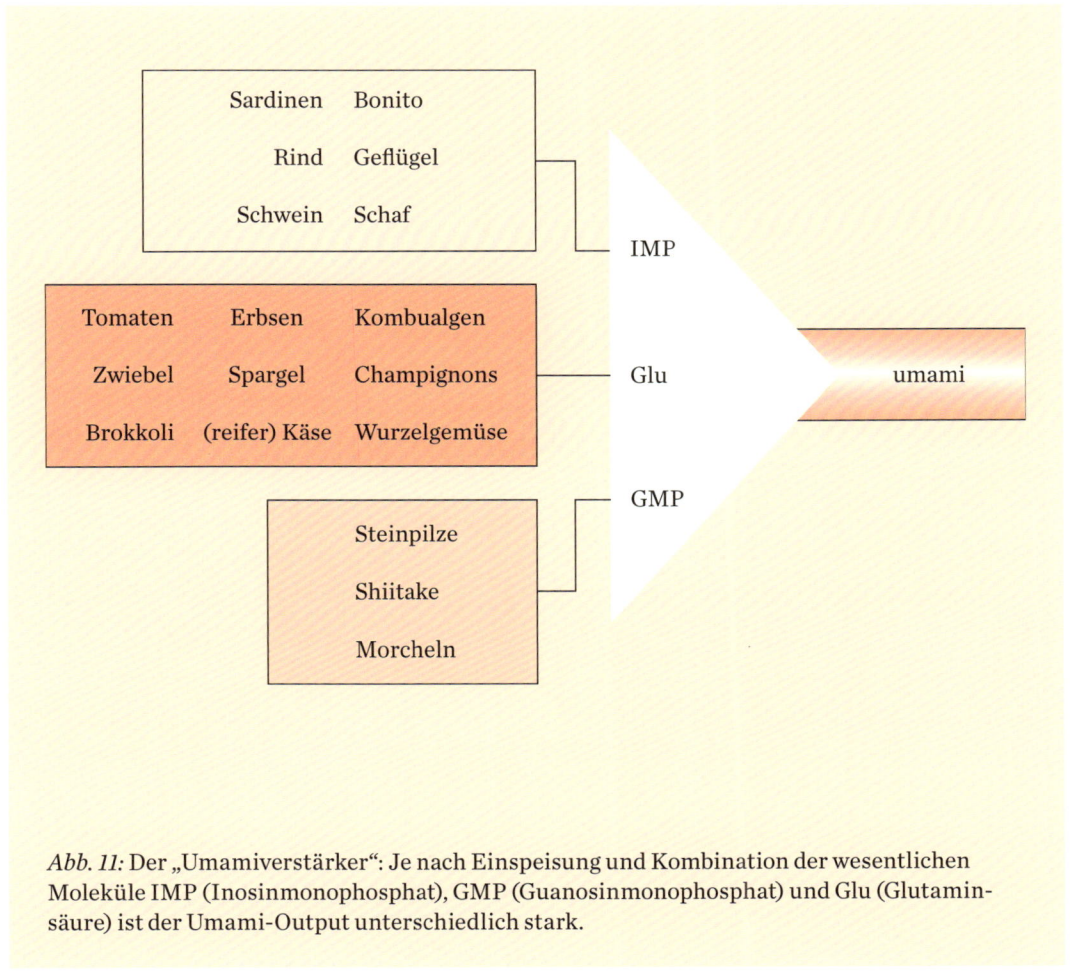

Abb. 11: Der „Umamiverstärker": Je nach Einspeisung und Kombination der wesentlichen Moleküle IMP (Inosinmonophosphat), GMP (Guanosinmonophosphat) und Glu (Glutaminsäure) ist der Umami-Output unterschiedlich stark.

Gemäß der Abb. 11 ist also der Versuch, einmal ein Stück Kombualge, getrocknete Rohwürste, Molkekäse (Handkäse) oder sogar die Rinde eines sehr alten Käses einem Schmorgericht zuzufügen, nicht verkehrt. Die Zunge dankt es.

Der Wunsch nach einem ausgeprägten Umamigeschmack ist in allen Kochkulturen tief verankert, und dies schon länger als der Begriff umami bekannt ist. Insofern widerspricht die Verteufelung der Geschmacksverstärkung allen Genusskulturen dieser Welt.

Der Aromatik und Mundfülle zuliebe: Fett!
Ohne Fett wirkt Fleisch fad. Schieres, mageres Muskelfleisch bleibt unabhängig von der Zubereitungsart oft ein wenig langweilig und bildet kaum spezifische Aromen. Der Unterschied zum fettdurchzogenen Fleisch ist gewaltig. Bereits beim Riechen lässt sich die aromatische Differenz schnell erkennen. Erst recht, wenn das Fleisch lang gereift ist: Aus Fett bilden sich durch Oxidation deutlich grüne, grasige, leicht käsige und vor allem pilzartige Noten, die jedem mageren Stück fehlen. Auch nach der Zubereitung wird der Unterschied eklatant: Während Fleisch mit hohem Marmorierungsgrad zwischen Zunge und Gaumen regelrecht zerschmilzt, müssen magere Stücke je nach Muskelfaserlänge und Cut deutlich mehr gekaut und bearbeitet werden. Marmoriertes Fleisch setzt während des „oralen Prozessierens" im Mund eine Vielzahl von Aromen frei. Mehr noch, Fett wirkt als Schmiermittel, sodass sich die Reibung zwischen Zunge und Gaumen vermindert.

Die Marmorierung wird durch das intramuskuläre Fett (IMF) verursacht. Es befindet sich in den Muskelbündeln und wird als letztes Fettdepot während des Wachstums der Tiere angelegt. Für Sensorik und Fleischgenuss ist das IMF entscheidend, es bestimmt einen Großteil von Textur und Aromafreigabe. In Japan wird der prozentuale Gehalt des IMF in zwölf Marmorierungsgraden gemessen. Aus diesen werden in den USA fünf Qualitätsstufen abgeleitet. Mageres deutsches Rindfleisch liegt nach diesen Maßstäben durchweg unter dem Durschnitt, was Textur, Geschmack und Aroma betrifft.

Das IMF eines gut marmorierten Stück Beef besteht aus einer Mischung von Triglyceriden gesättigten, einfach, mehrfach ungesättigten und Omega-3-Fettsäuren unterschiedlicher Länge, deren genaue Zusammensetzung rassen- und fütterungsabhängig ist. Da IMF als rasch zur Verfügung stehender Energiespeicher im Muskel dienen muss, ist sein Anteil an kürzeren, einfach und mehrfach ungesättigten Fettsäuren verglichen mit Talg deutlich höher: Es schmilzt daher bei deutlich niedrigeren Temperaturen. Daher schmilzt das Fett des Wagyūtatars bereits auf der Zunge.

Qualität	Marmorierungsgrad	IMF Anteil (%)
schlecht	1	0 – 3
unterdurchschnittlich	2	4 – 9
durchschnittlich	3 – 4	10 – 20
gut	5 – 7	21 – 43
excellent	8 – 12	44 – 56 und höher

Nicht jede Rinderrasse ist per se für die Einlagerung eines hohen IMF-Anteils geeignet. Natürlich steht Wagyū mit an der Spitze, aber auch Angus, Murray Grey, oder Shorthorns zeichnen sich durch höhere IMF-Anteile aus. Typische Fleischrassen wie Charolais, Holsteiner oder Simmentaler stehen deutlich zurück. Generell lässt sich feststellen, dass Färsen (weibliche Tiere) stets einen deutlich höheren Anteil an IMF aufweisen als Bullen. Auch sind Färsen erkennbar feinfaseriger als Bullen. Ochsen liegen beim IMF-Einbau dazwischen.

Einen ganz entscheidenden Einfluss hat der hohe Fett- und IMF-Anteil auf die Fleischreifung und die damit einhergehende Aromabildung. Insbesondere die ungesättigten Fettsäuren spielen hierfür eine große Rolle. Die Doppelbindungen sind chemisch instabiler und brechen während der Reifung mit höherer Wahrscheinlichkeit auf (Oxidation). Kleine Bruchstücke spalten sich ab und bilden wohlduftende Aromastoffe. Sie tragen maßgeblich zum typischen Aroma des gereiften Fleisches bei. Fettreiches Fleisch, insbesondere, wenn mehr ungesättigte Fettsäuren eingelagert werden (wie beim Wagyū-Rind oder einer anderen Rasse mit hohem IMF-Anteil), hat einen deutlich intensiveren, spezifischen (dry aged) Beefduft als mageres Fleisch.

Das Fett erhöht dabei auch indirekt die Mundfülle (kokumi). Aus den sich während der Reifung abspaltenden, langkettigen Fettsäuren bilden sich sogenannte Oxolipine, die ähnlich wie Schmorprodukte für eine deutliche Steigerung des Kokumi-Effekts sorgen.

Bei Tieren mit hohem IMF entstehen feinfaserige Muskelbündel, und eine langfasrige Fleischstruktur wird zugunsten der Zartheit bereits beim Wachstum verhindert. Das intramuskuläre Fett umgibt die Muskelfasern. Fleischsäfte können während des Garens weniger stark austreten, da sie die „Fettbarrieren" um die Fasern herum kaum durchdringen können. Wasserverluste sind daher geringer, die Saftigkeit bleibt erhalten. Die Zartheit wird durch das Wechselspiel zwischen intramuskulärem Fett und Fleischsäften gewährleistet. Mehr noch: Auch die beim Braten oder Grillen entstehenden Röstaromen lösen sich in hohem Maße im Fett. Sie bleiben im Fleisch und landen beim Genuss im Mund.

Fett hat noch einen ganz besonderen und neben den reibungsverminderten Textureinflüssen bisher weitgehend unbekannten/unberücksichtigten sensorischen Nebeneffekt, es wirkt als „Mundraumaromaspeicher". Fett kleidet Teile von Zunge und Gaumen mit einem dünnen Film aus (oral coating) und hält darin gelöste Aromen für eine gewisse Zeit fest, die den nächsten Bissen, sei es Fleisch, Brot oder Gemüse „nachwürzen". Fett wirkt in vielerlei Hinsicht als nachhaltiger und molekularer Flavourenhancer.

Und jetzt?
Der Umgang mit Fleisch und dessen Erzeugung erfordert in allen Phasen, von Weide und Stall bis zur Zubereitung, Sorgfalt und Respekt – sowohl aus Sicht der Kultur- als auch der Naturwissenschaften. Der naturwissenschaftliche Blickwinkel zeigt mehr als deutlich, was wir wirklich versäumen, wenn anonymes Fleisch achtlos in die Pfanne geworfen wird. Es macht vielleicht kurzfristig satt, zufrieden aber nicht. Und natürlich ist Fleisch wegen der vielen (essenziellen) Aminosäuren, des hoch bioverfügbaren Eisens und des Vitamin B12 tatsächlich ab und zu ein „Stück Lebenskraft". So lehrt es auch das große Buch der Evolution.

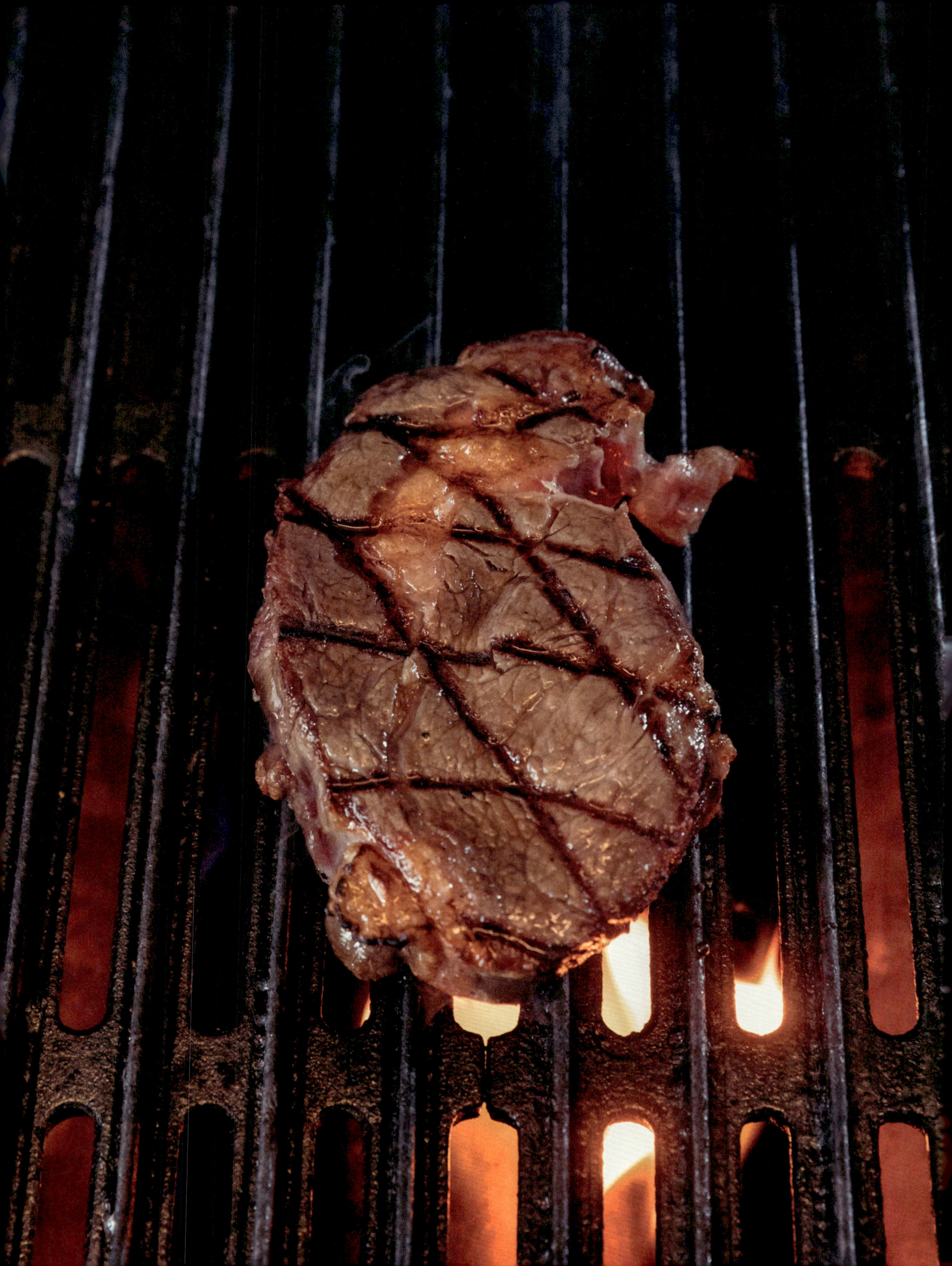

Meat—More Than Just a Slice of Vitality

Thomas Vilgis

Meat — From the Pasture to the Kitchen

Despite the many discussions about animal welfare, ethics, veganism, cooking techniques and varieties of vegetables, meat remains an essential "luxury food" in the gastronomy sector. Meat deserves much more notice than it is usually given in thoughtless overindulgence at one end or ideological debates at the other end. Far away from such questions, meat is a uniquely structured "biomaterial." From a completely sober, scientific perspective, its composition and structure let even hard-boiled gourmets be surprised with astonishment. In the world of micro- and nanometers, clear physico-chemical laws are exclusively applicable. And that is reason enough for a gentle approach to the hidden biophysical secrets, which lie deep in the protein structure, and that already reveal themselves during simple frying (fig. 1).

Before meat reaches the kitchen, it was a part of the musculoskeletal system of a living animal. Depending on its particular biological role, different sections are available for consumption: purely muscular meat, such as the heart or back, or cuts from the leg or shoulder, which are marbled with connective tissue. These visible differences can be traced back to their different demands. Meat from the muscles such as the loin is responsible for fine-tuning movements of the spinal column and therefore has little connective tissue. However, the entire weight of the animal is resting on the muscles of their legs and shoulders. Because these muscles are subjected to high loads, they contain a higher share of connective tissue (e.g., sinews). Thus collagen fibers have among the highest tensile strength and resistance to tearing. That means it is difficult, or even impossible, to chew them, and unlike steaks, they require more cooking time such as braising.

Then there is the fat: intramuscular fat (IMF) is an important "parameter" for enjoying meat. The sensory difference between a strongly marbled piece of Japanese Wagyū beef and a low-fat loin of beef is detectable by the naked eye. But what do these visible facts actually mean? The objective of this contribution is to understand meat more objectively. To do this, it is necessary to look deeply into meat, because the facts can only be clearly seen at a molecular level, if one does not want to resort to speculations or to make unclear statements.

From Muscle to Meat

The background of the selected piece of meat is of great relevance and far removed from such easy-to-answer questions as to the rearing, past life, breed or feeding. During the life of the animal, meat was an active muscle, after which it was transformed through a long-term and complicated process into in a cured piece of meat. The strictly hierarchical structure of muscular meat, which has been presented in a simplified manner in fig. 2, makes the cooperation between multiple proteins possible during movement. Every muscle consists of bundles of muscle fiber. These fiber bundles, and the muscle fibers themselves, are surrounded by a layer of connective tissue. Muscle fibers consist of myofibrils. Only when these have reached a length of a few micrometers can the fibrillar proteins actin and myosin be "identified."

Meat is approximately 75 % water and 20 % proteins. The latter can be subdivided roughly into three groups. The myofibrillar proteins, the backbone of the muscular structure, have the largest share in this regard with approximately 50 to 60 %. The second largest group of proteins, which is largely water-soluble, is located in the sarcoplasm, in the membranes and as part a of the content of muscular cells, and also in the myoglobin that provides color, as well as in a large number of enzymes, which are for instance responsible for transport or repair tasks in the living muscle. The connective tissue proteins, among which you will find—first of all—collagen, in the form of a triple helix, are insoluble in this native form. The water (the meat juices) is largely located in the inter-myofibrillar gaps, while a smaller share (below 10 %) is directly associated with the proteins and therefore strongly bound.

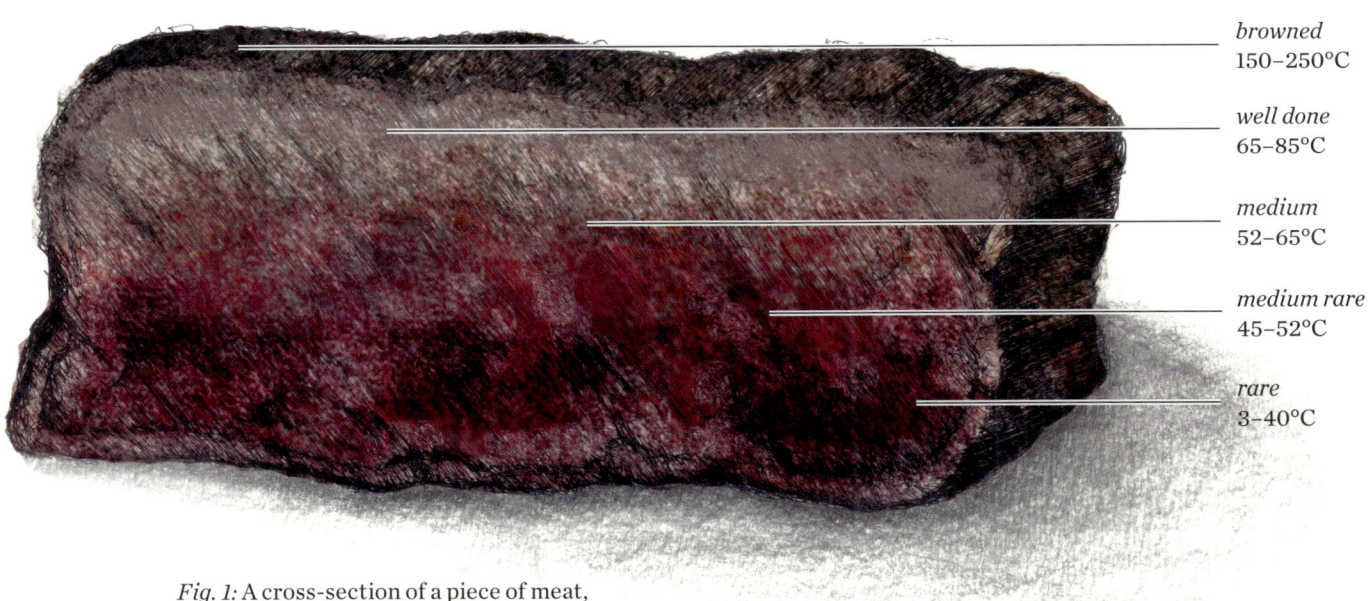

browned
150–250°C

well done
65–85°C

medium
52–65°C

medium rare
45–52°C

rare
3–40°C

Fig. 1: A cross-section of a piece of meat, which has been roasted gently, reveals a rough view of protein physics and the world of aromas.

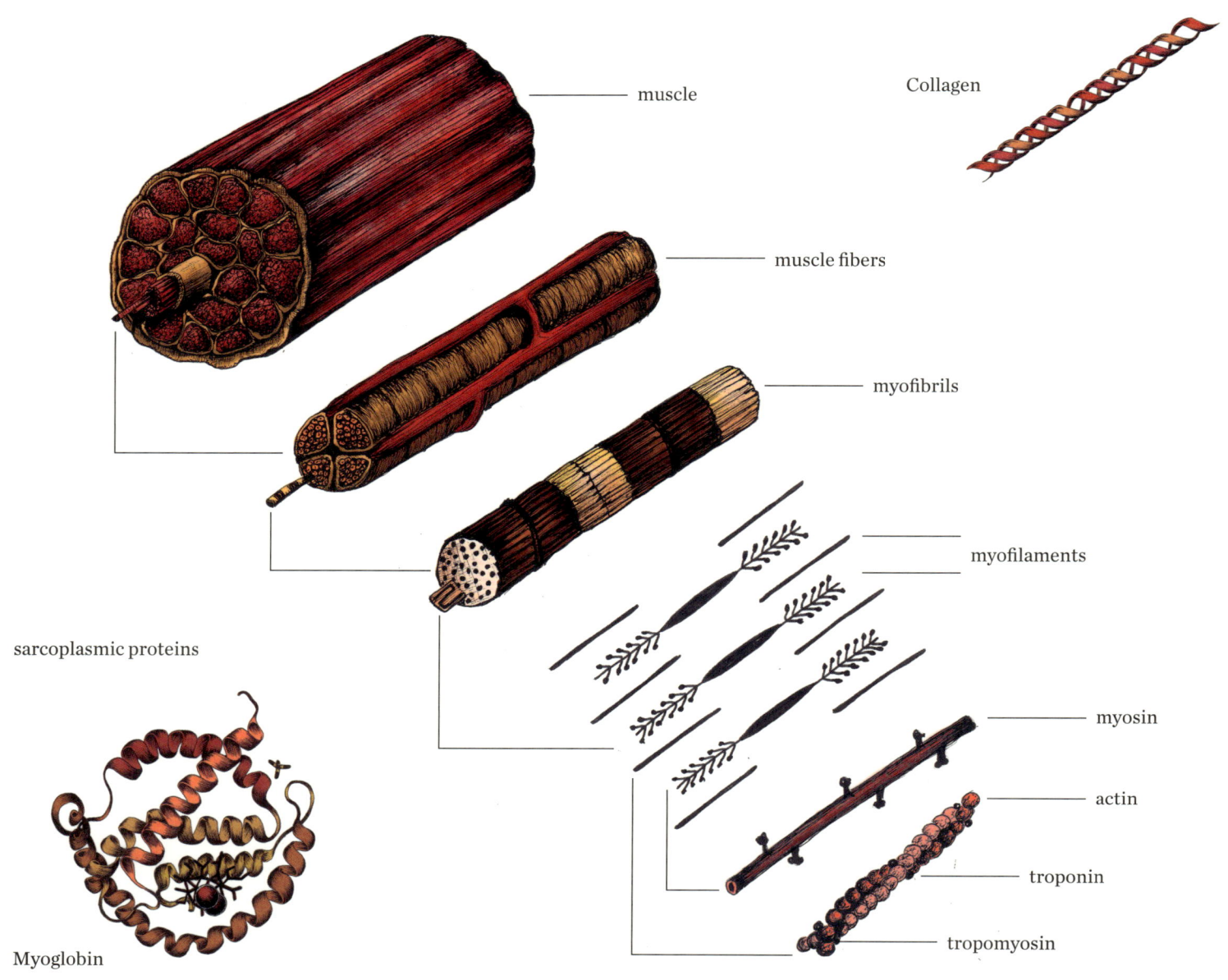

muscle

Collagen

muscle fibers

myofibrils

myofilaments

sarcoplasmic proteins

myosin

actin

troponin

tropomyosin

Myoglobin

Fig. 2: The hierarchy of proteins in muscle meat
In the macroscopically visible area, muscles on the length scale of 1 centimeter are detectable; individual muscle fibers have a typical size of 1 millimeter, and a thin but stable layer of collagen surrounds each one. Structured, micrometer-long myofilaments (individual proteins) control events on a scale of nanometers. The muscle cells are surrounded by a cell membrane. The interaction between the proteins actin, myosin, tropomyosin and troponin in the myofilaments forms the basic unit of the locomotor system in the living muscle.

Processes After the Slauther

An important role for the taste of the meat, especially after aging, is played by the "switching molecule" adenosine triphosphate (ATP), a quadruple-charged molecule (fig. 3) that provides and switches the energy of the movement in the muscle filaments. Muscle contraction and relaxation only become possible by its presence and action. ATP is a natural phosphate that consists of an organic adenine group, a sugar called ribose and the ionic component of triphosphoric acid.

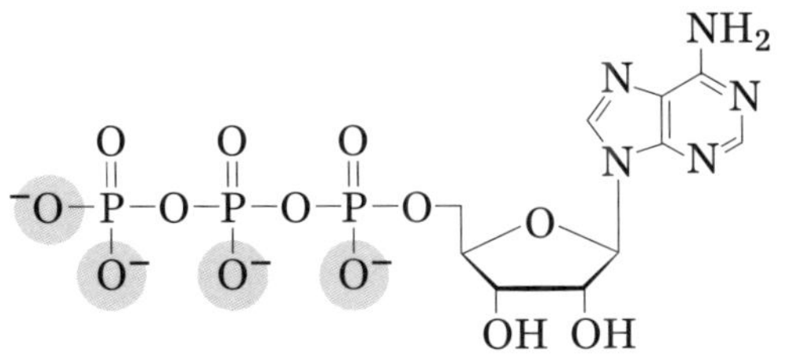

Fig. 3: The structure of adenosine triphosphate (ATP). The triphosphoric acid (P = phosphor, O = oxygen, N = nitrogen, H = hydrogen) has a quadruple (!) electric charge.

The enzymatic split of the ATP releases corresponding concentrations of triple-charged monophosphate ions (see fig. 4). During the decay of the ATP, a high concentration of triple-charged monophosphates is generated. This "hard chemistry" is certainly not mere theory, because the residues of the ATP are of decisive importance for the intensity of the hearty meat taste, or umami, and for all meat preparations, whether chopped (tartar), quickly grilled or braised. These issues will be explained later.

After the animals have been slaughtered, the oxygen supply in the muscle is cut off and the ATP decomposes without being renewed. Put in a very simple way, this has multiple consequences: after the decomposition of the highly charged ATP, the corresponding repulsion forces are missing to keep the small actin and myosin heads at a distance. As a consequence, and little by little, actin and myosin form strongly bound,

ATP: A Basic Element for the "Chemistry of Flavor"

Under physiological conditions, the triphosphoric acid has a quadruple negative charge. During muscular movements, the unusually high negative charge enters into an interaction with the double positively charged calcium ions Ca2+. While it can bind these, it nevertheless maintains a double negative charge. At the same time, the ATP correlates with the charged amino acids of the myosin, after which it can proceed to interact with the tropomyosin that envelops the corresponding amino acids of the actin, whereby the shifting of the myosin relative to the actin can generate a muscle contraction as an "elementary step". The ATP is successively converted into adenosine diphosphate (ADP) and adenosine monophosphate (AMP), each splitting off from the phosphate group. The effect is changed due to a reduction of the charge during this process: myosin can be bound, actin and myosin can be transferred during the binding phase of muscle strength, and they can then restart this process once more by binding a new ATP to the myosin head. Muscular work is only possible with ATP and under release of energy through its enzymatic hydrolysis.

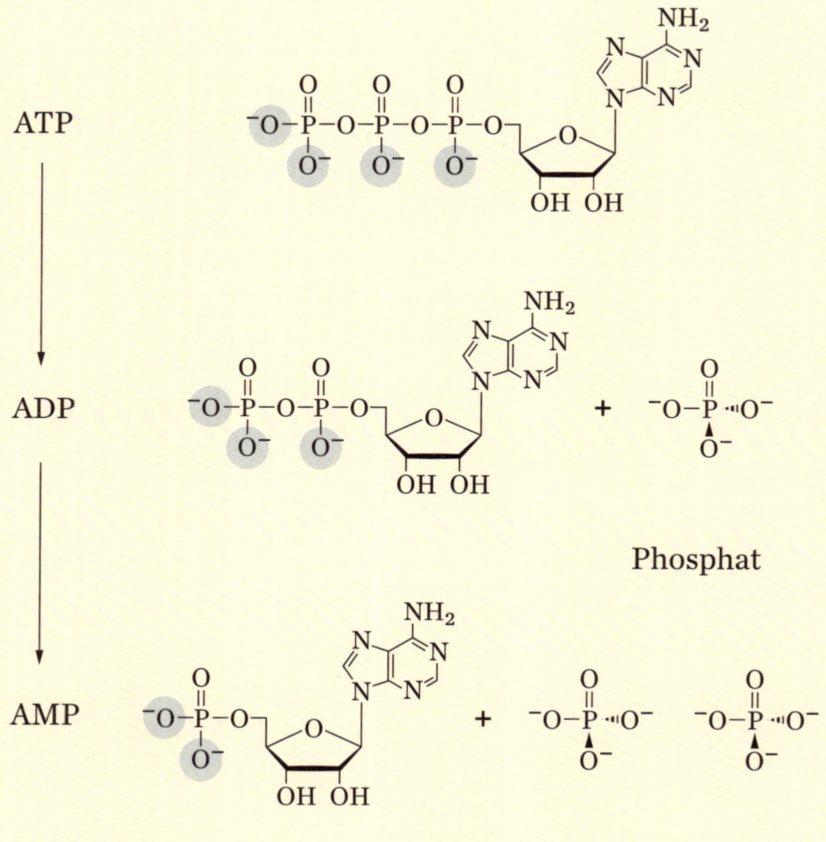

Fig. 4: The decomposition of ATP into ADP and AMP releases monophosphate with a triple charge, while the charge of ADP and AMP declines. Ultimately, the "flavor enhancers" inosine-5-monophosphate (IMP) and guanosine-5-monophosphate (GMP) are generated enzymatically.

rigid and insoluble complexes: rigor mortis ensues. Also, during the aging of meat, the strongly bound actin-myosin complexes cannot be dissolved. The enzymatic, biophysical processes that are in progress at that time, and which make meat more tender, do not concern the actin-myosin complex but rather the change of proteins in the muscle cell, the sarcoma for instance. Partial cutting of the connective tissue collagen releases and activates collagenase enzymes.

ATP causes a release of the binding points, to which the myosin head clings for a short time and which can cause muscular movement. Myosin itself consists largely of two helixes, which in turn are wound into helixes with a larger winding length. They terminate in a myosin head.

A basic understanding of the post-mortem processes, during the transformation from active muscle to meat, is of great importance for an understanding of making sausages. These have therefore been roughly summarized once again in fig. 5.

The transformation of the glycogen into lactic acid lowers the pH value of the meat to approximately 5. This changes the taste from slightly sweet to sour, and it also has a direct effect on the structure of the proteins. Their building blocks, namely the amino acids, are so-called dipolar ions, whose charge depends on the pH value. Acidity is transmitted via protons, namely positive charges ("hydrogen nuclei"). These positive charges insulate negatively loaded amino acids and "neutralize" them. Negative OH (hydroxyl) groups predominate in the alkaline, basic state (pH below 7) and weaken the positively charged amino acids. That is why a certain pH value exists for most proteins, at which all charges of the proteins are "neutralized." At this "isoelectric point," the overall charge of the protein is practically zero and it is electrically neutral. At this point, the cohesiveness of the protein structure is the weakest: it gives up its native structure and is partially denatured. This is also true for myosin, whose isoelectric point lies at an approximate pH value of 5. The myosin heads denature partially, but the solid actin-myosin complex remains.

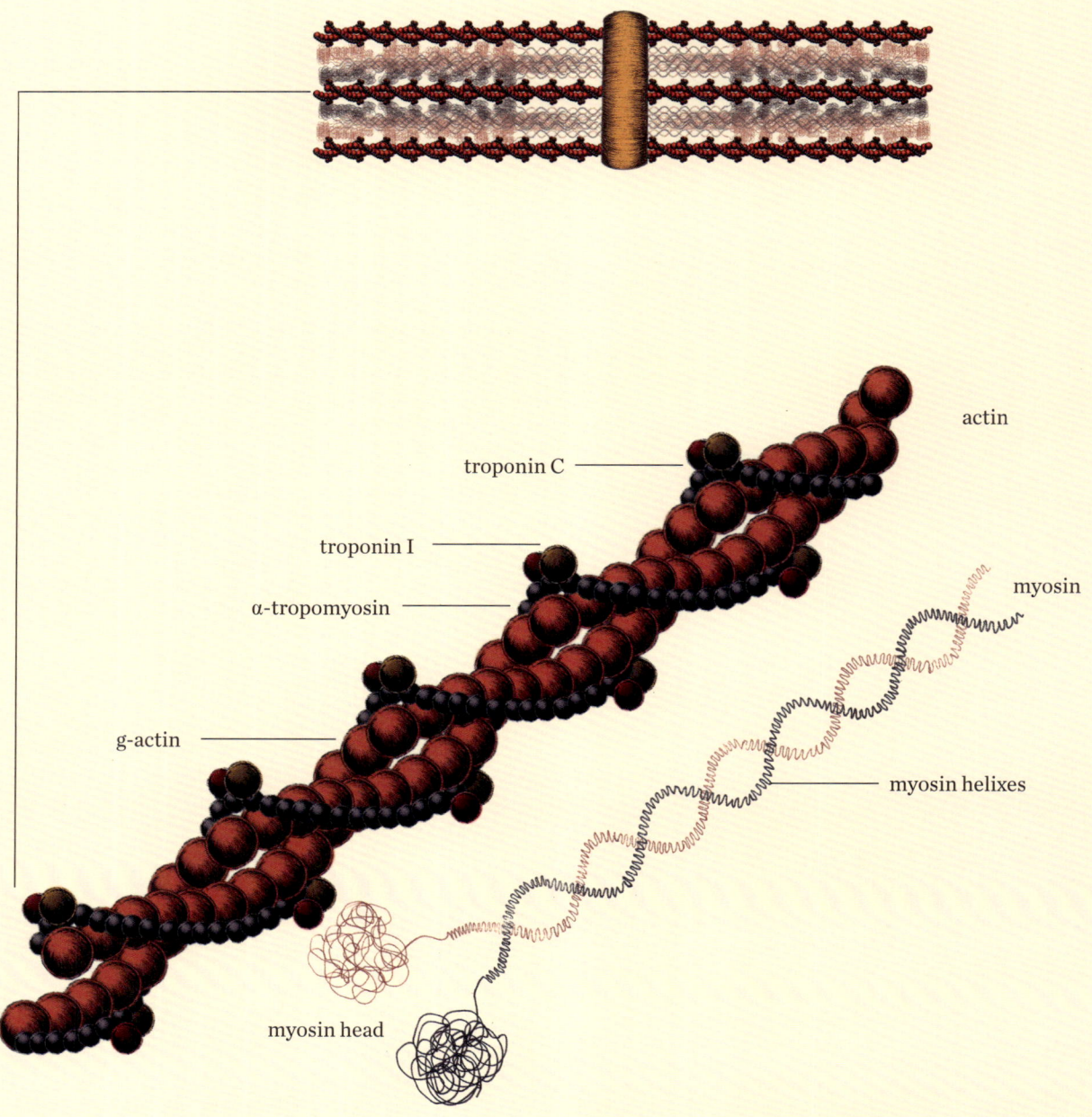

Fig. 5: A highly simplified presentation of the actin-myosin complex, in the myofibril of a muscular cell
Fibrillar actin consists of helix-shaped globular F actin proteins (light gray, ball-shaped
structures), which are surrounded by α-tropomyosin.

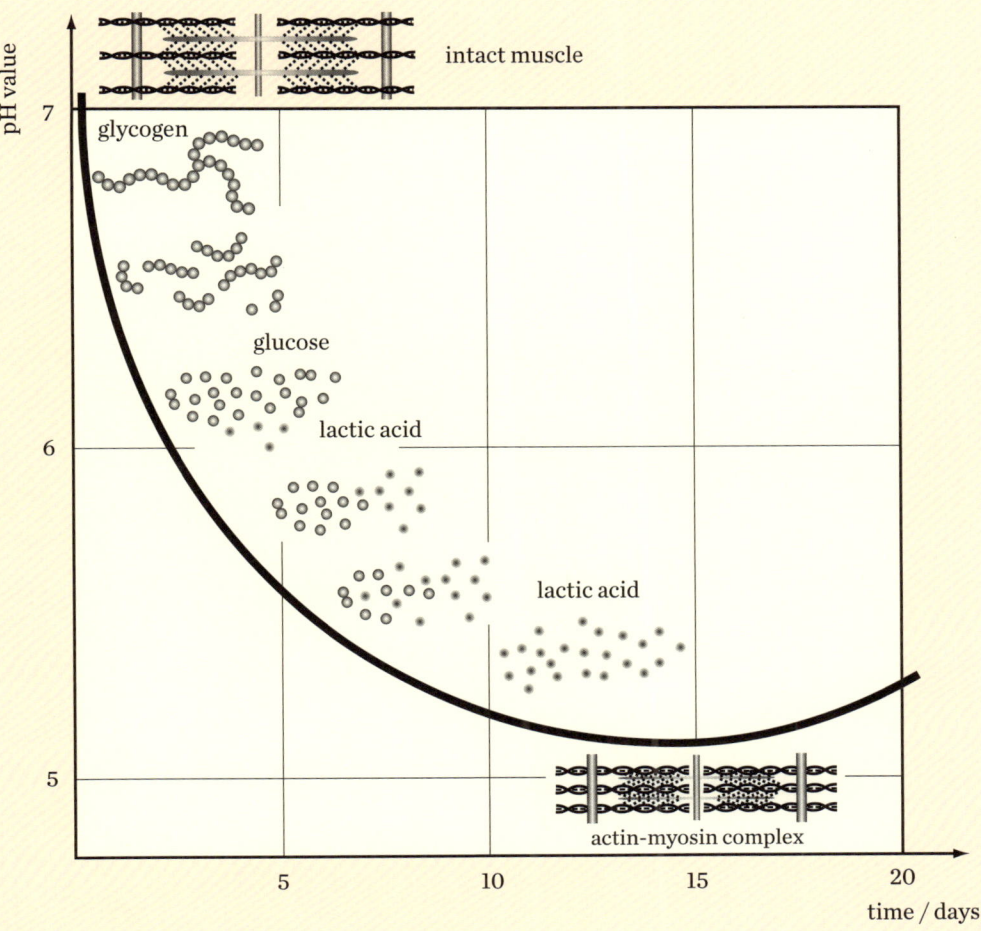

Fig. 6: Simplified presentation of post-mortem processes
The muscles are still intact immediately the animal is slaughtered. The full amount of ATP is available, as is the stored carbohydrate glycogen ("animal starch"). Glycogen is fragmented enzymatically into glucose, which is in turn anaerobically fermented by lactic acid bacteria into lactic acid, so that the pH value decreases. ATP decomposes rapidly; strongly bound actin-myosin complexes develop fully.

Meat: Thermal Changes of the Biomolecules

The thermal behavior of the individual protein classes is of fundamental importance for a clear understanding of molecular processes. The various proteins denature, or "cook," at different temperatures, in a range between 48 °C and 75 °C. The individual "balls" in the (fibrillar) actin consist of G actin, namely globular proteins. Perfect cooking is achieved through the change of exactly the "right" proteins.

A change in temperature has different effects depending on the negative form of the protein. In the case of globular proteins such as those present in sarcoplasm, this leads to their development and, with that, their exposure to hydrophobic amino acids. These can aggregate and, under favorable circumstances, can form a gel with a high water bond. When heated, extracted myosin also forms gels. In the case of elongated molecules such as collagen, the discontinuation of stabilizing hydrogen bridging bonds, which is caused by heating, can also lead to a contraction of the molecule for entropic reasons, as it is known from stretched polymer structures. This causes the collagen to shrink during a first step in denaturation before it dissolves and turns into gelatin when exposed to higher temperatures for longer periods of time.

With the help of differential scanning calorimetry (DSC), it is possible to follow these denaturing processes in the laboratory, as can be seen in fig. 7. If the temperature is slowly increased, then the denaturing process of the proteins begins. This "demands" energy, which can be measured with sensitive calorimeters via thermal flows. These are shown by the characteristic "peaks."

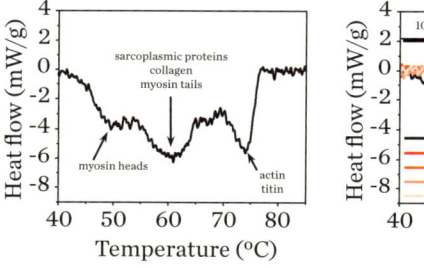 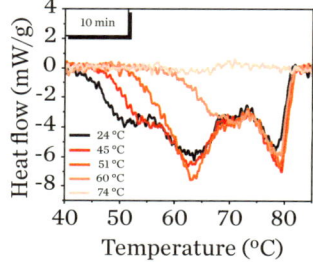 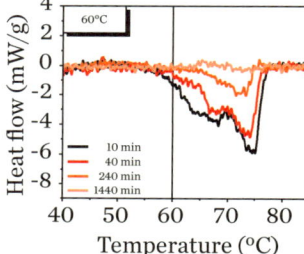

Fig. 7: Protein denaturation of pork
a) Various peaks can be seen with an increase in temperature, which are caused by the accompanying energy consumption. The protein groups are identified at the corresponding "peaks."
b) With the increasing temperature of precooking (for instance under a vacuum), less and less protein types denature. The peaks therefore disappear. c) Time also plays a large role here. If the meat is cooked at 60 °C for different and longer periods, then even the peaks that belong with high denaturation temperatures disappear. The widely accepted view that time plays no role, is therefore basically wrong. The cooking time under content time matters.

Due to the large number of available proteins, which partially denature at similar temperature ranges, it is not possible to assign these peaks to certain proteins. However, a rough picture is obtained. The globular components—the so-called myosin heads—denature first, which already happens at 48 °C. The denaturation temperatures of sarcoplasmic proteins and collagen are around 60 °C, and the helical myosin tails also develop in this temperature range. Actin and titin are the most thermostable: they only denature at temperatures between 70 and 75 °C. Even the cooking of individual proteins such as myosin occurs at different temperature ranges, as is clearly shown in fig. 8.

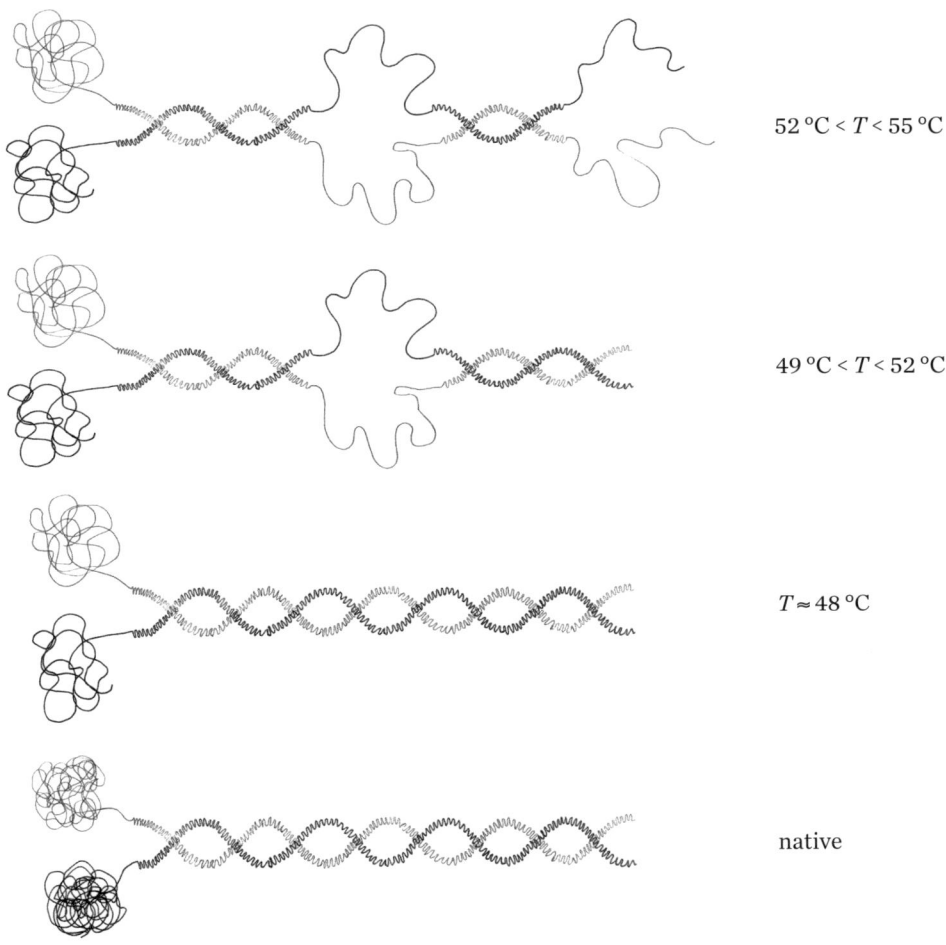

$52\,°C < T < 55\,°C$

$49\,°C < T < 52\,°C$

$T \approx 48\,°C$

native

Fig. 8: The most important denaturation stages of a myosin protein
The heads are the first to denature, losing their original structure and their former biological function. After that, the helix-shaped "tails" denature. The individual proteins themselves (presented in black and brown) have a twisted (helical) structure, which in turn twist into a "super helix," whose development and untwisting demands more energy: in other words, higher temperatures.

Dry Aging vs. Wet Aging

Only a few decades ago, no one talked about "dry aging": it was just called aging or maturing. It was the only method of choice for making tender beef and indroducing correspondingly fine aromatic traces of mushroom, or a kind of cheesy Camembert or earthy scent. Aroma and taste were already developed during the long time aging of the meat. Consumers only became accustomed to moist meat with a slightly sour note due to the bad habit of letting individual pieces of meat "age" in vacuum packaging. This was due to anaerobic lactic acid fermentation at low temperatures. While this is ostensibly an advantage for enzyme activity, a slow fermentation of the lactic acid already starts under anaerobic conditions and at low temperatures. The lactic acid bacteria, which are always present, form lactic acid and its corresponding typical aromatic combinations from sugars (e.g. from available remaining glycogen or glycoproteins). The meat, and the meat juices that slowly collect in the vacuum bag, typically have a "slightly sour" smell.

Wet aging has a certain softening effect on the meat, due to the declining pH value, but it also has a noticeable drawback during frying: the water content of the meat is high, while the water retention capacity of the meat is too low. Due to the increasing temperatures and protein changes during frying, the consequence is that a relatively large quantity of meat juice is released. When frying vacuum-packed meat, the meat juices that collected in the bag can, at best, serve as a sauce. When frying using pans, griddles, or grills, the released water is a disadvantage, as it evaporates. But the evaporation heat, which is lacking in the surroundings and the pan, is needed. The Maillard reaction—namely the browning reaction of the meat—is delayed: the meat is "steaming" as long as meat juices are being released.

These problems do not occur with cured meat, since the water content of meat has been reduced in two ways; at an aging temperature of between 0 and 3 °C, and at an air humidity of 80 %, water simply "evaporates" from the meat. Here, the water content falls from 75 % to approximately 65–67 %. In the case of liquid or vacuum maturation, the decline in the water content is limited to 1–2 %.

In dry aging, a significantly lower but perfect water content is achieved: the only water (meat juice) that remains in the meat is that which is able to bind to the proteins at the applicable temperatures and air humidity. After longer aging periods, the meat will always be in a "thermodynamic balance." The meat juice, which is more strongly bound in the meat, cannot evaporate as easily during frying, which means that it, together with the intramuscular fat, remains as an important "softener" during bleu (very rare), English (medium rare) and à point (rare) cooking processes.

Regardless of the taste and the aroma, the frying behavior of meat that has been cured for a long time is excellent: the frying meat does not generate clouds of vaporized water; proper frying is ensured by the thermal conductivity of the proteins and the fat (taking into account their conversions); the meat is browned quickly and evenly.

Wet aging may be an advantage from an economic point of view. The loss of weight is marginal. While the loss of weight is substantial during dry aging, positive effects on the taste and aroma prevail. Earthy, mushroom-like aroma compounds, fruit esters and pyrazines, with their nutty-spicy taste, are generated from the unsaturated fatty acids of the intramuscular fat during aging.

Individual pieces of meat can in the meantime also be "aged" without the use of special aging cabinets. The use of aging bags (made of semi-permeable, water-permeable outer layers) makes it possible to shrink-wrap meat. In that case, the meat "dries" slowly. This method is very safe: no fungus can form from the outside and the continuous reduction of the quantity of water prevents dramatic lactic acid fermentation.

Furthermore, semi-permeable aging bags are also suitable for the production of Bündner meat. Strongly vacuum-sealed, possibly lightly pickled in sea salt, sheer muscle loin cuts from breeds that have little intramuscular fat will be "dry" after two to three weeks, at which time it will correspond in color and texture to Bündner meat (even though the formation of aroma develops differently there).

The Umami Taste: Hearty and Meaty

The typical meat taste is derived from a basic flavor, namely "umami," which is a Japanese word construction for hearty, meaty and tasty. Actually, "umami" can be illustrated very easily using molecular details. Along with sweet, sour, and bitter, umami characterizes the flavor of all foods on the tongue. Umami is primarily triggered when glutamate stimulates the taste buds. However, glutamate is connected more with "taste enhancers" and the "China syndrome," and less with exquisite meat. Nevertheless, the small white crystals of (sodium) glutamate, namely the salt of glutamic acid, contain an important (but not essential) amino acid, which means they are a regular and ample component of every protein, both of animal and vegetable origin. If glutamic acid is bound in the protein chain, it does not stimulate any taste sensation. If it is separated from the protein and is therefore free, it activates the taste buds and signals umami, namely that hearty sensation on the tongue, so well-known from soy sauces and miso pastes, as well as broths and meat stocks that have simmered for long periods. All of these processes serve to separate out the glutamic acid in the proteins. However, free glutamic acid is already present in small quantities in meat before aging, giving raw meat a whiff of the umami taste.

Glutamic acid is not the only factor that determines the intensity of umami. In particular, it is the decomposition products and the products of chemical reactions in the ATP switching molecule of the muscles that provide the actual taste enhancer for umami, namely inosine monophosphate (IMP), which forms in large quantities in meat after the decomposition of the ATP after slaughtering.

From the point of view of flavor physiology, this is exciting: glutamic acid directly releases umami. If it interacts with the inosinic acid, then the umami taste increases exponentially, as has been shown by Japanese scientist Kenzo Kurihara (fig. 9).

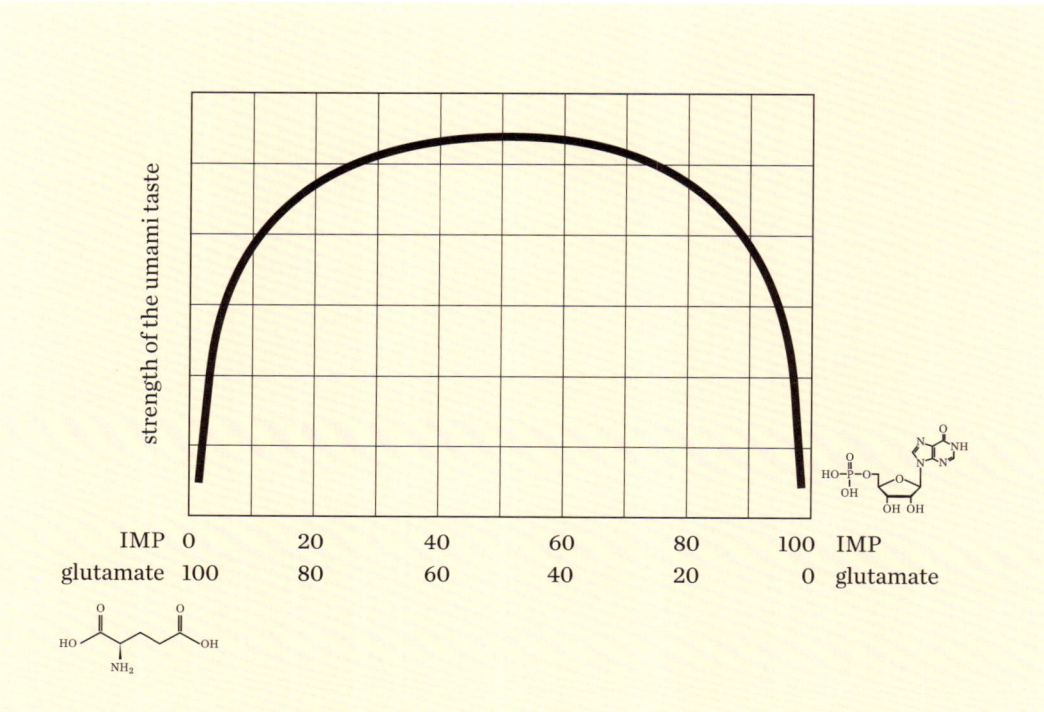

Fig. 9: Strengthening and synergistic effect of glutamic acid (on the left) and inosine mono-phosphate (IMP, also referred to as inosinate) increase. Both have a slight umami taste on their own, but the hearty taste sensation increases strongly if they interact. The strength of the umami taste can be presented as a bell curve. At a ratio of 10 to 90, and also 90 to 10, the taste sensation is strong, and it reaches its maximum at a ratio of 50 to 50.

Basically, and depending on the proportion of connective tissue, the meats can be briefly fried or braised for a longer period. The umami taste presents itself in a different manner in both cases, since the interaction between the glutamic acid and the inosinate is completely different. In this, the aging of quick-frying meat plays a particularly important role.

Cured Meat: Umami I
When exploring the taste sensation more precisely, aging of more than 20 days appears advantageous for several other reasons. During aging, enzymes split the proteins into amino acids, exactly as is also the case during longer braising and fermentation. During this process, the number of free amino acids increases. Free glutamic acid is formed during aging, which produces the umami taste.

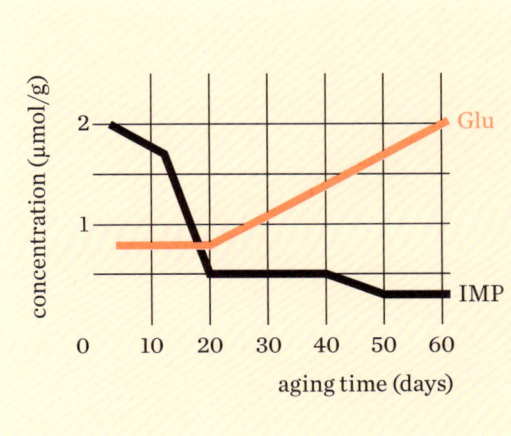

Fig. 10: During the aging of the meat, the concentration of inosine monophosphate declines in the first 20 days and then settles at a constant value, but a further decrease occurs after aging for 40 days. The concentration of the free glutamic acid (Glu) remains constant in the beginning, before starting to rise after 20 days. The umami taste intensity is most pronounced after aging of between 35 and 40 days.

In many cases, however, the intensity of the umami taste declines, despite an increase in free glutamic acid during aging and due to the decomposition of the umami taste-intensifying inosinic acid. Meanwhile, the "flavor"—the interaction between aroma and taste sensation—increases, since the number and concentration of new aromatic substances clearly increases during an aging of more than 20 days.

Furthermore, due to the long aging and via enzymatic processes, "precursors" of aromatic substances are generated. These do not yet have a special odor in this state, but do form a wide variety of aromas during subsequent aging, aromas that are missing during wet aging or shorter aging periods.

Fig. 10 shows the rough progress during the decomposition of inosinic acid and the simultaneous increase of free glutamic acid. After a long aging period, the decomposition of the inosinic acid "taste enhancer" is compensated by the umami taste sensation after an aging period of 20 days. The usual aging periods of less than 20 days have a rather negative effect, since inosinic acid is decomposed, but the increase in the glutamic acid can be tasted thereafter. However, an aging period of more than 40 days is counterproductive. Even though more glutamic acid is produced, the inosinic acid continues to decline, which—as shown in fig. 10—decreases the overall umami taste sensation.

Furthermore, not only are free glutamic acid produced during aging, but also additional free amino acids are generated; these are involved in the Maillard reaction and release new aromas. In contrast to glutamic acid, they ensure a umami taste sensation, even in fried crusts, because they are not converted into aromas. Cooked meat that has previously been cured for a long period therefore produces an above-average, highly aromatic intensity in comparison to wet-cured meat, regardless of whether it is fried, poached or vacuum-processed.

Braised Meat: Umami II
During the braising and cooking processes, the long-term exposure of the meat to heat releases glutamic acid from the proteins. The long simmering process means that the proteins split into increasingly small fragments. Glutamic acid that can be tasted is generated, including short-chain peptides, contributing to a mouth-filling sensation (kokumi). This phenomenon is well known. A clear beef broth still "tastes" bland after 20 minutes of cooking. However, after two or three hours of simmering, it will have a strong umami taste that is unbelievably mouth-filling, despite its watery characteristics.

During "real" braising, such as for Beef bourguignon, it is not enough to pay attention to only the meat to ensure it produces enough umami. All the vegetable ingredients—traditionally already added during the braising process—also add to the umami taste and an increased taste sensation: tomatoes, onions, mushrooms and, in some Mediterranean countries, a couple of anchovies. In particular, mushrooms should be mentioned here, because shiitake, morels and porcini mushrooms not only contribute glutamic acid, but also provide an added taste enhancer, namely guanosine monophosphate (GMP). This is an additional phosphate derived enzymatically from the cellular fuel ATP, which only differentiates itself from the inosinic acid in the adenine group.

Given this, the term "taste enhancement" can now be very clearly defined from a physiochemical point of view. Besides the weaker aspartic acid, glutamine acid (Glu) has a triggering effect, while the two ATP derivatives, GMP and inosinic acid (IMP), have an actual flavor-enhancing effect. As previously explained, IMP is mainly generated through muscular work. That is why the best sources of this "taste enhancer" come from the meat of animals and fish that are characterized as red meat. Bonito flakes (fermented, dried, and smoked) are frequently used in Japan, while sardines and anchovies are part of the Mediterranean kitchen. Dried boletus, morels, and other mushrooms, which contain micro-organic spores, especially shitake, supply substantial amounts of GMP.

As is generally known, glutamic acid occurs primarily in kombu seaweed, tomatoes, onions, mushrooms, pulses, and many root vegetables, which are frequently used and culturally entrenched additives during braising. This immediately explains the much-loved dashi (Japanese fish stock)—the combination of kombu (Glu) and bonito (IMP) provides a pure "umami" taste.

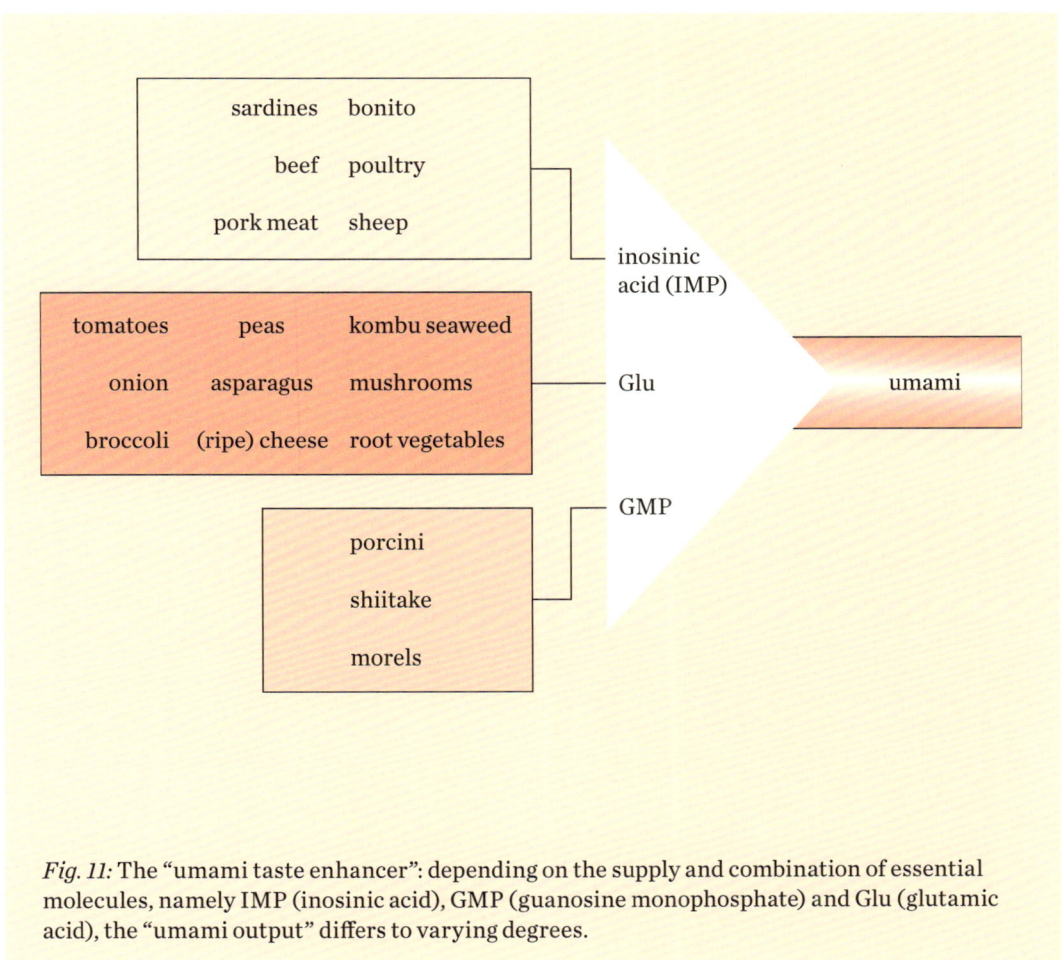

Fig. 11: The "umami taste enhancer": depending on the supply and combination of essential molecules, namely IMP (inosinic acid), GMP (guanosine monophosphate) and Glu (glutamic acid), the "umami output" differs to varying degrees.

According to fig. 11, an attempt to add a piece of kombu algae, dried raw sausage, traditional sour milk cheese (German: Handkäse), or even a rind of a very old cheese to a stewed dish will not go wrong. Your tongue will be grateful.

The desire for a pronounced umami taste sensation has been deeply entrenched in all cooking cultures, even longer than the term "umami" itself has been known. In this sense, the demonization of taste enhancers disagrees with all cooking cultures of this world.

For Aromas and Mouthfullness: Fat!
Meat is flavorless without fat. Independent of the type of preparation, sheer, lean muscle meat will often remain fairly boring and does not form any specific aromas. The difference between it and meat that is marbled with fat is enormous. This aromatic difference can be quickly recognized simply by the sense of smell, especially when the meat has been cured. Due to the oxidation of the fat, distinctly green, grassy, slightly cheesy and especially mushroomy taste sensations develop, which are missing with a lean piece of meat. Even after preparation, this difference is striking: while meat with a high grade of marbling will simply melt between your tongue and palate, lean pieces of meat clearly have to be chewed and processed longer, depending on the length of the muscle fiber and cut. During the "oral processing" of marbled meat in the mouth, a large number of aromas are released, and fat acts as a lubricant, so that the friction between the tongue and the palate is reduced.

The marbling comes from the intramuscular fat (IMF). It is located in the bundles of muscles, and it is the last fat deposit that is developed during the growth of the animal. IMF is decisive for the sensory system and the enjoyment of meat, because it determines a large part of the texture and the release of aromas. In Japan, the percentage share of IMF is measured in twelve levels of marbling. Five quality levels are derived from this in the USA. According to these standards, lean German beef usually lies below the average in terms of texture, taste and aroma.

The IMF of a well-marbled piece of beef consists of a mixture of triglycerides, saturated, simple, polyunsaturated and omega-3 fatty acids of different lengths, whose precise composition is dependent on the breed and feeding. Since IMF must be available in the muscle as a quickly accessible energy source, its share of shorter, simple- and polyunsaturated fatty acids is clearly higher than in comparison with tallow. The fat of a tartare of Wagyū beef, for instance, already melts at significantly lower temperatures, namely already on the tongue.

Not every cattle breed is per se suited to store a high proportion of IMF. Wagyū is, of course, among the leading breeds, but Angus, Murray Grey and

Quality	Degree of Marbling	IMF Share (%)
poor	1	0 – 3
below average	2	4 – 9
average	3 – 4	10 – 20
good	5 – 7	21 – 43
excellent	8 – 12	44 – 56 and higher

Shorthorn cattle are characterized by higher IMF shares. Typical meat breeds such as Charolais, Holstein and Simmental clearly rank lower. In general, it can be stated that heifers (female animals) always display a higher share of IMF than bulls. Also, the meat of heifers is recognizably more fine-grained than that of bulls. And oxen lie somewhere in between in terms of IMF incorporation.

A high fat and IMF share has a very decisive influence on the aging of meat and, with that, on the formation of flavor. In particular, the unsaturated fatty acids play a major role in this regard. Double bonds are chemically more unstable, and there is a high probability that they will break open during aging due to oxidation. Small fragments split off and form fragrant aromatic substances. They make a decisive contribution to the typical aroma of cured meat. Meat that is rich in fat, and especially if more unsaturated fatty acids are stored (such as with Wagyū or a different breed that has a high IMF share), has a clearly more intensive, specific (dry-aged) beef fragrance than lean meat.

Fat also indirectly increases the feeling of a good mouthfill (kokumi). So-called oxylipins are formed from the long-chained fatty acids that split off during aging, which, similar to the products of braising, ensure a clear increase of the kokumi affect.

Animals with generous IMF develop fibrillar muscle bundles, whereas a long-fibered meat structure is prevented during growth, increasing the tenderness of the meat. Intramuscular fat surrounds the muscle fibers. The meat juices are not able to leak out as strongly during braising, since they are unable to penetrate the "fat barriers" around the fibers. The loss of water is therefore reduced and the juiciness of the meat is retained. The tenderness is ensured, through the interaction between intramuscular fat and meat juices. Furthermore, when frying or grilling, the roasting aromas largely dissolve in the fat. They remain in the meat and land in the mouth when eaten.

Besides the friction-reducing textural influences, fat still has another, very special sensory side effect, which has been largely unknown or not taken into account up to the present, namely that it acts as an "aroma store in the mouth."

Fat covers parts of the tongue and the gums with a thin film (oral coating), in which it stores dissolved aromas for a certain time, thereby "adding some seasoning" to the next bite, regardless of whether it consists of meat, bread or vegetables. In many ways, fat acts as a sustainable and molecular flavor enhancer.

And Now?
The handling and production of meat requires care and respect in all its phases, from the pasture to the barn and all the way to its preparation—both from a viewpoint of our culture and the natural sciences. It is more than clear, from a scientific viewpoint, what we are really missing when an anonymous piece of meat is thoughtlessly tossed into the pan. While it may fill us for the short term, it cannot satisfy us. And because of the many (essential) amino acids, the high bioavailability of iron and vitamin B12, meat can sometimes really be seen as a "piece of vitality." That is what we also learn from the great book of evolution.

Autoren/*Authors*

Stuart Pigott

Nach seinem Master in Kulturgeschichte 1986 am Royal College of Art in London stellte Stuart Pigott fest, dass die einzige Möglichkeit, seinen Lebensunterhalt zu verdienen, das Schreiben über Wein war. Seit 25 Jahren lebt er in Berlin, und obwohl sein Name oft mit den Weinen von Rhein und Mosel in Verbindung gebracht wird, hat er auch in anderen Gebieten wie dem Médoc in Bordeaux, Hua Hin in Thailand und Nord-Michigan in den USA intensive Forschung betrieben. 2008/09 war Pigott Gaststudent an der berühmten Wein-Universität Geisenheim und kombiniert seitdem den wissenschaftlichen Ansatz, den er dort erlernte, mit dem von Hunter S. Thompsen inspirierten Gonzo-Journalismus. Er ist Redakteur bei JamesSuckling.com und Wein-Kolumnist der *Frankfurter Allgemeinen Sonntagszeitung.*

After receiving a master's degree in cultural history from the Royal College of Art in London in 1986 Stuart Pigott realized that the only way he could earn a living was to write about wine. He has lived in Berlin for twenty-five years and although his name is most closely associated with the wines of the Rhine and Mosel he has undertaken in-depth research in regions as widely contrasting as the Médoc in Bordeaux, Hua Hin in Thailand, and Northern Michigan in the USA. In 2008/09 Pigott was a guest student at the famous wine university in Geisenheim, Germany and combines the scientific approach he learned there with hardcore gonzo journalism inspired by the works of Hunter S. Thompson. He is a contributing editor to JamesSuckling.com and the wine columnist of the Sunday edition of the Frankfurter Allgemeine Zeitung.

René Pollesch

studierte Angewandte Theaterwissenschaft in Gießen bei Andrzej Wirth und Hans-Thies Lehmann. Von 2001 bis 2007 war er künstlerischer Leiter des Praters der Berliner Volksbühne. Pollesch inszeniert seine eigenen Stücke unter anderem am Staatstheater Stuttgart, am Wiener Burgtheater, am Thalia Theater in Hamburg, an den Münchner Kammerspielen, am Schauspielhaus Hamburg, am Schauspiel Frankfurt, am Schauspielhaus Zürich sowie in Stockholm, São Paulo, Tokio und Santiago de Chile. René Pollesch erhielt zahlreiche Preise. 2012 wurde er in die Akademie der Künste Berlin aufgenommen.

René Pollesch studied Applied Theatre Studies in Gießen with Andrzej Wirth and Hans-Thies Lehmann. He was the artistic director of the Prater at the Volksbühne Berlin from 2001 until 2007. Pollesch directs his own plays at the Staatstheater Stuttgart, the Burgtheater in Vienna, the Thalia Theater in Hamburg, the Münchner Kammerspiele, Schauspielhaus Hamburg, Schauspiel Frankfurt, Schauspielhaus Zurich as well as in Stockholm, São Paulo, Tokyo, and Santiago de Chile, amongst others. He received numerous prizes. In 2012, he was admitted to the Akademie der Künste (Academy of Arts) in Berlin.

Adriano Sack

leitet das Stilressort der *Welt am Sonntag.* Er ist der Autor mehrerer Bücher, die in diverse Sprachen übersetzt wurden. Als er 2001 nach Berlin zog, lernte er auf einer Hochzeitsfeier Stephan Landwehr und Boris Radczun kennen, die einige Jahre später den Grill Royal eröffneten. Er mag den Kopfsalat.

Adriano Sack is the head of the lifestyle departement at Welt am Sonntag. *He is the author of several publications, which has been translated in numerous languages. When he moved to Berlin in 2001 he met Stephan Landwehr and Boris Radczun, who opened the Grill Royal a few years later, at a wedding party. He likes the lettuce.*

Erwin Seitz

wurde in Wolframs-Eschenbach als Sohn einer Gastwirts- und Metzgermeisterfamilie geboren. Er besuchte die Benediktinerschule in Plankstetten, anschließend wurde er zum Metzger und Koch ausgebildet. Danach studierte er Germanistik, Philosophie und Kunstgeschichte in Berlin und Oxford. Er lebt als freier Journalist, Gastronomiekritiker sowie Autor „gastrosophischer" Bücher in Berlin. Zuletzt erschienen im Insel Verlag seine Bücher *Die Verfeinerung der Deutschen* (2011), *Kunst der Gastlichkeit* (2015) und *Naturnahes Kochen* (2018).

Erwin Seitz was born into an innkeeper's and butcher's family in Wolframs-Eschenbach. He went to school at the Benedictine school in Plankstetten followed by an apprenticeship both as a butcher and a chef. Afterwards he studied German studies, philosophy, and art history in Berlin and Oxford. He now lives in Berlin working as a freelance journalist, restaurant critic, and author of "gastrosophical" books. His latest publications include Die Verfeinerung der Deutschen *(2011),* Kunst der Gastlichkeit *(2015), and* Naturnahes Kochen (2018), *published by Insel Verlag.*

Prof. Dr. Thomas A. Vilgis
diplomierte und promovierte in Physik in Ulm, habilitierte in Theoretischer Physik in Mainz, arbeitete in Cambridge, London und Straßburg und lehrt an der Universität Mainz. Am Mainzer Max-Planck-Institut für Polymerforschung leitet Vilgis eine Arbeitsgruppe zur statistischen Physik weicher Materie sowie eine experimentelle Gruppe zur „soft matter food science". Vilgis publizierte über 300 wissenschaftliche Arbeiten zur Physik der weichen Materie und zur molekularen Lebensmittelphysik. Er ist Herausgeber der Zeitschrift *Journal Culinaire – Kultur und Wissenschaft des Essens* und Autor zahlreicher Bücher zur Naturwissenschaft des Kochens und der Physik und Chemie der Lebensmittel.

Prof. Dr. Thomas A. Vilgis received his diploma and his doctorate in physics in Ulm, followed by a habilitation on theoretical physics in Mainz. He worked in Cambridge, London, and Straßburg, and teaches at the university in Mainz. Vilgis is the head of a team specialized in static physics of soft matter at the Max-Planck-Institut for polymer research in Mainz, and leads an experimental group focused on "soft matter food science." Up until now he has published more than three hundred academic articles on physics of soft matter and on molecular physics of food. He is the editor of Journal Culinaire—Kultur und Wissenschaft des Essens *and the author of numerous books on sciences of cooking and on physics and chemistry of food products.*

Fotografen/*Photographers*

Maxime Ballesteros
wurde in Lyon, Frankreich geboren. Er studierte an der École supérieure d'art et design Saint-
Étienne (ESADSE) und machte 2007 den Ab-
schluss mit einem Diplôme national supérieur
d'expression plastique (DNSEP). Seine Fotografi-
en wurden in Einzel- und Gruppenausstellungen
in Frankreich, den Vereinigten Staaten, Belgi-
en, Russland, Deutschland, Großbritannien und
Dänemark ausgestellt. Ballesteros lebt seit 2007
in Berlin.

*Maxime Ballesteros was born in Lyon, France.
After studying at ESADSE, the Saint-Etienne
Higher School of Art and Design, he graduated
in 2007 with a DNSEP (national postgraduate
diploma in plastic arts). His photographs have
been featured in solo and group exhibitions in
France, the United States, Belgium, Russia, Germany, Great Britain, and Denmark. Ballesteros
has been based in Berlin since 2007.*

Florian Bolk
absolvierte bis 1989 eine Ausbildung in Fotogra-
fie am Lette-Verein Berlin. 1990 zog er nach Mad-
rid und arbeite für *El País, Marie Claire, Diario
16* und *EGM*. 1995 kehrte er nach Berlin zurück
und fotografiert seitdem für diverse Berliner
Tageszeitungen und das Magazin *Der Feinschmecker*. Bolk hat an zahlreichen Kochbüchern für
Tim Raue, Ralf Zacherl, Wolfgang Müller, Björn
Moschinski, Lucki Maurer und anderen mitge-
wirkt. Er ist außerdem Herausgeber des Food-
fanzines *Le Schicken* und der Kochbuch-Reihe
Die Stadt kocht.

*Florian Bolk was trained in photography at the
Lette-Verein Berlin until 1989. In 1990 he moved to
Milan and worked for* El País, Marie Claire, Diario
16 *and* EGM. *In 1995 he returned to Berlin and
since then has been taking photos for diverse Berlin
newspapers and the magazine* Der Feinschmecker. *Bolk has contributed to numerous cookbooks for
Tim Raue, Ralf Zacherl, Wolfgang Müller, Björn
Moschinski, Lucki Maurer, and others. Moreover
he is the editor of the foodfanzine* Le Schicken, *and
the cookbook series* Die Stadt kocht.

Stefan Korte
ist Architektur- und Porträtfotograf. Seine Arbeiten wurden in Magazinen wie *Numéro, W Magazine* und dem *Zeitmagazin* veröffentlicht. Aus
seiner Leidenschaft für Kunst und der Hingabe
an sein Handwerk sind Kollaborationen mit international bekannten Künstlern, Galerien und
Institutionen entstanden. Stefan Kortes Fotografien sind in zahlreichen Katalogen führender
Verlage veröffentlicht.

*Stefan Korte is a photographer focused on archi-
tecture and portraiture. His work has been published in magazines such as* Numéro, W Magazine
and Zeitmagazin. *Love for contemporary art and
dedication to his craft have led to collaborations
with internationally known artists, galleries and
institutions. Stefan Korte's work is featured in numerous catalogs by leading publishing houses.*

Peter Langer
ist als Fotograf auf erzählerische Stillleben spe-
zialisiert. Seit 2008 wird wöchentlich eines seiner Bilder im bekannten deutschen *Zeitmagazin* veröffentlicht. Er arbeitet für alle wichtigen
Mode-Publikationen weltweit. Zu seinen Anzei-
genkunden gehören Louis Vuitton, H&M, Dior,
Chloé und andere.

*Peter Langer is a photographer specialized in nar-
rative still life. Since 2008 Peter Langer's signa-
ture work is published weekly in renowned German*
Zeitmagazin. *He is working for all major fashion publications worldwide. Advertising clients
are Louis Vuitton, H&M, Dior, Chloé, and others.*

Robert Rieger
ist ein Fotograf aus Berlin. Er arbeitet hauptsächlich im Bereich Editorial und Anzeigen; seine
Arbeiten erscheinen regelmäßig und weltweit in
führenden Design- und Lifestyle-Publikationen,
darunter *T Magazine, Monocle, Condé Nast Traveler, China Adobe, 99U, Soho House Notes*, und
Real Living. Seit 2015 arbeitet er am Fotodesk
bei *Freunde von Freunden*, einem internationalen Online-Interview-Magazin mit tiefen Einbli-
cken und zeitlosen Geschichten.

Robert Rieger is a Berlin-based photographer. He primarily works in editorial and advertising, and is a frequent contributor to some of the leading design and lifestyle publications worldwide, including T Magazine, Monocle, Condé Nast Traveler, China Adobe, 99U, Soho House Notes, *and* Real Living. *Since 2015, he is working at the photodesk at* Freunde von Freunden, *an international online interview magazine driven by insightful, timeless storytelling.*

Impressum/*Imprint*

Redaktion und Koordination/*Editing and Coordination*
Uta Grosenick

Gestaltung/*Design*
BOROS, Berlin, Ingo Maak

Texte/*Texts*
René Pollesch, Adriano Sack, Erwin Seitz, Thomas Vilgis

Gespräch/*Conversation*
Stuart Pigott mit/*with* Andrea Kauk und/*and* Moritz Estermann

Fotografien/*Photographs*
Maxime Ballesteros (S./pp. 100–162, 168); Florian Bolk (S./pp. 200, 222); Stefan Korte (S./pp. 8, 14, 20–59); Peter Langer (S./pp. 174–183); Boris Radczun (S./p. 254); Robert Rieger (S./pp. 60, 80, 184, 192)

Illustrationen/*Illustrations*
Max Häckl (S./pp. 203, 204, 208, 225, 226, 230)

Lektorat/*Copy Editing*
DISTANZ Verlag

Übersetzung/*Translation*
Cillero & De Motta (S./pp. 223–242); Gerrit Jackson (S./pp. 169–173); Andrea Scrima (S./pp. 15–19, 81–98, 193–198)

Lithografie/*Image Editing*
Max-Color

Produktion/*Production Management*
DISTANZ Verlag

Die im Grill Royal zu sehenden Kunstwerke stammen von/*The artworks to be seen at Grill Royal are by* Johannes Albers (S./pp. 22/23 links/left, 46/47 vorne rechts/front right); Olivia Berckemeyer (S./pp. 30/31 vorne rechts/front right, 54/55 Mitte vorn/center front); Merlin Carpenter (S./pp. 40/41 rechts/right); Endart (S./pp. 38/39 rechts/right, 50/51 ganz links/far left); Keith Farquhar (S./pp. 22/23 Mitte/center, 38/39 Mitte/center); Francis Giacobetti (S./pp. 8, 20, 29, 34/35 ganz rechts/far right, 46/47 Mitte hinten/center rear, 54/55 Mitte hinten/center rear, 56/57); David Hamilton (S./pp. 14, 34/35 außer ganz rechts/except far right); Jonathan Meese (S./pp. 40/41 Mitte links/center left); Franceso Vezzoli (S./pp. 40/41 ganz links/far left); Andrea Zittel (S./pp. 22/23 rechts/right, 50/51 links/left); Der Hund heißt Pluto/*The dog is called Pluto* (S./pp. 130/131)

© 2018 VG Bild-Kunst, Bonn, für die Werke von/*for the works by* Olivia Berckemeyer, Endart, Jonathan Meese und/*and* Francesco Vezzoli

© 2018 die Fotografen/the photographers, die Autoren/the authors, and DISTANZ GmbH, Berlin

Gesamtherstellung/*Printing and Binding*
optimal media GmbH, Röbel/Müritz

Vertrieb/*Distribution*
edel Germany GmbH
www.edel.com
international-books@edel.com

ISBN 978-3-95476-193-7

Printed in Germany

Erschienen im/*Published by*
DISTANZ Verlag
www.distanz.de

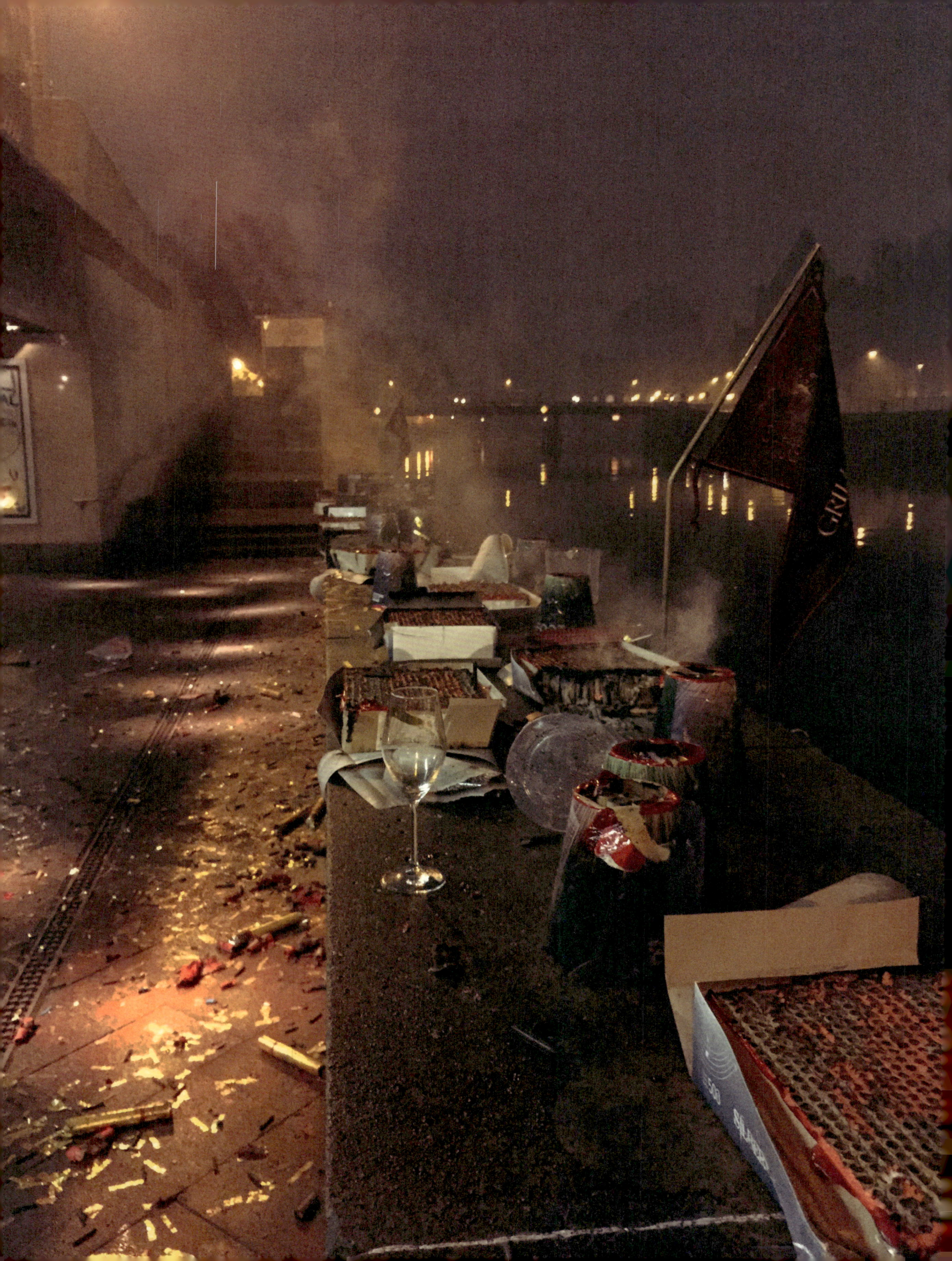